MUGABE'S LEGACY

/ AFRICAN
/ ARGUMENTS

African Arguments is a series of short books about contemporary Africa and the critical issues and debates surrounding the continent. The books are scholarly and engaged, substantive and topical. They focus on questions of justice, rights and citizenship; politics, protests and revolutions; the environment, land, oil and other resources; health and disease; economy: growth, aid, taxation, debt and capital flight; and both Africa's international relations and country case studies.

Managing Editor, Stephanie Kitchen

Series editors

Adam Branch
Alex de Waal
Alcinda Honwana
Ebenezer Obadare
Carlos Oya
Nicholas Westcott

DAVID B. MOORE

Mugabe's Legacy

*Coups, Conspiracies, and the Conceits
of Power in Zimbabwe*

HURST & COMPANY, LONDON

IAI　International African Institute

Published in collaboration with the International African Institute.
First published in the United Kingdom in 2022 by
C. Hurst & Co. (Publishers) Ltd.,
New Wing, Somerset House, Strand, London, WC2R 1LA
Copyright © David B. Moore, 2022
All rights reserved.
Printed in Great Britain by Bell and Bain Ltd, Glasgow

Distributed in the United States, Canada and Latin America by
Oxford University Press, 198 Madison Avenue, New York, NY 10016,
United States of America.

Epigraph to Chapter 10 from *Kleptopia: How Dirty Money Is Conquering the World* by Tom Burgis.
Copyright © 2020 by Thomas Burgis. Used by permission
of HarperCollins Publishers.

The right of David B. Moore to be identified as the author of
this publication is asserted by him in accordance with the
Copyright, Designs and Patents Act, 1988.

A Cataloguing-in-Publication data record for this book
is available from the British Library.

ISBN: 9781787387713

This book is printed using paper from registered sustainable
and managed sources.

www.hurstpublishers.com

For Brendan, Zrebar and Rojyar,
Defying the morbid symptoms as can no others

In Memory of

Wilfred Mhanda, aka Dzinashe 'Dzino' Machingura,
26 May 1950–28 May 2014

My hero, if there ever was one.
Without him? No history worth telling.
It just couldn't be caught.

Paul Brickhill, 8 July 1958–3 October 2014

Best Zimbabwean friend, raconteur and interlocutor: finally, those
80,000 words he wanted for his Anvil Press in 1991. And then some.
His eternal question: 'What happened to the democracy in our
National Democratic Revolution?'

David Sanders, 5 August 1945–30 August 2019

Who kept up the *vashandi* tradition.
Handing me Dzino's 'Prison Notebooks' in *c.* 1992 ensured that the
legacy on this book's cover would not be Zimbabwe's only one.

Bill Freund, 6 July 1944–17 August 2020

Sorry Bill, this didn't get out in time for you.
I hope it's wearing history's weight lightly.
Thanks for hiring me to a place close to my favourite one.

Joey Booysen, 4 June 1924–24 September 2020

Even after her age-mate Robert Mugabe died, Joey kept asking the
best questions about Zimbabwe.
Her engaging sense of humour will never be forgotten.

CONTENTS

ACKNOWLEDGEMENTS

If you wait as long as I have to write a proper book, there are simply too many people to thank. And one's memory fades. I will start, however, with those most immediately responsible. Toward the end of 2017, there was a coup in a small African country. It happened as an academic conference, about Africa, was taking place in Chicago. Zed Books then commissioning editor Ken Barlow asked my good friends, and excellent scholars of Zimbabwe, Blair Rutherford and Tim Scarnecchia, if they knew anyone who might be interested in writing about the coup. Individually or in chorus, apparently they mentioned me. Shortly thereafter, Ken emailed me to ask what I was up to. I began a lengthy reply about how I was engaged in a long intergenerational study of those Zimbabweans whose struggles opened up their country's democratic space—from the nationalists of the 1950s and the Young Turks of the mid-1970s, to activists at the turn of the millennium. Dog-walking time intervened.

On hearing of Ken's email, my partner, fellow dog-walker and superb political scientist Susan Booysen—to whom I owe beyond quantification: for the space, and so much to fill it—remarked to the effect of 'don't be daft: of course he wants you to write a book about the coup!' And so the following pages began. As they reveal, things moved on to—and back from—that blip in Zimbabwe's political history.

Many institutions and their dedicated, conscientious and efficient directors and workers helped the writing process. When Ken decided to include African Arguments managing editor Stephanie Kitchen in the task, I had no idea such a patient and optimistic person could exist and simultaneously exert the exact degree of pressure needed to loosen my

ACKNOWLEDGEMENTS

lethargy. When African Arguments moved to Hurst, I recalled that I had promised their managing director Michael Dwyer a book in 1996, at an excellent Adelaide restaurant. But Adelaide times were not propitious for such a task. I hope this is worth the wait, Michael. And to all the Hurst team, Alice Clarke to Daisy Leitch to Mary Starkey: many thanks.

Ade Adebajo offered me post-Zimbabwean coup sabbatical space at the University of Johannesburg's Institute for Pan-African Thought and Conversation—and allowed me to take refuge there from a minor office coup that postponed that sabbatical. When the longed-for leave period was resurrected in 2019, the Stellenbosch Institute for Advanced Study took me in—a bit later than expected. This was fortuitous: in addition to Edward Kirumira and his team's superb generosity, there could not have been a more conducive and convivial cohort of scholars of southern Africa, alternative political economists, philosophers, musicians and novelists—ever! A hard act for Clare Hall, University of Cambridge, to follow later in 2019. But my time there was special indeed, as were the good friends that I made, with interests far from the Cape of Good Hope, as well as in it (thanks to Lawrence Hamilton for that letter of sponsorship). Joost Fontein, head of my department at the University of Johannesburg, managed both to offer wise words on the first draft and to magically arrange my teaching duties so they did not coincide with the book's crunch times. Thanks too to all of my colleagues for a collaborative and friendly work environment, even during Covid. Lawrence and Joost go beyond merely being fellow institution members and into the category of friends.

Still in the realm of enabling institutions and the people in them, the UK's Public Record Office at Kew Gardens must be my favourite place in the world (next to Zimbabwe): for this amateur historian, simply a marvel. (Henry and Renee Bernstein's conviviality helped!) Close on its heels though are the National Security Archive at the George Washington University; the Labour History Archive and Study Centre at the People's History Museum in Manchester; the Churchill Archives Centre in Cambridge; the University of Stirling site of the UK National Archives; the London Metropolitan Archives; the Killie Campbell Africana Library at the University of KwaZulu-Natal; and the National Archives of Zimbabwe, whose glory will rise again!

Now the harder but most heartfelt part: first, of course, to Dzino's comrades (then and now), most of whom would not mind their names appearing on these pages, but I will keep them off just in case. Since the mid-1980s, they have helped immeasurably and enthusiastically—ever wondering (undoubtedly) when their help would see the light of day beyond a few academic articles. And later, not a few in *vashandi's* wake, whose brave updates on current affairs were extremely helpful and whose openness kept my spirits high. Further: the members of the March (1971) 11 Movement—whose fuller story will unfold! As will that of the 2000s generation, before they age further (I reckon Dan Hodgkinson will be first off the mark there).

For those to be named (with that, NoViolet Bulawayo comes to mind: thanks for the comments, good conversation, but mostly for your book!), the following are just a few. John Saul, for kicking it all off by marking ZIPA off from the Zimbabwean nationalist 'internecine struggles', supervising that dissertation decades ago—and for consistent debate and support since. Norma Kriger (a pillar!), Ian Phimister and Roger Southall for wise and encouraging words at the right moments. Of Zimbabweans, a truncated list: Brian Raftopoulos, for friendship and collegiality since 1985; all the Brickhills, Dumiso Dabengwa, Mike and Rob Davies, Ibbo Mandaza, Eldred Masunungure, Derek Matyszak, Strike Mkandla, Joshua Mpofu (only recently passed) and Zweli Mzilethi; Eliphas Mukonoweshuro; Judy Todd for the best of Bulawayo hospitality; Stephen Williams, and many more. Of the global North (in the South too), a short list. I will never forget David Galbraith's pithy comment at a Bulawayo restaurant with Stephen in 1985, that observing a bourgeoisie develop—in close proximity—is a harrowing experience. Linda Freeman—of course! Stephen O'Brien, Richard Saunders and Luise White (Blair and Tim too) for fun visits to this crossover point. Piers Pigou for helpful WhatsApps and more. Discerning journalists: Violet Gonda, Trevor Grundy, Michael Holman, Peta Thornycroft. Hazel Cameron and Stuart Doran for their brave exactitude on Gukurahundi. Gracious thanks, too, for the cover painting, 'The Last Moments', by Cosmos Shiridzinomwa, and the Zeitz MOCAA in Cape Town.

Last, but not at all least, I must thank my family in Canada, especially Mom. And Dad, who didn't make it to see even that dissertation, but whose support and encouragement helped it along (I could never have made it without that Amstrad he helped me buy for the last draft). Its legacy and—I hope—theirs, follows forthwith.

PROLOGUE

INTERREGNA: BEYOND THE LIMINALITY OF LEGACIES

Revising manuscripts is purgatorial. Heaven: publication! Hell? Well, Roman Catholic doctrine says purgatory is *purification*. Hell will not befall you. Limbo—now cancelled—was for unbaptised children, not adults.[1] For careful publishers, the proposal is baptism. Five rigorous secular priests of different faiths christened this book. The first draft's three to four reviewers (bishops?) took it to purgatory. Thanks in part to Covid-19's preview of hell this entailed nearly an eternity of tweaking, interrupted only by pleas to Peter or Petronella for deferrals.

This author's tendency to rewrite while revising exaggerated purgatory's immanent liminality.[2] That means heaven's guardian orders a purge: just seven to ten thousand words! External peculiarities contaminated the cleansing. The exciting (or sad) events that spurred this book faded into deep, silent structures—the same ones spawning them. Waning was inherent in their own history. The 'coup' that started this study transformed little in Zimbabwe. It seemed important in November 2017: not now. Beyond Zimbabwe, much changed. The world's thinking moved on. This work has ingested such alien particles, including scholarly considerations on 'truth', 'alternative facts', and the 'states of emergency' within long interregna.[3] Pertinent Zimbabwean examples exemplified these complexities. Readers can decide whether the modifications were beneficial.

PROLOGUE

The significance of coups and deaths—Robert Mugabe's causing the stretch to the loose, non-biographical concept of legacy—fades quickly. Time passed after the coup. When it was clear Mugabe would not live forever, with forever quickening on the horizon, his imminent death skulked to the front stage. Yet more time, and its events, passed. Books suffer when they cover too much. They drown in the depths of detail. If they don't sell it's hell. Purgatory's ablutions would be to no avail. 'Not another one about a tin-pot dictator', the book browser groans. Or: 'How many stories about a coup does it take to prove a point?' Concept and context thus prevail.

However, excessive abstraction can fly too high above apparent empirical flotsam. All forest, no trees—context cancels contingency. If the devil ducks under such detail, one must dive in. Rarefied pre-varication about the nature of the 'militarily assisted transition' (think 'wrestling MAT' to retain the muscly connotations) cannot persist. A goodly quotient of force removed Zimbabwe's president from his throne and ensured the victory of one of ZANU (PF)'s factions over another. An American Jesuit magazine's obfuscation—Robert Mugabe's defenestration was an 'unexpected, but peaceful transition'[4]—cannot rest in peace.

The state-run *Herald*'s blessing was quicker. The new regime's chief propagandist had changed *noms des plumes* many times. George Charamba had served the now dethroned commander-in-chief. Alongside the portly priest featured in the Jesuit magazine he was part of the MAT negotiating team under the president's 'Blue Roof'. He was probably the 'Radar' (soon aka 'Bishop Lazarus'), writing that ZANU (PF) had simply:

> [renewed] its leadership by way of recalling an errant cadre and a cabal and replacing them with newer and more focused faces ... [this correction] was neither a revolution ... Nor ... a subversion of a constitutional order, which is why our unique-coup-that-was-no-coup has become a global marvel.[5]

Such hubris embeds quickly in the hereafter of contested coup-like events, especially since the post-Cold War era has excluded them from the etiquette manuals of the African Union (AU) and the Southern African Development Community (SADC).[6] Such forceful transitions are unique only in their protagonists' efforts to deny that they are coups.

My hasty reflections on the 11/17 events could be too close to the Jesuits and putschists.[7] Noting the coup's 'very' Zimbabwean nature echoed southern Africans' parochialism, where everything political and historical is 'exceptional', given its 'colonialism of a special type'–and with Cecil John Rhodes's legacy peculiarly particular.[8]

Chris Mullin's *A Very British Coup* may have been invoked[9]–but serendipitously, given his mid-1970s research on the Zimbabwean 'freedom fighters', when Mugabe thought a coup was roiling. That moment is pivotal to this book; indeed, a turning point. Mullin was later an African affairs minister in the British cabinet: more coincidence.

I challenged the argument that all birds with a duck-like gait *are* ducks, ditto for coups, by noting that there are at least 140 varieties of the genus, including swans. Is not differentiation within a breed noteworthy?[10] That was another failed blow for unity among diversity. Legal scholars have more tactful field days with these debates.[11]

No matter: I soon boxed myself into a corner. Deprived of theoretical nuance by a television interviewer, I hummed and hawed: yes, it was a coup; soldiers were on the streets; people killed. Force joined persuasion. A change among power-holders had transpired. My momentary meander became immortalised with the moniker 'Teller of Obvious Truths'.[12]

I took up the coup contingent's cudgels happily, only noting some of this one's distinctions. I once thought it might have moved 'democracy' forward an inch. Its accompanying ecstatic albeit choreographed parades helped it look that way. Previous participatory gains assisted its relatively peaceful pace: but there would be no progress without further struggle.[13] That was an understatement: only gargantuan struggles will move this securocrat state that inch.[14]

Investigating Father Pollitt's 'unexpectedness' proved more interesting. I knew this tendency was not new soon after the coup. I had stumbled on the Baader–Meinhof syndrome: the realisation that something seemingly unexperienced has been ongoing.[15] This blended the coup-book with my long-simmering project exploring how (or how not) three generations of Zimbabwean political aspirants to power opened democratic space.[16]

These notions coalesced as work progressed: the 1970s–the liberation war years and the Zimbabwean nationalists' internecine struggles within them—were full of coups foretold as 'freedom' loomed. They were integral to Mugabe's means to power: thus Chapter 3. Indeed, this book's thesis rests on how Mugabe's handling of the 1970s' ideological and generational challenges—the *vashandi* movement marking that moment most[17]—scarred ZANU (PF) forever. Those generational issues are relevant now. Zimbabwe's elders give up power with little grace.

The 1950s and 1960s (Chapter 2) offer further hints to the making of Mugabe and his legacy. Chapters 4 and 5 chart the post-1980 years: in the 2000s especially the mounting conspiracies poised against Mugabe suggest that only a coup would rid Zimbabwe of its prime albatross—but that would be tricky. As Chris Mullin put it much later, 'sadly … most alleged conspiracies turn out to be cockups'.[18] The 11/17 coup's imagined predecessors were integral to the patrimony of the man soon to meet his political and biological denouement.

Conspiracies come with such manner of power's gains and losses. Lies are requisite. So are unprecedented accoutrements of privilege for the new rulers. Unbelievable conceits, including that people all over the world believe their deceits, accompany them.

That the 'Second Republic' was little more than a Mark II *déjà vu* was clear long before Mugabe stumbled off the mortal coil.[19] The coup victors may have intended the two violent spasms following the marred mid-2018 elections to consolidate the 11/17 intra-party shift.[20] August 2018 and January 2019 saw new versions of 'crowd control': but the coercive means of coup confirmation targeted the 'people' as well as a ZANU (PF) faction. Instead, more confusion ensued. Neither extra-nor intra-party conflict was quelled, but the putschists' own tensions were exposed. Thus the pattern of lies and corruption continued, albeit far less finessed than the old master could muster until he was too tired and flustered to exit his self-made mazes.

Half a year after Mugabe's final fall Covid-19 felled many more. The new regime gained an excuse to exercise its flagging muscles.[21] By the coup's third anniversary it seemed clear that even the death of this once important man carried less meaning than anticipated.[22]

The hopes that first Mugabe's sidelining, followed by his final cessation, would make Zimbabwe better have disappeared. Such dreams had simmered for long, as Roger Southall detected in 2013 as the cracks in ZANU (PF)'s edifice widened.[23] His magisterial study of the Namibian, South African, and Zimbabwean *Liberation Movements in Power*[24] ended with a precarious possibility. On Mugabe's death might the main opposition party (the Movement for Democratic Change (MDC), hyphened with a T, A, B, C or an amalgam thereof pursuant on its many splits and reconfigurations) and 'moderate' ZANU (PF) members create a new social contract? Plucking hope from even thinner air, Southall hinted that a Zimbabwean 'move back to constitutional democracy' could inspire 'a valuable corrective to [South Africa's] ANC inspired assaults' on such. That chance has slid by in Zimbabwe. The idea of moderation and the eternal search for its vectors—thus the mirages of 'social contract'—have melted to myth. Various actors have tried coalitions of convenience, but failed. More distant still, Southall cited the 2009–13 'inclusive' government's finance minister,[25] MDC Secretary General Tendai Biti's wish that 'the secret of good governance ... love and caring', might wend into a new Zimbabwe.[26] That has not approached either. Biti—featured in the following pages—once explained Zimbabwean politics in terms of 'magical realism'.[27] That assessment may well be the enduring Bitiism. The coup and post-coup chapters might bear this out.

The first chapter attempts to erect a conceptual structure on which the Zimbabwe 'facts' will sit. The rest explores what is magic, or tragic, about Mugabe's legacy.

When reading, remember Robert Gordon's quarter-century-old advice: 'Outsiders [i.e. academics] are typically estranged.' This 'leads to their best work ... precisely ... their ability to raise uncomfortable questions'. Social scientists are 'middle men *par excellence*' and as such 'suffer all the ambiguous advantages and disadvantages of people placed in such intermediary roles'. Academics—outsiders and knowledge brokers—are the 'tricksters of the modern bourgeois world. History purged of ambiguity is not history but ideology; society purged of tricksters is not society but a soul-dead mass'. If they are 'critically self-conscious awareness of this trickster role, they can do no better than follow the advice of Amílcar Cabral: "Tell no lies and ... claim no easy victories"'.[28]

Is Gordon's hope more than a glimmer? Can we tricksters raise enough uncomfortable questions to keep 'the power élite from becoming so enamoured of themselves that they forget their larger societal obligations and become complacent'? Yes, if their example illustrates the collective, difficult, effort needed to answer them.

1

INTRODUCING INTERPRETATIONS

'MEN' BECOMING HISTORY;
EVENTS BECOMING STRUCTURES

Interpretation is not a contemplative, calm, and disengaged activity; it is an active practice that requires an anarchic effort ... directed against those who call for alternative facts.

The death of the old ideologies takes the form of scepticism with regard to all theories and general formulae ... and to a form of politics which is not simply realistic in fact ... but which is cynical in its immediate manifestation.[1]

Robert Gordon's invocation of Amílcar Cabral's oft-quoted dictum about claiming improbable victories and telling no lies may not mean there is irrevocable truth.[2] It simply points to the fallacies involved in trying to pass off deliberate lies as positive facts. Fake doctoral theses would be the perfect example for academics. Politicians commissioning them and scholars accepting them are the worst culprits. That Zimbabwe—national pride bursting with intellectualism—is full of them may be the first warning needed for any historical, ideological or political study.[3]

The *longue durée* crept along after the oft-denied coup. The definite death of Zimbabwe's leader faded to the past. It became starkly clear that Mugabe's nearly eternal career in a profession where a week is a long time had inordinate influence over the three political generations I was interrogating before the 11/17 events. They started to look like a historical blip. The 'coup' sank into near insignificance as 2020 reached its end–'the Second Republic' simply repeated the tragedy of the first, although in exaggerated form.

It verges on cruelty to all those buried under ZANU (PF)'s steamroller to repeat Marx's verdict on the second rounds of stymied 'revolutions': farce follows tragedy. That nearly sums it up though. The various forces in oppositional political parties and civil society testing Marx and Zimbabwe's predictability seemed unable to transcend their miserable spell.[4] The 'arrogant and parasitic politico-military elite determined to cling on to state power and the access to wealth that it granted' that Roger Southall charted so carefully shows no signs of leaving.[5] This ruling group is more resolute than ever. However, its factions threaten evermore to tear it apart, thus stimulating more violence, more chaotic and confused than before. This factionalism is what many studies emphasising the Zimbabwean ruling group's cohesion miss.[6] Mugabe's especial forte was to create and dissipate factions almost simultaneously, but this skill faded with age. The fundamental thesis of this book's first draft still runs through it. The legacy of Mugabe's route to rule and his incumbency in that realm is one of many conspired coups and their detritus, followed by a real one with the sense that there are more to come. This was not a man of a mere moment. He was one who made an age, and it will make many others.

The famous French (and feudal) weather metaphor encapsulates the main point.[7] Louis XIV, or Louis XV, or perhaps Jeanne Antoinette Poisson, the latter's adviser and mistress more often known as Madame la Pompadour, coined it, and one can be sure many rulers have thought it.[8] Mugabe thought, and was encouraged many times to think, that *l'état c'est moi* and *après moi le déluge*. Remember, too, all states include the military, with its 'legitimate monopoly of force', and in Zimbabwe ZANU (PF) is entwined inextricably with the forcefulness of guns and gentler forms of political persuasion. For Mugabe, that famous statement stretched to include *les soldats et le parti*.[9] With the ultimate faction juggler fallen, the balls cannot remain for long up in the air, spinning in the momentum of his wake.

Time has passed, and with it the Zimbabwean *roi*. Those whom Mugabe juggled felled him. His dexterity slipped, hastened by his partner Grace and her Machiavellian 'Generation-40' acolytes. The coup was akin to spring rains, but it did not wash away the chaff.[10] Now the storms are brewing again, although yet to tear the party-state totally. The new leader hardly embodies the party-state complex and the networks in and around it in society[11]—at least not through consent rather than coercion (with corruption and chicanery between).[12]

One needs historical and theoretical buttressing to sort out the ephemeral from the lasting. Be the means of Mugabe's exit from power unique or a clone of many coups,[13] deeper thinking upon them and their context is required. Here follow, then, some efforts at theory-lite, taking into account the advice of one of Africa's best historians: beware theoretical fads, but wear the good and durable ones lightly whilst wading through the weighty matters of the past.[14]

Would such a dictum help us slip through the surface phenomena of a mere politician's death? John Saul has tried recently to disentangle 'great men' theories of history from their structurally determinist opposites.[15] Perhaps the proof of the impossibility of this counterfactual pudding is that it resides in its eating through those great men's assassinations (a bit like cannibalism, perish the thought). Most of Saul's list of murdered politicians bearing hope—from Cabral through to Chitepo and Sankara[16]—were offed far before their prime, and aside from Mozambique's we see little of the longer lists of less prominent people meeting bloody ends. The last line of Saul's ruminations on the long-term effect of Frelimo leader Eduardo Mondlane's murder is that Mozambique is now in the midst of a 'quiet assassination epidemic' (more recently, the new war in Cabo Delgado means collective assassination).[17]

These epidemics do not end in Mozambique. There were more people killed in South Africa's KwaZulu-Natal province in the months running up to the ANC's 2017 president-electing conference than even the highest (unofficial) numbers estimated in the Zimbabwean coup.[18] Life is sometimes short for South African environmental activists, too.[19] In Zimbabwe, such politicides could be a legacy of Mugabe and his peers, given the party-state's recent tendency to abduct young political activists—or their nephews.[20] The shadows linger, still, in the unresolved deaths of such leaders as Herbert Chitepo in 1975,[21] Josiah Tongogara as majority rule approached at the end of 1979, numerous car 'accidents', and the flame-engulfed demise of the 'kingmaker' who turned against the monarch.[22]

As Grinin, one of Saul's sources, put it, 'historical figures' are people who 'have such direct or indirect influence upon [their] own or another society'. They are recognisably significant because 'they left a noticeable mark (positive, negative or unambiguous) in history and in the further development of society'. This influence may be due to a range of factors, from their 'personal features, or to a chance, or to his or her social standing, or to the peculiarity of the epoch'. What are the social conditions in which they are most likely to emerge? During revolutions and the 'creation of a new order'. This is too misty: suffice that some leaders miss the moment created by the fluctuating systems (with myriad 'cultural' attributes) that have created the opportunities for them, some ruin the societies they gained, and a few manage to usher in a better order.[23] Saul does not discuss the old Marxist 'Bonapartist' line:[24] stalemates in class struggle often lead to the space for 'great' (or, mostly, horrific) leaders to rise to the top, sometimes thereby pleasing classes one might expect to be 'democratic' but that shy away at the thought of democracy's progress going too far. These leaders might even be 'progressive', as Gramsci's idea of 'Caesarism' allows,[25] but are prone to 'vanguardism'–or more simply, albeit bereft of ideological context, 'dictatorship'–instead of just 'good leadership'.[26] Nor does Saul discuss the moments in history that might make a mere man or woman a *leader* of many more mere mortals.

Does the idea of the 'conjuncture' help? Perhaps 'stalemates' can sometimes be conjunctures–when wide and deep tectonic plates collide so that the contingency and fortune battling in their cracks create nearly undreamt-of consequences. As Lenin–no little man–put it, these moments are when, in 'an extremely unique historical situation, absolutely dissimilar currents, absolutely heterogeneous class interests, absolutely contrary political and social strivings [merge], and in a strikingly "harmonious" manner'. These are the times constituting an 'abrupt turn in history' when 'such a wealth of content, unfolds such unexpected and specific combinations of forms of struggle and alignment of forces of the contestants, that ... there is much that must appear miraculous'.[27] Besnick Pula reminds us that, when we try to construct a 'complex, conjunctural, and multi-layered historical narrative,' we cannot 'anticipate in advance many of the key events that comprise sequences and processes of central analytical importance'.[28] It takes a long, cool and historically grounded gaze to pull out the 'coherent and connected sequences' and the consequences thereof. Difficult, too, to see which ones led to transformative, history-making episodes. Even more so to figure out the role of leaders making those calculations. And harder still for them to do so reflexively, on the trot. Few can marshal such chaos into a progressive pattern, without losing the wondrous spontaneity to stultifying bureaucratic order or worse.

Do these ideas take us very far when discussing what some have called 'Mugabeism'?[29] Not a few have placed this name within the realms of God, destined even to rule from beyond the grave.[30] Probably not far: both the agents involved and the structure that helps produce them need more delineation, beyond particular biographies and their context. This book is certainly not a 'biography' of the man about whom Norma Kriger says ten have been written.[31] Unfortunately, it will add to the 27 with 'Mugabe' in the title that, back in 2016, had Derek Matyszak wonder if this 'frequent inclusion' was a 'publishing imperative'. Be that as it may, Matyszak noted that 'the degree to which Mugabe's personal traits determine Zimbabwe's historical, political and economic trajectory is the axis around which much of the journalistic and academic literature on Zimbabwe revolves'. Matyszak posed the binary around this question nicely: those who think the Zimbabwean party–state amalgam was 'under the "personal rule" of Mugabe' will have a different idea of his aftermath than those arguing that a 'predatory elite' was (and thus still is) in charge. This is 'of importance for the question of succession and transition'. The 'personal rule' line 'implies a radical departure from the style of governance characterised by President Mugabe's 35 years of rule, the latter, continuity'.[32]

This book will take a more dialectical line: the post-Mugabe polity will not perpetuate his patterns seamlessly and eternally, but neither will it be completely different. It will not erase the man from history, but it will also dig deeper than the mere elite that is skating on the surface while also etching it markedly. Marx's tantalisingly ambiguous nostrum about people making history but not being able to choose the conditions in which they make it means avoiding psychology. Yet there are few who can even discern the cracks letting the light come through the fog and the walls–the ones Leonard Cohen sang about[33]– let alone lead a political project that will prise them open for all to see. Forging alliances across classes (permanently and conditionally 'progressive') and identities, and formulating the ideologies to help them bond and envision the other side of the battle is a task for more than one, and even a vanguard. Whoever they are, they must work within the broad parameters of the *organic* conditions that are cracking. Gramsci called this out. The following paragraphs will work up to his warning. That call will be followed by attempts to work out more recent theoretical considerations on whether this book's later fascination with the demonic details of Mugabeism's conceits, conspiracies and coups will rest on bases of 'states of exception' and the lies lying therein.[34]

What is this historically grounded–perhaps structural–theory for which we are searching? First, there is the 'Holy Trinity' making up Development Studies 101, as taught by Professor Toot (aka Teller of Obvious Truths: a new penultimate T could be 'teleological').[35] Primitive accumulation: Karl Marx is the Father of all comprising the essence of capitalism, as the main classes comprising it emerge from predecessors. Capitalists emerge, fighting among themselves as if in *The Godfather*, finally beating feudal restrictions to 'liberate' the surplus value taken from proletarian labour, to plough it through the imperatives of competition into innovative (or now 'disruptive') production.[36] The Son is the progeny of a Weberian and Gramscian marriage: nation-state formation and hegemonic construction; stably bordered territories with good bureaucracies and solidly monopolised violence buttressed by widespread acceptance that its rulers are fit for task. (War and other forms of violence are often the midwives of such means of governance and legitimacy; their acceptance is generated–through time, tales and taxes–materially as well as ideologically). The Holy Spirit is the democratic ghost hovering as ever more people struggle for full citizenship and participation in all aspects of their lives: working-class organisations help that process progress; well-meaning missionaries, whether otherworldly or of equally zealous secular varieties, are more likely to mess it up. Blood oozes–at times pours–from these pores on all sides of the trinity, not just the first.[37] As Michael Mann reads, democracy has as many dark sides as power has sources–the 'economic' base's pernicious partners are as pervasive and as many-hued in their redness as is primitive accumulation.[38] Indeed, as Perelman and Desai among many others argue, states are far from immaterial promoters of the various ways out of the dying modes.[39]

Of course the Holy Trinity's 'ideal type' is far too teleological, the end point being a pre-determined capitalist and liberal future that, hopefully for some (more then than now), set the foundations for the struggles leading to socialism. Dev 101 offers it because it is both the belief behind most of our analyses of African social formations and of globalised capitalism's spread as such, regardless of its original form or universality. Perhaps the only true believers now are World Bank and IMF workers and NGO types–and Marxist utopians who see another future. It is worth repeating Ernest Gellner's apt observation about the prevalence of this belief. Financial and humanitarian preachers pro-claim the 'historically eccentric' variants of Enlightenment values as 'self-evident': other socio-economic realities are 'not within the realm of the imaginable' for them and they are more than willing to force (or persuade) the benighted to be free. But they are rooted in settler-colonial societies such as Australia, Canada and the USA (where, Gellner neglects to say, capitalist ends followed genocidal means). As Gellner put it, where else but in Sydney (perhaps before obeisance to the previous custodians of the land) and other such cities 'if the words Bourbon or Romanov are mentioned, they can only mean whisky or vodka'?[40] Perhaps the moguls of the international financial institutions and their development industry minions are more sophisticated than that, but when alternative models of capitalist development are offered for World Bank Development Reports their final drafts redact them into thin air.[41]

Nevertheless, the model, with many caveats, still offers an outline of trends which, even at their best, are fraught with class struggle and violence: at worst, the battles freeze or reverse the process. To be sure, the endpoint could well have already passed, given finance and 'informational', fourth industrial (not so industrial) revolutionary forms of accumulation and production taking over capital's centres. As James Ferguson has it, the production motif has slipped by social for-mations such as Africa.[42] Ironically, the virtuous, semi-social democratic circle of capitalism and political liberal governmentality in the 'West' from the 1950s into the mid-1970s and some developmental 'policy autonomy'[43] in the decolonised world was enabled by a Cold War structured by undemocratic regimes that would have surprised Marx and Engels. However, with the fall of the Berlin Wall and a 'concatenation of falling profits and productivity, rising wages and prices and Third World assertiveness', what Desai and Heller called 'a couple of decades of unprecedented popular empowerment, progressive policy and prosperity' fell to capital's 'ferocious neoliberal counter-offensive'. The left could not 'overcome its historic divisions' and 'failed either to mount an effective defence of progressive post-war regimes or to develop them further'. The endgame appears to be 'a wave of right-wing and populist mobilisations of the discontents of neoliberalism that should have been the social bases of a reinvigorated left'.[44] Far less to the left, liberals (to the right of that ideology's ever-shifting centre) would alter that epitaph somewhat while bemoaning their hopes for a new start to history's end.[45]

Soon China will present a new type of capitalism on top of the world's array, probably without any form of populism informing its form of primitive accumulation.[46] It will remind us, however, that 'the hegemony of capital and the spectacle of consumerism' (or, basically, the welcome, if dull, compulsions of jobs) may have more pulling power than political participation or highfalutin ideas. Capitals laced with relatively heavy doses of force along with the international dimensions of hegemony—'renewed dreams of a *Pax Sinica*'[47]—of China's rise and the USA's relative fall means Development Studies 101 must also take into account 'world systems' thinking ranging from Arrighi and Cox to Frank and Wallerstein.[48] More precisely and analytically one can bend away from the tunnel (or dig new ones) by examining capitalism's many forms in 'East', 'West', 'North' and/or 'South'—or whatever geographical and temporal categories can still the process long enough for analysis.

The multitude of variations on transitions to and from capitalism's ideal form multiply when one investigates the many 'pre-capitalist' (the prefix 'non' would avoid unidirectional tendencies) socio-economic forms. It is here that Gramsci—with his Sardinian roots, hardly a stereotypical 'dead white male'—enters. His dichotomy between the state and civil society relationship in the 'East' (read Russia but by extension any unevenly developed social formation) and 'West' is well known, but too simple. The commonly cited binary is that, in the West (aka an advanced capitalist country with more than a modicum of democracy), a strong and vibrant civil society cements bourgeois hegemony: the media, schools, churches, popular and high culture, etc. helped the ruling class exercise the moral and intellectual leadership needed to govern via strong (and mostly ideological) consent. Force is ever lurking but hardly noticed, and the dull compulsions of economic survival are just that: not brutal. There are many 'bullshit jobs', as David Graeber had it, inherent in producing, buying and consuming hegemonic happiness, and they are a lot shittier in the world's nether parts.[49] 'Intellectuals' are often the biggest bullshitters of them all.

In the 'East', however, material pleasure is in short supply and Gramsci saw civil society as 'gelatinous' so the state is 'everything' (although when he mentions priests as 'traditional intellectuals' he indicates the solidity of feudal formations in the old West and others elsewhere). 'Wars of manoeuvre' can win these state–society complexes with more force than consent. Lots of 'education' can win over the hearts and minds later: they are ripe for the Modern Prince's picking and ideological cooking. Alternatively, in the 'West', civil society must be moved through 'wars of position' before the Modern Prince has a chance: even deep crises will not dislodge well-constructed ideological and cultural moorings.[50] In both West and East the 'organic intellectuals' keep busy fashioning viable alternatives to a faltering–or fallen–system. Those in the 'stratum which exercises an organisational function in the wide sense' in the realms of 'production … culture, or … political administration'[51] for one or other of the fundamental classes are tasked with reforming or rebuilding a whole society lost with neither moral and intellectual comfort nor coercion crude enough to wipe out any ideas. Economists are clearly one of the key professions in this group, needing clear analysis and steady hands to pull their charges out of crises: the point is, however, to locate their charges and judge how far they can go before they reach the edges of mutual destruction. As Priestland argues, if such intellectuals gain too much of an upper hand in the shifting alliances among themselves and the merchants and soldiers, political and economic crises are not far off.[52]

Just as with the simplistic version of capitalism's inevitable birth from the pains of primitive accumulation, however, on further reading the distance between the East–West poles of civil society–state relations collapses. Other of Gramsci's writings on this question are more complex. They foreshadow the discourse on the 'articulation of modes of production' that Harold Wolpe introduced from the French structuralists to South Africa.[53] For Gramsci, as the ideas and practices embodied in state, civil society and economic relations travel from the centre of the world capitalist system and become embedded in the periphery they create complicated hybrids. When 'a particular ideology'–take either liberal democracy or socialism as examples–'born in a highly developed country, is disseminated in less developed countries' it impinges 'upon the local interplay of combinations' in myriad ways. The interplay of these 'international relations ... with [the] internal relations of nationstates' creates 'new, unique, and historically concrete combinations'.[54]

Besides Wolpe's perhaps excessive focus on the ways in which these modes of production link together to enable capital to benefit from wages cheaper than the cost of labour's reproduction (fulfilled, in part, in the 'reserves'), the political and ideological consequences of such interplays are critical.[55] If the politicians taking over this multi-layered colonial state fail to nuance their power and ideologies and neglect to 'distinguish between historically organic ideologies ... which are necessary to a given structure, and ideologies that are arbitrary, rationalistic, or "willed"' they will run into serious trouble. They will create only 'individual movements, polemics' completely ill-suited to the terrain on which they tread. With luck, their mistakes can 'function like an error which by contrasting with the truth, demonstrates it'.[56] If they manage to maintain power without melding their practice with these 'necessary ... historically organic ideologies' that arise from already 'unique ... historically concrete combinations' and do not learn from their mistakes, they will rule in an 'arbitrary' way indeed. At times Gramsci seems more like Edmund Burke than Karl Marx.[57] Terry Eagleton has a better sense of humour than the above political theorists and practitioners (and most in their sway): if 'socialism' is one of the inorganic ideologies flying in to a 'Third World' country from overseas, its people should heed his warning. Socialism in one (poor) country is like 'being invited to a party only to discover that you had not only to bake the cakes and brew the beer but to dig the foundations and lay the floorboards. There wouldn't be much time to enjoy yourself.'[58] Perhaps only Cuba's Castro took such words seriously. As for forcing people to be free, as in Iraq and Libya lately, the less comedic Timothy Garton Ash was right to say that 'the road to hell can be paved with liberal intentions'.[59]

Wolpe too warned his comrades and compatriots trying to think their way out of the 'colonialism of a special type' trope—but ever so slightly. The 'virtual destruction' of the South African 'pre-capitalist mode of production of the African communities in the Reserves' and thus the source of 'cheap *migrant* labour-power' would create 'changes in and [the] functions of "tribal" political institutions', he wrote.[60] He went no further, although his thesis that the rise of the National Party's repressive ideology and practice was rooted in the cheap labour system's cracking might have included Africans. Today's examples of chiefly forms of authoritarian populism suggest he should have.[61]

I re-encountered Gramsci's cryptic call on arbitrariness and error in the context of a special type of post-colonial rule. It was in Zimbabwe, more than a quarter-century after I had employed his ideas on these interplays in a doctoral thesis long wilted in the mouldy mists of time. Information permanent secretary and Chevening alumnus George Charamba (aka Nathaniel Manheru)[62] utilised them in an editorial blast at the MDC,[63] robbed of an election once again. Quoting Gramsci's above words prolifically, Charamba said the MDC would never win the hearts and minds of the Zimbabwean electorate because its ideology was too Western—too foreign, too liberal—for those who would rather rejoice in the ruling party's ideas.[64] A perfect example of deceitful conceit, Charamba's diatribe elided ZANU (PF)'s well-deserved reputation for election-time violence with its cheating and chicanery.[65] Charamba could have been channelling, but deflecting, Gramsci's idea of the 'corruption/fraud' lying between ideological hegemony and the state's iron hand. This mid-way strategic constellation includes 'the demoralisation and paralysis of the antagonist (or antagonists) by buying its leaders—either covertly, or, in cases of imminent danger, openly' thus sowing 'disarray and confusion in his ranks'.[66] Therein lie the variations within Gramsci's always dialectically blended poles of consent and coercion as the various contenders for power attempt to forge illusive historical blocs–harder to weld in the 'third world' of heterogeneous modes than in the first. When the elisions and corruptions are too evident, rulers resort to strategies reliant on purer force–immediately devastating to those resisting, in the medium term mutually destructive, but ultimately losing.

As Bernard Dubbeld has recalled the history of 'revisionist Marxism' in South Africa, Archie Mafeje and (later) the 'social historians' took umbrage at the 'nomothetic enquiry' encouraged by Marxist abstractions.[67] Dubbeld goes to E. P. Thompson to counter their objections successfully enough, but there is ample ammunition in Gramsci's weaving in and out of real history too. Furthermore, it relates to how differing but bound-together modes of production and reproduction work out their co-existence–or do not. Indeed, reading Zimbabwe's self-styled 'organic' intellectuals such as Charamba imposes an imperative: their arrogance forces us to dig much deeper than their attempts to capture, create or anticipate official discourse. Concepts such as primitive accumulation and the articulation of modes of production (and others embedded in them at various degrees of distance such as the politics of arbitrary states and 'patriotic–ideological–history')[68] help the digging. More than a few (perhaps mostly anthropologists) work hard in the trenches.

Blair Rutherford's use of 'modes of belonging', as he interrogated farmworkers' strikes in the midst of Zimbabwe-wide political and ideological contestations, must have roots–sometimes deeper in 'production' than others–in the 'articulation' discourses stretching back to the late 1960s.[69] As Perry Anderson reminds us, Robert Cox, who in the 1980s initiated Gramscian international political economy, counted twelve 'modes of social relations of production'.[70] He did not count the ways out of them. He did however echo Foster-Carter's concerns that 'each Andean valley [could have] its own mode of production', with residents changing them as often as their underwear.[71] Nevertheless, as the networks of power and accumulation across Africa are examined, the blends of historical times present us with clans, royal families, totems, *nyangas* and *sangomas*, and 'modern' means of politics and business, all linked and simultaneously apart. The modes of mayhem Rutherford analyses so carefully in his *Ground of Politics* is a stark reminder that an 'elite' study such as this book reflects the tip of subaltern realities, intertwined as they are.

In southern Africa especially, 'race' is the identity flowing across and through all of these elements. It is the hegemonic twist in the tales of primitive accumulation and democratisation.[72] Although many Marxists may attempt to sublimate it to less visible and more silent class struggles, as Friedman discusses,[73] it is the tail wagging the dog now. Until 'Africans' become equal to their white compatriots in the realms of property ownership and proletarian socio-economic positions–until, as Michael Mann puts it, the horizontal struggles will subsume the vertical ones[74]–the state will be their 'democratic' avenue to hasten that end, an end that is as chimerical as the many shapes into which it changes.

Yet regardless of the many ways these articulations can mix–for a long time–rulers' discourses repeat the platitudes of 'development' through the tunnels of their tutors in the industry built on its promise. Zimbabwe's 'Second Republic' promises 'middle income' status by 2030 (if only those sanctions would go away 'opening for business' would wave a wand), and the opposition's budget proposals in the 2018 election manifesto prophesised growth rates surpassing China's.[75] The Marxist modernists are not as fantastical, but do see light at the tunnel's end. Few of either tendency appreciate the gap between Marx's historical idea of capitalism's progress in its 'homeland'–not to mention its 'different aspects' and 'various phases' around the world– and the language through which those years are expressed.[76]

A close read of Marx's chronicles of capitalism's victory over the feudal muck of ages suggests schizophrenic slippages between spasmodic and nearly eternal transitions. He notes the centuries–going back 'not ... very far' to the fourteenth or fifteenth century when capitalism began 'sporadically'–but proceeds to proclaim that the 'epoch making revolutions' were *moments* tearing the 'mass of free proletarians' from their old subsistence plots to '*hurl*' them as free and 'unattached' workers to the labour-market. All of this all was '*forcibly hastened*' by the royal powers. The price of wool's '*rapid*' rise gave the 'direct *impulse*' for the serfs and crofters' expulsions. The nobility was '*devoured*'–not masticated and digested slowly. Money, the 'power of all powers', speeded up the process of expulsion even more. Further quickening impulses ranged from the 'colonies, the national debt [hastened by war], the modern tax system, and the system of protection', all utilising state power.[77]

What can bring on primitive accumulation in Africa? Can smart-phones, footloose finance capital and slippery states hasten this histori-cal project? Are the classes emerging within and fighting over these colonially created states too 'unproductive'–maybe 'comprador', pos-sibly 'predatory', perhaps 'neo-patrimonial'[78] or 'prebendal'[79]–to cre-ate the classic social relations that produce real capital?[80] As Colin Leys asked, who could superintend 'the mass dislocation and conflict that would ... [result] from a rapid programme of converting land and labour into commodities' constituting primitive accumulation? Even the colonial powers dared not do this.[81] What comes out of the com-plexly articulated modes of belonging that artificially imposed colonial borders brought together?[82] Are we stuck with the contemplation of the marxisant melancholic optimism emanating from London's School of Oriental and African Studies?[83]

There are also magical realism's prevarications, hoisted too on the optimism/pessimism petard. Jameson thinks that a 'conquest of new kinds of relationships with history' is possible. This could make good sense of the 'overlap or the coexistence of pre-capitalist ... features' with the 'radical fragmentation of modern life and the destruction of older communities'. Gramsci's 'interplays' would thus be 'not neces-sarily based on absolute loss or impoverishment'.[84] That is more opti-mistic than Doctorow's sweeping claim that magical realism expresses the 'exhaustion of meaningful choice'.[85] Jameson's reworking is pre-cisely that, and lots of very hard work. More than that of replacing one ruler with another–especially if they, their comrades and foot soldiers be of the same cloth. Besides their long teleology and too-complex lineages, linkages and breaks, the accumulation and articulation inter-pretational grids fail to bring us close enough to this book's subject: the making of a man and his legacy of coups, conspiracies and conceits. One needs an interpretive lens with finer focus.

There may well be new means–universal enough, yet with closer grain *and* depth of field–enabling closer examination of the time and space of the above structured and processual phenomena as they wrapped around Robert Gabriel Mugabe's enigmatic 'agency' and its effects. The cure from excessive abstraction and context-and-thought-less empiricism could be recent academic indications of a renewed

Gramsci. Combine them with theories of alternative truths, and one has a less vague idea of Mugabe and his moments.[86] Percolations from a particular event—which also led me to extend this book beyond the coup to more about the man who was soon to die—inspired this way of thinking. Following a rendition of the meeting that generated many variations on searches for truths, I will attempt to 'interpret' them given the current age of extended interregna[87] and 'alternative facts'.[88] If interregna stretch beyond imagination then so can Clausewitz's dictum that the difference between politics and war is only a matter of means. Likewise, that truth is the first casualty of war (be the expression's originator Aeschylus or a Johnson)[89] bears similar semantic elasticity.

This particular event, a mid-2019 Chatham House conversation with Zimbabwe's foreign affairs and trade minister, serves up a couple of illustrations. The most important one has been transcribed and YouTubed for eternity.[90] Others circle around the state–civil-society–politics Gordian knot, which gets tighter the more it expands. Sibusiso Moyo (who died of Covid-19-related illnesses just as I was tweaking the last revisions on this book),[91] famous while as a Major General he announced the 'militarily assisted transition', adept at defusing a demonstration threatening to move towards the State House,[92] and later touted as a prospective president, was on the deck. He performed as well as one tutored by a World Bankish soul in the British embassy could ('long-term gain after short-term pain', etc., etc.).[93] However, shaken by journalist Violet Gonda's fiery questions, he faltered further when I asked him two more.

The first was about the roots and consequences of the economic crisis, arguably the source of the many crises in his country. The land invasions that started the new millennium, perhaps? Maybe earlier: the 1998 intervention to assist Laurent Kabila in the war against Rwandan-sponsored 'rebels', wherein army officers (and Emmerson Mnangagwa, and he) got rich via what the United Nations called the 'plundering' of the DRC's minerals?[94] Second, I asked him if he was worried about the international reputation of a country where in January at least seventeen people died in a chaotic series of demonstrations, riots and killings sparked by a spike in the price of petrol. I wanted to know if a 'briefing' his office had apparently released after that, seemingly laying the blame at the feet of a group of democracy missionaries named 'Canvas', indicated his take on the root of Zimbabwe's existential threats.[95]

His answer(s) veered in and out of the scripts prescribed by the dictates of development discourse. He did not want to repeat what he had said a few months before at Chatham House regarding Zimbabwe's economic woes, but did claim that 'we learnt to unlearn the past, and as a result, we then managed to chart our way forward'. Chuckling, he remarked that 'there are so many things, I'm sure, which have happened in your life, since you were born'. There were 'many factors' contributing to the crisis, 'which came to be to the boiling point, particularly in 2008'. Fundamentally, though, 'it was a country under sanctions'. Second, however, 'some of the issues were, also, the manner in which we dealt with specific matters ... our own faults could have contributed'. After he said he wished he was rich, he uttered the following fascinating lines:

> but all I can tell you is that all these issues, which have been taking place, are issues which were as a result of perceptions and other, which then developed into real truth or false truth, whatever the case may be. But all I can tell you is that it's very straightforward and transparent.

I thought at the time that this was the answer to my second question. On reflection the minister might have still have been considering the DRC situation, which as far as he was concerned was all wrapped up because now 'we are very close' to Rwanda's president: the war was 'nothing personal, it was an organisational response ... to that particular issue'. Still, his final words seemed indicative of one of Mugabe's legacies–lying. Was this what 'Operation Restore Legacy' (the coup) was resuscitating? Of course, being economical with the truth is a component part of coups and conspiracies. The conceit is that your power means everybody had better believe you. Yet there are many indicators of doubt within such utterances: 'all I can tell you', twice; 'perceptions and other' unnamed contingent approaches to veracity; and after the separation (or lack of it) between real and false truths, the second 'all I can tell you' was a promise that 'it's very straightforward and transparent'. What was 'it'?

The minister's confusing words have bothered me for a long time. As well as explaining a lot about the twists and turns in Zimbabwe's political history, they also spoke to a universal concern. The scourge of 'alternative facts' as they spewed forth from the mouth and Twitter account of the past president of the United States has generated much thinking about how truths are constructed. Before trying to deal with some conceptual takes on the generality of real and false truths, however, the other two alternative truths around this particular communication event may be worth recounting.

Starting at the beginning might present a more rounded picture. When I arrived at the Chatham House meeting, I passed a small group, presumably of exiled Zimbabweans, demonstrating against the minister and the regime he represented. Violet Gonda was inside. The seat beside her was free. I took it. She was exuberant at scoring an interview with the minister, albeit on the side of the Chatham House meeting or another with members of the Zimbabwean diaspora at Zimbabwe House on the Strand that evening. Minister of Foreign Affairs and International Trade, Lt. General (Retired) Dr Sibusiso Moyo's diary was quite full, but we guessed that since his primary reason for being in London was to attend a media freedom conference, he would deign to keep his promise to converse with a journalist seen to be solidly in the opposition's camp.

Ms Gonda's bold questioning gave me courage to stumble along with my queries. But as the meeting closed, she received a message cancelling her chances for further interrogation: no interview for her. Her manner was too confrontational. 'Crestfallen' barely manages to indicate her sentiments on that news. We left together, made some inquiries of the demonstrators, and I went to another meeting. While I was occupied in Regent's Park a protester sprayed water on the minister as he approached his car. Ndabaningi 'Nick' Mangwana, the regime's permanent secretary for information (perhaps ironically, a United Kingdom citizen),[96] tweeted a condemnation of such wanton violence; Gonda heard that she was blamed for an organisational role in the demo. Tweets in her support revelled in the irony of her curtailed interview just after the minister's participation in the media freedom conference.

The day went on. Minister Moyo's meeting with the diaspora was next. The guest list was poorly organised, so I found it was easy to get in without an invitation. There was Violet Gonda, the intrepid journalist, in animated conversation with a couple of women showing off the latest wedding pictures of cabinet minister Dr Sekai Nzenza (who once worked for World Vision in Australia). After Minister Moyo announced the imminent one-stop investment window, another question period came up—mostly about business opportunities, for the good of the nation of course. When Minister Moyo belittled a journalist's scare-mongering questions that morning, Ms Gonda fired back with the issue of her cancelled interview. Soon her erstwhile friends, and many others, were booing, hissing and telling her to sit down. The moderator from Chatham House suggested she get to her question. S. B. Moyo looked perplexed. When the hubbub abated, he said he had never instructed Mangwana to call off the interview: had it taken place, he and Ms Gonda would have been friends. Another false truth exposed.

What did they all mean? The message from a public-relations hack who thought he could protect a powerful minister (who, as with any one-time military leader, is never fully retired from the organisational means of force, but liked to talk to journalists) from a journalist's ostensible bad manners. Thus resulted social media wars, sullying the Zimbabwean 'second republic's' claims to media freedom, and a confused minister in front of a crowd. The fickle crowd turned on a dime against the outspoken journalist. Real truths; false truths; a legacy of lies: *and* a promise to make it all 'straightforward and transparent', possibly among 'friends'. A crowd that guaranteed the conceits of power. Was this day a microcosm of Zimbabwean politics *in toto*? To consider that this was simply the contemporary condition of world politics and its culture in miniature (there were assuredly more tears and wars in the Trump camp) might be taking things too far. So too would John le Carré's contention that a swindling father could well relieve a son or daughter (in this case him) 'of any real concept of the truth. Truth was what you got away with.'[97] It is not enough to repeat the story about Mugabe's father abandoning him to understand the tangling of truth and power in his case. Who knows S. B. Moyo's psychohistory?

In any case, it was clear by that day's end that I would have to interrogate more than the coup. Its context and consequences would extend far before and after it. Mugabe's certain death also meant that more emphasis needed laying on the legacy already outgrowing him. The theories at hand seemed too big for that task. A few months on—during the purgatory phase of re-writing—new waves in those waters began to crest. They might help to unpack the uncertainties and untruths displayed at the London houses of Chatham and Zimbabwe—and the November 2017 events wrapped up in them.

What then could be a way to break the theoretical logjam? There needed to be something more than just 'conjuncture'.

Fortuitously and fortunately, a number of interpretations of the context and conditioning of lying on a grander scale than usual appeared during the liminal moments (including a peremptory pandemic!) between the first and post-review drafts of this exercise in historical reconstruction. As indicated above, a number of new (not a few short on historical materialism)[98] visits to Gramsci's idea of 'the interregnum' have arisen in the wake of the new world disorder and the rise of the ultra-right on its tides. What were once considered relatively short periods between the reigns of kings and queens are now often deemed protracted periods, betwixt and between modes of production or world orders, approaching an uncertain 'normality'.[99] Thus there are many 'projects' yet no class force powerful enough to lead one forward; in short, as Joseph Femia put it years ago, not even a 'minimal hegemony' to keep the rulers together.[100] Indeed, when one re-examines the *longue durée* Marx set (in his sober moments) for capitalism to emerge from the depths of feudalism, and indeed the indeterminate bounds even Gramsci placed on his many morbid symptoms, this new wave of 'interregna thinking' should not be surprising. It has long-term precedents: I recall my 1980 honours paper supervisor discussing Gramsci's monstrous prognosis.[101] We wondered when his interregnum—the organic crisis—would end, in terms of theoretical prognosis or diagnostic empirics. For those yet to encounter the idea in full, its repetition is worthwhile, even though it raises nearly as many questions as it pulls in from the thin air of melted certainties:

> The crisis consists precisely because the old is dying and the new cannot be born; in this interregnum a great deal of morbid symptoms appear … a problem caused by the 'crisis of authority' of the old generations in power, and by the mechanical impediment that has been imposed on those who could exercise hegemony, which prevents them from carrying out their mission.

> The problem is the following: can a rift between popular masses and ruling ideologies as serious as that which emerged after the war be 'cured' by the simple exercise of force, preventing the new ideologies from imposing themselves? Will the interregnum, the crisis whose historically normal solution is blocked in this way, necessarily be

resolved in favour of the old? Given the character of the ideologies, that can be ruled out—yet not in an absolute sense. Meanwhile physical depression will lead in the long run to a widespread scepticism, and a new 'arrangement' will be found.[102]

Rather than interrogate this enigmatic collection of concepts as an eternal truth, it is best to remember them and apply them to concrete historical situations.[103] In Zimbabwe, what were and are these 'generations'? What is this 'mechanical impediment' and how does it prevent 'those who could exercise hegemony … from carrying out their mission'? The 'war' could be that which enabled a form of democracy based ostensibly on fully franchised elections and their attendant freedoms. That modicum of a new reign was not fulfilled. Did more force fill the gap? Think of Gukurahundi and the thousands killed therein, and the repression following the emergence of the MDC at the turn of millennium. What were the 'new ideologies' Gramsci indicated? Think of the 'ZIPA moment's'—especially its *vashandi* element—abrupt ending in the middle of the liberation war, involving a new generation.[104] Was it, as well as Gramsci's concrete reference, an 'ultra-left' symptom of maleficence, or were those ill tidings rooted in fascism's early stages? As for the new ideologies now emerging in Zimbabwe's long interregnum, are there spaces between neoliberal nostrums, evangelical eternities, and whatever vicious *Weltanschauung* ZANU (PF)'s younger cadres wield? What, given the still-uncharted terrain of an 'African' mode of production (or—wider—'belonging'), could a 'historically normal solution' be? What would one heading to uncharted territory appear; how and why might it be blocked? If 'Mugabe's legacy' answers the latter question convincingly, we might go some way to answer the questions raised by paradigms ranging from 'personal rule'[105] to 'the overdeveloped postcolonial state'.[106]

The morbid interregna syndrome has certainly arisen with the global right and the fears emanating from it. It will not disappear with a new and slightly liberal American president (at 78 years of age, hardly a harbinger of a new era). That these new interregna—just as well labelled 'organic crises'—are recognised as such should be taken as indicators of the possibilities of Bonapartes or Caesars emerging. They may be more worrisome than a Trump or a Boris Johnson. It is notable, too, that they are applied mostly to the centres of advanced capitalism, even though there is much in Gramsci that is useful for the study of 'unevenly developed' social formations, as indeed was Italy and the home of the Comintern when he practised the politics of praxis, and wrote.

Today's analyses of our long purgatory have many post-Gramscian twists, too (some speaking his prose without knowing it). Santiago Zabala's interpretations of the 'age of alternative facts' could be indicative.[107] Could this journey from a Heidegger remaining mostly beyond me (*Dasein?* Huh?) to the undefined idea of a broadly churched leftism going back to Ernesto Laclau (and thus Gramsci via Althusser) *c.*1977, yet to sunder the class and hegemony nexus, assist?[108] Would Zabala's detour through Agamben's states of exception and 'bare life' in a global concentration camp help examine the Zimbabwean predicament? Would it add something to a Gramscian analysis thereof (or vice versa)?

I had previously dismissed Agamben's ideas as preposterous and fetching only for the theoretically promiscuous. But it hit me that life in the training camps for Zimbabwean guerrilla soldiers and some of their political leaders might resemble existence in concentration camps.[109] Could the camps in Mozambique, Tanzania and Zambia demonstrate that Agamben exaggerated the distinctions between 'bare' and 'political' life, as an Aristotle specialist claims on different grounds?[110] Certainly, their 'sovereigns' had to hold on to the reins of their reign in exceptional ways. Those who contested it faced consequences without constitutional mediation: 'rebels' were punished in many ways—on the hoof—some reliant on the host state's overarching sovereignty and violence, others by spontaneous and very arbitrary rulings. Ironically, the war waged against Ian Smith's emergency was prepared in 'states of exception' based in Zambia, Tanzania and Mozambique (again, varying sovereignties) where colonial forms of order were replaced by emerging ones. The arbiters of the new order certainly retreated to their shells (i.e., the ones fired out of guns) when their 'alternative truths'—themselves charged with uncertainty and insecurity, à la Gramsci's gelatinous blends of West and East—were challenged. The emergent leaders were creating another 'frame' demonstrating their 'imposition of truth through power'—their order (ordered with the help of guns).[111] This was the root of *their* lies, coups, conspiracies and conceits, poured over an existing cocktail of Rhodesia's version of 'colonialism of a special type'.

They squashed other, also emerging, versions of truth that might have led to a 'Modern Prince' transcending nationalist muddles to reach what Peter Thomas has called a 'creative phase of the constitutions *ex-novo* of a collective will that aims to institute genuinely new political forms'.[112] Some of these moves in the camps challenging the early efforts of the Zimbabwean nationalist 'old guard's' to construct their hegemony demonstrated the *potential* to cut the knot binding those living the 'bare life' to the 'sovereign', in other words to free political thinking from the 'aporias of sovereignty'.[113] They were working their way to a new 'history of man'.[114] But the new sovereign—"who decides on the exception ... the production of the biopolitical body" that can be killed with impunity'[115]—arose in the camps. Was it one man who created the legacy that lasted long into the post-colonial era? Zimbabwe since 1980 has experienced many years of literal 'states of emergency', with 'popular' and top-down versions of sovereignty therein challenged to varying degrees.[116]

Zabala's account of Agamben's Benjaminesque state of emergency may assist the discovery of a route out of this theoretical rabbit-hole, and an escape from Zimbabwe's long descent to dissipation.[117] The transition out of Agamben's state of exception/interregnum—a 'no-man's-land between public law and political fact, and between the juridical order and life'[118]—is more likely to move into rather than out of totalitarian modes. The 'emergency' enabling the military coup-makers to slip into the space all but vacated by the doddering nonagenarian president could be Agamben's 'protected democracy'. They claimed an aim of preserving the constitution's and (initially) Mugabe's sanctity from the 'criminals' surrounding him. If so, we should remember that such prophylactics bear no resemblance to democracy: they serve 'instead as a transitional phase that leads inevitably to the establishment of a totalitarian regime.[119] Timothy Scarnecchia's prediction of a fascist future for Zimbabwe could well eventuate.[120] Zabala could be following Scarnecchia.

The role for Benjamin's Zimbabwean tyrant will be 'to replace the unpredictability of historical accident with the iron constitution of the laws of nature'. These 'accidents' are when those trampled by the tyrannical states of exception realise that the emergency is 'fake'. They see that the real crisis is indeed their oppression and repression, which hide the genuine emergency. However, the veneer of the new rules outside the law cannot be seen as legitimate for long. The 'subalterns' may not have a utopia designed for the future, but they certainly want to escape from the horror of history that its angel has revealed. The 'real' emergency arrives when their violence emerges. For Carl Schmitt (responding to Benjamin), this emergency requires the 'sovereign' to intervene. Indeed, he is justified to go outside the law in order to preserve it. Fortunately or not, the dictator's aims are doomed to fail. "'At the first opportunity ... [this] mad autocrat and symbol of a disordered creation'" will reveal his incapability to decide how to 'avert the state of emergency.'[121] His 'gestures of executive power' will be revealed immediately as 'hopeless'.

For Zimbabwe–as in pre-fascist Germany–it remains to dig deep historically to find the roots of this 'disordered creation' and the role of one man in planting them. When that is determined, we still need to know how the one tyrant who created a particular form of 'exceptional' rule simultaneously set the scene for the bathetic coup and death that cut him completely from any threads of hegemony that remained. The coup-makers said without irony that they were 'restoring' this legacy. Perhaps Benjamin would have said all of these efforts were and are 'hopeless', but this was not and will not be revealed 'immediately'. They served to enable lucrative modes of accumulation for those who tailed Mugabe and his state.

The legacy of all this is their scrambling to keep their avenues of accumulation from each other. Before an account of this history proceeds, however, one could outline the legacy's legs, the tripod on which the Holy Trinity rests. S. B. Moyo's search for the 'very straightforward and transparent' truth follows a road full of bends and with unclear ends. The path is far from straight, be it during wars of 'liberation' or post-colonial eras barely gaining momentum to decolonial discourses, let alone originally 'African' modes of materiality.[122] The Zimbabwean rulers are almost undefinable. They are far from a classically productive capitalist group. They carry little in the way of feudal *noblesse oblige*: ask the artisanal miners who encounter the presidentially linked al-Shabaab gangs around Kwekwe.[123] Its chiefly elements display more vassalage than *ubuntu*. Can the label 'securocrats' apply to them all? Perhaps now, if one deigns to call those who lost to the coup 'intellectuals' and cronies that needed not the soldiers (note too that the 'civilian' security branches–intelligence and police–did not win). Whatever the label, they do not seem to be much of a 'father' in the developmental triad.[124] Primitive accumulation, dependent on the separation of peasants from their sources of production, had a shaky start with apartheid-style industrialisation, its partial proletariat, and its stalling of original agrarian capitalists. Come 'fast-track land reform' in the 2000s there went most of the old settlers' big farms and the industrial mode in the linkages ahead and behind them. As Terence Chitapi has written, the new settlers on mid-size farms are far from being agrarian capitalists. They are finding that accumulation takes place 'outside of agrarian production'.[125]

Nevertheless, those who think they have a hold on this mode of belonging barely consider constructing and maintaining a coherent state and ideological or materially based hegemony within it: all else but the power to accumulate is contingent. Coercion and co-optation can work when they must. The in-between modes of corruption work well enough for now. The national 'son'? Perhaps naught but the Terence Ranger version of history ever asserted that; disavowed by default in his 'patriotic history' trope and more explicitly in his memoir.[126] Genocidal missions are not the way to build a nation;[127] balancing ethnic divides does not last either.[128] Can a social formation with some sort of boundaries between it and other blends of states and societies be a nation when it had to abandon its worthless currency, and more than a decade later has no breath to resuscitate it? On the 'son's' ideology side, Marxism of various adopted sorts? Not even given a chance to learn from its errors. The efforts to make a cohesive ideology of 'the Third Chimurenga' (the land invasions, or retaking, were to be the source of pride inherent in the last war against the white settlers) have not convinced the millions escaping the porous borders around the economic meltdown and political repression. Their money, though, keeps their remaining families alive.

And the democratic Holy Ghost? At its basic level, what is the count of stolen elections? Six. How many were free of coercion and chicanery? None: and the 2008 version saw at least 170 killed, with thousands fleeing the military's punishment for voting the wrong way (many voting for ZANU (PF) MPs but not the president).[129] The Cold

War; the one-party state; new rulers' humiliation at having to imitate 'Western' forms of democracy; agreeing to follow their naïve enthusiasts road to the end of history rather than be the 'founders of something original themselves':[130] all of these elements tended to diminish the prospects for participatory politics. Compounding it all was donor fickleness and oppositional mimicry.[131]

All in all, a rather unholy trinity. A state of exception to be sure.

That is about all we can say about the conditions that have created the terrain on which men like Mugabe tread; they do not determine how they will walk, with whom, nor a single path. No interregnum, conjuncture, class stalemate, oddly articulated complex of modes of production or 'emergency' can create a predictable Bonaparte or Caesar.[132] Plenty of contingencies and Fortuna accompany them. We can however chart the ways in which the Mugabes of the world make their mark on their roads, and judge if they have altered the subgrade— how their political coups, conspiracies and conceits in their societies' superstructures change their structures. Something approaching historical exegesis may assist this mapping.

Stuart Doran, the definitive historian of Gukurahundi's deep dark shadow, said during a recent lecture that we might only know the real story 'when ZANU (PF) falls apart'.[133] That is as close to prediction as any historian would let slip, and parallels the ones about the coming storms. Readers can judge if the following pages substantiate those informed guesses.

2

MUGABE'S ENDS

Siphiwe Gloria Ndlovu's extraordinary *The History of Man* ends with 'what makes a man is his life's story'. Those writing their own want some parts well known and others to 'remain hidden'. They would portray themselves 'in an objective but empathetic style ... kind ... even where ... a less forgiving lens would be best'.[1] When a man's story includes most of a country, much that he wants unseen will eventually be uncovered. Mugabe may have thought his legacy would last as he wished. Others believed that since the Zimbabwean state had indeed been all his, 'a new era [would begin] with his fall'.[2] Falling between, one could argue that much of his legacy will stay. Chinks in his post-mortem armour will crack in time. This chapter's stories might widen those gaps. They will not match the narrative Mugabe would write.

Sometimes people slip up all by themselves. Mugabe spoke his last public words on his 95th birthday, 21 February 2019, fifteen months after the coup deposing him from his presidential pedestal. He would die in seven months. His celebration brought the concept of 'conceit' to mind–a simple version, unlike Chabal's critique of Western reason.[3] This universal one speaks of the transformative–or revelatory–qualities of power. As Acton might have put it, its absolute form corrupts totally, but it comes with a thesaurus of additions ranging from vanity to tyrannical arrogance. Conceit also means an over-stretched, 'fanci-

27

ful' and 'strained' metaphor.[4] How about 'So Blair, keep your England and let me keep my Zimbabwe' for a far-fetched feudal fantasy?[5] The idea that one leader can subsume popular sovereignty is a conceit. Did enfranchised Zimbabweans consensually grant part of their autonomy to ZANU (PF) and government organisations, or even *a* 'sovereign'? You'd need to lie, and maybe even believe it, to continue with that conceit. In Mugabe's Zimbabwe, this belief became the polity's organising theme: political decisions had his indelible stamp. This was Mugabeism. Those who practised it imagined that *everybody* believed it. Only a malevolent force could create unbelievers; indeed, transformed into unsuspecting or corrupted puppets. Mugabe's 95th birthday party had to be viewed through the lens of conceit.

Bulawayo 24's photo showed no great party, costing millions, as in years past.[6] No 'February 21 Movement', when kids sharing that anniversary trooped like little Kim Il Sungs to the festive table. There were the sons, minus the $60,000 watch and the champagne with which to douse it.[7] A couple of grandchildren were with their mother, Bona. Dr Grace Mugabe—she of the ghosted PhD—was perched aside her husband, gazing to the photographer's side. The fly in the ointment that destroyed G-40's elevation to the party's pedestals was hoist on her own petard. A glazed Marie Antoinette. No cake in sight, unlike the previous thirty or so presidentially pretentious parties. She smiled vacantly, still bemused at missing the guillotine.

Shrivelled and small, the man of the moment was dwarfed in a throne-like chair haloing his head with a cockerel-like crown. His disproportionately long legs pushed his knees into his shrunken trunk and pulled up his trousers' hems far above his ankles and his long, shiny, shoes. Was it really Mugabe, who had been in power for four cocky decades? This family portrait would warn off any pretender to more than two terms on the throne.

Elegiac as it was, the picture spoke no thousand words. Mugabe's final, macabre bon mots were enough. Just over a couple of dozen, dripping with sarcasm but draped in lies, said it all. They painted him into the corners constructed by his conceit.

One supposes such words would suggest how he wanted his memory to remain, in contradistinction to the views of the man who stole his throne. Violent demonstrations and killings had racked Zimbabwe a month before the ex-president's final birthday. The conflagration occurred in the wake of a huge rise in petrol prices, anticipating the second round of hyperinflation in a decade. At least seventeen people were killed and as many women raped. Hundreds more were beaten and arrested, to attend mass trials of hundreds at a time. The protagonists seemed a chaotic mix of soldiers (some fake), police, looters and agents provocateurs: few had a clear idea of who killed and beat most. President Mnangagwa had taken a convenient trip to Eastern Europe, Russia and the annual Davos celebration, leaving his subordinates to mind the mess.[8] Mugabe thought his successor was behind it all.

The distinctly disenchanted and obviously weak Mugabe rasped: could Mnangagwa not 'do without seeing dead bodies'? What sort of person could 'feed on death'? Repeating his tired refrain on his imagined separation between soldiers and politicians, Mugabe admonished:

> I say to soldiers be followers of the people you want to lead, you are not even qualified to lead them. Take your places in recognition that you are not trained to lead but to follow the people, to protect them.

This was a concoction repeated since at least 1976, as Mugabe eliminated 'a people's army' that he feared, but knowing he would have to manage another one to quell the threat. Even then, he lied about where his control lay.[9]

More personally, he warned his once-obsequious retainer:

> You want to shower yourself with praises despite being at the top? You are not God ED. Today you are at the top, tomorrow you will be at the bottom, keep that in mind. God has his own way of punishing rogues and cruel people.

One takes some pleasure when the powerful fall into pathetic bathos. The emperors are slow to realise they have been bared to the bone, but are aware they have lost their crown, robes, thrones and aura. Having said his last words, Mugabe must have decided that death finally made sense. There would be no more sense in 'living so long'.[10]

With so much history wrapped up in one man, can his final metamorphosis reveal deeper manifestations of transformation?[11] A coup, even if called one that was not, indicates more possibilities of change than a subsequent death. Death always arrives, although, as Joost Fontein knows, its material and symbolic forms vary significantly and it stays longer than expected.[12] Perhaps Mugabe's *political* death made his corporeal one anticlimactic.[13] Many think coups bring big changes. Zimbabwe needed the latter. Coups are quick, require careful strategy and tactics, are risky, and they kill–all the while promising a new beginning on a new terrain in a new world. Deaths dwell on the past. By the time Mugabe died, much of the hope for a new start had died too. Mugabe's death was a double death. His real death created more memories than aspirations. To mangle Marquez thereby foretells the future[14] ... unless, unless, one can go some way to ensure the books (and unordered truths) are not burned and/or buried. Not just archival trails of vicious colonial lies, but of nationalist travesties too.[15]

A magical realist or other fantastical notion of death might explain how I learned of Mugabe's departure. Mugabe died in Singapore barely over six months after his 95th. He often graced the 'dictators' den' at Gleneagles Hospital. On 5 September 2019 Joost Fontein and I dined together. We wondered how Mugabe's anticipated passing would alter our books.[16] I forgot to set my alarm that night: unwise, given the slothful sunrise in Johannesburg's September. At about five to seven, I awakened with a start. As I reached to turn on the radio, the phone fell to the floor, breaking the screen protector in near-perfect halves. It rang precisely then. It was Mdu Maqubela, the producer for SAFM's 'Sunrise', not the alarm.

'Prof,' Mdu exclaimed, 'Robert Mugabe has died, can you speak to us in a few moments?' I asked, 'Are you sure?' Such rumours often preceded the facts. 'Yes, BBC has confirmed.' I ratified readiness as thoughts of British cultural hegemony crossed my mind. I had plenty of time. Mugabe and his array of admirers and critics were always a big deal in South Africa. Well-known Zimbabweans would precede this cosmopolitan's interloping.[17]

Aside from extra-sensory phones, this particular moment is unimportant but for Tendai Biti being the first of the instant obituaries. South Africans knew him best as a leading light within the MDC's various permutations and from 2009 to 2013 as Zimbabwe's finance minister during its 'government of national unity'. I remembered his long and consistent opposition to ZANU (PF). He exemplified his generation of radical university students, including Trotskyists like him, Maoists, Fanonists and liberals, who did so much to start the

National Constitutional Assembly (NCA) and get the MDC off the ground: to get Mugabe thinking about life on such political terrain. It clicked: Biti was the perfect embodiment of Zimbabwe's third generation of democrats–that pillar of the trinity with holiest hues–now with their father gone.

Furthermore, as a lawyer, he had represented one of the *second* generation's finest rebellious souls. Wilfred Mhanda was one of the first to meet Mugabe's wrath while encountering the 1970s *vashandi* challenge. Mugabe's response? Mozambique's prisons. In the 1990s Mhanda, the ginger group's *éminence grise*, demanded 'war veteran' status. As the MDC and opposition politics arose, in part the product of the Biti generation's work, Mhanda took the leading role in an alternative war veterans' group, the Zimbabwe Liberators' Platform.[18]

Mugabe's death generated relief, celebration, despair and digging into the past. Biti disappointed in the last-mentioned. He was the first to remind me that the 1970s were as much as forgotten. Here was a history of new truths unfolding the morning after Mugabe died. However, Biti's fulsome praise for Mugabe snapped me out of my historical reverie.

He had only praise for Mugabe's great contribution to Zimbabwe's liberation. Mugabe was our 'founding father', Biti said. He 'shepherded us for all these years'. In comparison with the people now ruling Zimbabwe–those who put him to the side with their soft coup–'we appreciate him'.

Biti and his student-generation political leaders arose in Gukurahundi's wake, when ZANU (PF) swallowed the opposition ZAPU and embarked on its aim–always challenged–toward a one-party state. His route to the opposition party that came closest to dislodging the self-appointed 'party of revolution' shared much with his generation and legal vocation. Unlike his contemporaries, however, he had risen to the post of Secretary General of the only party to challenge ZANU (PF) seriously. Few could manage his next step: finance minister in a government incorporating the MDC.

Biti did say Mugabe had imprisoned and tortured him, but offered no details. Then the MDC Secretary General, he faced treason charges (and more) at the end of March 2008. After what became the first round of Zimbabwe's first 'harmonised' election (combining municipal, parliamentary and presidential contests), he announced an MDC victory too soon. The MDC had won the parliamentary race, with 99 seats to the ruling party's 97; fewer than a dozen went to an MDC splinter and an independent. Biti's declaration–only the day after the count–announced a victory slightly over the 50% line for MDC president Morgan Tsvangirai. This was too much for those habituated to and protecting Mugabe's sovereignty. Many 'official' counters said off record that they tallied 56%. Stephen Chan's openly published accounts recorded similar results from his networks,[19] Zimbabwean public intellectual Ibbo Mandaza–by then a disenchanted veteran of many ZANU (PF) years–said so at Southern African Liaison Office (SALO) meetings. The ZANU (PF) minions were undoubtedly preparing for a long count to reach a state-sanctioned number. Their colleagues with guns were readying the vicious Operation Makavhoterapapi ('Where did you put your cross?') for the presidential run-off, during which hundreds–including those who voted ZANU (PF) for an MP but Tsvangirai for president–were killed and tortured, with many more forced out of their residences.[20]

Strangely, Biti's announcement was also disconcerting for civil society election watchers. On the next Monday–to meet journalists' frenzy or dampen ruling party wrath–a consortium of election NGOs hurriedly and statistically sloppily announced a plurality for the near-president: Tsvangirai's 47% versus Mugabe's 43%. This entailed a run-off presidential contest. The Zimbabwe Election Support Network (ZESN) and its donors had rushed to fill the gap Biti had created between civil society's counting techniques and the party-state machines' auditing routine. The former tested the new regulation that each voting station post its 'V-11' results in public view. The latter (although not of one mind on the ends desired) relied on any means needed. Suspicions remain. Why did ZESN put on this show?

Six weeks later–a long time to count election ballots!–the Zimbabwe Electoral Commission's counters accentuated these doubts. Zimbabwe's official but sneaky election body cut Biti's 50+% tally to just over 47%–very close to civil society's monitors. The run-off election and Operation Makavhoterapapi ensued. Mining shares worth around $100 million had been through many hands and indigenisation laws to supplement the ZANU (PF) war chest earmarked for the task. *Primus inter pares* with dirty fingers was Billy Rautenbach, well-known Zimbabwean facilitator and beneficiary of similar transactions ranging from the DRC to South Africa.[21] Sometime around then I heard a story about the same chap handing over a few million bucks to Morgan Tsvangirai for his party, to be passed on to Roy Bennett, the MDC treasurer. A month or so later Rautenbach asked Bennett if he had received the money. Bennett did not know about it. Just a story, albeit from well-informed folks; besides, a good capitalist supports all sides of a democratic project, combining self-interest with the political probity the new era of democracy welcomed.

Never missing an unintended consequence, Norma Kriger noted that the 2008 violence was 'a sad paradox of the effort to bring transparency to elections ... post[ing] the election results outside the polling stations enabled the ruling party to target those villages or farms or resettlement areas which had voted for the opposition'.[22] These included many ZANU (PF) members who had voted for their party in parliament but not for their party's choice for president.

The pre-election violence forced Tsvangirai–after long consultation with his party–to withdraw from the run-offs. Biti was tortured, interrogated about the MDC's plans, and denied medication. Mugabe would 'win'–with a 42% turnout delivering a 90% 'victory'[23]–but the regional and continental multilateral bodies finally had enough of his shenanigans. Thus arrived the GNU (actually a TIG, or transitional inclusive government), with Biti as finance minister. ZANU (PF) gathered its wits and augmented its power while the MDC slipped.[24] ZANU (PF) 'won' the 2103 elections.[25] Biti left the MDC to form his own party. By the 2018 election he was back in, this time part of the MDC 'Alliance'. By 2019 the MDC was born again in a more formal reunification.

Soon after his 2008 release, Biti wrote that reading Ngũgĩ wa Thiong'o's *Mũrogi wa Kagogo* (*Wizard of the Crow*) could help one understand what he had just experienced. For him, Ngũgĩ's Abhurian State 'brilliantly described' how ruling classes in post-colonial Africa fill the vacuum of nationalist ideology:[26]

> Faced with the frustration of failing to transform the colonial state during the national democratic stage of the struggle, nationalism degenerates and decomposes into neo-patrimony, clientelism, the imperial presidency and patronage. In short, it converts the state into a rogue

state where violence, corruption and personal accumulation become vehicles for the continued reproduction of the state.

He cited Chinua Achebe's *A Man of the People*, Ousmane Sembène's *The Last of the Empire* and Ayi Kwei Armah's *The Beautyful Ones are Not Yet Born* in his critique of nationalism's death throes.

At that stage, the highest level of decomposition, nationalism needs to be saved from itself or it will take the nation with it. That is exactly where Zimbabwe is at the present moment. ZANU (PF) needs to be saved from itself or it will annihilate the construct that Zimbabwe is.

Biti took us through all theories from the Marxism of the National Democratic Revolution (meaning: 'sorry, if you think you can impose socialism on a society that has yet to reach capitalism's potential, reset')[27] to neo-patrimonialism into horrific beyonds. He had experienced them all. He had two choices left: populism or liberalism. Collaboration with dyed-in-the-wool liberals such as Greg Mills and Jeffrey Herbst, a re-dyed Olusegun Obasanjo,[28] and Washington beltway think tanks (not to mention the World Bank), along with the once social-democratic MDC, suggested he chose both. Yet just over a decade after prison and embarking on the GNU's constraints, when Robert Gabriel Mugabe died Tendai Biti sounded very much like a nationalist. Does this nationalism occlude the phase incubating the coup-makers who wanted to 'restore' its legacy?

Elinor Sisulu's sober remembrance followed Biti's superlatives, but she also remained in the post-1980 script. Long-time human rights defender and in the 1980s also a university student council president, she started her criticism with the biggest blots on Zimbabwe's landscape. First was the 1980s genocidal Gukurahundi massacres.[29] The bulldozing of thousands of houses and the removal of hundreds of thousands of their residents during Operation Murambatsvina ('Clear out the trash') after the 2005 election was second. She refrained from declaiming Mugabe's permanent hero status.

When I was in university, he was a hero ... but that changed ... now I feel sad for all the people who were tortured and died. ... He did play a big role in the liberation struggle but that does not give him the right to kill people.

My contribution? I said that Mugabe was *a* father of the nation along with Joshua Nkomo and Ndabaningi Sithole. I noted that when he started on his road to lead ZANU in late 1974 Samora Machel, just arrived on the statehood scene, wondered if he had committed a coup in prison. I summarised Mugabe's facility at managing the many contradictions within the Zimbabwean ruling group until it caught up with him. I probably repeated my favourite line about him and the clouds roiling in his wake: *après lui les déluges*.

Recalling the sceptical response of one of the victims of Mugabe's 1977 outrage to my query regarding *The Conversation*'s early 2019 commission to ready an obituary for the nonagenarian, I recoiled from *extreme* negativity. He asked: 'Why would you want to do that? You'd just be known as the guy who couldn't find anything good to say about Mugabe when he died.' Cultural taboos on speaking ill of the dead did not go quite that far, and anyway interpretations thereof are mixed. Tinashe Nyamunda claimed that *wafawanaka* means 'the dead are now exorcised of bad doings and therefore we can only speak of their good deeds'.[30] Ruth Murambadoro differs: when one dies 'people are expected to come forth and clear the debts that they owe and are owed by the deceased before burial. *Wafawanaka* (death is the ultimate rule)' also means that the dead's 'transgressions and good deeds' accompany them to the grave.[31]

I did not fear contradicting the platitudes of politicians too proximate to their past power.[32] However, at seven in the morning they had yet to appear–and the obit was out very soon, without the cuts I had promised weeks ago. I could only anticipate them. Did anyone believe that rote anyway? With excessive praise floating around various media forms (less, though, on the youth-driven messaging outlets), I figured it would not be bad to be known as the naysayer. Even the purveyors of relatively nuanced news could be countered. For example, if one knew more about ZANU and ZAPU relations during the liberation war in the 1970s (and before), how could one claim that their 'very toxic relationship', including Gukurahundi, began only in 1982? How could one say that if the 'Mugabe of 1980 were to meet the Mugabe of 2000 and 2017' they would have a long argument, because 'over the years he had 'transformed, transformed, and transformed'?[33] Only if you thought that metamorphosis meant getting older and more blatantly tricky–but weaker in mind and body. Mugabe certainly did transform just about every facet of Zimbabwean politics, policy and general life:

from dog tales to tobacco, the environment, and of course ethnic relations, as Dande and his co-writers chart.[34] Zenzo Moyo may however
have summed up a young, post-nationalist generation's consensus:
'Mugabe was an educated man who refused to learn.'[35]

Percy Zvomuya's exception proved the rule that few of the racon-
teurs on the death of this man of history reached below the magic 1980
cut-off date.[36] Zvomuya recalled a story recounting that even Mugabe's
mother warned his fellow nationalists back in the early 1960s. Mbuya
Bona Mugabe wondered why they thought her son cared about 'your
politics'. She told them that 'he doesn't care one bit about that. You
don't know how cruel my son is. You don't know him at all.' Of
course, the issue rests on more than what a mother knows. As Zvomuya
cited Graham Greene (apparently one of Mugabe's preferred reads),
'a man isn't presented with two courses to follow: one good and one
bad. He gets caught up.' That brings us back to what is special about
the maelstrom that sweeps up a very intelligent son. It involves the
biographies of many people, spread far and wide in space and time.

Zvomuya also took the mid-1970s as a missed turning point. He
cited Robert Bolaño's warning about waiting too long for the stages of
history to unfold as if to counterpoise the 'infantile and ultra-leftist'
line Samora Machel impressed on the young political soldiers daring to
cross Mugabe.[37] We were on the same track, although I am still unsure
if they were childish and extreme or the best indication of how the
National Democratic Revolution might have worked had it a measure
of time and space.[38] Much depends on definitions of 'infantile'. If
Frelimo's brand of 'democratic centralism' foreshadowed their future,
it was hardly for Machel to invoke Lenin's swipes at those who sneered
at parliamentary democracy when it was a viable option. Frelimo's
economic policies were far from Bukharin's too. The vashandi feared
ZANU (PF)'s road dead-ended at democracy.

Zvomuya raised his radical vashandi hopes with decolonial-guru
Sabelo Ndlovu-Gatsheni, who also dared dive before 1980.[39] First,
though, they traded explanations for Mugabe embracing 'violence as a
mode of rule': Nietzsche's monsters (colonial ogres or the brutality of
the liberation war?) or hamartia? Ndlovu-Gatsheni chose a safe fence:
perhaps a fundamental flaw, maybe 'sociogenesis–political socialisa-
tion'. The ambiguous combination remains: not further ahead than

Giddens' 'structuration' blending agency and social determination. Yet Ndlovu-Gatsheni was keen to emphasise the authoritarian 'school' of the liberation struggle—mentioned seven times at least—as if it was uncontrollable. The 'tribalism' trope came in too, but nearly, neatly, omitting the Ndebele and ZAPU.

When they got to Zvomuya's question, Ndlovu-Gatsheni praised the radicals' ability to suss out the falsity of the old guard's Marxism-Leninism, but claimed they had fallen into the colonial trap of accepting the Westphalian idea of the nation-state. Ironically, however, the *vashandi* question relates directly to Ndlovu-Gatsheni's claim that Abel Muzorewa and Ndabaningi Sithole 'lost it' because they were unwilling to 'worship the barrel of the gun'. Sithole and Muzorewa's losses were a direct result of the ZIPA (Zimbabwe People's Army) ginger group's dismay at the possibility of their leadership. This, to carry the irony to a second level, was a large component of Mugabe's ladder to his coronation. Sithole—from 1964 until the 'coup in prison' retired him in 1974 the leader of the breakaway party that eventually ruled Zimbabwe—'lost it' in the wake of ZANU national chair Herbert Chitepo's assassination in Lusaka in March 1975.[40] He abandoned 'his' soldiers to the Zambian army's guns and disappeared to the USA, apparently to visit his sick daughter. On return, he scurried to Nyerere in Tanzania to claim his due, and then the Mozambican camps to curry the soldiers' favour. He was too late.

Denied the freedom fighters' support, in the late 1970s neither Sithole nor Muzorewa hesitated for a second when the Smith regime offered the vicious 'auxiliaries' to pave the path to one of the most short-lived governments ever.[41]

Muzorewa's story is sad. The liberal and nationalist forces of opposition to a plebiscite on a mild-mannered constitutional proposal pulled the (American) Methodist bishop out of his pulpit in 1972 to preside over their 'no' campaign.[42] Edgar Tekere told me that the imprisoned nationalist leaders approved—indeed suggested—Muzorewa thinking it was an interim measure for an umbrella grouping.[43] Yet Muzorewa hung on long after the Pearce Commission, treading water out of his depth until dumped. Well past his sell-by date, his last letter to Margaret Thatcher pleaded for his family's sustenance. In mid-1981 his ephemeral prime ministership in the hybrid 'Zimbabwe–Rhodesia' long gone, he asked for $25,500. His sons' university education needed cash. Kent State was about to expel one for non-payment of fees, the one in London was expensive. Five months on, he demanded $30,000 for Durawall fencing, security guards and a chauffeur, because the Zimbabwean state no longer provided these. In March 1980 Peter Carrington had donated $100,000 towards the residence. The negative reply–for which the poor prelate had to wait another month, if he got it at all–was for the Harare-based high commissioner to deliver orally: 'it would be a mistake in [Carrington's] view to commit any response to paper'. This should, Carrington relayed to Thatcher, put a stop to the perception that there is 'something of an open-ended commitment' in train.[44] Whatever their ends, neither Sithole nor Muzorewa decried guns as means. Why did Ndlovu-Gatsheni say that their refusal to 'worship' them was why they failed?

Zvomuya's final conversation with Ndlovu-Gatsheni concluded with the Bible. If God planted the tree of knowledge in Eden, 'knowledge creates reality'.[45] We were back to alternative truths, seemingly out of thin air or holy breaths. It could be worthwhile to return to their pasts, to see which ones made history. That might take us beyond fleeting moments of idealist fantasy.

Reminiscences of people of Mugabe's generation, who had witnessed or even helped Mugabe to the heights of Zimbabwean power but were also able to situate him amidst a host of determinations, might bear closer to a truth.

Long-time ZAPU stalwart Reg Austin's life span and experience surpasses all of the above. Perhaps given his long legal and other service to ZAPU and the cause of unity and democracy in Zimbabwe (and globally), Austin's perspective on Mugabe's rule was 'pragmatism'– with a Machiavellian polish–and lots of context. Austin noted that Mugabe was rumoured to keep *The Prince* by his bed. (In fact, Zimbabwe Institute of Development Studies employees remember him borrowing the book. They do not know where Mugabe kept it, but report that Machiavelli never graced ZIDS' shelves again.) For Austin, ZANU (PF)'s '40 years in control of the party/state suggests his was a complex, *deliberately contradictory* [emphasis mine] hybrid of philosophy and pragmatic practice'. Hobbes is a better fit for that, he argues: Mugabe seemed to be think that human–'particularly Zimbabwean'–

nature needs the Leviathan to lessen its nastiness and extend its years. But Austin then asks, were these 'Hobbesian convictions also able to infect, infiltrate and pervert our democratic constitutional institutions— executive, administrative, parliamentary and judicial?' The ruling party 'controlled and moulded them for over 40 years. They are part of his celebrated "legacy".'[46]

Austin's idea of Mugabe's deliberate construction of contradictions sounds like an elaborate creation of economical truths, the consequences of which would lead to unintended self-immolation. Austin's sense of the complex and extremely frustrating historical processes and structures making Mugabe brings necessary context to usually one-dimensional pictures. The conditions—aside from two—within which he struggled were not conducive for him to maintain his 1950s vision of nationalist utopia. From the Thatcherite insistence on the preservation of property rights when the issue of land came up at the 1979 Lancaster House negotiations, to South African destabilisation as 'freedom' came only half-way, to the evaporation of the 1960s dream of untouchable one-party states for which he had killed thousands, Mugabe's makings in history were severely constrained.[47]

Only power was left, and it boxed him in. The two fast-receding facilitating conditions were the Cold War and South Africa's liberation—the latter simultaneously enabled and constrained by the former. Ironically, they allowed Mugabe and his party-state to proceed with the Gukurahundi slaughters and spend as if 'structural adjustment' would never arrive.

Although reading Machiavelli indicates brainy application, Austin did not assess the degree of Mugabe's intellect. Many others are wont to do so. This should not be surprising given Zimbabwe's long political history of 'egghead vs. lowbrow' aka 'elite vs. populist'—and at times slipping into 'patriot vs. sell-out' conflict—dating long before then-journalist and later minister of information (and much else) Nathan Shamuyarira in 1960 welcomed members of the former to the National Democratic Party.[48] Perhaps it started when Goromonzi High School opened in 1946 to groom the prospective elite: forty years later, a young scholar there told me that 95% of his classmates wore glasses although few needed them. He needed neither, he said, 'I know I am smart'. The year before, I met a young ZAPU cartographer; masking tape kept his spectacles intact. A gang of ZANU youth beat him up during the pre-election period. As they ground his glasses to the ground they taunted: 'Do you think you are an intellectual? Are you as smart as Mugabe?'

I first met Joshua Nkomo sometime between these meetings, in his Bulawayo bungalow not far from the tracks that had so recently divided white and black. He and his acolytes were discussing the day's newspaper. One of ZAPU's politicians had crossed the floor: 'You can never trust these intellectuals,' Nkomo growled. The next time I met him, in a similar Harare house, I attempted to raise the history of the March 11 Movement of 1971, which mirrored ZANU's *vashandi* in many ways. He muttered something similar, adding 'cowards' to the discourse.[49] Morgan Tsvangirai's memoir is scattered with evidence of similar tensions, and Tendi's many works on the politics of 'public intellectuals' indicate unwavering conflict in this realm.[50] The problem with them all is that they make little attempt to link this social group to the main classes in society, except by default to an undefined state. This is yet another symptom of Zimbabwe's ambiguous interregnum, and the hopes conjured therein. As elastic as they are, Gramsci's ideas on the organic (or not) qualities of this stratum would stretch to snapping point at the celestial claim that 'a new political value system' is needed in Zimbabwe, apparently in the realm of thought alone.[51] Do intellectuals make history and its values? Do they not have material roots? What is the force behind a propagandist's version of historical truth?

Perhaps one of Mugabe's legacies is the intelligentsia's diminished status. Whilst so many politicians and their partners buy their doctorates or zip them through a distance-education university in some faraway Pacific island, serious thinkers fear the tarnish of a Dr before their name. David Priestland's argument that societies failing to get the balance of sages, soldiers and merchants right will fail may have nailed Zimbabwe.[52] Even in 'developed' capitalist societies, however, intellectuals may have an inflated notion of their and their global peers' importance. This might account for the European Zimbabwe-watching cultural and diplomatic brokers' fascination with Mugabe's cognitive capacities.

Dennis Grennan, a working-class Labourite who developed friendships with African nationalists whilst at Ruskin College and established the Ariel Foundation to help their cause, had known the future Zimbabwean president since meeting in the mid-1960s while advising Kaunda. Sarah 'Sally' Mugabe resided at his London house for three years for part of Mugabe's imprisonment. He helped find her a job teaching African dressmaking and as director's assistant at the Africa Centre. Later, Grennan was intimately involved in the regional and international politics of Zimbabwe's liberation war, thus well able to compare Mugabe with his peers. He thought Mugabe was extremely intelligent. The caveat, however, was that he was 'not as intelligent as he thought'. As for ideological depth, Grennan snorted, 'he had no ideology. He was a pragmatist. Or put it this way: he was an opportunist'.[53]

Richard 'Dick' Cashmore was more of the British middle class than Grennan. However, his father, born a proletarian but becoming a bishop in Calcutta, gained infamy for inviting Gandhi to the Calcutta Club. Cashmore had just retired from the FCO's Zimbabwe desk when I met him in early 1986.[54] Toward the end of our interview—where he revealed that Mugabe had postponed the 1985 elections so he could travel to London to SOAS or LSE to write the exams for another of his many MAs—he bent to his knees in supplication. 'It all hinges on Mugabe, that intellectual *manqué*', he prayed, worried that such a precarious insecurity could lead to trouble. I wondered if Mugabe was a Marxist. No, he said, the Shona intellectuals loved arguing about these philosophical matters, keen to be *au courant* with the latest theories. None mattered much in the end. 'Besides,' he remarked, 'Terry Ranger's piece assured us that Mugabe was really alright.' He was referring to Ranger's 'changing of the old guard',[55] which attested to Mugabe's Castro-like qualities, countering leftist scholars' allegations of his vacillating petty-bourgeois characteristics. Ranger relied heavily on an early 1976 meeting Mugabe had in London with the Zimbabwe Solidarity Front, run by what the eclectically radical southern African *Zimbabwe Information Group* called 'a group of two Mad Maoists and running lapdogs'.[56]

How could an article attesting to Mugabe's Marxism be good news to the Brits? I would have been better prepared had I read Ian Phimister's critique,[57] although it bears noting that at least one liberal holding off support for the declared Marxist-Leninist—Maoist was

41

pleased to learn of Phimister's adjudication of Mugabe's fey socialism.[58] Norma Kriger's work,[59] too, would have disabused any romantic notions anywhere on Zimbabwe's spectral ideological spectrum.
David Caute's scalpel on Ranger's *Peasant Consciousness* and his efforts
to erase the ethnic–political perceptions and realities presaging
Gukurahundi should have sounded a loud warning bell too. How,
Caute asked, could Ranger mark his friend's 1985 election victory
celebrations as a 'relaxed' and culturally diverse occasion? Maurice
Nyagumbo had arranged for the axing to death of his ZAPU opponent
'during a week of terror for the supporters of opposition parties in
Mashonaland' (note: this was not Matabeleland).[60] Had I attended
meetings at the Royal Commonwealth Society or the Britain-
Zimbabwe Society contingent with Caute's caustic piece I might have
witnessed Ranger dismissing Gukurahundi as journalistic exaggera-
tion, with Caute on the attack.[61]

   In January 1977, a year after theorising with London's choplogic
Marxists, Mugabe threw the radical leftists in his own ranks into
Mozambique's prisons. Cashmore spoke from experience.

   Perhaps Per Wästberg, editor of Sweden's prime newspaper, novel-
ist, PEN stalwart, adviser to the state on southern African matters, and
later a member of the Nobel prize for literature committee, knew
Mugabe best.[62] The Rhodesians expelled him during his 1959 student
exchange trip for writing critical articles for Swedish magazines. He
kept in touch with Mugabe via Amnesty International's letter-writing
programme, and when the UK Home Office made life in London difficult for Sally, he and his family took her in through Amnesty's sponsorship programme.[63] Mugabe's intellect may have been responsible
for the Swedish state recognising ZANU as well as ZAPU (normally,
the first movement on the block, with firm relations with the ANC in
South Africa, would have remained the sole 'authentic' beneficiary of
Swedish largesse). As Wästberg, consulted on the matter, put it,
ZANU's recognition 'very much was due to the fact that Mugabe was
seen as a forceful intellectual'. Wästberg might have argued with
Cashmore and Grennan about Mugabe's ideology: 'although he was a
Marxist, he was a Western intellectual that one recognised and talked
to'. Joshua Nkomo, ZAPU's leader, 'was eating too many desserts'.
Of the other Zimbabwean nationalists, 'Sithole was an extraordinary
drunkard and Muzorewa was a sell-out, more or less'.[64]

Much later, Wästberg noticed a problem shared by many insecure intellectuals. He told Zimbabwean journalist Itai Dzamara–later to disappear at the hands of Mugabe's agents–that Mugabe 'doesn't like people. He prefers being alone ... Mugabe is a fearful intellectual who is very intolerant.' Wästberg said that he had parted ways with Mugabe in 1994. 'We no longer had any common views and approaches' on issues ranging from term limits to Mugabe's 'clear dislike of opposition [and] lust for power'.[65] By 2017–contiguous with Mugabe's ouster– Wästberg thought that Mugabe had become 'Africa's Ceauşescu', whose survival in power was 'the only thing that mattered. ... Hatred was his hard currency.' He wondered, 'how could a freedom movement end in such moral dissolution?', and he queried his own role in this 'story that never ended ... he had a part in [it], even though I was spared from its sharp edges'.[66]

In fact, both Grennan and Wästberg had clear-cut roles in Mugabe's making, and probably Cashmore did too, although evidence of such might not be in the open. His missives in the FCO files indicate one of the best minds there.[67] If indicative of wider trends, Cashmore and Grennan suggest progress vis-à-vis Mugabe since 1962, when the UK's man in Salisbury wrote to his Whitehall colleagues that Mugabe was a 'sinister figure with a Ghanaian wife'.[68] The diplomatic corps in the dust of empire might have moved on from Liberal MP John Bright's 1858 description of the Victorian foreign-policy regime as 'a gigantic system of outdoor relief for the aristocracy',[69] and Wästberg's role in Sweden indicated what might have been a liberal form of social democracy at its zenith.

As usual, however, Americans have the last word. By the middle of the 1970s some Democrats there were getting a grip on southern African politics. In July 1976 junior Congressman and member of the sub-committee on Africa Stephen Solarz, with Johnnie Carson, deputy head of the US mission in Maputo, flew to find Robert Mugabe in Quelimane, Mozambique. How and why they visited is for another chapter to tell: their impressions are the thing here. Solarz thought Mugabe was an 'impressive, articulate and extremely confident individual [with a] philosophical approach to problems and ... well-reasoned arguments'.[70] That is perhaps the highest accolade recorded on these pages. Solarz did not know that Mugabe was a liar. He had

43

misled the naïve American (think Graham Greene's quiet one) with his assertion that he had the guerrilla soldiers in his hands. He told the Americans that they should take a leading role on the diplomatic front to stave off the sort of militarism encouraged in Mozambique by the other side of the Cold War divide. He indicated that he would be a democrat of the Zambian or Tanzanian sort. And ... so ... on. Fortunately, or not, America has more than one voice. Solarz's may or may not have had impact.

A year earlier, Mugabe's cousin James Chikerema—who had broken away from ZAPU a few years earlier in a quixotic quest to merge the nationalists (or the Zezuru group among them)—had been looking for him too, to no avail. They did manage to exchange letters though. Mugabe's reply chastised his cousin for joining with Nkomo during détente, but commended him for breaking away again.

> I am glad you and George [Nyandoro] have finally done it and done it with a sting! Let the chopping and slashing campaign go on and when there is finally a fall, what a big thud there will be? [sic][71]

If Solarz and Carson—with Grennan, Cashmore and Wästberg—had read that letter, they might have had a different idea about Mugabe's impressive philosophy. Unless, that is, they were happy with a 'split-and-rule' run.

3

KNOWING MUGABE

Graham Greene's historicism beats Edenesque fantasies. One finds history's webs and works the best way possible within them, changes them, or exits. Who finds whom in those labyrinths, and how do they work for or against each other? For Mugabe and his Zimbabwe, we need to know more about the stage on which his workings were constructed during the early decades of nationalism and the liberation struggle–and the actors acting (not just thinking) on them. Contra Greene, history did not just catch them up. They were catching up. Some won the race. Others were ahead of it but beaten by it: that might be the meaning of 'infantile ultra-leftism'.

Was Mugabe the only one in Zimbabwe who caught history, and made it fit his hands perfectly? Maybe for a moment: they soon went on their separate paths. The political historian's questions should be when and why.

The mid-1970s, when my somewhat hagiographied heroes appeared–and disappeared, accused of coup-like propensity–would take pride of place (for me) in the study of Mugabe's, and Zimbabwe's, making.[1] Besides its formative place while Mugabe caught up to history, the 2017 coup-makers claimed the famous 1975 Mgagao Declaration as core to their project. That was Mugabe's flag of guerrilla legitimacy. It declared Sithole finished. The guerrilla soldiers pronounced Mugabe an 'outstanding' member of ZANU's executive. He could serve as a 'middle

45

man' through which they could talk to other ZANU leaders. Key *vashandi* folk crafted it.[2] The 2017 putschists ignored this inconvenient fact—and indeed took credit for extracting the *vashandi* thorn from Mugabe's side as he threw most of the Declaration's creators aside. Now the coup-masters said they were 'restoring' that legacy from the despoliation meted by the 'criminals' surrounding the president, if not by himself. Clearly, the legacy needed unpacking (or deconstructing).

Of course, this distinct and rather unsavoury legacy has roots deeper than the 1970s. They spread far beyond the man making himself, and the colonial redoubt constructing him. Many men and women around the world—also bounded by conditions outside their choice—helped make Mugabe. Their experience and opinions cast more light on his construction. They refracted the complex and contradictory 1960s and 1970s, which produced empire 'insurgents' similar to those Priyamvada Gopal traced in earlier times.[3] Cashmore and Grennan were somewhat of that lot, illustrating the complexities involved in the matter of ridding the empire of its retrograde elements (read: Ian Smith and company) and keeping its remnants out of enemy hands (read: 'the Communists'). This all contributed to Mugabe's makeup. So too was Wästberg in Sweden.

Another man made Zimbabwean history and was caught up in its larger webs. They killed him. Wästberg included ZANU's national chairman in an interview with the Swedish historian Tor Sellström on his country's role in southern Africa's liberation. Herbert Chitepo was 'the main ZANU figure in exile and ... a very likeable man'.[4] The first black in the semi-colony to gain a law degree—and that at Gray's Inn—he had (mostly) been in British good books since at least 1954. The empire's servants knew they should not stymy a smart lawyer's upward path. At one point, the London contingent of the colony tried to persuade their Southern Rhodesian colleagues to alter the Land Apportionment Act so Chitepo could practise as an advocate rather than a lowly attorney. One letter among the score or more figuring out how to solve this problem noted that Chitepo had become 'somewhat embittered by the obstacles he has met in trying to set up as a professional man on equal terms with Europeans. He has not been a political extremist, but has associated himself with various protests and manifestoes [sic] by people like Stanlake Samkange.'[5]

In 1960 the African-American Institute–similar, and linked, to Grennan's Ariel Foundation–invited Chitepo to the bulwark of frontier democracy. London's FCO officers requested their Salisbury colleagues to assist him 'in every way possible to make useful contacts during his visit'. Their missive ended with a broad hint of their Cold War reasoning. If the Federal or Southern Rhodesian (these were the Central African Federation days) authorities did not 'approve of Chitepo and would not wish him encouraged' they could be reminded 'that ... if we do not guide him into the right channels, he may come under less desirable influence'.[6] A subsequent letter from the British embassy in Washington reports Chitepo joining the National Democratic Party (same nationalist party; new name after the state banned the old one) on his return to Salisbury, 'whose arrested leaders he is now busy defending'. The author, pleased with the emerging consensus, repeated his psycho-political diagnosis:

> He will add intellectual power to the party and be, one hopes, a moderating influence (though he is a good deal more bitter and disillusioned than he used to be). I doubt, however, whether he has the political personality or force of character to assume the leadership.[7]

ZANU politics definitely put him to the test–to his untimely end. In 1964 he was elected national chairman (the *Gwelo Times* listed that position in third place, ahead of Secretary General Mugabe: on the next day it was fourth). He left soon after to head the Tanzanian public prosecutor's office. By 1966 he was in Lusaka, leading a party very junior to the one from which it had split over two years before. The British and their friends across the Atlantic were still watching him.

The British representative in DC reported on Chitepo's 1967 trip: he had 'it on good authority that he came on a United States Government grant'. Chitepo 'pressed strongly' for 'more active American support'. When the British wondered why ZANU needed backing, the Americans argued that without it 'the Russians will establish control over them'. Thus 'we suspect ... the State Department (no doubt in conjunction with CIA) are considering' Mr Chitepo's request. The cable recounted the State Department's regard for Chitepo as 'one of the more competent and articulate Rhodesian Africans in exile', but also its 'slight disappointment' with his 'good [but] superficial impression', lacking 'substance underneath'. Chitepo had 'presented his case in relatively

47

restrained terms' to liberal congressmen 'in contrast to his performance at the rather strange meeting in a Chinese restaurant'.[8]

Restraint was not a winning strategy for the Zimbabwean leadership
stakes (unless one is good at long, cautious waits). ZANU's bi-annual
meeting in 1971 was very hot, leading, in part to the fissiparous rise of
the Front for the Liberation of Zimbabwe (Frolizi)–the Zambian liberation movement minders labelled it the Front for the Liaison of Zezuru
Intellectuals. In three years, Kaunda and Vorster's détente effort meant
to deflect the Angolan and Mozambican decolonisation model (read:
too much Soviet influence) led to Zimbabwean nationalist leaders'
release after their decade in Rhodesian jails.[9]

The worms in the nationalist leadership can had multiplied in those
ten years. They included the failed Nhari–Badza revolt, the consequences of which resulted in between 60 and 250 punitive executions,
against which Chitepo argued.[10] The imbroglios resulted in his assassination on 18 March 1975, shortly after Kaunda brought together his
neighbouring sovereigns to meet the released Zimbabwean detainees
and make a moderate plan: a car bomb killed him as he set off in his
Volkswagen Beetle.

Thirty years after Chitepo's assassination–suspicions lingering
still[11]–Kenneth Kaunda told me, without irony, that Chitepo would
have made the best Zimbabwean president.[12] The alleged murderers
blamed Kaunda, given his efforts to choose leaders for them in collaboration with Smith and Vorster, and wrote the damning *Price of Détente*.[13]
Dick Cashmore read it, and remembered that in 1971 (after the March
11 Movement, similar to *vashandi*, was quashed) 'Kaunda handed over
to Smith nearly 150 freedom fighters whom he subsequently argued
were only a bunch of Rhodesian spies and layabouts'.[14] It was in May
2005 that Per Wästberg wrote in his notebook that he had played a part
in Mugabe's making.

It was sharper than he indicated. Just two-and-a-half months after
Chitepo's assassination he penned 'Where is Mugabe?' for the influential *Dagens Nyheter*. Sally Mugabe had asked him for help. His article
argued that 'many observers have seen him as the best possible leader
of a united African front and as the first President of Zimbabwe'.[15]
Mugabe was in political purgatory. Samora Machel and Julius Nyerere
were not sure who had ousted ZANU president Ndabaningi Sithole in

a Salisbury prison coup, as they had learned as the détente limped to a start. The hunt began, spreading to London and Washington over the next year. By the time of Wästberg's article Frelimo had allowed Edgar Tekere and Mugabe to rusticate in Quelimane, after they deemed it wasteful to stay in Rhodesia as détente had allowed. Mozambique's new rulers were still awaiting revelations regarding the future of Zimbabwe's best possible leader.

Sally Mugabe was the key to much of her husband's 1970s successes. She was also the link between Wästberg's Swedish milieu and Dennis Grennan's in London–not that these men knew it. How did this unusual servant to Her Majesty end up hosting the woman he called 'ZANU's best diplomat' for at least three years in his own house? I first encountered Grennan in Simpson, Smith and Davies' underrated *Mugabe*, wherein he accommodates Mugabe as 1976 began.[16] London's National Archives hosted the next happenstance twenty years on.[17] There was a telegram from Whitehall to the high commission in Ghana, dated 9 November 1967. Upper-case letters reveal that 'Mrs. Sarah F. Mugabe, Ghanaian born wife of Robert Mugabe, Secretary General of Z.A.N.U., has been invited to visit Britain by the Ariel Foundation', which would fund her stay and her secretarial studies. Mrs Mugabe needed a letter from Ariel 'who are well known to us'. Given the short notice, the FCO officer hoped this telegram would substitute for a direct letter. A scribbled note on top of the typed copy read, 'Eric, were you consulted abt. this?' More penned flurries wrote, 'Would you wish to have this on one of your files? If not, it can be destroyed,' and, in another hand, 'can we now destroy?' A larger scrawl notes that 'Mr. Reiss of IRD despatched this tel. It was not cleared with us. Ariel decided on their own initiative to help Mrs. Mugabe.'

A conspiracy website sends scrollers to Stephen Dorril's 'inside story' of M16,[18] wherein the Ariel Foundation was said to be a CIA front, rooted in Grennan's mid-1960s days as the National Union of Students president as he tried to keep the Soviets out of European student unions. Resembling the curate's egg, such versions of truth are good in part–Grennan later acknowledged the early assistance from across the pond, but the Ariel Foundation had no need of the CIA's peanuts: corporations were more generous.[19] Meantime, the archives indicated more files on Sarah Mugabe needing special permission for retrieval. They arrived with the fanfare of the National Archive's New Year list. I revisited the Grennan trail just under around a year later at one of Sue Onslow's 'Witness to History' discussions in the same building. I raised the 'Dennis Brennan' [sic] and Ariel question to the table around which sat many of the people I would later learn held a dislike for Grennan–and it was mutual.[20]

I repeated the telegram's message (and Dorril's claim), asking if anyone at the meeting knew Grennan and/or his relationship with the Mugabes. Robert Jackson answered my queries, as well as earlier discussions about ideologies and the Cold War during the liberation war. Jackson had been a Conservative MEP in the early 1980s and a special adviser to Lord Christopher Soames when the British ran Zimbabwe–Rhodesia in the months between the 1979 Lancaster House settlement and Zimbabwe's first election in April 1980. Jackson affirmed 'that there [was] a great deal of ideological fluidity and international affiliations. All those people were pretty opportunistic and highly flexible. That was probably more or less generally recognised. What you said about American involvement seems highly plausible.'[21]

Jackson continued on the Ariel Foundation. He had not heard of it before his Zimbabwe mission, but on writing a *Daily Telegraph* article about his tenure during the transition the foundation invited him to its final meeting, in Guernsey. 'It was really a group that had been constituted to apply pressure on the British to do the "right thing" in Rhodesia.' The meeting hosted parliamentarians from then UK, USA and Canada, and 'was rather a celebratory meeting. I was received as a kind of great man who had just come from the great event in Zimbabwe and the success that it represented.' He recalled 'a discussion about future models for development, led by a black American Congressman. He talked about different models and said that there was a Yugoslav model and a North Korean model.' Jackson felt 'totally out of court … and became like the man in the Bateman cartoon' on suggesting 'that rather than those models there might be a question of African countries rather following the Haitian model, and I spelt out what that was'.

Jackson did not mention Grennan, but the man ahead of me at the coffee table turned around to chat. What he said indicated some of the class and ideological contradictions Grennan would confirm later. I paraphrase but remember the key words very well: 'Grennan was an obnoxious radical pest: on one of our missions to Zambia we made sure he was sent off to Angola, a much more congenial place for him,' he said. That comment sealed my desire to meet Grennan, but a bomb at King's Cross the next day stymied that plan.

It would be more than two years before we met. More Grennan connections appeared in the interim. A Lusaka conference a month later offered the opportunity for archival research in addition to me spouting off much too insolently in a paper about Zambia's rough treatment of the Zimbabwean armies it hosted.[22] A telegram at George Washington University's National Security Archives had pointed out Grennan again, keeping an eye on Kaunda and Vorster's efforts to get the Ian Smith and Zimbabwean nationalist gangs together on a train perched over Victoria Falls.[23] A certain Wilkowski sent an elated cable to the American Secretary of State, Henry Kissinger, and embassies all over, announcing that Kaunda's foreign affairs adviser, Mark Chona, had just phoned him. Chona reported that his president and Vorster would be in Livingstone 'tomorrow August 26 [1975] prior to opening session at Victoria Falls and will attend this first bridge meeting between Ian Smith and ANC nationalists'. Kaunda had decided to 'take the final plunge and pay the highest price to avert the worst'. The 'direct overseeing by Vorster and Kaunda should make it clear to the world who is responsible party if the talks break off'. On hearing this news the British high commissioner said, 'from now on its [sic] up to the British'. Wilkowski concluded: 'understand Dennis Grennan, Callighan's [sic] special assistant from FCO is standing by in Lusaka while UK Hicom Miles is waiting around in Livingstone.' Wilkowski seemed to have no idea that the Zimbabwean attendees to the conference on a bridge were fast approaching irrelevance. The 'militants' would soon disavow their less adventurous colleagues. Robert Mugabe (he of the 'coup in prison') would hitch his wagon to their stars—and would in turn disown them almost immediately.

Long-time Zambian left-wing activist and politician Simon Zukas[24] listened patiently to my intemperate presentation on the tragic Zambian–Zimbabwean duet, and informed me afterwards that he would give me Bente Lorenz's telephone number. Mrs Lorenz—an artist and potter—was the widow of architect and Danish honorary consul

51

Erhard Lorenz, who had designed Herbert Chitepo's house in Salisbury when they both resided there. The Lorenz family moved to Lusaka in 1964, seeing the Rhodesian right's writing on the wall before the 11 November 1965 Unilateral Declaration of Independence. Mick Pearce had moved north too. He had upped his mother's early support for ZANU by running guns and much else for its fighters.[25] Lorenz and Pearce established an architectural firm.[26] Some time during those years Pearce's lecture at London's Royal College of Art inspired Nigel Wakeham to join the struggle in Lusaka too. He later designed ZANU's flag. Wakeham became ZANU's main photographer as well, but he left hundreds of his pictures and negatives behind when, after Chitepo's assassination, life became too difficult for anyone associated with the roiling party that was beyond the Zambian state's control.[27] In the best of worlds, ZANU (PF)'s 'Shake Shake House' (its headquarters resemble the waxy 'traditional beer' containers) would have an architects' hall of fame: however, Mick Pearce's open support of the MDC in 2000 would have had him taken off the walls.[28] Lorenz and Wakeham would probably sign off, too.

Chitepo had visited the Lorenz home on the last evening of his life.[29] He enjoyed talking about art, his days at Gray's Inn, but little of politics, over a dram of whisky during his frequent visits. Mrs Lorenz remembered a rare political discussion when Chitepo said, regarding the militants in the party who rejected détente, that they were right to continue the armed struggle. She also told me about Daphne Park, an employee of the British high commission, who had asked Erhard in 1964 if he might store some arms for her. He refused. I thought, conspirationally, that they were for ZANU, but the former foreign affairs permanent secretary Mark Chona told me in 2013 that the request was most likely in anticipation of the 1964 Lumpa 'rebellion'.[30]

Dame Daphne Park, heralded widely as 'Jane Bond',[31] answered my fax from the University of KwaZulu-Natal to the House of Lords the next day—by telephone. We arranged to chat when I got to the UK next. When we did, she regaled me with her technique for gaining information from the Zimbabwean nationalists: holding extended parties on the stoep of her rented farmhouse on Lusaka's outskirts. She remembered the then ZAPU Lusaka head James Chikerema (Chitepo was still in Tanzania) in particular, with his repertoire of Zimbabwe

History and Anthropology lessons. Lusaka must have been a relaxing post after Leopoldville as the Lumumba and Mobutu saga reached its nadir. She liked Lumumba, she said, but when he smoked too much hashish he got a bit crazy. Regarding my ultimate quest, she gave me economist Michael Faber's phone number.

Faber had taught Economics at, and by 1959 been expelled from, the University College of Rhodesia and Nyasaland. He joined many of his radical compatriots five years later in the new Zambia. Along with the Owenite co-operative socialist Robert Oakeshott, he saved the country just under £50 million: they caught out the British South Africa Company's attempts to overcharge the copper mines' nationalisation deal.[32] Professor Faber was very happy to tell me Dennis Grennan's phone number.

Grennan warned that he was not supposed to reveal much; then he smiled and said he had a big ego and not enough discipline to write on his own reflections. I thought, what could be wrong if Daphne Park, whom he knew very well, approved? Grennan's father was a bare-knuckle boxer in the Warrington slums west of Manchester, arrested many times. He did not take up his grammar school scholarship because his parents could not pay for transport or lunch. He had no kneecaps: malnutrition atrophied the cartilage around them so the surgeon removed them. His Irish mother was the local Labour Party's secretary. His visceral dislike for the Communist Party was due to its thugs' propensity to trash her office, not the Tories'.

During the Second World War his mother arranged for her 16-year-old son to move from a chemical factory's noxious fumes to a clerk's post with the National Health Insurance. His union activities there and Labour Party campaigning—for Harold Wilson's first election campaign in 1945, during which they formed a friendship—led him to a scholarship for Ruskin College's diploma programme. That introduced him to African nationalists, including Julius Nyerere. Joan Wicken was a classmate. She chose to spend the rest of her life in close proximity to Nyerere, becoming his personal assistant and founding a Ruskin-style college in Dar es Salaam.[33] While in Tanzania, Wicken maintained contact with Grennan and Peter Mackay (another character for inclusion in an updated Gopal study),[34] and was a constant source of Whitehall's information on southern and eastern Africa's politics. As

53

well as being a key figure in the relationship between Oxfam and the Tanzanian state,[35] the FCO copied her on hundreds of communications with its far-flung offices. She died in Bradford shortly after moving from Dar es Salaam, leaving her papers, but willing them closed for fifty years.[36]

Grennan wanted a proper university degree besides the Ruskin diploma, so he enrolled in Politics at Southampton University, soon to head the National Union of Students: he recalled the *Daily Telegraph*'s headline reading 'Father of 35 Heads NUS'. His second newsworthy utterance was after the Chinese failed to invite him to their World Students' Congress. He publicised the embassy's advice that imperialism's paper tigers were not welcome. Grennan proceeded to rid the NUS of Communists, using CIA funds to organise summertime student conferences around Europe in competition with the USSR's. He also joined the commission that established the university grant system, of which he was justifiably proud. The commission introduced him to some the bigger British capitalists, including British-American Tobacco (BAT): they would help with the Ariel Foundation.

On leaving Southampton, he and a triumvirate of bipartisan politicians started the Ariel Foundation. Funded partially by the Ditchley Foundation (apparently retaining none of Ariel's records), as well as some of the industrialists on the student loan commission, its major purpose was to introduce African nationalists to leading members of the British establishment. This would counter reactionaries such as the far-right Conservatives supporting Ian Smith in the Monday Club. Grennan thus shared much—including funding—with the African-American Institute in the United States, which did similar work and led to Dow Corning's money. He said Her Majesty's Service recruited him around this time—casually, at a Westminster cocktail party. When Wilson showed him a letter from the Russian embassy stating he was a spy, he laughed and said, 'Well, who sent this to you and why?'

He headed to Zambia along with Faber and similar Fabians to advise Kaunda, while Daphne Park settled at the high commission. A 1966 Whitehall missive labels him Kaunda's private secretary.[37] A year later, FCO bureaucrats exchanged over thirty letters sussing him out: his special access to both their prime minister and Zambia's president were difficult to understand. His plans to establish a unions' college along the lines of Ruskin and Wickens' one in Tanzania seemed not to take off.[38] By 1975 he was still a 'special assistant' to prime minister Callaghan.[39] He met Robert Mugabe during his early years in Zambia—first, he said, at Zambia's State House and later in Salisbury's prison. Mugabe was at the beginning of a decade of incarceration. When Grennan asked Mugabe how he could help, the answer was, 'Please look after my wife.' She had no real home. It was too risky, not to mention unpleasant, to stay in Rhodesia. Ghana held memories of the recent death of their son Nhamodzenyika, whose funeral the Rhodesians denied Robert leave from prison to attend. Thus eventuated the Ariel Foundation's request to Whitehall and the telegram at Kew Gardens.

Martin Meredith records that Sally moved to London to study Home Economics and work for the Runnymede Trust. She 'spent her evenings in libraries copying out passages from books' for Mugabe's prison reading.[40] Perhaps Mrs Mugabe's schooling plans changed to nursing: a 1988 file records her husband's fighter-jet-shopping visit (the competition: 'Red China') coinciding with her kidney treatment—or better, a new kidney. Given her past employment with the National Health Service, the NHS would assist the search but 'the costs of the operation will be met privately'.[41] During other years of the 1980s, while Gukurahundi raged, Mrs Mugabe would witness the Greater London Council unveil Nelson Mandela's bust or address a ceremony marking Marcus Garvey's centenary.[42] Grennan found her work at the latter venue soon after her arrival. She taught dressmaking and was the assistant to the director while also studying on a student visa. She gained a teaching diploma from Queen Elizabeth College, the University of London's division devoted to women's education.

These arrangements threatened to unravel at decade's end.[43] On 11 December 1969 the Home Secretary's office (with James Callaghan as the minister and Merlyn Rees his junior: Callaghan kept quiet) decided Sarah Mugabe must go. The Home Office's under-secretary denied her early October request to stay to work. She had until the end of the year to leave. Her study visa had expired while she was still in the UK and her marriage to a Rhodesian did not warrant her proper citizenship in the rebel state, so the UK could not offer her other than Ghanaian status. She would have to leave the country and re-enter with a job offer. That offer's utility to the British economy would determine her voucher's class. A teaching diploma would probably not suffice as a scarce skill.

Mrs Mugabe (at 20 Madeley Road, Ealing Broadway, presumably Dennis Grennan's residence) wrote letters via the Royal African Society to Maurice Foley, parliamentary under-secretary of state and a founding member of the Ariel Foundation. Thus began a long battle with the Home Office. He won a stay of her departure date, dependent on the resolution of the war. Mrs Mugabe pushed Foley harder. 'I still feel strongly that you can do your best to change the negative reply,' she pleaded. 'I am completely at a loss to know what else I could have written to touch the hearts of the decision makers.' How, she wondered, could she live 'whilst this scrutiny goes on?'

Midway through 1970 her husband–still imprisoned–entreated directly to the top (Harold Wilson, prime minister), as if to a king with Victorian sentiments who could 'exercise [his] mind' to get around the Home Office's 'legal technicalities completely deprived of morality'. Presaging his feudal imaginings that prime ministers owned their countries,[44] Mugabe pleaded with Wilson to 'recognise her status and grant residence permit till my release from political detention'. That was congruent with the British state's 'moral responsibilities towards ... persons in my circumstances (and) their wives ...'. Robert Mugabe closed with a request: 'Sir, that you personally exercise your mind on the case ... so that justice is done to my wife and myself.'

Wilson lost an election before he could decide what to do about the supplication. Yet the Tories picked it up. Three reasons may have encouraged them. One: Colin Legum reported in *The Observer* that Ian Smith's stepson had managed to pick up a visa whilst on a short trip to Eire. Two: 'stretching the point' on a Rhodesian passport (lost in transit, said Robert) might ensure that Wilson, leader of the opposition, would not speechify. Three: Robert Mugabe had just risen to the peak of Zimbabwe's nationalist pyramid. He had reportedly become the leader of an amalgamated ZANU and ZAPU, upon 'the stepping down of Mr. Nkono [sic] and the Rev. Sithole'. Perhaps with high hope for Frolizi, the FCO officer anticipated Mugabe's rise by only six years. Nonetheless he thought that 'the Home Office are reconsidering' the 'bad effect on her husband' her liminal status would cause, as well as probable embarrassment for the FCO and its political masters if they forced her to leave the country. A scribble at the bottom of the note read that the news of a new twist in Robert's fortunes might 'reawaken interest in her case in in parliament and elsewhere'.

The Sarah E. [sic] Mugabe issue moved out of London's hands during the next year, although Frolizi's effervescence took slightly longer to dissipate. The organisation that in 1985 Mugabe would call 'Amnesty Lies International' came to his wife's rescue.[45] Per Wästberg reappeared. He started the Swedish branch of Amnesty International (AI) in 1963. AI allocated Mugabe to Wästberg and his partner Margareta Ekström (a writer as well) when he was imprisoned. Ekström wrote the letters to Salisbury prison, given that Wästberg was *persona non grata* in Rhodesia, and they both sent him academic books. Mugabe's letters were often smuggled out of jail by sympathetic warders, so they learned much of his political thinking. The prominent members of Sweden's literati invited Sarah for a long visit. Robert did not want her in licentious London (he did not mention Home Affairs problems). Amnesty International sponsored her to a place where Lutheran uprightness had waned long ago.[46] Sarah tended Ekström and Wästberg's children for a while as they focused on writing. Soon, however, the Swedish International Development Agency hired her to travel between schools giving lessons about Africa. Her 'laconic Swedish but eloquent sign language and good English from her Ghana upbringing' served 'with great success'. A flat in central Stockholm came with that job.

Thus a big step to finding the political pilgrim.

Wästberg cannot recall how Sarah got back to London. Regardless, Mugabe was catching up to a lot of history. He arrived to London in January 1976, saying he needed to visit Sarah in hospital. Robin White's BBC interview on the 21st aired Mugabe's claim for the guerrilla soldiers' full support and his denunciation of Kaunda's perfidy for accusing the wrong people for assassinating Chitepo.[47] Within three days the world that was watching could read a letter from the imprisoned nationalists confirming his account, affirming their loyalty to the new leader, and promising to 'join you in the field'.[48] On the same day, ZANU's DARE (War Council) repeated the sentiment, albeit noting Mugabe's provisional leadership status and asserting the 'organising principle ... of a unified political and military command, in order to guarantee victory'. Three more days passed before Radio Lusaka's short-wave band released a stern critique of how this particular member of the African National Council external wing's Central Committee 'wanted to make Zambia a battlefield where Zimbabweans would butcher each other for political supremacy'. Mugabe had become an ostrich, 'burying his head in the sand' to the reality that Kaunda was trying to ensure Zimbabwe would not meet Angola's fate of civil war. He should apologise.[49]

Soon after that he addressed the 'mad Maoist' Zimbabwe/ZANU solidarity group on the theoretical nuances of military–political relations, and embarked on a tour of some Western European capitals.[50] From a somewhat qualified response from his party's warriors (implying unity with ZAPU and their people's soldiers line) to Zambia's outrage onto Maoism's pedantic sophistry and then diplomatic pretence: certainly a good crash course in the art of bullshitting.[51]

Wästberg made it to Maputo in February with a Swedish government mission and spoke on the phone with Mugabe, back in his Quelimane retreat. He was angry with Samora Machel, who 'thought him amateur and irresponsible'.[52] Sarah could visit Mugabe at his 'home'. She was soon to stay with him in Maputo, where the travails of war were closer than in London or Stockholm.

Meanwhile Mark Chona, Zambia's permanent secretary for international affairs, could chat with James Callaghan, then Secretary of State and head of the FCO but soon to be prime minister, advising him that Mugabe was 'not the guerrilla leader; if he had been he would not have visited Europe when he did'. The new military High Command of ZIPA (the Zimbabwe People's Army), uniting the armies previously divided between ZAPU and ZANU, 'were politically unknown quantities ... under both Chinese and Soviet influence, although the Russians were at an advantage because they could supply more sophisticated weapons'. Chona continued with an ideologically loaded warning: 'It would be very unfortunate if all Rhodesia's future leaders were drawn from the younger generation of guerrillas.' This could lead to '"socialism with a vengeance" and the European farmers and those who defended them would simply be swept aside'.[53]

Chona was no Swedish social democrat, nor even an American-style democrat. As noted in the last chapter, a young Congressman of that tendency wended his way to meet Mugabe. Perhaps Solarz heard of the BBC interview, or the ZANU representative in the USA surprised him with the suggestion for a trip. The British in Maputo helped arrange matters with Frelimo. When he made it up to Quelimane with Carson, they were impressed with Mugabe's philosophy but uncertain about his claim to control the guerrillas. By the end of the year they would be sure of that. Mugabe had lied, but he had predicted the truth. The uncertainty still lies with the question of how that truth arrived. For that, more on the 1970s conjuncture—which made so much of Mugabe and he in turn formed—needs examination.

4

VASHANDI

THE OUTSIDE VIEW

'If you can pull this off where we have so often failed, it will be a major coup.'
Anthony Crosland to Henry Kissinger, 21 October 1976.[1]

Henry Kissinger is famous for two witty–if cynical and probably unoriginal–observations reflecting on his life and the world at large. The first: 'Academics fight so viciously because the stakes are so small.' The second is 'Power is the greatest aphrodisiac.' Only the select among those who pour over the massive records of American foreign policy makers' meetings could know the third.[2] Kissinger uttered his third witticism as he handed over to incoming Secretary of State Cyrus Vance in early 1977.

The Geneva conference of 28 October–15 December 1976, called to bring an early end to Ian Smith's rule and the guerrilla war, gained neither objective. Kissinger is hardly famous (or infamous) for it, although a book for business and state negotiators heralds the conference as the ultimate model of its kind.[3] However, it did present Robert Mugabe to the world, controlling the most militarily powerful component of the nationalist armies–and winning over the various factions of the gestating Zimbabwean ruling group.[4] Kissinger worked tirelessly and cleverly at setting the stage, on behalf of the British, to get that far.

His words, in a personal letter to his British counterpart Anthony Crosland, revealed the 'big picture' prescribed in the negotiating textbook for the grand strategists in Kissinger's wake. 'The whole enterprise', he hectored Crosland (privately), seemingly missing the forest for the trees, 'only makes sense as a firebreak to African radicalism and Soviet intervention.'[5] As he said later, for the record, 'We don't give a damn about Rhodesia. The only reason we got into it is to set a pattern for the rest of Africa.'[6]

The Young Turks who restarted the war during the ceasefire accompanying 'détente' embodied this 'African radicalism'. Ironically, they also bore a great deal of responsibility for casting Mugabe as the lead man on the ever-shifting stages of Zimbabwean power. To keep there, Mugabe would have to recast them as minor extras with their bit parts expired. Regarding 'Soviet intervention', their attempts to forge a united and 'political' army from the separated Zimbabwe African National Liberation Army (ZANLA) and Zimbabwe People's Revolutionary Army (ZIPRA) would have enabled Soviet arms of solidarity to embrace all the Zimbabwean nationalists. ZANU would no longer rely only on the Chinese and global social democrats. ZAPU would share its tougher military infrastructure with ZANU; the latter would attract larger numbers of human fodder.

One cannot tell if the 'ZIPA moment', or the *vashandi* ('the people' or 'workers') sub-group within it, could have stretched further into time. Suffice to say it died trying, and would remain in Mugabe's brain as a 'counter-revolutionary contradiction'. Only the axe could restore the apostates to harmony. Whilst felling the blunt instrument he would forever spout radical rhetoric ranging from Marxist-Leninist-Maoism to the 'Third Chimurenga' and Africanist sovereignty, while for as long as possible easing into the global and regional strictures militating against them.

Kissinger's brutal, duplicitous realism may have been Mugabe's first exposure to these constraints, replete with the full array of force, persuasion and corruption only the very powerful can marshal. Primary among the philosophical paroxysms entailed in these traps was the classic liberal separation of 'guns and politics'. Even whilst reminiscing on his denouement coup, the ruse remained. He wondered why it failed him.

VASHANDI: THE OUTSIDE VIEW

In March 2018, as Mugabe seemed to be inventing a new party to restore his throne, the *Zimbabwe Independent* reporters asked him if he had 'brought the military into politics and what has happened to you is a logical culmination of that'. Mugabe forgot the early 1977 arrangement with ZANLA commanders Josiah Tongogara and Rex Nhongo to extract the thorns in his side. 'Ah,' he bloviated, 'we never said they should come into politics. We always said the gun should be led by politics. They've come into politics now.'[7]

The fissure's final flouting came with Mugabe's forced retirement. The reporter's crunch question, fusing long-term reflection with the palace coup's immediacy, encouraged more misleading: 'If you saw the military meddling in politics, why didn't you take decisive action to thwart them? Did you see the coup coming?' Mugabe reverted to his first, pedagogical, profession: 'No I never saw it. With the education we had given them.'

Two score and a year before, Kissinger was as confused as that reporter must have been. His joke to Vance in 1977 was that his efforts to herd the Geneva conference toward his horizon were 'a bit like dealing with the Harvard faculty'.[8] As for Mugabe, Kissinger fumed: Mugabe was 'out of control. He's absolutely untrustworthy. ... If I could have picked someone from the beginning, it would have been Nkomo. Nkomo is the best. What I don't understand is, is he just a figurehead for Mugabe or does he have power of his own?'[9]

Dennis Grennan, entitled 'Special Adviser on Africa' on the 10 December 1976 what-do-we-do-about-the-not-yet-completely-failed-Geneva-conference meeting's guest list, had already answered. Nkomo 'assumes he can control Mugabe. That's ... his mistake.' Kissinger agreed. Discussing possible meetings with the two Patriotic Front leaders, Grennan advised Mugabe and Nkomo's simultaneous presence. 'They will never meet except together.'[10] Grennan held great admiration for Kissinger (and Mugabe) but very little for Nkomo. Nkomo made him scramble to cover his London expenses: £1,000 for a particular weekend, he recalled, adding Nkomo's penchant for the best hotels, business deals and women rather than the political grind.[11] (The many admirers of Mugabe's asceticism might have remembered Shakespeare's contrast between lean and hungry politicians and 'fat, sleek-headed men and such as sleep a-nights'.)[12] Grennan's first response to Kissinger's wonderment vis-à-vis the Nkomo–Mugabe dance was 'he hasn't got any guerrillas of his own'. Nkomo had misread the PF 'situation'. It was only after Kissinger advised not assuming 'he's made a mistake; I'd ask what it is that makes him think it's in his interest' that Grennan came in with the vaguer idea that Nkomo might think he could handle Mugabe. Grennan could not have believed Nkomo had no troops. He might not have been averse to shifting the truth game's goalposts to score for his friend's husband.

He stepped in quickly when Ivor Richards, chair of the conference chaos, opined that 'it would be quite monstrous if in the end the Patriotic Front came out on top when the Bishop has the votes'. Grennan riposted that this was 'Chona ... talking. They're wrong.' Zambia's rulers desired a settlement dearly, however. As Mozambique was discovering quickly, hosting Ian Smith's enemies cost enormously. Chona told me that in the midst of the Geneva conference he flew to London to convince Margaret Thatcher to reverse her assertion that the Tories would never recognise a settlement dealt by the Labour Party. The next morning, a 10 Downing Street aide called and asked if he had seen the morning paper. He rushed to the newsagent on the corner to read the good news. Three years later the Lancaster House agreement brought that news to life.[13]

Kissinger may not have read Solarz's rosy report from his and Carson's July trip to Quelimane; if he did, perhaps he dismissed it as the work of idealist Democrats. They were not the only careful assessors, though. A good number of the documents preceding and accompanying the conference cautioned against such abrupt and negative analysis of Mugabe. Only a few days later, in Geneva, after finishing as ambassador to Nigeria, Assistant Secretary of State for Public Affairs Dr John Reinhardt had at least half of the story. He was quick to note 'Nkomo's seeming impotency; and ... an unyielding and influential (in Geneva at least) Mugabe'. The other half he may have misread: 'The nationalists', he wrote, 'particularly the Mugabe crowd, have run wild.'[14] A new member of the State Department's Africa mission 'shadowing and supporting the British effort', as he put it 36 years later, reported that the real plays were backstage. On 12 November Frank Wisner II reported that 'the less visible, but perhaps equally important conference involves the black battle for leadership of an independent Zimbabwe'.[15] In 2013 his memory of Mugabe differed from Kissinger's immediate recollection: 'diffident, stand-offish, smart, intellectually acute and by far the most impressive' compared to Muzorewa, Nkomo and Sithole. Mugabe had 'the coldest, clearest eyed approach'.[16]

Nor did Wisner remember–or he remembered to forget–the young radicals of 1976 and 1977. As he put it, 'I can tell you no policy maker in Washington was thinking about the interstices of the Zimbabwean rebel military forces: this was not on anybody's screen.'[17] Nor did his November report note them. However, he had received a telegram from Stephen Low, the American ambassador in Lusaka, accounting for them at length, if underplaying their role and misreading the nature of their alliances.[18] Low thought that 'Nkomo, Mugabe, and Muzorewa [were] more realistic and reasonable political leaders, [but] one would at the same time have to recognize that all three are weakened by more radical elements within and outside of their organizations.' As for the man approaching his moment, 'Mugabe himself is supposed to be more reasonable in private than in public.'

This reckoning may have reached America's diplomatic residence via the British deputy high commissioner in Lusaka. Jeremy Varcoe– the recipient of the 1970 note about Sarah Mugabe's visa issues stating that Mugabe was the new leader of a united ZAPU and ZANU–had hosted Simon Muzenda, one of Mugabe's key allies, Stephen Solarz and *Observer* journalist David Martin in the previous few months.

At June's end, a couple of weeks after ZIPA's unity sundered, 'Simon Mzenda [*sic*] came in to deal with passport problems' but left crucial information behind. He confirmed reports of 'inter-factional fighting in the Tanzania training camps ... the ZANU and ZAPU groups have now been completely separated'. In Mozambique, too, ZIPRA soldiers and ZAPU members of the joint command have no 'effective say in either the policy or the conduct of the guerrilla war'. ZAPU leaders were in Lusaka, probably planning a third front, although Varcoe did not know if Zambia 'agreed that they should operate as ZAPU, i.e., as a separate entity, from here'. Muzenda was adamant there was 'no prospect of any unified structure capable of embracing those actually doing the fighting'. He had spoken with both Mugabe–still under guard in Quelimane–and 'the Karanga leaders'. He was not sure if Mugabe could visit the soldiers' camps to gain more acceptance.[19] By mid-August ZAPU–still named the détente-inspired African National Council (Zimbabwe)–reported to the Organisation of African Unity (OAU) Liberation Committee that the May and June battles and deaths in the Tanzanian camps confirmed ZIPA's part in a Chinese and Tanzanian plot to wipe ZIPRA out. 'Within a short time [of ZIPA's formation]' the delegation claimed, 'it became obvious that ZANU intended to eliminate us.' The Chinese instructors' 'puppets' were bent on murder and destruction.[20]

Varcoe hosted Stephen Solarz six days after his Quelimane visit: given Muzenda's news, Mugabe may not have exaggerated ZAPU's exit. Yet Varcoe thought Mugabe lied to Solarz regarding his claims to control ZIPA despite reliable information circulating that he was 'in close contact with the freedom fighters'. Varcoe agreed with Solarz that ZANLA would be the force to wrest power from the whites, and that if Smith remained intransigent 'the Communists were once again likely to gain a political victory' in the region, although possibly short-lived.[21]

David Martin did not partake of Varcoe's hospitality until September closed and the Geneva conference was in sight. Varcoe listened to Martin's take on Mugabe as 'certainly much softer in private than in his public statements ... [although he] still had a lot to learn politically ... this was the main reason for his intemperate public statements'. Yet Varcoe had misgivings about Martin's claim that Mugabe would soon preside over his party and army's harmony: he doubted 'Mugabe's claim to be a political representative of the ZIPA cadres' as indicated by a list of ZANU leaders drafted by Mugabe and displayed by Martin. 'So far as I can judge there was only one person who could be said to represent ZIPA,' wrote Varcoe. This meant 'there could still be differences between ZIPA and ZANU on political issues'.[22]

Wisner would have been privy to such correspondence. Perhaps, as he said in 2013, the State Department would pay no attention to a mere Congressman's report, but there could be no denying the discussions with the cross-(northern) Atlantic meetings later. Meanwhile, Reinhardt reported breathlessly from Geneva soon after his 17 November arrival. In spite of keener eyes, sharper ears and better contacts than Wisner, he fused 'the Mugabe crowd' and the entity 'running wild'.

He might have been twisting Mugabe's line to a Canadian television journalist. She asked if whilst in Geneva he was in direct contact with the 'fighters' in Africa. He replied firmly, hesitating only slightly:

Yes of course ... we are, the head of [eyes closed a second] ah, the, ahhh, army. ZANU is running the war. We started it. We have a majority [slightly inaudible], and therefore it is our war. ... [The commanders are] in the field, because commanders know how the job should be done. But uhh, it's in accordance with the policy of the party that there should be a war, and armed struggle ... it's derived with the support of the masses of the people ... who are actually participating in it.[23]

Reinhardt recorded that the observers, too (the Frontline and other states supporting the Zimbabwean dream, but unsure who could realise even its lowest denominator) had been 'persuaded of ZIPA's importance [and] have embraced the more extreme, Mugabe-spouted militant demands'. The Nigeria veteran argued that 'the wild men' had almost deadlocked the conference. 'They know their power. They are aware that intransigence over time will result in substantial front line and other African support.' As for the Mugabe/Nkomo Patriotic Front alliance (the political, not military, version), 'no one doubts' that it would split 'perhaps even at the formation of a transitional government'. That might not matter, though, because 'there is still a prevailing attitude among Mugabe's more extreme subordinates that the new Zimbabwe should rise phoenix like from the ashes of Rhodesia to which they set fire'.[24]

The half of the picture Reinhardt missed, however, was that Mugabe and 'the wild men' were far from fused, nor were the latter very willing to be his subordinates. They had tried to refuse to attend and thus legitimise a conference destined not to go far on the road they wished to travel. Had the diplomats read Dennis Grennan's advice in a mid-October note, they might have seen the gap. Grennan had participated in conference preparations, and knew both Mugabe and Nyerere—from the Ruskin College and early Lusaka days—far more than did the diplomats and politicians. Tanzanian high commissioner Mervyn Brown passed on a conversation about ZIPA's extreme reluctance to attend the Geneva 'sell-out'. Brown's cable reported Grennan's advice: 'Mugabe's worry was that he would be disowned by ZIPA.' Nyerere agreed. Mugabe did not control ZIPA, 'although he pretended that he did, and therefore we should not over-estimate him'. Nyerere implied:

> ... i ittt wwould [sic] not matter greatly if ZIPA were not represented at Geneva. The five presidents would back a solution, not individual leaders. Africa would judge the conference by its results and [if] these were satisfactory, i.e. achieving a genuine transfer of power, then ZIPA would be powerless to oppose it.[25]

Ironically, the *vashandi* group's ideological and strategic propensities militated non-attendance, but Nyerere had also given up on them. As Hashim Mbita, his trusted Secretary General of the OAU Liberation Committee told me in 1997, ZIPA had 'done its job':[26] ended the ceasefire; persuaded the soldiers at Mgagao to dump Sithole; by default got the USA on the stage; and assisted in the release of those accused of murdering Chitepo. Also ironically, those men helped Machel and Mugabe force the 'wild Palestinians' to fly to Geneva so Mugabe could show the world they were at his command.

Perhaps Nyerere was responding to an idea Mugabe was spreading around. Mugabe told John Lewen, the British ambassador in Maputo, that:

> ZIPA guerrillas would not necessarily obey an order from Machel or the other front line Presidents to cease fire if they did not like the look of the Rhodesian settlement of which the cease fire would be a part, and they were prepared to go on operating in these circumstances whether the Mozambicans liked it or not.[27]

Mugabe hoped he had got Lewen thinking about two cats among the pigeons. One was the possibility of the ZIPA soldiers disregarding *any* politician's decision—Mugabe included—to move towards moderation. The second feline finesse was the Soviet bogey. Mugabe made it clear that he was no fan of Soviet scientific socialism or military intrusion, and those in tune with global politics saw little threat in Chinese connections (Kissinger had already accepted Mao's China into the 'international community'). Lewen knew of the imbroglios in the Tanzanian camps, and ZIPRA's exit. Thus the fear of across-the-board Soviet help should have dissipated, but Mugabe told Lewen that ZIPA still received funds (if not arms) 'indirectly through the OAU by the Russians, who directly support ZAPU, and hence the ZIPRA element of ZIPA'. Thus, Lewen continued, 'there are mixed yellow and red perils for those ... impressed by them'. He wondered how long ZIPA could hang on without Mozambican logistical support, but 'in theory they could turn out to be African Palestinians'.

Was Mugabe raising more fears than reality about the Soviet menace? He was sounding like the liberal Centre Party in Rhodesia. In April, just after ZIPA had revived the war from its ceasefire slumber, its memorandum to Ian Smith and any interested Rhodesians warned 'that should the guerrilla leaders be allowed to get out of control, the politicians may find themselves beyond the power to influence events and may be finally replaced by military leaders'.[28] Smith, however, saw Mugabe as the politician needing the wariest of watching.

As the Geneva conference loomed a fortnight away, Smith arranged for his representative in South Africa to send Crosland, Kissinger and Vorster a vitriolic letter expressing his fears about a Mugabe dictatorship. Smith reasoned that the guerrillas were shepherded and the ascetic Mugabe held the staff. He forewarned that the 'failure of [Rhodesian Africans] ... to reach any agreement among themselves is a forewarning of coming power struggles' but jumped to his claim that Mugabe would corral consensus among them. This would not be a good thing, because:

> This man has a long record of Communist affiliation and he is now emerging as the apparent spokesman of the terrorists based in Mozambique. His recent statements and those of the terrorist leaders can leave no room for any doubt as to their real intention, which is to establish a Marxist-type military dictatorship in Rhodesia on the model of that in Mozambique.[29]

Solarz's post-Quelimane visit to Salisbury had no moderating effect on Smith, nor would David Martin's bromides from elsewhere. Rhodesian attacks on ZIPA's camps in Mozambique—as well as Mozambican villages—were evidence enough of that. The UNHCR estimated the Rhodesian soldiers' horrific 9 August 1976 Nyadzonia (or Nhazónia) raid, as young refugees and/or trainees were celebrating ZANU's anniversary, to have killed 670 and injured 500. Later approximations approached 1,028 dead.[30] Charles de Chassiron—workload at the British embassy doubled due to ambassador Lewen's heart attack–reported these atrocities assiduously and sympathetically. He noted the Rhodesian propaganda claiming that the Mozambicans faked the 'atrocity photographs', but doubted if the real story would reach as widely as did the Portuguese massacre at Wiriyamu in 1972.[31]

Back in the London–Washington corridor as 1976 ended, ZIPA's import remained unclear to the Anglo-American consortium. As the conference closing *sans* closure loomed, the Crosland–Kissinger group's 10 December meeting mulled the options. The inability of the Zimbabwean nationalists to agree on much loomed in the background. Grennan thought the Frontline presidents would have to agree before the Zimbabweans could, but 'second, and perhaps more important, is one's estimate of ZIPA'. He did not believe Chona's estimate 'of 4–5,000 well-trained men and only 1,000 will go back'. Richards sniffed: they were 'school children' and would return to class. Grennan moved an inch: true, they had not been fighting for a decade, like the MPLA. A British embassy counsellor asked whether the Geneva negotiators were 'battle-hardened Marxists really'. Richard re-placed the ball in the Frontline presidents' court and all agreed that said presidents might not enforce the agreed formula. Grennan broke in: 'ZIPA isn't such a problem.'[32]

Mugabe visited Romania on his return from Switzerland to confirm his control in the camps.[33] No problem. American foreign policy abided dictators annoying the USSR.[34] In 1983 Ceauşescu nearly became a Zimbabwean landlord.[35] The television images of his gory 1989 departure unsettled Mugabe.[36]

As if to confirm Grennan's assessment, at the beginning of 1977 the CIA's National Intelligence Estimate assessed the ZIPA story. It diagnosed Rhodesia's post-Geneva prospects, and then prescribed some changes. The NIE saw Tongogara and ZIPA (linked) as part of the Mugabe delegation, itself bound loosely to the Patriotic Front. The NIE was uncertain about the guerrillas' post-settlement role, but was sure that it would be important. ZIPA leaders would demand a meaningful, perhaps even leading, political role. Even in a democracy, ZIPA radicals could persuade voters 'susceptible to simplistic and inflammatory rhetoric' of their good intentions. The report painted Nkomo as a moderate, but his prospects were 'inversely proportional to ZIPA's strength'. Mugabe seemed indeterminate, but not necessarily 'radical'. Who could reduce this threat?

We believe that the front-line states would agree to restrain and disarm many of the guerrillas, thus diminishing their leaders' own hard line regarding, and claim to power in, the interim government. Conversely, Mugabe would not necessarily have a better chance at assuming the leadership if ZIPA were not defanged: the guerrilla high command would probably put forward its own candidates. In that case, internecine struggles between guerrilla factions would likely ensue.[37]

Cleansed of double negatives this reads 'ZIPA's removal *would* mean Mugabe's chances at ZANU's leadership *would* improve'. If the second 'not' is a typo, the 'estimate' moots the possibility of co-option forestalling further 'internecine struggles'. Coincidentally or not, ZANU carried out both of the dentist's prescriptions. It removed its own self-diagnosed bad teeth and offered to fix up a few of them for reinsertion. When a recalcitrant one or two refused repair–or even to accept the diagnosis–the revolutionary dentists threw them all away. The surgery was finished ten days before the American intelligence community produced its consensus.

Grennan remembered nothing of ZIPA when we conversed in his Hexham flat. Viewing a picture of Dzinashe Machingura, the firebrand ZIPA political commissar and *vashandi* guru who must have made some impression when he finally arrived at the conference, he indicated only the slightest sign of recognition.

By 2013 Wisner had forgotten ZIPA too, as did he the National Intelligence Estimate. In any case, he said, they are not policy documents but provide background alone. Their summaries of all the agencies' analyses might not be 'on the agenda of issues to be addressed by policy makers'.[38] So much for academics Rosenbach and Peritz's analysis: for them the SNIE is the 'most authoritative written judgment on national security issues ... [produced] after consulting with all intelligence community members through an interagency process' and distributed to 'key policymakers in both the executive and legislative branches'.[39] Policy makers would consider such a collective consensus carefully.

Perhaps one can only discern the Cold War hammer with written, archival, historical distance. A couple of letters help. As 1979 and a new Zimbabwe glimmered slightly around the corner, two resolute Rhodesia watchers remembered ZIPA–as a warning. Readers have yet to meet Dame Rosemary Spencer, at the time on Whitehall's Rhodesia desk. She moved from her Nigeria posting directly to the Geneva conference and its wild and fractious men. When I met her in Salisbury (the original, in the cathedral's shadow) in July 2014 she remembered Dennis Grennan well, as well as Keith Evetts.

Rosemary Spencer's two-page New Year greetings to 'Dear Keith' in Maputo, and copied to five others including Dick Cashmore of the FCO Research Department, thanked him for the 'batch of letters' she had received in early December 1978.[40] She zeroed quickly into a discussion of Evetts's assessment of 'ZANU, the Mozambicans and the Russians', and ZAPU and ZANU relations in that regard. Spencer assessed an August 'secret meeting' between the two nationalist parties (still in the Patriotic 'Front' but hardly united) to which Evetts referred, the context being possible ZANU relations with the Soviet Union. The USSR seemed to be taking 'a greater interest' in ZANU than before, but 'their money still seems to be on Nkomo'. ZANU and the Soviets were extending 'feelers' towards each other, and in Eastern Europe more widely the former was looking around 'with their eyes fully open' (no mention of Romania was made). Spencer was not impressed with ZANU's public image in the West: perceived as a Marxist proxy for the global carriers of that brand and appearing 'too convinced of the infallibility of their cause', it was hard for ZANU to 'indulge in the soft-sell'.

However, Spencer reported cheerily that 'reports ... which have reached us through other channels' say ZANU's leadership had stabilised 'at least to some degree ...'. She said that 'tribal rivalries' were still important, as too were the personal relations between the political and military leaders–'particularly of course between Mugabe himself and Tongogara'. Spencer remarked that there was a 'possibility that a leader might emerge from among the younger military commanders, but ... it is impossible to deal with anyone but leaders of the day' because of ZANU's organisation and 'the present state of our relations with them'.

Her talk of a younger generation may have reminded her of Evetts's earlier remarks about ZIPA. She concluded: 'We share your views about the consequences of the formation of a new ZIPA, although we doubt it is a likely development in the near future. We should be grateful if you and Lusaka could keep an eye open for any moves in this direction.'

Evetts's reply arrived two months later. In the meantime, one of his letters passed on ZANU's 'surprisingly warm reception' of the humanitarian aid for refugees Spencer had arranged in 1978. The Central Committee's collective response that 'at last the imperialists are thinking of helping us' hid differences of opinion regarding relations with the UK. Some members, including Eddison Zvobgo—that 'charming rogue' who had to be 'holier than the Pope' to dispel suspicions of his American 'capitalist education'—wanted to keep the UK at arm's length. Those with 'somewhat shorter arms', including Mugabe and Nathan Shamuyarira (with a Princeton PhD) overruled such sentiments, and were not shy asking the British ambassador when the 'sausages' would arrive.[41] Evetts was glad to say the Russians had not delivered any.

Evetts responded fully to Spencer's query by 1 March. His 'ZANU (Mugabe) Potboiler'[42] celebrated Mugabe's failure 'to secure arms supplies from the Soviet Union and its closest allies'.[43] The Soviets, he claimed, 'clearly do not wish to risk their investment with ZAPU and would only answer Mugabe's request for arms if the Patriotic Front was united (with the Russians' man at the head of it)'. Neither Machel nor Nyerere had 'exerted significant pressure on ZANU to unite'. One of his colleagues who knew the Cold War enemy well was 'convinced that the Russians are exasperated with the Zimbabweans'. Nkomo was annoying them: he had 'made little progress (and … his reputation is in decline)'. The Russians did not believe Mugabe had control over 'liberated areas', they were 'frustrated by their inability to get PF unity', and they would rather not let 'both ZANU and ZAPU' have arms 'since the two wings of the PF would probably shoot at each other'. The ambassador had reported that his Russian counterpart was contemplating the idea of a peaceful settlement in hope.

That both Spencer and Evetts were concerned about 'another ZIPA' emerging suggests it was an important element of southern Africa's struggle. Evetts's March 1979 letter shows why. It was all about the Russians. It was about the Cold War. It was—perhaps indirectly—about 'divide and rule'. If ZANU and ZAPU had truly united—if ZIPA, particularly the *vashandi* group within it, had lasted—the USSR would have been assisting one fully integrated nationalist movement instead of one destined to play a relatively smaller role in Zimbabwe's political path. Another counterfactual is that Gukurahundi would have been less probable than the horrific and far from inevitable history that caught thousands in a deathly grip. As Evetts surmised, the Soviets' fear of putting guns in the hands of both armies suggests that the risk of civil war was commonplace.

For this book's purposes, however, the importance of the 1970s' track–particularly the 'ZIPA moment', as Saul has it[44]–is elsewhere. The question is, how did those years contribute to Mugabe and his party's collective fear of, but entrapment within, conspiracies, the coups they presage, and the conceit that all will work out with power and privilege? Whether this power leads to chances to accumulate resources, if not 'capital' in its full array, or has its immanent attractions, is a question far too philosophical for a pursuit such as this. This is a lower-order question: how did the patterns set in the 1970s regarding generational change become entrenched in Zimbabwe's broad political order, specifically in terms of how Mugabe himself dealt with real and imagined challenges to his authority?

Given that the speechwriters for the 2017 the military intervention ensuring Mnangagwa's takeover employed the 'restore legacy' discourse, referring to the 1970s and *vashandi*, that decade is doubly important. The putschists claimed the Mgagao Declaration, that they had rescued Mugabe and the struggle from counter-revolutionaries, and hoped their 2017 effort to rescue him from the 'criminals' who had captured him would be accepted with like gratitude.

Vashandi in and of itself, then, warrants a closer look.

5

INSIDE *VASHANDI*–THEN OUT

As indicated in Percy Zvomuya and Sabelo Ndlovu-Gatsheni's brief discussion of the *vashandi* and those who desacralised the gun, the Mgagao Declaration symbolises one era's end and a new, rocky road to another.[1] Parker Chipoera, Dzinashe 'Dzino' Machingura, James Nyakadzinashe and Saul Sadza escaped the wake of Chitepo's assassination in Zambia to reignite the liberation struggle. Détente seemed only to accelerate the rise of untrustworthy and inadequate leaders, and Zambia seemed to be doing everything to hasten them to power. The foursome and their comrades had organised hunger strikes among the ZANLA soldiers imprisoned in Mboroma camp and witnessed Zambian soldiers killing them. Sithole did nothing to challenge the Zambians about the crackdown, and indeed tried to persuade them to go to a meeting where the Zambians had planned to arrest them. They met Chitepo's alleged killers–a good proportion of the ZANU and ZANLA leaders–in their prison and agreed on Sithole's incapacity, and the way forward to fight again. They left Zambia soon after.

While in Tanzania and Mozambique preparing to advise Tanzanian president Julius Nyerere about their plans, they heard that Sithole had returned from visiting his sick daughter in the United States. He was heading them off. Mhanda and Nyakadzinashe returned to Mgagao camp to draft the now famous declaration. It finalised Ndabaningi Sithole's demise, but it took a lot of discussion and argument to agree on the next in line. They finally wrote: 'We can only talk *through* [my emphasis] Robert Mugabe' to the other–moderate–leaders compromised by détente. He was a 'middle man', through whom the soldiers could talk to various parties. To do otherwise would have gone against the Lusaka prisoners' commands and indeed the party's hierarchy, but they were wary of endorsing a man unseen. In the meantime, they stretched poetic licence by attesting to Mugabe 'defying the rigours of guerrilla life in the jungles of Mozambique'.[2] Perhaps those weeks waiting to cross the Rhodesian border *to* Mozambique might have counted, as would rustication in Quelimane. It could be that they just did not know, but assumed. Not a good omen for living in hope by stretching veracity. In any case, they were able to present their plan to the OAU Liberation Committee headquarters just before Sithole's arrival, and thus the next phase–their moments in the maelstrom, Mugabe's rise, and their demise–began.

On meeting Mugabe–smuggling him from his house arrest in Quelimane to meet the cadres of the new 'people's army'–the young political soldiers began to realise their mistake. Those whom Mugabe later loathed were disappointed with him on the first trip. According to the driver, all Mugabe wanted to do was ascertain the tribal identities of the new players. He did not talk too much, but took everything in to himself.

Encouraged by Nyerere and Machel they started the war afresh from Mozambique. They created Wampoa College–based on Stalin's 1920s idea for the Chinese nationalists and communists to make the National Democratic Revolution work–to proselytise their ideological path. Wampoa was the site for ideological change (and, as is often the case, the students tended to take the instructors' lessons far beyond their intent). Within a few months, however, the battles between former ZANLA and ZIPRA soldiers in the camps stymied their efforts at unity. Mhanda's fiery interview with the Mozambican press agency, soon published around the world by left-wing solidarity groups but circulating in the FCO almost immediately, must have warned off the guardians of global capitalism and defenders of the non-Communist mode of freedom.[3] One can only guess whether their left-wing ideology contributed to their expulsion, but one cannot expect people of Mugabe's ilk to appreciate the suggested subtleties of their relation to the emerging imperialist intrigues. When Tongogara–later out of jail and restoring his sense of order in the camps–heard people talking about the negation of the negation he wondered aloud if this meant people could return from the dead. Then he advised that these too-philosophical people be negated in turn.[4] Their refusal to attend the October 1976 Geneva conference unless they did not have to support only one leader (Mugabe) sealed their fate. However, they were forced to attend the conference, as indicated above, to show the world that they supported Mugabe and to ease the pressures of war on Mozambique. Soon after it ended–without resolution–their future with the 'party of revolution' met a resolute finality.

In January 1977 they were taken to a kangaroo trial in Beira and sent to Mozambican incarceration facilities, and eventually to relatively open confinement in Cabo Delgado where they rusticated until released in advance of the 1980 elections. While kick-restarting Zimbabwe's war in early 1976, their hosts wooed and celebrated them. When they became a nuisance, they were chewed up and spat out. *Vashandi*'s progenitors were thrown into the bins of history–more precisely, into Mozambique's jails–as hopeless 'ultra-leftists', as Machel called them. For the Frontline states they had done their job of getting the war going again. However, Mugabe did not forget them. They were not killed, as had happened to many in the Nhari–Badza rebellion. Chung claims Muzenda–a 'Karanga' most adept at corralling his otherwise fractious ethnic peers to side with Mugabe–intervened to save their lives, but Mhanda says Muzenda did not.[5]

Perhaps this brief eulogy to *vashandi*–intended here to illustrate Mugabe's ways more than to the ginger group and its leaders per se–should begin with the immortal words Mugabe spoke as he announced their closure. He inaugurated his new 'enlarged' Central Committee after ridding the camps of the *vashandi* and arresting perhaps 600 of their supporters, and passed judgement on the recently incarcerated ginger group.[6] He repeated Hegel's negation notion and condemned

... destructive forces ... who arduously strive in any direction that militates against the Party line or who, in any way, seek, like the rebels of ... 1975–76 to bring about changes in the leadership or structure of the party by maliciously planting contradictions in our ranks. ... Their actions are a negation of the struggle. We must negate them in turn.

This is ... the negation of the negation. ... The ZANU axe must continue to fall upon the necks of rebels when we find it no longer possible to persuade them into the harmony that binds us all.

The 1984 party congress was the first constitutionally correct one in the two decades since ZANU hived off from ZAPU. It was another opportunity for Mugabe to explain away the 1975–7 maladroit moments. He called the 'Dzino revolt' the work of 'treacherous ... counter-revolutionary elements [and] trouble-makers'.[7] He laid down a long list of charges. One was that the ZIPA group had reneged on the promise to allow those imprisoned in Zambia under suspicion of assassinating Herbert Chitepo a return to their high positions. Mugabe claimed that the group told General Tongogara, just released with his fellow suspects in order to attend the Henry Kissinger-enabled Geneva conference in October, to apply to ZIPA as an individual. He maintained that the *vashandi* accused the Central Committee members who attended the Geneva conference of treason. ZIPA members were caching arms for a revolt, said Mugabe. They 'called themselves *vashandi* but dubbed us the *zvigananda* or bourgeois'. As if this last was the straw breaking his back, Mugabe continued thereafter: 'It thus became imperative for us to firmly act against them in defending the Party and the Revolution.' Mugabe repeated his axe metaphor—and the negation of the negation chant—to the thousands of ZANU (PF) members assembled. The Beira meeting that sent the *vashandi* to prison

> was attended by all members of the Central Committee, former members of Dare [the War Council] and the ZANLA High Command from Lusaka, and by members of ZIPA themselves. After this meeting, we had all the ZIPA trouble-makers detained with the permission of the Mozambican government. The list finally included Dzinashe Machingura (Dzino), Elias Hondo, J. Nyikadzinashe, Augustine Mudzingwa, T. Pfepferere, D. Todhlana, Bindurazvina Musoni, P. Chipoera, and several others. This exercise was followed by a politicisation programmed in the camps. We warned any person with a tendency to revolt that the ZANU axe would fall on their necks: '*Tino tema nedemo*', was the clear message!

But the 'coups' were not finished. In early 1978 what Constantino Chiwenga nearly forty years later called *vashandi 2* met a similar fate. The 'real' *vashandi* members call them the 'donkeys who come to the water but refuse to drink', because they had been warned of a similar fate when the early 1977 moves were under way against the 'Dzino rebels'. Instead of joining the Dzino gang they chose to stick with Mugabe, soon enrolled in his 'enlarged' Central Committee. *Vashandi 2* started with a letter to Machel (repeated in another sent to London in time for the Lancaster House conference at the end of 1979) complaining about how the new committee was distorting the struggle.

Rugare Gumbo drafted it. He returned to ZANU in Zambia in 1973 from studies in the USA and Canada courtesy of the African-American Institute. Gumbo took up a key media role, publicising the party's Marxist inclinations and faced flak for putting the picture of that white man with a big white beard on a *Zanu News* cover.[8] The letter to Machel argued that 'the decision to isolate the ZIPA commanders was in principle wrong. ... Genuine efforts by ZIPA were interpreted as to usurp power or engineer a coup. ... When contradictions develop, they must be solved.'[9]

The 'Gumbo–Hamadziripi plot'—or coup attempt–took place while Mugabe and others were at another Anglo-American conference in Malta. It had taken the convenors of the Geneva conference that long to arrange a continuation: Mugabe was busy cleaning up the debris from what he thought was *vashandi*'s coup. Much of the FCO correspondence then reads like Wästberg's 'where is Mugabe' article. Mugabe describes the events as follows: 'On the night of 30 January 1978, the counter-revolutionary group ... [including] some disloyal members of the General Staff, organised an operation for the seizure of power.' This band of troublemakers kidnapped central committee members Edgar Tekere and Herbert Ushewokunze, but second-in-command Rex Nhongo and 'loyal ZANLA forces' saved them. According to Mugabe, they were ready to assassinate at least six leaders, including Tongogara and Nhongo. 'Some 133 persons were in all arrested and many of them tried by a constituted Central Committee Court.'

The opposing version is that the Mozambicans arrested Gumbo and Hamadziripi after submitting their complaint. Comrades in the camps kidnapped Tekere and Ushewokunze as bargaining chips.[10] Two decades after Mugabe's 1984 speech, Tekere told me at his home in Mutare that the Gumbo and Hamadziripi gang had faced immediate

MUGABE'S LEGACY

execution, but that he intervened. Tekere advised waiting 'until we are in our own country'.[11] The second-best option was the pits (literally) for six weeks, until Mugabe and company arranged with Frelimo they join 'vashandi 1'. The two groups remained together until a letter they smuggled out via an English volunteer teacher reached Tony Benn. Benn handed it over to Peter Carrington, the Tory chair of the Lancaster House conference. Where did left-winger Benn meet arch-Tory Carrington? At their club, I was told.

The prisoners—seen by many as bonded by their 'Karanga' rather than their political and ideological identities—were released to Zimbabwe along with a Rhodesian prisoner of war before the results of that last conference were consummated in the 1980 elections. The conference organisers did not think it would be a good idea to invite them to the conference itself.

Mugabe's last few words in his 1977 and 1984 speeches illustrate his flexible fusion of Antonio Gramsci's struggles with that blend of coercion and consent constituting the hegemonic centaur.[12] His axe promised to be harder than an iron fist gloved by velvet, but he had relatively few people killed in his coup-squashing exercises. The brutal quelling of the Nhari–Badza rebellion, as discussed in differing ways by Gerald Mazarire and Blessing-Miles Tendi, was a major cause of Zambia's discontent with ZANU, and a big factor in the build-up to Chitepo's assassination.[13] As discussed previously, the complex contradictions of the relation between the 'the gun and politics' was to dog Mugabe—and the party and polity he played with unnerving and finally enervated passion—until he met his private version of God, who perhaps along with Mugabe's Jesuitical confidant, would solve the problem.[14]

Other ZANU veterans (and observers) thought of the vashandi differently than did Mugabe. Fay Chung's memoir (Mhanda was discussant at the launch) describes Mhanda as 'a brilliant analyst and highly articulate speaker ... implacably opposed to any form of corruption or compromise with the colonial masters'.[15] She portrayed him as he arrived—unwillingly—at the October 1976 Geneva conference that would seal his fate as Mugabe demonstrated his mastery of the Young Turks:[16]

Wilfred Mhanda arrived in Geneva dressed in Che Guevara style with a black beret and blue jeans. He habitually shaved his head completely [actually he was born bald and remained so]. Short and stocky, bristling with intelligence and with ideological righteousness, he exhibited a high level of puritanical restraint as compared to other leaders who had just emerged from jails or from the battlefront.

To be sure, Chung saw the problems such puritanical brilliance could cause. According to her, this 'formidable intellectual and brilliant speaker' was 'uncompromisingly against having anything to do with the old nationalists'. He and his comrades believed that 'these old politicians would betray the socialist revolution'. They were too 'apprehensive about the new post-*détente* ZANU leadership'. Chung thought 'Mhanda's group was particularly opposed to Robert Mugabe', judging him as 'an old-style nationalist who would create in Zimbabwe a neo-colonial regime'. They were wary of his pretence to 'socialist credentials and feared he would become a fascist dictator'.[17]

Perhaps Chung was not present at Mugabe's interview with a BBC reporter when Mugabe displayed his gradualist take on socialism as well as his liberal credentials.[18] He started with his principles of non-racialism. When asked if his party was socialist—a 'fully socialised society'—he replied almost flippantly. 'Oh yes, sure; as we have said and as every African Delegation here has said.' The interviewer—either oblivious to the notion of non-capitalist land tenure or who had studied the history of the 'purchase area' class—asked if black farmers would go on with their individual farms. Mugabe would not push the revolution: 'one would have to adapt here to a major adaptation of socialist principles. You cannot start off by taking control of everything, of every individual enterprise.' As for elections?

> Yes, of course, why not? We are fighting for democracy. We would like to see a democratic state established in Zimbabwe and this means a state based on the wishes of the majority of the people. The best way that people can demonstrate their participation is by voting and elections are quite a necessity.

If Mugabe could fool Stephen Solarz, why not the world? Perhaps he was very good at saying what his audience wanted to hear—except when he knew the audience was in no shape to answer back. Certainly, his London reconnection with Sally Mugabe was bearing political fruit, and his relationship with the 'Third Force' was being widely considered. At first, the new initiative gained some supporters. In early May, for example, Dennis Grennan met his Ruskin chum and Nyerere confidante Joan Wicken, in Bonn.[19] She reported the Nyerere perspective:

> The four presidents had recently agreed that all the freedom fighters would be trained together in one country and as far as possible in the same camp. This should help to get over tribal divisions and create a sense of unity on the basis of common objectives, training and experience. ... The training would take place in Mozambique.

Soon after, Machel was contrasting the 'fighters' unfavourably with the African National Council politicians emerging from the Lusaka détente process and hoping to win big pieces of the political pie. British ambassador Lewen reported that Mozambique's young president 'referred scathingly at an airport press conference at Lusaka' to these politicians, vowing that 'Mozambique will help the Zimbabwe combatants, not these incompetents'. Also, on his return from an OAU Liberation Committee meeting, foreign minister Joaquim Chissano declared that said politicians had 'insulted the four [Frontline state] presidents in an attempt to cover up their own disunity'. Chissano said that the ANC leadership 'was practically dismantled, and the factions claiming leadership were pursuing personal ambitions for power and not the liberation cause'.[20] The Mozambican leaders were not yet certain if Mugabe should be included in that gang, however. Mugabe and Tekere were still cooling their heels in Quelimane, except when the new carriers of the torch deigned to drive them to the camps.

Almost simultaneously, all sorts of actors besmirched ZIPA. Rhodesia's 'liberal' Centre Party sounded like Ian Smith. In April, its memos decried an ill-defined 'military' rule. By June's end, their fears focused on a familiar threat: 'the Russian Communist system' was on its way to Rhodesia. The leaders of the Third Force were 'training to take over the civil administration' hoping to eliminate 'the mainly Christian and more realistic political leaders'. The Highly Confidential memo claimed that 'a number are already believed to be under political instructions and indoctrination in Havana and possibly Moscow'.[21]

Joshua Nkomo was only a step removed: he told his FCO interlocutor in May that he feared the Young Turks 'ran the risk of turning Rhodesia into a second Mozambique' (he was supposedly under the Soviet thumb!). Little wonder the FCO officer noted with some angst: 'If parts of my note appears somewhat obscure, this is because it was no means clear at points in the conversation what Mr. Nkomo himself was really trying to say.' Nkomo's professed fear of the reds was similar to that of Ted Rowlands, the Minister of State for the Commonwealth, who combined ethnicity, ideology and global political history rather too neatly. He warned of a 'second Vietnam' if the 'Mozambique-based Karanga, under Frelimo guidance, w[ould] rapidly come to the top in a new Zimbabwe'. Rowlands repeated Nkomo's assertion that 'Mugabe was quote controlled by the young men unquote in Mozambique'.[22]

Mugabe must have realised he should drive a wedge between himself and ZIPA. Maybe Solarz's visit clarified his ideological thinking: he painted himself liberal whilst those around him were red. The mid-July 1976 meeting discussed previously sheds more light on Mugabe's philosophical and empirical dexterity.

As if to verify Grennan's probable recommendations to the African-American Institute, with which he worked often (Dow Corning apparently contributed a lot to Grennan's Ariel Foundation and the African-American Institute), and Per Wästberg's query in Sweden, Solarz and Carson forayed to Quelimane. It was like a Graham Greene novel, Johnnie Carson wrote.[23] He and Solarz were 'squeezed into the back of a tiny, single-engine plane flown by two white South African pilots in the early hours of July 7'. They did not know 'quite where we were going' and were 'unsure of who and what we would encounter when we arrived in northern Mozambique'. The pilots of their rudimentary plane 'followed the coastline north for several hours before turning inland and west before finding our landing spot—an abandoned dirt airstrip on an old coconut plantation'. They must have been pleasantly surprised to find such an urbane—but tough—host.

After meeting Mugabe, Solarz and Carson were convinced 'that he was a force to be reckoned with, and that he had what it took to come out on top'. Carson had witnessed Joshua Nkomo 'from the back benches'. Compared to him, 'it was clear that Mugabe had overcome more hardship and possessed more political grit—energy, determination, strategic thinking, and seeming alignment with the fighters on the ground—to challenge and overtake Nkomo's seemingly dominant position as Zimbabwe's top black liberation leader'.

Solarz and Carson's cable reported Mugabe's contention that he had no truck with Mozambique's 'military state ... we do not want military rule'. He would prefer 'a civiial [sic] government, democratically elected, and similar to what Tanzania has today'. Zambia, too, looked better than Mozambique. Mugabe said Machel's idea that Zimbabwe's guerrilla conflict should be a 'protracted struggel' [sic] was not on. He stated emphatically that the 'third force [i.e. ZIPA] High Command was composed entirely of ZANU military leaders who were loyal to him'. It was 'controlled by himself and ZANU Central Committee'. Mugabe dismissed the idea that ZANU and the 'Third Force' would invite foreign troops (implying the Soviet Union or its allies) to assist in liberating Zimbabwe. As for the foreigners he saw playing an important role, he said that the UK had lost its chance to help resolve the Rhodesian problem. It was time for the United States.

Mugabe decried the idea of unity that he thought Kaunda had imposed 'on threat of extinction' for the late 1974 détente attempts. There were no more ZIPRA soldiers, he said: they had 'turned out to be completely worthless'. They had refused to fight 'while their chief, Nkomo, continued to negotiate with Smith. Most of them eventually left the camps.' Mugabe denied that the ZIPRA soldiers 'were being chased away', although acknowledging the 'friction between the ZANU and ZAPU cadres in the camps'. He told Solarz that there were 20,000 'youngsters over seventeen' trained or under military instruction.

Solarz's next comments indicated that the 'Third Force' was clearly of concern and that it was important to ascertain its leadership: 'Whether Mugabe is or is not the leader of the third force, he is ... staying close to the fighters and building his bridges for the future. There is no question that he will have to be reckoned with in Zimbabwe's post-independence sweepstakes.'[24]

Solarz informed Mugabe that his next stop was 'Saliburg' [sic], where he would try to meet Rhodesia's prime minister, Ian Smith. He asked Mugabe if he had suggestions for the meeting. Mugabe replied that Solarz could shoot Smith.

Carson's telegram arrived at the FCO as it reached the State Department. Given their longer time with the Zimbabweans and slightly less naivety, British views differed somewhat from Solarz's. Ambassador John Lewen wondered in his 12 July report just how close Mugabe was to the soldiers. Lewen learned from the UNHCR representative that Mugabe was a member of ZLA—meaning 'Zimbabwe

Liberation Army'–High Command, but noticed that 'Mugabe does not figure' on the list of its leaders he had seen. Lewen had concluded that Mugabe was a 'political rather than a military leader'.

Two weeks later, Robert and Sally Mugabe dropped by to chat. On 26 July Lewen reported on his and de Chassiron's meeting with Mugabe 'and his wife'. He suggested that Mugabe's 'Catholic and ... humane grounds' deterred him from the idea of protracted war. Mugabe told Lewen and de Chassiron that, unlike Frelimo, ZANU had not come out of a guerrilla war. The Zimbabwean nationalists 'were politicians'. They had 'only taken to armed struggle in despair of a political settlement'.[25] Mugabe elaborated on the now complete 'divorce between the ZANU and ZAPU soldiers who "never wanted to fight" and often gave themselves up to the Rhodesian security forces and served them as informers'. Those who did not desert were in separate camps. As for Solarz's visit, Mugabe took a different tone than he had used in Quelimane: 'he remained suspicious of American motives', remembering that in 1970 the USA had vetoed the Security Council's efforts to sanction Rhodesia.

Lewen and de Chassiron were still unsure of Mugabe's relations with the 'freedom fighters or the Mozambicans, but he certainly seems to rate higher than Muzorewa or Sithole'. The British diplomats 'found [Mugabe] quite an impressive and likable man, but rather mild and modest', sharing none of the 'swagger or ruthlessness of Machel'. While in Maputo, Mugabe had addressed a UNESCO seminar on the region. Warwick University professor John Rex opined that Mugabe's presentation on the history of African nationalism in Rhodesia was 'masterly'.

The British seemed to know that ZANU's man in America, Eddison Zvobgo, that 'charming rogue' with whom Evetts would soon enjoy a chat, had a hand in arranging Solarz's visit. Their records do not mention his sponsors.

The British diplomats were happy to help Mugabe's best friend Edgar Tekere exit Mozambique to visit Solarz's homeland. London worried that Frelimo might not have approved of the Congressman's visit and thus might make trouble for Tekere, who had gone missing. 'We should be grateful for any news you can glean about his fate–perhaps a *faux naif* telephone call to Quelimane would shed some light?'[26]

The call was made, and eventually Didymus Mutasa (in Birmingham and referred to by his first name) met with FCO officer Barlow and Tekere at Whitehall. Tekere was accepted as 'Robert Mugabe's principal lieutenant' and found to be 'an impressive character, unlike his companions [including Mutasa], who are typical minor black Rhodesian political organisers in exile'.

Yet Tekere showed how hard it was for anyone to understand Zimbabwean politics. He spouted an anti-American line in direct contrast to Mugabe's sweet talk to Solarz. Tekere 'did not like the idea of US involvement. They were showing too much interest, and ... he was "angry" about this. They might have been encouraged by the Zambians, but the further the Americans stayed out of the problem the better.'[27]

He told the Whitehall meeting that he and Mugabe had advised Solarz 'that the best thing for the US would be to keep out of Rhodesia'. Meanwhile, more efforts of ingratiation followed. Perhaps to apologise for the intrusive phone call, the UK's second secretary in Maputo sent Mugabe copies of *The Economist*. Mugabe was gracious in his thanks: the magazines were 'extremely helpful and so far they happen to be the only English newspapers we are getting. I hope you continue the good work'.[28]

As discussed above, Lusaka high commissioner Jeremy Varcoe did not like Mugabe as much as did his Maputo friends, and he was slightly sceptical about Mugabe's 'big impression' on Solarz. His ideology was 'socialist ... with all land nationalised and the dismantling of privilege'.[29] He was not convinced Mugabe would be able to hold off the red hordes, and Smith's intransigence would just create an environment conducive for more. Furthermore, he wondered if Mugabe really represented the political soldiers in ZIPA. The list of Mugabe's choices for a new Central Committee that David Martin had shown him only had one person bearing resemblance to a ZIPA personality (not that Varcoe was very clear on the quickly shifting Who's Who of the nationalist leaders). The 'hardliners' in Martin's list consisted of men in Lusaka's prisons waiting for their trial regarding Chitepo's murder. Their release, Varcoe noted, was still uncertain. He did not think the British view would see their presence at 'any meeting' as helpful, but it would be 'equally ... embarrassing if ZANU insisted on their release as a precondition to attending any meeting and the Zambians still held out'.

All things (including the ethnic card) considered, Varcoe thought Mugabe was

> certainly one of the people that we (and the Rhodesian Front) will have to deal with in the coming months. Nevertheless I have reservations about his ability to remain on top of an organisation containing so many embittered men whose principle [*sic*] aim has been to seek victory by military rather than political means. Moreover, as a Zezuru Mugabe could face a Karanga backlash if things go at all wrong. Meanwhile we can only take some comfort from the fact that Mugabe is one of the most moderate and sensible of the current ZANU leaders.[30]

The polar opposite of such sensible moderation had been expressed a week before. The Mozambican Information Agency (AIM) had published Dzinashe Machingura's interview on 22 September.[31] This was about a month before the Geneva conference that Crosland and Kissinger hoped would save the region from an Angolan and Mozambican end. It took the British embassy's second secretary just two days to send the 10 pages of perfect English, stamped by the Mozambican Ministry of Information, to their eager readers in London. They reached Whitehall on 3 October, with Charles de Chassiron's introduction. De Chassiron praised Machingura: 'fluent and extremely intelligent. The interview needed little editing.'

Yet de Chassiron doubted 'Dzino's' originality. He thought it was too close to 'Frelimo's political vocabulary'. As well, ZIPA's political structures 'parallel those created within Frelimo during the liberation war'. The event and the discourse had 'obviously been stage managed by the Mozambicans'. De Chassiron noted Machingura's 'hostile atti-tude to current attempts to find a settlement', too, and argued that this would be hard to 'break down', even if the Frontline presidents agreed to and endorsed a ceasefire.

De Chassiron did not analyse AIM's interview with a Marxist lens, or even one with liberal coating. Machingura's ideas about the National Democratic Revolution (NDR) may have jumped a few more stages than experts in Sino-Soviet discourse would allow. He claimed that the semi-liberated zones were a beacon of participatory democracy.[32] The 'masses [were] organised in units and ... democratically conducting their day-to-day business under the leadership of ZIPA'. He did not mention some of the disciplinary measures ZIPA had carried out.

Closer to the bone, however, was the ZIPA deputy commissar's label for the African nationalists salivating at a quick settlement. They were 'puppet Africans serving the Smith racist regime'. Mugabe's philosophical disquisitions with the likes of Solarz did not go that far. However, de Chassiron saw some light at the tunnel's end: Machingura's statement 'did not ... entirely square with the indications we have had that the guerrilla leadership may not be so determined to continue fighting as Machingura claims'. One can surmise that Mugabe was looking better all the time to those following the Solarz path.

As Mhanda recalls, that interview with the Scotsman cum Frelimo enthusiast Iain Christie may well have been *vashandi*'s undoing.[33] Christie was with Mozambique's Radio Free Zimbabwe, for which the interview was intended. However, the local weekly picked it up and it went viral—with, as de Chassiron noted, near-perfect English translations coming in fast. As Mhanda recalls, he had taken an 'unambiguous ZIPA platform rather than a ZANU position', consistent with Nyerere and Machel's idea of a 'Third Force'. Mugabe and Tekere were incensed, and demanded that Mhanda retract and state his fealty to ZANU. He took the matter to the Military Committee, which took an 'unequivocal stand in support of my stance and agreed ... we could not pander to their whims'. That would have risked 'abandoning our principled position but also ... sacrificing the support we enjoyed from Presidents Nyerere and Machel'. Mugabe and Tekere received the memo 'signed by all the members of the Military Committee', including ZIPA's head, Rex Nhongo. Nhongo delivered it, too: perhaps that is when he denied his agreement. 'Admittedly,' Mhanda—never one to mince words—confessed, 'the memorandum was emotionally charged, with the liberal use of strong language to convey our views.' It was 'turned around as ammunition against us, used to accuse us of harbouring designs to transform ZIPA into a political party'.

One with a suspicious mind could surmise it was all a trap.[34]

One question remained—and is still to be resolved with certainty. De Chassiron and many of his peers thought ZIPA was Frelimo's creation. This goes too far, but Frelimo met, welcomed and supported ZIPA before Mugabe came into the circle. Yet Frelimo abandoned them and packed most of its leaders off to the Geneva conference. On return: repentance or prison.

Regarding Mugabe, the remaining question is, when did he know he could strike? On 17 October the alleged Chitepo assassins were released. The Zimbabwe Detainees' Defence Committee had recruited British lawyer John Platts-Mills for the case. As Fay Chung puts it, his 'political acumen' and knowledge of Commonwealth politics helped build up his case. He argued successfully that the torture applied to the suspects annulled the trial, so they were free.[35] Mugabe could not have known what these 'soldiers' would do. Immediately thereafter, ZIPA's leaders, who had arrived to Lusaka with position papers for Geneva almost prepared (some still wanted to go to Geneva with ZANU, some did not—preferring to abide by Nyerere's suggestion to just keep fighting), were told that the Patriotic Front, with Robert Mugabe and Joshua Nkomo at the top, was a *fait accompli*. It was just for *tamba wakachenjera* or 'buying time', but they would have to go as ZANU cadres.

Mugabe felt secure enough to head to the Geneva conference.[36] However, when the *vashandi* returned to Mozambique they decided not to go to Geneva under Mugabe's banner in spite of Machel's lecture to them about their ultra-leftism, and that they would have to move right into Rhodesia if they did not go to Switzerland. Indeed, seemingly with Nyerere's blessing they wrote a blistering press statement at the end of November—with the conference well under way—denying that they were under the control of any particular leader.[37] 'None of the traditional political leaders exercise any political leadership over ZIPA and the broad masses of Zimbabwe,' they wrote. We 'do not take our orders from any of them. Anyone who pretends to lead ZIPA is an unscrupulous politician,' because they had their own 'chain of command completely independent of the traditional leaders and movements in Zimbabwe'. The release—signed by Nhongo under duress—said the soldiers' contingent 'flatly refuses to be associated in any way with the imperialist treachery and conspiracies ... being hatched in Geneva with the connivance of the Zimbabwe traditional leaders'.[38] That—and many conversations, to be sure—inspired Mugabe to send the 'Karanga' members, recently freed from prison, from Geneva back to Mozambique to work with Machel to the end of sending them packing for the conference. The ZIPA leaders had to signal their arrival with a telegram to Mugabe attesting to their unequivocal support for:

the stand which you and ZANU delegation took in Geneva talks. You have forced the enemy to shift its position and accept the principle of independence ... As we are entering a new phase of the talks aimed at dealing with the mechanism of transfer of power, a delegation composed of members of the Central Committee, ZIPA officers and fighters will come to Geneva in order to strengthen the party position at the talks.[39]

Immediately afterwards, Radio Free Zimbabwe, now run by *vashandi* man Abel Sibanda, broadcast an explanation. ZIPA had not changed its strategy or given in to 'the racists and their imperialist supporters'. Rather, it had a 'national duty to prevent the racists and their imperialist allies and the apologists of monopoly capitalism from neo-colonizing Zimbabwe'. Listeners should not interpret this as abandoning 'our principal strategy of armed struggle as the only viable strategy that will bring about genuine national independence to the struggling masses of Zimbabwe'.[40]

Back to the long haul of the National Democratic Revolution.[41]

Mhanda felt that Kissinger had convinced Machel and the British that Smith would concede: the *vashandi* held no such illusions. Machel was moving towards the idea that Mugabe would be a good leader: the *vashandi* was peddling backward on that one. Unity had not worked out very well: there had been fights and killings in two camps, leading to ZIPRA's withdrawal. It could well be that the *vashandi* pushed too hard down the non-partisan, but socialist or Marxist, ideological line. It also could be that they were not attuned to the old guard leaders' visceral hatred for ZAPU. Mugabe shared that hatred, as his 1975 letter to Chikerema indicated and his actions after 1980 verified. As the first two decades of the twenty-first century ended, stories emerged that Rex Nhongo, ZIPA's military commander, told the 'ZANLA' soldiers in ZIPA that if they were in a battle with Rhodesians and former ZIPRA soldiers they should shoot the latter first.[42]

A course guide from the short-lived Chitepo College, established after Teurayi Ropa (aka Joice Mujuru) supervised Wampoa's closure with the burning of all its books,[43] indicates ZANU's extreme dislike for ZAPU. It said that 'ZPRA' forces planned to let ZANLA 'smash the Racist State Machinery single handed'. Thus the 'social imperialist' USSR-aligned nationalists would gain 'breething [*sic*] space so that after victory it will apply the Soviet formulated "USSR Operation 1 Zero Hour" to crash [sic] ZANLA and seize political power'. ZPRA's cadres would lure ZANLA fighters with promises of beef and other 'pleasures ... like cigarettes, matches, radios beer, drugs' and even educational trips abroad. They would propose 'love to ZANLA female comrades with the hope of extracting Party secrets from them, the "Ndebele cause"'.[44] Cold warriors in the UK and USA, knowing nothing of these sentiments, would have seen unity as unwanted because it would bring Soviet support to a large, united army instead of a smaller one of two. Divide and rule was never far from their minds, but there were few rules and many divisions regarding the ever-splintering Zimbabwean nationalists within the diplomatic and intelligence corps of powerful states. In any case, with ZIPRA gone those in ZIPA who wanted real unity had no base. The political 'patriotic front'—claimed by Mhanda as a *vashandi* idea but at a broader level so Ian Smith could not hive off Geneva with a Muzorewa or a Sithole (which he did)—soon died a vicious death, to be reborn after Gukurahundi as close to a one-party state as Mugabe could manage.[45]

At the end of the day, however, the Rhodesians' attacks on the camps in Nyadzonia and Chimoio could well have moved Machel to extreme caution instead of enthusiasm. Exasperation with the faction-ridden guests could be another. It was not the £15 million in loans, interest free for fifteen years, that ambassador Lewen presented to Machel in mid-1977. They had been on the way since early 1976, to mitigate Mozambique's losses through sanctions.[46] Some of the ZIPA veterans talked of some large shipments of American grain greasing Frelimo's palms vis-à-vis the defanging operation, but concrete evidence thereof awaits confirmation.

Indeed, Machel had a good inkling of more trouble ahead whether Geneva worked or not, so he called those who did not want to attend 'ultra-leftists' and said that if they did not go they would have to fight in Rhodesia, with no backing from him. So they went, and Mugabe was able to show the British, the Americans, and the most of the Zimbabwean political actors who went to Geneva that he held the soldiers in hand (even though some observers thought they were *all* 'wild men'). If so, did he have to take the extra step in January to prove the case and to guarantee the outcome? Mhanda did not trust any of his prosecutors' offers of pardon, so it is doubtful if the co-option alternative was feasible. If the Mugabe group arrested 600 cadres during the January 1977 purge,[47] Mhanda and company had a lot of support. They would not be trusted unless they exercised force against their former followers. Nor would they be allowed to fulfil the demands of a national democratic revolution in a Zimbabwe with full franchise.

As it is, we see the axe on high, ready to fall on dissenters seen as coup-plotting traitors. At the same time, we hear a teacherly helmsman preaching Maoist Marxist-Leninism. In his 1977 lecture to all and sundry he advised his new Central Committee members to hit the books!

Back in the UK, the ZIPA story gained traction. A month ahead of Solarz and Carson's visit to Quelimane, Chris Mullin—then a journalist—and Abdul Minty of the Anti-Apartheid movement sent reports to various Labour Party recipients regarding rumours of radicalism in southern Africa's hottest spot.[48] Mullin's five single-lined pages to the party's international relations section did not benefit from a trip to Mozambique, but gained information from the *Observer*'s David Martin, who had spoken at length with Machel and was 'virtually the only Western outsider to have visited the camps'. Mullin had not heard of ZIPA's battles in the camps, as he considered Nhongo (aka Mutusuwa [sic]) and Mangena as its leaders still. He did say that the barrister [sic] Mugabe was the 'best known of the leaders ... who it is alleged was several years ago elected leader of ZANU in place of Sithole', the latter being deposed 'when ... Kaunda and Nyerere refused to accept him'. He got the soldiers about right: they, he said, held most of the nationalist politicians in 'contempt [due to] their inability to unite'. They would have to fight to the finish, but had no political programme and were 'bitterly divided along tribal lines'.

Abdul Minty's apparently unsolicited two pages reached deputy leader Michael Foot a week before Mullin's formal commission to Labour's international division. Minty claimed to know people who knew ZIPA (ZPA, for him) and could verify its socialist credentials. But the soldiers were hobbled by their inability to politicise the masses 'in depth ... prior' to armed struggle. This led to peasants' 'apathetic unwillingness to become actively involved in the struggle', and thus rampant informing. Nyerere and Machel had 'hijacked' the ZPA and sent it prematurely into this unpromising environment so they could siphon foreign aid. The solution? Negotiations, even with the moderates, and 10 to 15 years so Mugabe and the socialists (seen as one force) could wage what others—including *vashandi*'s key thinker—have called the National Democratic Revolution.[49] For Minty, too, tribal issues might derail such a process: he warned about a 'dangerous flashpoint between the Karanga and the Manyika'. He did not mention the Zezuru, but thought Mugabe, although a 'southerner at heart', could be a unifier. Foot declined gracefully to pass on the advice: if Anthony Crosland and his FCO crew saw it they might think 'Marxist Mozambique' was invading Rhodesia.

No wonder the FCO officers developed sangfroid and Freudian slips. A 'note on ideology' may have spoken for many:

> If you are a Marxist you believe that your victory is inevitable. If you are a FRELIMO Marxist you have just proved it. If you then look at ANC dissensions you will see the contradictions inherent in racist society inflected in petty bourgeois individuals (a bishop, for instance) and you will seek power[purer] leaders (Mugabe, a teacher?). It will not, however, seem to you that these bourgeois impurities (or the death rattles of neo-colonialism causing incidents on your borders) are anything more than temporary obstacles to the invincible progress of dialectical materialism in Southern Africa. And you may be right.[50]

Fifteen months later, after the 'failed' Geneva conference, efforts at humour had not diminished: 'The Secretary of State asked why the guerrillas could not cut the Rhodesian railway line to South Africa. It was explained to him that they were not very good guerrillas.'[51]

Kissinger's imperative was what was needed was to cut to the chase. As Sisman's biography of Le Carré suggests, the Americans thought the British were naïvely unconcerned about the Soviet threat.[52] Frank Miles, high commissioner to Zambia for some of this time, told me, 'We thought this was just an ordinary decolonisation process.'[53] Kissinger was unconcerned about the internecine struggles of the Zimbabweans: recall his joke about Harvard and his comment that for him Rhodesia was a test case for bigger things. Kissinger's sense of the hunt was global in scope albeit constricted in its Cold War conjuncture. His angry letter to Crosland during the Geneva conference said as much as 'it's the Soviets, stupid!' With such stakes, cabinet approval was a nuisance. Kissinger told Crosland that if the British failed, it would confirm 'the general fear that every potential peaceful Rhodesian settlement is built of sand'.[54] Crosland replied that he would not 'cramp your style' but the continental crusader should be 'tolerant of our difficulties' with the democratic demands of cabinet approval for major steps. In the presence of such executive privilege and global power, Crosland bolstered Kissinger's confidence with the coup metaphor if he could unseat Smith and company when the British had lost every battle. Neither Kissinger nor Crosland's proxies did pull Geneva off, but the process did identify the Zimbabwean emergency maker who Kissinger thought was uncontrollable and unreliable.[55]

Who was more accurate: Kissinger and/or Solarz, with their rather Manichaean views, or the subtler sympathies of the Grennans and Wästbergs? And how did these diagnoses affect Mugabe's making? Perhaps a 2020 (date and hindsight coinciding) review by two relatively liberal participants in the Rhodesian realms of intelligence seeking is the least wrong of them all. Besides offering a trenchant critique of Ian Smith and company's reactionary efforts to reverse history, Ellert and Anderson's *A Brutal State of Affairs* spares no objectivity about those hastening it—or botching it for any of a hundred reasons. They reproduce a curate's egg-like intelligence report; relatively balanced on the battles in the camps, albeit with too heavy a primordial dose, but with too much emphasis on Machel and Mbita's aims to create a 'Marxist military dictatorship' in Rhodesia.[56] Their own analysis has longer terms in mind.

They write that 'under the dominant (Vashandi) command from late 1975 until late 1976, [ZIPA's] major doctrinal and operational changes ... essentially restarted the war (after Détente)'. This led to 'significant progress' before Mugabe was allowed to leave Quelimane and head to Geneva. After 'outwitting the Vashandi leaders such as Wilfred Mhanda' and persuading Samora Machel to get them out of the way, 'Mugabe, who had no interest in collaborating with ZAPU, acted ruthlessly, crushing and disbanding ZIPA'.[57]

Just as Mugabe and Machel were dealing with the *vashandi*, Eshmael Mlambo had lunch with an FCO employee.[58] Peter Mackay had helped him out of Rhodesia while he escaped the ramifications of the 1966 university activities.[59] Well known as the author of an excellent analysis of Zimbabwean nationalist parties up to the end of the 1960s, Mlambo had been economic adviser for ZAPU since the Geneva conference.[60] He worked for the OAU in Geneva, travelling to London every weekend. He thought he should advise his host about the two main nationalist parties' ideological makeup. Mugabe and Nkomo were not Marxists, he said, but they cannot say so because they need arms from the Communist countries. 'Britain', he advised, 'ought to make it plain to the world that the Patriotic Front were not Marxist-oriented.' As is common and enjoyable (if legible) to readers much later, there were scribbles at the bottom of the host's letter to his superior. 'I am inclined to agree with Mr. Mlambo's assertion that Mugabe is not a Marxist. But some juniors who surround him possibly are.' By the end of the month, worries on those grounds disappeared—although the weapons would go to separate parties.

Ironically—or perhaps not, given the omniscient view of 'patriotic history'[61]—nearly forty years after that lunch and just a few years before Ellert and Anderson's assessment, a ZANU (PF) apparatchik read and critiqued Wilfred Mhanda's (aka Dzinamrira [*sic*] 'Dzino' Machingura) memoir. As if channelling Mugabe's 1984 words, Arthur P. T. Makanda said *Dzino* was in the same camp as the 'angry Rhodesians who ... do not believe that they were defeated in the battlefield by the blacks'. Mhanda's 'prime motivation for writing his book' was to 'complement Rhodesian literature and curry favour with reactionary forces that he has joined'. Its 'tone and ... agenda ... have apparently been set by someone else [so] we cannot rule out a third white hand in Dzino's memories'.[62] *Dzino* is narcissism writ large: Mhanda saw himself as the 'personification of the war ... the instructor, commander, cadre, the injured, the dead, the survivor who lived to tell the authentic story'. Such a tale fits perfectly, says Makanda, with Zimbabwe's 'oppositional voices ... rehears[ing] the theatre of a political comeback'. This would be, of course in the 'interests of minority whites ... still clutching on to a molesting vision of coming back to usurp the land that the nationalist leaders have distributed to the people of Zimbabwe'.[63]

Even Terence Ranger was not spared: he was 'the link-man ... shaping ... British opinion and foreign policy towards Zimbabwe', lending the book 'a broad theoretical thumbs-up'. Mhanda must have been one of the many 'self-seeking people' on the 'lucrative commercial venture … sponsored by the British' trashing the liberation struggle.[64] Professor Ranger, who passed away before being able to read the poorly edited chapter,[65] would have been surprised at his role in the UK, sharing Mhanda's view of the National Democratic Revolution. It would have been interesting if Makanda had read Ranger's 'Changing of the old guard',[66] more so Mhanda's prison writings 'Treatise'.[67]

More interestingly, the chapter suggests how the 'blame everything on the imperialists' discourse ensnares many within Zimbabwe's intelligentsia—and their ability to keep within the 'revolutionary party's' bounds of respect. Makanda's only empirical snippet is fascinating too, especially given the 2017 coup's reminder of the *vashandi* moment and the flexibility of party members when singing and voting for their leaders. Just before expounding on Mhanda's 'celebration of American values'[68] (Kissinger would add this to his jokes) Makanda records the lyrics to the songs chorused by musical soldiers to celebrate Dzino's unveiling. They illustrate the efforts involved by rulers-in-the making trying to construct hegemony during various states of emergency—and how fleeting they can be. To be sure, music is always an important component of such strategies, especially in times of war.[69] Yet it may be unique to bring songs into 'internal wars' absent show trials. Makanda shows the second-guessing such choirs inspire. He suggests— dismissing the heresy quickly—that the singers 'in concurrence with the decision taken to banish [Mhanda] were ignorant of his misdeeds' or that they might have been 'coerced into singing against their conscience by an atavistic conglomeration that was pitted against his achievements'.[70] Makanda takes their chorus as proof of ideological and alliance-building hegemony. But if 600 people supporting *vashandi* and singing songs that worried even the *vashandi* leaders were arrested in the Beira trials' wake, can he not be mistaken?[71]

What can be made of these lyrics, which place 'Dzino' side by side with the man who, after being disciplined for wayward behaviour on the front, abandoned the guerrilla soldiers and returned leading the Rhodesian Selous Scouts to attack Nyadzonia camp?[72] 'Dzino', asserts Makanda, 'fell into this category of selling out Zimbabwe', as his recitation avows.

Haiwa isu tinoti pasi naNyati–we say down with Nyathi
Wakatengesa Zimbabwe–who sold out Zimbabwe

Ndaizoibata ndaizoidhuutsira–I will carry a gun and shoot
Murungu pasi naNyati–the white man down with Nyathi
Pasi naNyati wakauraisa macomrades–down with Nyathi who sold the
comrades to the enemy

Vana Dzino vakatemwa iwee–Dzino and others were axed
Vana Dzino vakatemwa nedemo–Dzino and others were axed by
Demo redu reZanu–our Zanu axe
Nedemo demo redu reZanu–by our ZANU axe
Saka toti pasi navo iwe–so we say down with them
Saka toti pasi navo ivo vana Dzino–so we say down with them, Dzino and
others
Ivo vana Nyathi waiona hondo.–Nyathi and others have seen the war.

KaDzino kakatemwa kuBeira–little Dzino was axed in Beira
Woye woye hondo yarongwa neZanla–ooh ooh the war planned by ZANLA

Vana Dzino vakatemwa iwee–Dzino and others were axed

Vana Dzino vakatemwa nedemo–Dzino and others were axed by
Demo redu reZanu–our ZANU axe
Nedemo demo redu reZanu–by our ZANU axe
Saka toti pasi navo iwe–so we say down with them
Saka toti pasi navo ivo vana Dzino–so we say down with them, Dzino and
others
Ivo vana Nyathi waiona hondo.–Nyathi and others have seen the war.

KaDzino kakatemwa kuBeira.–little Dzino was axed in Beira.

Makanda summed up his copies of the songs with this: 'The import
of labelling one a sell out and declaring him an outcast would then
place one in the same category with the enemy, hence his summary
killing was popularly sanctioned.'[73] Neither Dzino nor his comrades
were killed. Nor was Nyathi. Who was?

The 11/17 parallel? Has anyone ever seen whole political parties rally
so quickly–district committee after district committee–to fire a vice-
president and anoint a new pantheon of leaders? And to vote to sack
them all in around two weeks, as that unemployed vice-president awaited
'the voice of the people' to supplement the military means to rise to the
peak? There is concurrence of coercion and conscience involved in both
cases. As Gogol (and William Kentridge, not to mention Bukharin)
might have put it, then 'the horse is not mine and I am not me'.[74]

At the very least, examination of Zimbabwe's 1970s allows us to know that the array of possibilities at similar conjunctures may appear to be endless, but some more than others can hasten a better end. How the agents of the changes within them handle their power and their opponents can be as good as any indicator of that. Some of the less powerful within those moments can perceive the nightmares that they lack the capacity to stop. Some of the *vashandi* political soldiers realised as their fate unfolded that they had made a big mistake by not working hard enough to bring the security sectors to their side—the same ones who distrusted their intellectualised motivations for joining the struggle as they told their 'biographies' to their interrogators so many months before. This was a lesson the 'G-40' had not learned by late 2017. One imagines they had by the end of November.

Some with power between the pyramid's extremities can shift the sands beneath them. Dennis Grennan said he might have had that sort of influence. As it campaigned in the elections that would kick off the next phase of Zimbabwe's long democracy game, Robert Mugabe's ZANU (PF) engaged in much violence. The suffix PF did not indicate unity with ZAPU, but an attempt to maintain its pretence after Mugabe declined to pursue harmony at that level. The parties would run separately and Mugabe would pursue the 'chopping and slashing campaign' until the big thud he had promised his cousin five years before.[75] Joshua Nkomo of the newly named PF–ZAPU brought this violence to the attention of Christopher Soames, the temporary British governor. Soames sent his notes back to London. Nkomo's 'complainet [sic] ... was that throughout the Shona-speaking areas Zanla had instituted a reign of terror.' Mugabe's *mujibas* (young male 'messengers' recruited during the war but now armed) still carrying arms were kidnapping and killing Nkomo's supporters. Soames and Robin Renwick consulted, later advising Nkomo to go public with his concerns.[76]

The British ambassador in Washington summarised Assistant Secretary of State for African Affairs Richard Moose's perspective. 'Entirely in character', he wrote, 'quote vintage Nkomo opportunism unquote'. Nkomo would 'privately ... encourage measures against Zanu from which he would be the principal beneficiary' and be reluctant to 'support such measures in public since he doubtless appreciated the danger of being branded in Africa as someone prepared to desert a former ally'. More broadly, Moose dictated, it was necessary to 'keep Mugabe in play'. Even the South Africans 'were coming to accept that it would be better to deal with a regime which included Mugabe than to see continued instability in Zimbabwe'.[77] The Americans were to open an embassy in the new Zimbabwe, only 12 hours after accreditation began. According to Moose, 'Robert Mugabe's election was probably the greatest reverse the Russians have suffered in Africa in years'.[78] Kissinger may or may not have agreed.

Grennan may have had as much claim to this great reversal as his colleagues across the sea. Soames's team of advisers argued at length about Nkomo's claims, he said nearly three decades later. Deputy governor Anthony Duff apparently argued that Nkomo–backed up by military intelligence reports[79]–was right and the British should consider serious action. Grennan, however, argued that all the parties had blood on their hands and ZANU (PF) would probably win anyway. The war would recommence if Soames cancelled the election, with no change in the balance of forces.[80] I did not triangulate this particular truth, but what remained with veracity was Grennan's disappointment that Robert Mugabe never thanked him. One supposes Sarah did.

The real decision, however, was made before these arguments carried out by the messengers of empire at its outposts as it neared its finish. Toward the end of our interview I asked Mark Chona if I had missed anything important. He said yes, he thought that his lunch with Josiah Tongogara, after the Lancaster House conference and before they left London, was interesting. He was surprised to hear Tongogara say Nkomo had made the best contributions to the conference–better than Mugabe's.[81] About a decade before that interview Edgar Tekere told me about the last time he spoke with Tongogara. It was at a meeting just after Lancaster House. Samora Machel presided. Mugabe, Tekere and Tongogara were at the table with him. Machel asked if they thought the Patriotic Front should stick together for the election. Tekere told me that he spoke first–indeed, many presumed that his outspoken nature articulated Mugabe's unsaid thoughts. He was opposed, adamantly so. Why, he asked rhetorically, would we want to ally with Nkomo? He talked with Smith when we were at war! He was betraying us. Machel then turned to 'Magama' Tongogara–who had cried 'no, I couldn't have' when Tekere and others grilled him about his culpability in Chitepo's murder–and asked him 'who would be the leader' if the front stayed together. According to Tekere, Tongogara said 'the senior'. Mugabe said nothing. Shortly thereafter Tongogara was no more.[82]

6

COCKROACHES, KIDS AND COUNTING DOWN

1980–2000

A link or three (missing or not) concerning guns, politics and politics

Before delving into the three Cs (coups, conspiracies and conceits) of Mugabe's legacy as it evolved alongside ZANU (PF)'s post-1980 trajectory of power and accumulation, some links between the 1970s and the 1980s–and before–are worth noting. Towards the end of 2004 some evidence of what Mlambo and Raftopoulos call Zimbabwe's 'multi-layered crisis' was piling up.[1] Zimbabwean citizens were constantly looking upward to see if Tony Blair's fighter jets had come over from Iraq to invade their space. The MDC threatened to withdraw from the parliamentary elections looming in March: an oft-used electoral strategy for Zimbabwe's opposition parties, but mostly unsuccessful. A Victoria Falls candidate thought this would only benefit ZANU-Ndonga–a remnant of the Ndabaningi Sithole days. It did work once, when the Patriotic Front refused to contest the election leading to the hybrid Zimbabwe-Rhodesia. That lasted for a few months in late 1979. The PF had guns then. The vicious but sloppy 'auxiliaries' for the parties that had lost the guerrilla soldiers' confidence in 1976 could not match them.[2]

By 2004 the 'fast-track' land reform process arising from ZANU (PF)'s 2000 referendum loss and close election was moving towards a

101

new agricultural mode.[3] Over 1,500 white-owned large-scale commercial farms were now 127,192 households on 'A1' plots with use rights and common grazing land, 7,260 'capitalists' with leasehold and a 'proposed option to buy', and a few hundred big chefs gaining most news coverage. Nearly 250,000 people waited for this land while more than 4 million starved. Productive and white commercial farmers decreased from 4,500 in 2000 to under 500 in 2004. Wheat production fell to 170,000 tons from the former 300,000 average, the commercial beef herd went down from 1.2 million to approximately 150,000, inflation increased to 600%, and unemployment had gone up to well over 80%. As Rob Davies measured, Zimbabwean income per head fell to 53% of the 1996 level: if rates of growth had remained at the 1996 rate this figure would have been 97% higher (he did not calculate changes in the Gini coefficient). Inflation and the dismemberment of official and real exchange rates were working their way to a wrecked economy. It hit bottom by 2008's end. Soldiers rampaged when their very late Christmas bonus afforded a loaf of bread. Zimbabwe could not afford to print enough notes to maintain its currency sovereignty.[4]

Mugabe held a press conference after his party's 2005 78 to 41 seats victory.[5] A reporter asked him how long he would stay in power. Then a sprightly 81, he answered, 'Until I'm a century old'.[6] April to June 2005 witnessed a drastic slide: petrol cost Z$3,500 officially, but Z$30,000 at 'World Bank' rates on the streets. The informal exchange rate for the American dollar rose from Z$13,000 to Z$28,000 from March to May. In 1980, when Mugabe had performed his reconciliatory gestures, the Zimbabwean dollar was worth twice the American. If Zimbabweans accepted that scale for weighing the merits of past and present then by 2005 life was 56,000 times worse than in 1980. The negative consequences of Mugabe's continued reign were even clearer within weeks of ZANU (PF)'s 'victory'.

The first four years of Zimbabwe's new millennium—and 'fast-tracked' land reform—witnessed 128 murders, 37 attempted murders, 3,849 torture cases, 619 abductions, 2,042 arrests and detentions, 712 assaults, 259 displacements, 26 rapes, 33 disappearances and 190 death threats in the cause of ZANU (PF)'s continuing leadership. That was a slow burn: after the 2005 election came Operation Murambatsvina ('drive out the rubbish'). The punishment meted out to urban opposition supporters included 22,000–30,000 urban *siya so* ('leave it as it is') traders arrested and the destruction of their homes and businesses. Between 200,000 and 300,000 were homeless in winter's midst.[7]

This moment would be a mere shadow of the very dark 2008. Besides marking the first stages of Zimbabwe's economic regress and the ways in which liberal or social democratic models of opposition politics transmogrified, it witnessed one of the more public displays of 'regime' change inside ZANU (PF).

In August 2004 I met Patrick Kombayi in Gweru to talk about ZANU (PF) politics. He had been a railway worker on the line to Lusaka, where he established a restaurant. He supplied the liberation parties when they moved north. Fay Chung's account of the (18 March 1975) Chitepo assassination's wake says he showed 'exceptional courage and brilliance', heading committees supplying weapons and food to soldiers in Zimbabwe and the imprisoned comrades' families in Zambia. However, years later he crossed Mugabe when he demanded recognition as a leader for his troubles—and further when, refused, he wanted his money back.[8] On returning to Zimbabwe he bought Gweru's main hotel and became mayor. He joined Mugabe's erstwhile best friend Edgar 'Two-Boy' Tekere to lead the Zimbabwe Unity Movement (ZUM), the country's second substantial opposition party (after ZAPU). When running for ZUM in the 1990 election, at least four employees of various ZANU (PF) appendages (one the Youth League, another the Central Intelligence Organisation (CIO)) ambushed and shot him. He hobbled with a cane after recovering.[9]

Framed photographs of him with just about every nationalist of the early years covered the hallway to his office—weddings, rallies, celebrations of political victories, reunions on airstrips with long-lost comrades. The happy ones ended at Tongogara's smashed car—at the end of Rhodesia in 1979 and the beginning of Zimbabwe in 1980—with the carnage on the road, and the funeral, which Kombayi arranged. The horror of brutalised MDC supporters' slashed backs, buttocks and smashed heads completed the gallery. As his story unfolded, he remarked in passing that he was glad to have British assistance for ZUM. The struggle to go beyond the one-party state was a mutually held ideal: he had experienced their failures where he had lived.

The link? Rex Nhongo aka Solomon Mujuru, ZANLA's military supremo, or near to it, ever since he crossed over from ZAPU as it began to splinter in the early 1970s. Sixteen years after Kombayi's tale, Nhongo would be the subject of Blessing-Miles Tendi's fascinating biography, emphasising his role as soldier and kingmaker.[10] Mugabe is the king, of course: clearly, understanding *the* man demands the same of his makers. One can read Nhongo as the archetype of Mugabe's efforts to separate the two halves of Gramsci's centaur—indeed, the biography's title indicates such. But the account bifurcates the heart of humankind's second profession. It severs the part-man, part-beast blending force and persuasion—coercive domination and consensual hegemony. Thereby it points directly at Mugabe's attempts to do the same: a liberal conceit at the heart of an increasingly illiberal and possibly frozen interregnum.[11] Mugabe started it while addressing the Maoists in London as he was about to defang the *vashandi* 'terrorists',[12] and repeated it ad nauseam as he would declaim the superiority of the bullet over the ballot and his degrees in violence but then complain if the soldiers bothered him.[13] Nhongo would be a key player in that process, revealed intimately in the biography. Thus his heroic kingmaker moniker for restoring 'politics' to ZANU and ensuring Mugabe was at its head. However, when Mujuru tried to persuade Mugabe to retirement, Mugabe seemed happy at his death via furious fire. This crossed the thin line between 'politics and the gun' for the zillionth time, but Mugabe (along with many liberal academics, and cultural Gramscians)[14] seemed unable to deal with that dialectic.

Seven years after the heated death, Mugabe fumed at what he saw as the efforts of Mujuru and his physically-but-not-politically separated wife Joice to capture the party—to be kings and queens, not just his acolytes. Mujuru's fiery death in 2011—on the same August night that Wilfred Mhanda launched his memoir—has inspired much speculation.[15] Not for Mugabe, though. 'He just died', he told the *Zimbabwe Independent* journalists. He added, enigmatically, 'What is fortunate for the party is that it happened away, on his farm.' Mugabe careened down memory lane, back to Geneva and the fire in Mujuru's room. Fay Chung writes that ZANU 'believed [the cause was] a Smith agent, a young over-friendly lady with revolutionary pretensions who had somehow found her way to one of the commander's rooms'.[16] Mugabe was sure it was Mujuru all on his own:

He was a terrible guy. Very selfish. And a smoker. A smoker, I think this is what killed him. In Geneva, we burnt down a hotel and it was Mujuru again. Well, we managed to avoid trial, but it was his smoking that almost got us killed. … He was a careless smoker. An investigation established that the fire started in his room. But we denied it and said no no.[17]

Eleven months later, on his last birthday, Mugabe wondered how and why soldiers got involved in politics.[18]

Kombayi's tale got to the roots of a theory fusing the gun and politics, aka coercion and consent, *and* the political economy of accumulation. He revealed the triumvirate of the conceit within ZANU (PF) power: coercion, consent and corruption. This is the Holy Trinity Mk II, in the shadows of primitive accumulation, hegemonic construction/ nation building and democratisation. It entails the contradictory processes of resistance, alliance building and co-optation spreading political participation around contending social groups. The fantasy that we can split power between politics and 'the gun' arbitrarily ties the trinity together. Kombayi added 'accumulation' to the equation.

We were discussing corruption. He told me how Zimbabwean soldiers and politicians learned that the 'gun meant money'. Rex Nhongo was the head of ZIPA, not happy with the intellectual, ideological and smart-ass members of the *vashandi* tendency. He invited Kombayi to the camps in Mozambique. Since the adjacent zones in Zimbabwe had opened up, ZIPA found it hard to feed the huge influx of young volunteers (and conscripts from mission schools). As Kombayi put it, hundreds were dying of kwashiorkor. Nhongo and Kombayi asked Samora Machel for permission to kill some elephants in the national park to make elephant stew. The plan worked well. It worked doubly: Nhongo realised he could sell the tusks in the Gulf states en route to London, where he could access the party's bank account. The guns that killed the elephants replenished ZANU (PF)'s bank accounts as well as the future soldiers' stomachs. As Mhanda and his comrades remarked often, Nhongo was very popular among trainees and guerrilla soldiers in the camps because he was sure to be seen dispensing food and supplies. Kombayi thought this was the perfect example of corruption's genesis in ZANU (PF), and the soldiers' role at its conception. That was Nhongo in the 1970s. Rhodesian officers excelled at this too.[19]

As for the link with the 1980s–the elusive tomorrow had arrived out of an unfinished Rhodesian past–the gun and the man with its trigger play an even larger role, albeit pointed in a new direction. The moment of its second revelation was in the new peacetime and involved money as well. Ellert and Anderson report on the meetings that created a new Joint High Command in April 1980. A year later Robin Harvey, the CIO's representative on the JHC, reported on the Domboshawa Brigade's pay and promotion complaints. Mugabe told Nhongo to attend to the matter. Nhongo reported back the next week: the problem was resolved. The soldiers 'causing the unrest had been shot'.[20] A good start to labour relations in a Marxist–Leninist–Maoist regime.

That sort of industrial relations was to take especial hold when combined with politics writ large. Given the Zimbabwe Congress of Trade Unions' (ZCTU) umbilical cord with the ruling party, a longer history of conflict in that regard[21] and complex international ramifications, ZANU (PF)'s portrayal of some trade union activity as rather like a coup was nearly predictable.

In March 1985, 14 union activists, including the president of the General, Engineering and Metal Workers' Union, were arrested and imprisoned. They had been pushing for more democracy and less corruption. This threatened the ZCTU leadership, tied to ZANU (PF) too. The black Zimbabwean unionists–one a tried and true ZANU (PF) war veteran–were tortured in prison. Their South African and Dutch comrades, expelled from the South African ANC for working outside its strictures with trade unions abroad, were also incarcerated. Their torture was to hear their black comrades scream through the walls; their interrogators told them there was one obvious way to stop it. The British Council library's copies of *The Guardian* told the story, but *The Herald* cooked up its own version six weeks later. It claimed that the Southern Africa Labour Education Project (SALEP) was a proxy for the British Labour Party's left-wing irritant, the Militant Tendency. The vigilant Zimbabwean state had stymied a coup. Its foreign instigators were deported. The local activists stayed to face more music.[22]

British Labour Party leader Neil Kinnock was about to meet Robert Mugabe in Addis Ababa at a July 1985 OAU conference. At the end of April, however, a group of Labour Party members and unionists flew to Zimbabwe. Guests of the Ministry of Labour at the May Day celebrations, they were shocked to hear Mugabe denounce their party and its 'alleged connection' with Militant Tendency. They cabled the TUC's international committee head, advising him to rebut the charges immediately. As Kinnock prepared for his Ethiopian foray, the party advised that, 'to get off to a good start' with Mugabe, he had better 'ensure that Mugabe understands that we do not support or condone SALEP ... [nor] the Militant Front in Zimbabwe. ... After getting the Militant issue out of the way,' the prompting continued, 'it might be worthwhile spending time congratulating him on how well Zimbabwe has done': the beleaguered president was 'fed up with all the carping from Britain'.[23] The ZCTU's leadership collapsed soon after.

However, Labour's soft-pedal was short-lived. The Labour Party noticed ZCTU leader Morgan Tsvangirai's 1989 arrest. He had addressed a seminar on the pitfalls of the one-party state, led by University of Zimbabwe student leaders Arthur Mutambara and Enoch Chikweche (aka Munyaradzi Gwisai)[24] already arrested. The party's National Executive Committee (NEC) demanded that Kinnock write to Mugabe in this regard. The NEC memo claimed that Labour *had* supported the SALEP 1985, and the liberation struggle before. It cut a critical swathe of ZANU (PF)'s retrogressive labour legislation and security laws 'inherited from the Smith regime'. Kinnock's letter to Mugabe attached the NEC's strident emergency resolution, noting its dismay and disquiet. Yet the personal note said the NEC resolution contained 'some errors of fact ... as I and other members pointed out'—on which Mugabe might wish to respond.[25] Mugabe did not.

Note: this issue had nothing to do with white farmers, the Ndebele people and ZAPU, nor land, nor a party full of puppets (unless the Militant Tendency was on some strange strings). All of these accusations came more than a decade later, against other counter-forces, as ZANU (PF)'s slender thread of hegemony thinned further.[26] The contradictions of the 'neo'-liberal economic policies (albeit with foreign exchange controls belying that label) and 'liberal' political dreams would lead to the conflagrations consistent with the clashes within the Holy Trinity all over history.[27] The Labour Party—in power with its Cool Britannia dressing—would cause more damage than the Militant Tendency and its comrades. So too would students in the Mutambara and Chikweche generation—as they did in the 1960s and 1970s as well.

The final link reaches back into history (especially of campus confrontations). Michael Holman, a young Rhodesian covering the Geneva conference for the South African *Financial Mail*, met Eddison Zvobgo on a plane. He did not write an article about that, but had done so with Josiah Tongogara.[28] The guerrilla commander came out as a perfect liberal: 'Do you want the capitalist system eliminated in Zimbabwe?' Holman asked him. Tongogara replied:

> The people will tell us in which direction to go ... I want to see Zimbabwe free and then we can sit down and see what sort of line we should take. I have gone to Eastern countries–probably you would call them communist. ... But I don't come back as Mao or Fidel or as Che Guevara.

No vanguard for him. He would soon show that a pre-figurative National Democratic Revolution was not in his cards either. Holman was a 'graduate' of the mid-1960s days at the University College of Rhodesia and Nyasaland, which was more an island of revolt than 'non-racial learning', as chronicled by once vice-chancellor Michael Gelfand.[29] In that respect, it resembled its counterparts in the 'West'. However, the radical white students' home was in (or beside) the 'third world', and they realised some of its problems earlier than most of their peers. While in 1966 ZANU and ZAPU incursions and Judy Todd's speeches around the world caused havoc for the state,[30] demonstrations against UDI and for the African nationalists disrupted the idyllic island of meritorious scholarship. Authorities confused the ZAPU supporters on campus (some running guns, etc.) with the lecturers and students' ruckus about UDI resulting in arrests and worse as the police sifted through the finer grains of dissent.

In March, hundreds of students marched and boycotted to protest against the UDI state and for the nationalist parties. When they confronted vice-chancellor Walter Adams at his campus-based house, they formed a 'Committee of Six' (four black students with an Indian and a radical white–he being Michael Holman). Journalists were deported. Josiah Maluleke, a trade unionist and student, escaped from Gonakudzingwa prison camp in April and returned to classes. Adams supported Maluleke. His minister forbade that; Adams nearly resigned.[31]

Coincidentally or not, encouraged by the OAU's promise of funds to the nationalist groups if they would take some action, ZANU launched its now emblematic Sinoia attack. ZAPU's July incursions to Sipolelo and Mount Darwin, where Herbert Chitepo's father Johannes met the guerrillas, followed. 'Foreigners' Peter Mackay and Giovanni Arrighi had assisted them in the preparatory stages.[32]

A July demonstration at a graduation ceremony was replete with roughing up the 83-year-old Lord Malvern.[33] Ten days after the campus demonstrations, on 27 July, the police arrested and detained nine lecturers and ten students. They included an Italian, Giovanni Arrighi (whose writings on Rhodesian political economy remain essential reading); a Canadian, Gerald Caplan; a Norwegian, Axel Sommerfelt; a naturalised Briton, Jaap van Velsen; a Rhodesian, Timothy Curtin; and four British citizens, Ian Henderson, Christopher Hill, Richard Whitaker and Elizabeth Joyce. Among the students, the Rhodesian Basker Vashee was detained while nine more were restricted for a year: C. M. Ushewokunze, I. S. Mudenge, E. M. Mlambo, J. W. Murisi and N. Moyo went to Gonakudzingwa. A. J. Wilkinson, M. R. Ward, W. H. Godwin and S. Morar were restricted to various areas of their residence.[34]

John Conradie's lover's jealous girlfriend spilled the beans on the bombs (small ones: grenades) he and Arrighi had transported from Zambia. The South African assistant history lecturer and Arrighi had started their visits to the exiled ZAPU leadership in Lusaka in 1964, relaying communications with the prisoners in the newly constructed and easily accessible Gonakudzingwa prison camps. Border guards' racism favoured the cause. The grenades and other arms arrived a couple of years later. Stashed at Conradie's to avoid discovery during the student and lecturer ruckus, they cost him a twenty-year prison sentence. (In 1978 the short-lived Zimbabwe-Rhodesia regime released and deported him. He worked with 'Education for Production' projects in collaboration with Patrick van Rensburg in Botswana, returning to Zimbabwe briefly in 1980).[35] The courts declared Arrighi and Drama and English lecturer John Reed leaders of a ZAPU cell, but they were lucky to be out of the country. Arrighi was gone: the lecturers involved in the campus demonstrations had been deported, and he had a job interview elsewhere anyway. Reed had just taken up the University of Zambia's English chair.

Along with fellow troublemaker Peter Mackay, Terence Ranger had left Rhodesia a couple of years earlier. Ranger, expelled, moved to the University of Dar es Salaam's History department, leaving his ZAPU cell and editorship (with Reed) of *Dissent*. His memoir recalls his days with this group, but deflects their arms-related activities with discussions about Marxism's (ir)relevance.[36] Peter Mackay, once in the Black Watch and a Scots Guards officer slated to very high positions among the United Kingdom's guardians, left the military for a Rhodesian tobacco farm. Ill-suited at that, he started writing for an agricultural magazine. There, as the Capricorn Society's organiser, he met 'eggheads' such as Nathan Shamuyarira and the Samkanges.[37] Moving leftward–intellectually towards Owenite views such as those of his friends Robert Oakeshott and Joan Wicken, and actively towards military involvement–he published a magazine for the Malawian and Zimbabwean nationalist parties. That, and refusing the draft, had him leaving the country to newly independent Zambia, where he set up a refugee camp. He transported many escapees from the Rhodesian and South African versions of 'separate development' tracked by the British South African Police as they wandered in Botswana to safety. He also ferried arms to Arrighi and friends as they hoped to start ZAPU's sabotage. His memoir ends in the late 1960s, too early for a man whose career extended well into the 1990s with a health NGO in Zimbabwe's north-west. When I asked Dennis Grennan if he knew Mackay the answer was: 'Hmmm, I think he went AWOL about then.' That was probably when he started working with ZIPRA's communications contingent at his house near the Lusaka airport.[38]

Ranger's memoir leaves Arrighi and Mackay 'clash[ing] violently' over the merits of going home to the Sardinian revolution versus 'romantic adventures' in Africa:[39] no mention of guns. Arrighi was soon to teach at the University of Dar es Salaam, where John S. Saul found him: their *Essays on the Political Economy of Africa*[40] are the first written record of their long comradely friendship.[41]

The postscript to Arrighi's foundational study of Rhodesian political economy refers obliquely to his freedom-fighting days. Could, he asked, 'an African revolution ... halt the trend towards an *apartheid* society in Rhodesia?' The chances of 'protracted guerrilla warfare of the traditional type [were] unlikely to succeed in directly toppling the regime', largely because aside from Zambia the colonies surrounding Rhodesia were 'sympathetic to the regime'. Arrighi 'presum[ed] this is consciously or sub-consciously realised by the African population'. Thus Africans would 'lapse into resignation' or channel their 'widespread discontent ... into terrorist activities' (distinguished from guerrilla warfare as mainly directed against the civilian population while the guerrilla aim is '*mainly* [emphasis Arrighi's] directed against regular forces').[42] With the combination of guerrilla war in Angola and Mozambique with the Portuguese coup changing that dynamic, Arrighi would have changed his prognosis. That would leave the ideological dispositions of the nationalists in a more determinant position. Perhaps our 2004 conversation outside the Johns Hopkins University cafeteria shed light on those possibilities. Arrighi recounted another of his early diagnoses. During his time in Rhodesia, the tensions in ZAPU leading to the Ndabaningi Sithole group splitting were apparent. His perspective differs from Ranger's account of the Nkomo–Sithole divide: Ranger records Reed as 'disheartened [by] Mugabe saying that the masses don't understand and will accept anyone as leader'.[43] Arrighi took this further. He and his comrades agreed that Nkomo was a bit of a buffoon, but ZANU was CIA.

Sports enthusiast, English student and adamant non-racist Holman was close to it all. After the Committee of Six ordeal, he and ex-pat lecturer Paul Nursey-Bray edited *Black and White*[44] while he was also the student union's president. Nursey-Bray's anonymous poem inspired the university and police to send Holman to Gwelo, confined to his parents' house. Scotsman Malcolm Rifkind–later to serve in British ministries with global reach–lectured at UCRN while writing an MA on Rhodesian land issues.[45] His visit to Gwelo led to Holman's Politics MA at the University of Edinburgh, after many cables and letters, well watched–and assisted–by the FCO.[46] Cabinet discussed Holman's case. Some ministers thought the 'renegade ... had the makings of a very militant opponent'; perhaps he should be kept home. The winning argument was that this denial would make him a 'hero and martyr [making] him more important than he was at present and give him *entre* overseas to numerous subversive organisations'.[47] Holman returned with his MA to Salisbury, reporting for the liberal South African *Financial Mail*.

Six months after the Geneva conference, a Rhodesian civil servant remembered the renegade: Holman's attempts to gain the draft's exemption had failed. Perhaps his interview with Josiah Tongogara marked him out. A 'friendly source' in the Special Branch advised him to leave—quickly.[48] He did so, soon to start as London's *Financial Times* Lusaka correspondent. Eventually he became the paper's Africa editor.

It was a short, casual interview with Zvobgo, the future minister of many portfolios and designer of the constitution that made Mugabe think he could rule for a tenth of Ian Smith's dark dream—and who drew close to the MDC as his life neared its end. Holman asked him how he gained a first-class seat. Zvobgo—the 'charming rogue' in the Evetts and Spencer correspondence; the Harvard-trained lawyer; the poet arranging Solarz's visit to Robert Mugabe—answered perfectly: 'Nothing stands in the way of the struggle.' Had the conversation continued, Zvobgo might have revealed Solarz's travel details. Perhaps he also knew if Mugabe crossed to Mozambique with Special Branch permission. According to Ellert and Anderson, the local officer was 'instructed ... not to interfere with Mugabe existing [*sic*] the country'.[49]

With an adieu to Mugabe like that, Zvobgo would have to change the pro-'ZILA' stripes he had displayed brazenly—albeit alongside salutations and letters from the man of the future—a few months previously in the new San Francisco edition of the *Zimbabwe News*.[50]

Holman could have asked if Amnesty International covered Zvobgo's luxurious seat. In 1972 the human rights organisation reminded the FCO of its promise to Zvobgo and five others (including Joshua Nkomo): 'airfare and all other possible assistance' if released from Rhodesian clutches. The Pearce Commission window might have allowed for that. The Amnesty correspondent advised the FCO that these struggle stalwarts would leave the country so 'could hardly pose a threat' to Rhodesia's security.[51]

Zvobgo would not be alone in dropping the ZIPA qua *vashandi* fusion. In April 1977—just months after the *vashandi*'s incarceration and during the camps' cleansing—an American university audience heard Nathan Shamuyarira praise a ZIPA *sans vashandi* and embedded within ZANU.[52] A few months later, in the post-Chimoio *Zimbabwe News*, Shamuyarira blasted 'armchair revolutionaries' Arrighi and Saul as 'sworn enemies' of Zimbabwe's revolution. He fingered an early

1977 celebration of the *vashandi* view Saul wrote for an American solidarity magazine, criticising Crosland and Kissinger's preferred petty-bourgeois leaders in ZANU. Too late to help the ginger group, it fed in to the ZANU eggheads' arsenal.[53]

Back to the cockroaches

Due or not to Dennis Grennan's advice, the realisation that Mugabe and his 'wild men' would soon be Zimbabwe's governance interns trickled down slowly. The die-hards' plans ranged from ballot stuffing to the coup-like Operation Quartz. The latter included shooting down Mugabe's plane on its arrival from Mozambique, killing 100 ZANLA troops in Salisbury, and eliminating the 200 ZIPRA and ZANLA 'along with their commanders (Rex Nhongo, Dumiso Dabengwa and Lookout Masuku)' residing at the Audio-Visual Arts Building near the University of Rhodesia. Ellert and Anderson's 'rise and fall' chronicle argues that 'Nkomo was considered more amenable, [so] the ZIPRA men would be given an opportunity to escape'.[54] The plotters cancelled their plans at the last moment: the British and their Rhodesian allies (some also British) wanted no blowback.

Coups and conspiracies surrounded Robert Mugabe as soon as he gained his Zimbabwe. Yet during his first prime ministers' meeting with his British counterpart, he did not complain about scheming whites. A few weeks after his inauguration, he and Margaret Thatcher proclaimed his transmutation from terrorist to Statesman. Mugabe praised the Rhodesians—'senior commanders in particular had behaved admirably'—but not his erstwhile Patriotic Front partner.

> The real problem lay with ZAPU and ZIPRA. It was not clear that Mr. Nkomo was responsible but some members of his organisation were not prepared to accept the new situation and wanted to continue the fight. They had been responsible for a number of very silly acts, some involving deaths. Those responsible had been arrested. But there was still a strong element who were tempted to resort to sabotage in the hope that the ensuing chaos might lead to new elections and the overthrow of the ZANU government.

Some of these problems emanated from the assembly points (APs). At one, 1,500 of the 2,000 had disappeared. Others were clearly ZIPRA territory, for example, Mike AP in Lupane, north of Bulawayo:

113

'[A] few ZANLA men had decided to be bandits and were being hunted out. But the number of *dissidents* [emphasis mine] from ZAPU and ZIPRA was increasing all the time. Moreover, there seemed to be a political basis to their activity. The government might have to act against them soon.'[55]

Mugabe was unclear if the 'dissidents' were *within* ZAPU or *from* it, meaning they had left. Jocelyn Alexander traced ZANU (PF)'s dissident discourse at Zimbabwe's dawn. The disaffection in the APs did not warrant such a label in early 1980. In May and June regular ZIPRA forces rounded up at least 400 'errant' soldiers and delivered them to the local prison. As Alexander records, the 'dissident' label 'was more or less officially adopted from March', but with Parliament's opening came the overtly political arguments.[56] Thatcher was among the first to hear it, with its clear implications. Just the day after the two prime ministers met, the *Bulawayo Chronicle* noted parliament's discussions about ZAPU's unhappiness with the election results leading to violence. Two weeks later, Mugabe complained that 'organised bands of ZIPRA followers' refused to acknowledge his government's sovereignty.[57] The rabid anti-ZAPU discourse evolved quickly thereafter, leading to the first major intra-army confrontation at Entumbane in November. Yet a mid-March 1981 memo from the FCO to Thatcher regarding another meeting with Mugabe avowed that 'his firm handling of the recent clashes involving dissident elements of ZIPRA and ZANLA' meant that the 'security situation has returned to something like normal'.[58]

These conversations presage Zimbabwe's horrific Gukurahundi, but it is unclear if Thatcher was already wilfully blind, as Hazel Cameron labels the British during what Mugabe later called a 'moment of madness'.[59] Scores of archived notes between the FCO, Defence, the prime minister's office, and high commission representatives in the early 1980s take the 'dissident' issue very seriously. Many more agonise over the Five Brigade's training sessions, the British citizen being interrogated roughly for his participation in the South African and ex-Rhodesians' devastating attack at the Thornhill air force base, and selling more Hunter aircraft. More correspondence than usual demand special viewing permission.[60]

The London and Harare diplomats' sarcasm alleviated their worries. A Harare officer proffered advice on how to dissipate Mugabe's 'steam' after an 'intemperate, irrational, and emotional performance' (in late 1983, when enraged about British concern for the man accused of blowing up the Thornhill fighter jets). A good lunch and an 'entirely amicable talk' with minister of state for security Emmerson Mnangagwa would dampen the furies.[61] A more serious note—from London at 1982's close—reflected Cold War tensions. The Soviet threat was the last, but lengthiest, concern on the list. Business was first: 'Zimbabwe could well become UK's third most important export market in Africa (after Nigeria and South Africa)'. The Lancaster House agreement's good vibes must remain. A total Zimbabwean collapse or civil war would render the UK with few choices aside from cutting ties. Africans would then see the UK as supporting 'white Africa'. The penultimate and scary idea was that there was 'no successor [to Mugabe] of comparable stature in prospect'. The memo presented the Soviet issue as follows.

> Limiting Soviet and Communist Influence. If we refuse military sales and aid, Mugabe will turn elsewhere, possibly to the Soviet Union despite his reluctance to do so. If the security situation got bad enough, he might feel obliged to follow the example of Angola and Mozambique and accept large-scale military help from the Soviet Union and Cuba. Other Front Line states would also draw the lesson that Western help cannot be relied upon and be more ready to look to the Soviet Union. The US Government attach particular weight to this danger. The worst case scenario would be a virtual Soviet world monopoly of certain strategic minerals and Soviet domination of the key sea lanes around the Cape.

Options to keep Zimbabwe on track? A Zimbabwe–UK business association? Could a 'leading university' offer Mugabe an honorary doctorate? More university scholarships to Zimbabweans? Try persuading moderate ministers such as Bernard Chidzero to remove the Herbert Ushewokunze-style radicals from cabinet. Could we convince our media to stop reproducing Ian Smith's rants?[62]

Dumiso Dabengwa, recently heading ZIPRA intelligence, had a different view: he thought such prime ministerial chats were evidence of a concerted strategy to keep the Ndebele people on power's receiving end.[63] Stuart Doran's monumental study of the genocidal mid-1980s sees them as evidence of Mugabe's remarkable 'determination and skill' to pursue commonplace nationalist and one-party-state aims. His 'intellectual ability ... absolute commitment to violence ... patience and shrewdness ... [and] aggression was controlled and organised', to play 'rivals and threats one against the other'.[64] This combination of attributes worked during the 1970s battles for ZANU's top job. It would do so again in the 1980s. By pitching the 'original' nationalist parties and their reinvented ethnicities against each other—again— Mugabe postponed the construction of a Zimbabwean 'nation' by decades or more.[65]

The cockroaches? In 1983, just over two years after Mugabe and Maggie chatted about the bothersome ZAPU, the man who is now president of Zimbabwe addressed an audience in Victoria Falls. He was then minister of state security and in charge of the CIO (often called 'the President's Office' and somewhat jokingly claimed to employ one tenth of working-age Zimbabweans). Well before the Rwandan discourse about unwanted but persistent ethnic groups, he said the dissident/bandit menace facing Zimbabwe was like an epidemic of cockroaches and bugs. DDT would rid Zimbabwe of these pests: that would be the North Korean-trained Five Brigade; many others played lesser roles.[66]

Mugabe and his minions massacred anywhere from 5,000 to 20,000 residents of the Matabeleland and Midland provinces, while thousands more experienced the slightly lesser consequences of what Mugabe claimed was a temporary instance of insanity. There has been no official reconciliation process or investigation published, and the current regime seems able to divide civic organisations' efforts.[67]

While on an environmental awareness tour in early 2020, Zimbabwe's post-Mugabe president, known for his slow-burning brutal temper—one of the reasons for his nickname 'the Crocodile'—but not his humour, advised villagers to rid their homes of cockroaches.[68] Students of the late-1970s Chitepo College curriculum could have predicted that the cockroaches would be on the way to something worse than a coup.[69]

During Gukurahundi, former head of the Rhodesian Special Branch David 'Danny' Stannard, who told me he stayed on in the security brief after 1980 to help keep Communism at bay, had only one complaint about his co-director. Mnangagwa, Stannard said, treated the areas under siege as 'liberated zones'.[70] Mnangagwa exercised no disciplinary constraints on the soldiers, still hearing the Chitepo College chorus of crash [*sic*] or be crushed, and reeling from the battles at the barracks on the dawn of freedom.[71]

After swallowing ZAPU in 1987 in the 'Unity Accord', guaranteeing 'ZAPU' one of the two vice-presidency positions, Mugabe and ZANU twisted and turned in the contradictions exacerbated by the 1990s structural adjustment policies that Cold War and South African considerations had delayed. Those tensions hit the fan at as the new millennium arrived. The rise of a strong, civil-society and trade-union-based opposition party, combined with the aggrieved war veterans' anger and simmering discontent over the distribution of land, gave Mugabe—slipping slightly from his pedestal—a tail he could twist to his benefit.[72]

However, as the first two decades of the twenty-first century slipped by, his grip failed—albeit not as quickly as his country's material base and social structures. This all accentuated the misleading conceits on which his and his party's power were constructed. The conspiracies about coups and the coups that never happened were once Mugabe's means of maintaining power, but they failed him as the times and the means got leaner and meaner. The real coup arrived, led by men with more conceit, but less cognate capacity, than Mugabe had.

The consequential conjuncture means more confusion and chaos than hegemonic construction: an 'emergency' of a Bonapartist crisis with no dictator capable of hammering it into Caesar's shape. Perhaps an investigation of nearly two decades of conceits and conspiracies—more within the ruling party than from without—may find a pattern, and paths leading out of it.

And the kids …

With the forced unity agreement of 1987, university students' radicalism sharpened focus. So too did Mugabe's responses to their displays of Marxism with a libertarian and eventually multi-partied tone. Perhaps a non-authoritarian style of the Trotskyism wound its way to campus, assisted by arrivals such as Rehad Desai. On encountering a colourful case of University of Zimbabwe students misbehaving in the early 1990s, Mugabe responded in an authoritarian patriarchal mode.

They were 'a bunch of rapists, drunkards and drug addicts who could not be allowed into the city because they were given to violence. ... They are our children. We will discipline them our way.'[73] This was far from his 'axe will fall' discourse after *vashandi*'s destruction and students were small potatoes after Gukurahundi. It did display his priggish side: not up to the student's Bakhtinian carnivalesque.[74] Indeed, on gaining the state he ordered hippy-inspired occupants of public office, many recipients of Western university scholarships, to wear dark suits. His prudishness went far beyond dress codes. As early as 1983 the police swept more than 3,000 single women off the streets. A Non-Aligned Movement meeting was on the way.[75]

At the university, such stuffy sentiments made their way to Mugabe's interpretation of Marxism. Dan Hodgkinson's excellent doctoral dissertation on university student activism cites Mugabe's warning of a 'dangerous intellectual bourgeoisie in our midst'. He recommended ZANU (PF) begin a 'process of cadre formation' to create the correct 'socialist, people-centred orientation'.[76] Perhaps the intellectual vanguards at the university did flaunt their superiority: the Goromonzi syndrome. As Hodgkinson puts it, university student leaders tended to claim a 'political authority ... through [a] reconstituted form of political studenthood in which they were the key agents of the revolution'. Their combination of educational privilege and 'socialist critique ... reifi[ed] ... the university's liberal traditions'.[77] Yet as the student leader the British Labour Party tried to protect put it, they had no choice. Arthur Mutambara reflected that Zimbabwe's 'material conditions and history' imposed this 'de facto social role' on them. The young politicians striving for Gramsci's organic intellectual status were 'cognisant of the problems, material conditions and aspirations of the toiling masses and are the barometer of socio-political consciousness'. The Student Representative Council thereby was obliged 'to provide a platform and a forum for the voiceless and disorganised by vehemently declaring and venting their problems and aspirations'. This 'aspiring intelligentsia [is] equipped with the tools of scientific analysis'. It should 'explain the socio-political and economic bankruptcy characterising our nation'.[78]

ZANU (PF) did not fully test turning a potentially dangerous bourgeois vanguard leftward via a 'cadre formation' process. In the mid-

1980s Brian Raftopoulos, then in the Ministry of Manpower Planning and Development, was drafted to lead a study on the prospects for a national youth service scheme. The task force included technocrats from the education, women's affairs and youth ministries, as well as an army officer. They visited Cuba, Yugoslavia and Tanzania to compare their schemes. Their negative recommendation, on economic grounds, was accepted. As Raftopoulos put it later, the team 'kept our arguments at an economic and technical level' although the programme's 'likely politics' worried them. In the 2000s, though, the idea 'took on the more grotesque form' of ZANU (PF)'s National Youth Scheme.[79] That turned out to be the Green Bombers' recruiting camps. Whether its earlier implementation would have engulfed future leaders of civil society and the MDC is best left as a counterfactual.

If a 'liberal tradition' extended to a vanguard blending structural determination, obligation and meritocracy with an anti-authoritarian Marxist–Leninism such that today's version is 'thought leadership'–the purveyors of which, says Richard Poplak, are best met by instant projectiles of vomit–so be it.[80] Vomit is better than Gulags, but a shaky bulwark against the alternative-fact factor. Nevertheless, Angela Cheater's comments on Zimbabwe's legislation attempting to stifle such liberal traditions are worth remembering. It was characteristic of many universities in similar circumstances: 'Destroying universities is ... a necessary precondition to strengthening not only the state, but also those who, however temporarily, control the state ... irritating university "dissidents" must be silenced'.[81] Such silencing is brutal.

Tim Scarnecchia's article on Zimbabwe's nascent fascism cites Tinashe Chimedza's eight arrests during his 2001–2 national student's union headship.[82] A later American State Department report promoted him. He was a professor 'addressing students on academic freedom' in April 2004. Police arrested and assaulted him. His lawyers were watching, but denied access after his arrest: while waiting the charge was changed to 'inappropriate dress'. Chimedza's email account expanded the meaning of 'arrest' (and such reports). The US report was

wrong as usual. We were having an Education Forum at Mt Pleasant Hall. They surrounded the Hall and hundreds of students were milling outside. We tried to reason with them; they denied us the hall, forcing people away; we tried resisting; got nabbed; dragged to the room behind the hall and they had a party on me. That is how I ended in a private hospital with a machine gun guarding the door. My girl-friend's extended family summoned her and instructed her to cut [our relationship] off. [83]

A Human Rights Watch report records the 2006 silencing process. Two hundred students arrested while demonstrating at Bindura University; 15 tortured. In Harare: 15 trade unionists beaten and arrested. Two hundred Women of Zimbabwe (WOZA) activists arrested; 63 detained for three days. In Mutare, 180 NCA members arrested while demonstrating for the unionists. Another 200 faced the same fate in Harare. Promise Mkwananzi, then the national student president, told the NGO of his five days at the Bindura police station:

> They beat me with baton sticks, clenched fists and kept kicking me. … Every night they would threaten … 'We will kill you tonight' [and] … would strip me naked and then handcuff me with my hands between my legs so that I would not be able to move while they beat me. Sometimes they would be three people beating me, then two or at times four. [They said] I was trying to facilitate regime change and working for the opposi-tion. … They finally released me without charge. [84]

Fortunately, a future vice-president was not supervising a book-burning ceremony, unlike at the closure of Wampoa College in 1977.

The British Labour Party's NEC's instructions to its leader to notify Mugabe of their concerns regarding the students did not fail to note Morgan Tsvangirai's subsequent arrest. The guardians of the ZANU (PF) party-state also accused him of being a South African agent. This indicates the fusion of civil society organisations, and ZANU (PF)'s fear of foreign intrusion. So too does the MDC, the party causing the most headaches for Zimbabwe's rulers. [85] Academics and other civil society organs have chronicled the travails of Zimbabwean civil society well. What concerns the rest of this chapter is how these and other factors exacerbated ZANU (PF)'s tendency to see conspiracies and coups everywhere. It may be too teleological to see the particular denoue-ment of Mugabe's rule in 2017 as inevitable, but it is hard to avoid a trajectory towards that end. Of course, one element of this part of Mugabe's legacy is the conflation of challenges. A complaint about a policy or a person is considered a threat and thereby linked to the whole ruling party. Since the ruling party (and its leader) embody the people and nation's sovereignty, those challenges are sponsored in turn by outside forces and thus tantamount to treason. When these worms of dissent are *within* the otherwise perfect ZANU (PF) rose, pesticide is the only remedy.

On the long road to the coup

The equation of political opposition with foreign powers extended to Edgar Tekere and Patrick Kombayi's Zimbabwe Unity Movement—which, as Kombayi recounted, shared democratic aspirations with the UK and accepted some of its ideas and pounds.[86] ZUM fared well at 26% of the 1990 urban vote in spite of the violence measured out to it.[87] A lesser phenomenon interested the conspiracy theorists. ZUM arose out of Tekere's apparent anger at ZANU (PF)'s corruption, exposed so embarrassingly in the 1989 Willowgate scandals, when journalist Geoffrey Nyarota uncovered cabinet ministers selling their bargain-priced cars at near-market prices to various friends.[88] The CIO thought ZUM resembled South Africa's historically important (and Marxist) National Unity Movement (NUM) too closely to be trusted. Abdul Latief Parker was rooted in the NUM environment, and indeed was on the editorial board of the Glasgow-based *Critique*, an offshoot of the South African variant of the Trotskyist tradition. He was also one of Edgar Tekere's friendly funders.

Parker told me he moved to Zimbabwe in 1986 from his Cape Town home to 'see how socialism worked in Africa'. He kept his foreign exchange shop in southern England and other interests in South Africa intact, and traded asbestos in Harare. He diarised his Wednesday lunches with the Cuban ambassador meticulously. His sessions with CIO officers in the Jameson Hotel's bar debating the ABCs of socialism (about which his fair-weather friends knew nothing, he told them, proceeding to lecture) were more haphazard. The CIO seemed to think Parker was a South African spy, although he was more akin to a wealthy, theoretically sophisticated and serious pursuer of Communist utopias and their failed realisations. Tekere expressed profuse gratitude for his help at the back of his book—a catalogue of friends with money they liked to advance to Mugabe's one-time friend—even thanking Parker's partner, a doctor, for her medical assistance to Anne, Tekere's wife. Parker said Tekere was lying.

He had good reason to do so, as he probably denied this in prison too, deposited there twice and interrogated many times, perhaps regarding running guns. When released on condition that he could not return, he advised the local BBC reporter of his flight to Gatwick. When the waiting reporter asked when he would return to Zimbabwe his answer was 'When it is free.' Local security operatives trailed him and Tekere when the latter visited him in Cape Town.[89]

Perhaps the 'war vets' visit to State House was a coup, twenty years before the real thing. It did not replace a ruler, but changed his mind. By the middle of 1997 the war vets were as dissatisfied as anyone with the effects of structural adjustment. They had been insulted too. Media had revealed the corruption swirling around payments distributed since 1995 for medical ailments suffered during the war. Dr Chenjerai 'Hitler' Hunzvi, who trained in Poland with ZIPRA, gained support within the veterans' association by signing medical certificates. As Chirombowe has it, Hunzvi widened the programme beyond the 'privileged few' who accessed it first.[90] He certified many false injuries. Presto, he was president. When Mugabe, thus notified, suspended the scheme in March, the war vets were 'the laughing stock' of Zimbabwe.[91] Thus humiliated, Hunzvi mobilised the war vets into action. They were ready for a revolution.

As Thabo Mbeki put it, the lumpenproletariat war vets took power.[92] Mugabe needed them because his party had lost faith. The 1990s Economic Structural Adjustment Programme (ESAP) had taken its toll. People blamed Zimbabwe's rulers: they called the neoliberal IMF medicine 'eating shit amidst plenty'. The ZCTU even persuaded the civil servants to join as they struck in 1996. By 1997 the war vets demanded pensions and land, and had even made a deal with the ZCTU: the workers would support them as long as it did not hit them in the pay packet.[93] They booed Mugabe at the August Heroes' Day ceremony. They threatened ZANU (PF) leaders all over the country. Later in August, the war vets used force to back up their demand for a State House meeting. There, Mugabe acceded to demands for pensions of $2,000 per month (then about £125) and huge lump-sum payments of Z$50,000 (about £3,000)—and land.

Land analyst and fast-track reform enthusiast Sam Moyo told a UN news outlet that the deal was made 'more or less at gunpoint'.[94]

Important ZANU (PF) leaders were under armed guard at their homes. Those claiming to be in the know say that armed war veterans held retired air force marshal Josiah Tungamirai hostage. It is not hard: VIPs of that stature in the party-state have armed guards from the military. If indeed the war vets on the street had allies in the formal military, it would be easy to 'borrow' uniforms and stand in for their friends: twenty years later the coup-makers played a similar tactic. Didymus Mutasa, a nationalist stalwart since the 1950s 'seminars' at Guy Clutton-Brock's Cold Comfort Farm and in 1997 Speaker of the House, perhaps the most important ZANU (PF) leader in Manicaland, was probably under guard too.[95] Was this the victory of the gun over 'politics', as Mugabe might have put it?

As one of his long-time challengers said, Mugabe could turn a 99–1 defeat to a win. If it was a coup, Mugabe turned it to his advantage. Yet even if he had turned it, the victory was short term and self-centred. It would set a path to penury in place. It might have been the most ruinous coup in Zimbabwe's history. The outlay could have been handled, given that the money would circulate through the economy. There was more, however: the war vets wanted the long-delayed land issue resolved, and Mugabe saw that as a vote getter.

He granted that demand too, and 20% of it would be for them. On 14 November—the day has been known as Black Friday ever since—the act to get that land was gazetted. The state would take around 1,400 large commercial farms and pay due allowances for 'improvements'—all allowed constitutionally but never implemented. The value of the Zimbabwean dollar fell by 75%. Breaking the bonds of private property did the trick.

A week before that, British aid minister Clare Short replied rather abruptly to a Zimbabwean minister's letter asking for some help on the much-delayed land issue. Her answer was a qualified 'no'. She said her government would be willing to 'support a programme of land reform that was part of a poverty eradication strategy, but not on any other basis'. The 'no' was directed at the idea that the UK owed Zimbabwe anything for its colonial past. Tony Blair advised: stick to lots of consultations with all the stakeholders and don't forget the market. More than anything else, Short's tone put a stop to meaningful discussions with the old colonial power. The historical ups and downs of relations with Albion started on a long slide down.[96]

Who would pay the pensions? Mugabe soon made sure there would be no worker–peasant–lumpenproletariat alliance.[97] There would be a levy for the pensions. Combined with the removal of subsidies on maize meal (neoliberalism still had some bite), that led to the food riots in early 1998–the first time soldiers shot citizens. Opposition forces recruited hundreds of high-school students to the streets. The terrain for the social democratic seeds and flowering freedom tilled in the universities and unions throughout the 1990s was beginning to green. By February 1999 the Workers Convention vowed to create a workers' party, and the NCA mounted a campaign for a new constitution.

The September donor conference on land shepherded quietly by South Africa's president Thabo Mbeki might have broken the logjam,[98] but naught transpired. All donors except the World Bank (allocating $50 million to a stillborn pilot project) thought that the excessive state control would only help ruling party potentates, leaving the poor in penury.[99] Some think this was punishment to ZANU (PF) for taking Kabila's side in the second–just started–DRC war. ZANU (PF) did nothing: it had no funds for the improvements demanded by the administrative courts for the farms the war vets wanted.[100]

The DRC war cost $1 million a day. This instigated the IMF's withdrawal: its fungible funds fled to the war. Fiscal rectitude was abandoned as uniform makers, transport companies and diamond dealers related to the generals made a killing (no pun intended).[101] Journalists were tortured when in late 1998 they reported army discontent: 23 upset soldiers in the DRC were jailed for inciting mutiny against Mugabe.[102] One soldier told me that their diet in the DRC sometimes consisted of the food prepared for the army's horses back home.

A retired police officer who spoke to me many years later happened to be on duty at a December 1998 Central Committee meeting in Victoria Falls. He recalled the buzz of expectations on Mugabe airing his retirement. It might have been a good time for Mugabe to leave the mess to someone else. However, it was clear that a strong opposition was about to be born, and with lots of foreign help. Mugabe decided that his party and his pride would not survive his departure. Bonapartism indeed: as Marx would have said–about the Zimbabwean political class if not the peasantry–Mugabe had become the 'master ... an authority over them ... an unlimited governmental power' protecting them against all their enemies and to 'send them rain and sunshine from above'. Marx was certainly no clairvoyant vis-à-vis Zimbabwe, but he did write that after 'a vagabondage of twenty years and after a series of grotesque adventures' somewhere, someone would be 'their ... final expression in the executive power subordinating society to itself'.[103]

The MDC was born on 11 September 1999, just as the constitutional referendum was unrolling. A parliamentary election was due by mid-2000 at the latest. At the last moment before the referendum vote in mid-February, Mugabe overruled the commission and removed the two-term clause. The land would go back to the original tillers, with compensation for the more recent ones if possible but if not, by crook. Just over 54% of the 26% of the registered voters defeated it.[104] None of the usual applause greeted Mugabe at the next cabinet meeting. A few weeks later, he pulled out the stops for the land invasions.

The retaking of the land may have assisted ZANU (PF) to win the June election. Killings and cheating—at the early stages—helped too. The MDC did very well: 57 of the 120 seats. Not all ZANU (PF) party members and supporters were pleased. The real conspiracies for coups started soon after.

7

RUMOURS OF COUPS

2000–7

If *The Guardian*'s Hugo Young was not one to spend time on or to visit Zimbabwe, his connections with British politicians were tight and trusted.[1] He wrote about a soon-to-be-hatched coup just before Mbeki's July 2001 screed about the lumpenish consequences of Mugabe's precipitous actions: the southern African convert to a fiscally prudent yet social democratic 'third way' advised IMF rectitude and a fair presidential election in March 2002 for his northern peer.[2] Young claimed in May that Zimbabwean 'senior army officers' informed their southern peers 'that they might launch a coup against Robert Mugabe if the growing political and economic crisis results in riots'.[3] October's maize shortages conjoined with a 'bitter struggle against the opposition' would mean that the police would side with Mugabe against a people's uprising. Increasingly upset over its misuse in the DRC's war, and in the context of the defence minister's death by car accident, the military side of security would refuse Mugabe's orders to join the other armed arm. Young reported on Pretoria's belief that Mugabe's waving away of the IMF indicated 'personal withdrawal from the real world'. Young put some hope in Colin Powell's barbs pointed at Mugabe's 'totalitarian [and] terrorising' methods. He did not say if Mbeki's flirting with Anthony Giddens' and Blair's versions of politics and economy held an iron fist in his foreign policy glove.

Perhaps Young's journalistic profession meant he knew the current British high commissioner to Zimbabwe, Peter Longworth. His interview in the Churchill College, Cambridge, collection of diplomats' reminiscences does not reflect his reputed showering of generosity to the MDC, but young MDC recruits do. The record is however clear about the differences of opinion between his kind of diplomacy and Clare Short's abrupt moralism and the cash-strapped realists in the FCO.[4]

Young's two articles about Zimbabwean politics ended with an eloquent tribute to its voters' tenacity whilst the Commonwealth waited for the presidential election's tally to test its resolve. Would it ban Zimbabwe from its club?

> Where, in our own continent of ingrates, would people queue for 15 minutes, let alone 20 hours, to make their point? Where ... has any other leader gone to such lengths as Robert Mugabe to confer democratic legitimacy on himself? While he serially violates the substance of democracy, he can't do without its semblance. Each side, voter and dictator, pays tribute to what democracy is meant to be. It could be called a kind of apotheosis.[5]

Young feared that the Commonwealth would prevaricate on the issue of democracy's universality and lose 'its last remaining purpose'. The Commonwealth did keep its promises, with little avail—aside from many students unable to get its scholarships—but Mbeki did not follow through with his recommendations.

Zimbabwe's election team proceeded with enough violence and underhandedness to make Mbeki commission a *second* report given the first's blindness (rumours had the South African observers' technical team taking dictation from their president). It took a dozen years in South Africa's courts to see the new one. Only then could the Khampepe Report confirm suspicions that the elections were far from free or fair.[6]

Zimbabwe's ruling group made moves to bring in the opposition after the 2002 election.[7] When something like this fails everyone involved says they had nothing to do with it, and memories fade automatically. Conjecture, misspelling, obfuscation, and unnamed sources replace hard searches. Retired colonel Lionel Dyck was a source, along with some anonymous non-retired officers and double-tracking politicians. Much seems to depend on the then recently retired (now late) general Vitalis Zvinavashe. Apparently he was keen to restore economic liberalism to its rightful place in a country on its way to ruination (perhaps he had been born again since his stint at the trough in the DRC).[8] One question: did he start the process on his own, or did his commander-in-chief inspire him? Mugabe may have wanted to test an offer to retire–but slowly and ceremoniously, in a symbolic presidency perhaps with both Mnangagwa and Tsvangirai by his side, in that order.

If Dyck is misspelled Dycke or Dyke, reports on such plots might bear no credibility.[9] A 'prominent South African businessman' remains mysterious to date. So is an 'obscure' and 'relatively unknown ANC politician': 'Patrick Moseke' is found only in reference to Allister Sparks's baffling article.[10] Another incorrect spelling? Is he the very wealthy Patrice Motsepe? The latter visited the president of an 'inclusive' government in 2010 to tell him he was 'very confident and optimistic ... that there will be huge investment in this country' shortly.[11] Be that late promise as it may, as soon as Tsvangirai 'smelled a rat'[12] during the post-2000 discussions, all involved held their noses. Yet before Sparks' piece Tsvangirai told the *Washington Times* he would be willing to consider an interim government 'whose sole task would be to restore law and order and arrange fresh elections'.[13] Tsvangirai thought Washington might send a 'special envoy' to help things move along. Mugabe–perhaps he started the project in the first place–sniffed 'counter-revolutionary'.[14] Jonathan Moyo, running Zimbabwe's information ministry, said all this was 'tantamount to plotting a coup in the glare of the media'. If the protagonists had 'hatched a plot to *force* the president to step down they should face the full wrath of the law'.[15] Two years later Moyo would divulge more.

Patrick Chinamasa, proud proclaimer of ZANU (PF) patriotism, denounced these moves as 'an attempted coup d'état ... [that] will not be tolerated'.[16] A ZANU (PF) insider asserted there were many contenders in a new 'war of succession'.[17] Is this what crocodiles do to suss out where the pickings lie? Both Jonathan Moyo and Emmerson Mnangagwa were soon accused of contriving coup-like concoctions.

The 'plotters' were angry with Tsvangirai, blaming him for agreeing, then backtracking. David Coltart and Roy Bennett had apparently advised Tsvangirai that the agreement would place him in a weak, undefined position in a government resembling a junta more than a democracy. Perhaps they had even jammed the plans of the coup's alleged co-sponsors in the Anglo-Atlantic alliance. Walter Kansteiner, then US Assistant Secretary of State for African affairs, is said to have described Coltart as 'that evangelist' who foiled the talks. In 2004, innocent and ignorant of these imminent coups, I interviewed Kansteiner and various Washington thinktankers. The latter offered the impression that southern Africa needed the Zimbabwean state to be strong and steady to buffer the winds of terror heading to South Africa. They saw Tsvangirai as incapable of maintaining the bulwark. If elected, hell would reign.

Yet, neither was there unity in DC, even among the Republicans. Kansteiner recalled that when George Bush the Younger visited Thabo Mbeki in July 2003 he took two speaking points.[18] Secretary of State Colin Powell's, articulated soon after he misled the United Nations about Iraq, advocated spreading the American democratic dream. He wrote in the *New York Times* that 'South Africa and other African countries ... can and should play a stronger and more sustained role' reflecting the urgency of Zimbabwe's crisis.[19] They should urge Mugabe to 'dialogue with the political opposition'. If they did not, 'he and his cronies will drag Zimbabwe down until there is nothing left to ruin'. His analysis was better than on Iraq, but he was running against national security advisor Condoleezza Rice and her director for African affairs, Jendayi Frazer. They wanted Mbeki to lead with his 'African solutions for African problems'. Rice and Frazer won: Zimbabwe's civil liberties lost to persuading the Nigerians to deport Charles Taylor to The Hague, with its particular form of punitive global liberalism. Mbeki was, as Bush put it, 'the point man on this subject ... an honest broker'.[20] The Zimbabwean media snipers could retain the 'Uncle Tom' affixed to Powell.[21] Opposition journalists wondered what had happened to Kansteiner's promises of more manna. Mugabe's ability to skulk just below the 'international community's' sights won the day again.

Yet unity talk had not died. Mbeki slipped it in during the Bush meeting: they were 'absolutely of one mind' on the need to address Zimbabwe's issues: 'We have urged the government and the opposition to get together. They are indeed discussing all issues. That process is going on.' R. W. Johnson, always hearing unsaid lines between those spoken, cited 'unconfirmed' reports from Harare with Mbeki predicting 'Mugabe would leave office in December during his party's annual conference'. Elections would follow in March.[22] It only took a decade and a half for the fruition of that forecast. Even then, would Mugabe have stumbled off the stage had the 'extraordinary conference' planned for December 2017, but cancelled because of the coup, actually happened?

This 2002–3 vignette is included here not only to indicate the tentative start—and nature of—the 'unity' vs. 'let the people vote free of fear (and let the ballots be counted fairly)' divide. Nor is it to show Mugabe's ability to shake things up, seemingly behind the scenes. Rather, it might shed light on that most horrific of elections in 2008, the second round of which resulted in at least 170 people killed and hundreds if not thousands more drastically brutalised and displaced.[23] It propelled Tendai Biti to a long stay in a miserable jail followed by the state's stages as finance minister.

The 2008 election may also go down in history as the time when another member of Biti's generation showed that youth is no guarantee of a new dawn. Biti was 55 in 2021. Saviour Kasukuwere, the most ambitious and probably richest member of 'Generation 40', was 51. He announced late in 2019 that he would contest the 2023 election from South Africa.[24] Rumour had it that unhappy vice-president Constantino Chiwenga supported him, and that perfidious Albion was up to its tricks with him too. Within a week in late 2019 two social media outputs concerning Kasukuwere hit the phones: his Tweet condemned the police bashing around ten MDC supporters at their leader's banned speech. The other, a forwarded WhatsApp copy of Lance Guma's much earlier SW Radio Africa submission,[25] was in clear contradistinction. Another journalist very familiar with the terrain it trod attested to its veracity, aside from the nine farms claimed for Kasukuwere. Kasukuwere was the MP for Mount Darwin South and the youth and indigenisation minister in 2008. Guma's report follows his march through the CIO. Apparently he was fired, but kept an office and used a retinue of officers on his coercive campaigns. A truncated version of the nearly 1,200-word report follows, worth absorbing even if only half true. As Guma concludes, it 'it exposes him as a violent thug'. Kasukuwere has two nicknames: Tyson, for obvious reasons, 'Paraquat' because he orders his charges to rub the herbicide into their victims' wounds.

Mainly in the Mashonaland Central province, from 2000 to 2008 he (not content to direct from afar, he participated) and his militia gangs specialised in the use of iron bars to batter and kill opposition activists. He and his sister Sarah established and supported a ZANU (PF) torture base. Twenty-eight young men stayed in his campaign manager's house as the 2000 parliamentary elections approached. On 25 March–even before ZANU (PF) called the June election, but just a few weeks after ZANU (PF)'s failed constitutional referendum–candidate Kasukuwere and 200 youth and war vets met at the Madondo Hotel. They proceeded door to door with a list of MDC-T supporters they would pummel. On an April night the gang burnt down a Mount Darwin MDC chair's house: while escaping the flames, he was hacked nearly to death by axes. Mugabe's method of political harmony raged again.

A couple of days later, just before an MDC rally, Kasukuwere ordered the police to mount roadblocks and turn back everyone heading to the rally. The defiant MDC supporters fought their way through the police roadblocks and hundreds of ZANU (PF) youth and war vets. Having gone through the first roadblock and the teargas fired by police, the MDC supporters ran into a second ambush, this time mounted by Kasukuwere and a gang of CIO operatives. Four pick-up trucks and a maroon Mercedes belonging to Kasukuwere blocked the road. The CIOs, including Kasukuwere, pulled out their pistols and began assaulting people while police officers looked on.

An activist called Albert testified: 'Kasukuwere took an iron bar and began hitting my windscreen. He broke through the window and then the bar hit me on the face.' When the MDC supporter stepped out of the car, Kasukuwere 'hit me in the eye. I have now lost an eye.' He proceeded to smash the windscreens and lights of the next car in the queue.

Eight years later, just over a month after the March 2008 election results humiliated the ruling party, Kasukuwere ferried over 300 militia in his lorry to Chaona, in Mazowe. They proceeded to kill 'Tapiwa Meda, Alex Chiriseri, Joseph Madzuramhende, David Tachiwa Mapuranga, Patson Madzuramhende, and Joseph Jemedze', beating dozens more. Wearing 'Tyson's' campaign T-shirts, the gangs were 'helped out by uniformed soldiers led by Major Cairo Mhandu'. The same group murdered MDC-T supporters Fischer Chitese, Bright Mafuriro and Sairiro Kamufuto eight days later. Eleven days after, MDC activist Phanuel Mubaira was assassinated.

Kasukuwere '[ran] his ministry like a mafia organisation'. He smuggled 'more than 11,000 youth militia onto the civil service payroll and deployed them countrywide, to intimidate opposition activists'. On one day alone—25 May 2008, just a week away from the run-off that Tsvangirai had to abandon—he hired 6,861 youth militia.

There are more preludes to 2008. Events gone sour post-2002 and immediately in 2008 led to fury on high. There was more botched unity plotting (referred to by Moyo as *coup*-plotting) and party-fixing to come.

If there were plans for a GNU (government of national unity) afoot in 2007, their failure bearing relation to the horrific second election in 2008, their medium-term roots were planted three years in advance. That would be the messy affair around the Tsholotsho Declaration of 18 November 2004. Its ghost, its sometimes-professorial chronicler recounted, would soon be 'haunting ZANU (PF) succession politics'.[26] One might hazard that it still is. Tsholotsho is the constituency about 100 kilometres north-west of Bulawayo, where Five Brigade soldiers killed Jonathan Moyo's father. Professor Moyo has often been the MP there. The Tsholotsho affair suggests what happened in ZANU (PF) when Mugabe's mortality sank in. It is a good case study of ZANU (PF) politics because the person who is widely seen to be one of the main characters in what led to the 2017 coup has written about it publicly—a rare practice in a paranoid party, populated by more than one illeist.[27] Moyo, almost politically destroyed by the processes towards power in 2004, chose to expose it widely while with a chance of the grand master's forgiveness. His view veers widely from David Coltart's—a lawyer who had done much to expose Gukurahundi's horrors in the 1980s, in 2004 a parliamentarian in the one and only MDC.

Moyo reveals the links between 2002 efforts to ease Zimbabwe from its Mugabe- and war-vet-inspired crisis, indicated above with the Dyck/Zvinavashe tale, and the hell of 2008. 'Some [ZANU (PF)] reformists', Moyo writes, formed a subcommittee after the 2000 election scare and 'open[ed] dialogue with the MDC on constitutional reforms'. The context? Failed inter-party talks brokered by South Africa and Nigeria–in 2002–and the MDC's failed 'Final Push' campaign after the close 2002 presidential election.[28] Coltart also mentions a trip to South Africa for the mission.[29] From there, however, their tales have little in common.

Vice-president Simon Muzenda (fixer between Mugabe's Zezuru side and his own fluid 'Karanga' since war days; supervisor of Patrick Kombayi's near assassination) died in September 2003. Besides proving that even ZANU (PF) leaders were mortal, his passing meant ZANU (PF)'s VP gap needed replenishing (the second VP had to be formerly ZAPU, and never in line for the top post).[30] Coincidentally or not, back channelling with Londoners started again with the parliamentary speaker: Emmerson Mnangagwa. He was then ZANU (PF)'s administration secretary. He had been Mugabe's sidekick since the post-*vashandi* days. By the 2000s he was Kwekwe's cruel kingpin,[31] not very successful at winning votes. By 2017 the 'soft coup' landed him in Mugabe's seat. He was (and still claims to be) a 'moderniser'–meaning he knew fast-track land reform without private tenure was not music to capital's collective ear, especially if it had been taken from white farmers. Mugabe and his lumpen war vets might have to go.[32] Such transitions are better from within, not without, ZANU (PF). Was British support for the MDC just another way to pressure ZANU (PF)?

David Coltart recounted that Mnangagwa, aka Ngwena or 'the crocodile', had a plan to gain the vice-presidency. As ZANU (PF)'s administration secretary, he circulated it to the provinces. It promised equitable ethnic rotation forever. All of the various (re)invented ethnicities would taste power in strict order. Above-board patron–client relations would rule the distribution of office and its perquisites. There would be no more pretence to a singular national identity. It is hard to freeze such fluid entities, but Mnangagwa tried. 'Shona' did not appear as a solid entity. He listed all the sub-groups under that linguistic umbrella. He noted 'Ndebele' but not 'Kalanga'. 'Kalanga' was born of a missionary lexicographer's mishearing 'Karanga' (the group to which Mnangagwa 'belongs'). Its members are seen as more Ndebele than Shona. The bearers of that identity reside at the crossroads of a century and a half of ethnic translocation and transliteration (aka 'nation building')—one politician from the Midlands said she was from 'Europe' given the blurred ethnic identities there. Perhaps Mnangagwa, in the 'Karanga' construct, did not want to think too hard about the 'Kalanga', who made up some of the more powerful members of the military on whom he would rely in years to come.

This ethnic fixing would not have appealed to Mugabe, who, although perceived as 'Zezuru' (if not, by some enemies, Malawian!) and a superb ethnic-identity manipulator in practice, liked to believe he thought in terms of 'my Zimbabwe'. He wanted to be the father of a family not of petty 'tribal' factions but a nation as sovereign and united as the one he imagined for Tony Blair.[33] Mugabe's was a more feudal than cool construction however—why else would he want to rule forever? He pretended to rule a governing group bound to him in fealty, as with Ian McEwan's imagined British prime minister, whose members and values 'he understood and loved. ... They were precisely his own. Bound by iron courage and the will to succeed. Inspired by an idea as pure and thrilling as blood and soil. Impelled towards a goal that lifted beyond mere reason to embrace a mystical sense.'[34] If McEwan's conceit was so grand as to require a metamorphosis, so too was Mugabe's, but his would be in more measure facetious and fractious. Moyo could not crack it. He did however foresee the contradictions thereof in his doctoral thesis. Its introductory notes discuss Africa's 'crisis' in terms of tribalism (among much else). The 'cleavages', he wrote, 'between clans, tribes, and nations ... [are] ... an obstacle to the search for common solutions ... to problems such as Africa is having [because] tribalism ... espouses values that are incompatible with the nationalistic aspirations of the modern state'.[35]

Who would lead this search, and how? It would take 'a new generation of post-independence leaders ... able to foster a sense of common values and purpose among ethnically diverse and burgeoning populations [by] ... develop[ing] and design[ing] innovative policies and strategies that provide for sharing of the benefits of economic growth among ethnic and other socioeconomic groups'.[36] Moyo did not recommend coups—i.e., 'forced (usually violent) removal'—to hasten the demise of a leader hanging on too long and the rise of the saviour generation: 'Quite the contrary, the African military men—often members of a single ethnic group—have tended to engage in "nation building" based on the repressive use of official violence [sic] than on the mobilization of popular support and responsiveness to public demands.'[37] There are however charismatic leaders who fill the gap between militarism and democracy. In time, they who have gained 'mass support [in the] one party states [that] have been the rule rather than the exception in most of Africa' will pass, as will their parties. Due to their tendency to retain power until death or coups, 'radical reversals of policies including the elimination of prior political parties' follow them. Embedded in the 'personal rule' trope of the time,[38] Moyo wrote that 'most ... political parties are closely linked with the personalities of the leaders [sic] than with independent human ideals which could survive the mortality of the leaders'.[39]

A PhD thesis does not map its author's path to power, but Moyo's 1988 efforts—just after Mugabe and Mnangagwa's genocidal campaign in his neighbourhood and ZANU (PF) had swallowed ZAPU into the closest approximation to a one-party state possible—are remarkably prescient. The next words in the banal tome (no mentions of the hundreds of left-academic takes on state–class relations in post-colonial Africa) on bureaucratic 'craft-literacy and craft-competence' are telling. They suggest that democratic and constitutional means could 'solve [Africa's] ethnic and, ipso facto, political problems'.[40] Nigeria's federal solutions could hasten Moyo's bureaucratic utopia. How to reach a civil service that could encompass 'the crux of democratic reality', that would have the 'capacity to be, more than its being' and would be 'a dynamic process in flux, and not a rigid and unmovable system'? This African utopia must have 'the attractive potential of eliminating the prejudice of personalism and putting in its plea [sic: place?], a system of accountability at both the technical level of competence, and the moral level of responsibility'.[41]

What then was the professor proposing in 2004, unleashing the fear and loathing of what those angered thereby ('glibly', responded Moyo)[42] called a coup? The Tsholotsho idea proposed democratic voting, with secret ballots, at the congresses.[43] Coltart focused, however, on the Solomon Mujuru factor. Mujuru was Mnangagwa's main competitor for much more than vice-presidencies. Mujuru revealed the Moyo–Mnangagwa strategy to Mugabe. Mujuru had used such strategies to keep his relationship with Mugabe intact in times past: he was, as Tendi's mesmerising biography argues, the ultimate kingmaker.[44] Mugabe created an addendum to the rules for the roster at the top. There would have to be a woman next to the top. That would be Joice Mujuru, maritally separated from Solomon (aka Rex Nhongo) but politically betrothed.

According to Coltart, on learning that he had been exposed Mnangagwa decided to avoid the meeting called at Tsholotsho school to discuss the scheme. Thus he dumped his partner-in-plans, information minister Jonathan Moyo. The Crocodile later denied it all and called the plot 'stupid'. On losing his seat during the next election he was appointed to head the lowly rural housing ministry. Moyo too lost his seat at the high table: Mugabe sacked him. On receiving Mugabe's firing fax Moyo declared that he was 'falsely accused' of concocting the plan to win the vice-presidency for Mnangagwa. He accused Mugabe of trammelling the Tsholotsho people's will to remove him. 'It is notable,' his open letter started,[45] '... and I am sure history and posterity will record the fact that my service to the President started at a time when the presidency, the ruling party and our nation were individually and collectively facing an unprecedented onslaught from a number of hostile foreign interests and powers.' Moyo claimed 'the honour and privilege' to have been of the 'very few' in ZANU (PF) to play a key part of 'the fight to preserve, defend and protect Zimbabwe's sovereignty and democracy'. Now it was better for him to be 'with the people ... to work for them'. No longer would he be 'hostage to the whims and caprices of the politics of patronage'.

Moyo's history nearly persuades one of many ZAPU folks' conspiracy theories: the CIA installed him to destroy their eternal opposition (or maybe to 'modernise' it, possibly tantamount to the same thing). Mnangagwa repeated that tale in 2017, after Moyo's flashy video presentation to the Politburo about the VP's 'Blue Oceans' strategy to take over, with which one supposes he intended to disgrace Mnangagwa into pleasant retirement.[46] Moyo had once joined the liberation struggle, but escaped (although he denies it)[47]—twice, the last time for good—the camps in Tanzania. Soon after, he gained the resources to travel to the USA (some say he is related by blood or marriage to Ndabaningi Sithole, the first leader of ZANU, who had ties across the Atlantic). The clincher for the conspiracy theorists is his post-doctoral forays to Stanford where he visited Condoleezza Rice and Jendayi Frazer.

While teaching Political Science at the University of Zimbabwe he contributed columns to *Parade* magazine, wrote a liberal book on 1990s elections, and left for the Ford Foundation offices in Kenya after double-air-ticketing in a joint degree programme with Denmark and India. It is generally agreed that he misused Ford's funds in Kenya (but no one can understand how, if there are charges against him there, he manages to live his post-coup life in Mombasa). After leaving the scene of those crimes, he gained a Kellogg Foundation research post for Johannesburg's University of the Witwatersrand–and proceeded to rip them off for millions of rand. Mugabe saved him the consequences of that misdemeanour, however, with an appointment as spokesperson for the constitutional commission called to stave off the NCA's challenges. From there Moyo directed ZANU (PF)'s 2000 parliamentary election campaign against the fast-rising MDC. Only 'alienated urban intellectuals' would vote for the MDC, he told me then.[48] He seemed indispensable to the otherwise flagging ruling party (although the election was close and, many close observers feel, stolen). While information minister thereafter he proceeded to shut down–maybe even blow up–alternative sources of truths and falsehoods.

The Tsholotsho flop nearly caused Moyo political extinction. His *Zimbabwe Independent* columns–graciously granted to the denier of media freedom–closed with his prediction that Tsholotsho's 'burning fires threaten to leave ZANU (PF) in political ashes unable to turn around the economy and to restore Zimbabwe's international reputation'. All he wanted to do, he wrote, was to regularise the ethnic nature of ZANU (PF)'s internal politics so all shades would get their place in the sun and by the trough in good time. ZANU (PF)'s top leadership positions–the president and first secretary, two vice-presidents and second secretaries, and the national chairman–would rotate, reflecting 'Zimbabwe's regional diversity and ethnic balance between and among the country's four major ethnic groupings, namely Karanga, Manyika, Zezuru and Ndebele'. Secret ballots would do the rest. For Moyo, this was consistent with a non-hierarchical and constitutional rule of law, as discussed at countless party meetings. These ideas, he said, had been brewing since 2000, when serious consideration arose regarding the need for democratic and modern renewal rather than 'current ZANU (PF) clique's … tribal and village politics'.

'Part of this process', Moyo continued, included 'vigorous attempts spearheaded by some politicians linked to Solomon Mujuru' pressuring Mugabe to retire at the December 2001 congress, ahead of the 2002 presidential election. They had continued up to 2003. The 'Mujuru faction' touted the seemingly technocratic and non-assuming Simba Makoni.

The still-employed professor's second column suggested that by August 2004 the arrows towards the next VP position pointed—correctly and constitutionally, while the Tsholotsho ideas ran smoothly—in Mnangagwa's direction.[49] However, the Zezuru crowd geared up. (Dr) Nathan Shamuyarira 'is said' to have suggested a woman's place in the presidium. The politically-correct Princeton graduate reckoned this would keep Mnangagwa out. Mugabe and Grace, his wife of nearly eight years, announced this idea at the Women's League congress. Things still looked as if the (non-feminist) modernising tack would take the course: they had more provinces behind them than did the Zezuru clique. However, before the Tsholotsho meeting could happen Mugabe called an emergency meeting to take Mnangagwa to task over his and Moyo's plans.

Moyo's newspaper stories halted with his firing at that point, although he did fire off a 'full text' via his website. He launched his campaign as an independent by closing his text with: 'There is a rock somewhere upon which we can all develop a better Zimbabwe.'[50] He *nearly* found it more than 12 years later.

Moyo's career without ZANU (PF)—including two victories as an independent MP and a limp attempt to start a party called the United People's Movement[51]—ended with re-joining ZANU (PF) and losing his Tsholotsho seat to the MDC in 2013. He skipped a beat at the early stages of the 'gamatox and weevil' battles in 2014.[52] Then, he realigned with Mnangagwa to unseat Joice Mujuru.[53] The 2017 coup saw him stick with Mugabe as the 'G-40' blew their anti-Mnangagwa plot—and that was it. The real coup applied somewhat more force to him than he had encountered previously. He fled to Kenya (surprisingly, given his unresolved trials there) but remained in cyberspace. The 2017 loss may not be his final metamorphosis. ZANU (PF) was still two parties in 2021. He is part of one, loosely speaking. He carries the status of a top intellectual. Civil society groups like his crowd-pulling abilities for webinars.

Meanwhile, more huggermuggering was happening, contributing to the fearsome debacle of mid-2008. As the carnage-ridden run-off approached, speculation about coups escalated—including the 'guns and votes' debate again.

There is a continuing debate about who made the decision to go into the second round of the presidential component of the 'harmonised' 2008 elections with guns blazing, machetes whacking and bludgeoning batons—and why. Was it the 'soldiers', thus cementing their increasing control over the party and winning the empty 'guns vs. politics' argument, or the ageing president and his coterie of amateurs at violence? If Kasukuwere's activities above do not settle it—he was a 'politician' but more of a thug than 99.9% of soldiers—perhaps the events of 2008 do.

If one accepts (temporarily, for the sake of argument) that there is a dividing line between 'politics and the gun' in interregna such as Zimbabwe, 2008 could be a turning point. It was when the 'securocrats' consolidated their grip on Mugabe to tighten it until the real coup. Ensuring the MDC's president stayed out of the office he wanted was Mugabe's cut of the deal. (Ibbo Mandaza, starting the process in 2000, may be a contrarian but thereby nearly dissolves the border and the argument.)[54] Besides strengthening their grip on much of the economy, they gloved the polity as well.

Popular wisdom has it that the 'generals' forced Mugabe to crack down and guarantee his victory. The violence convinced Tsvangirai—in much consultation with many party members—to throw in the towel. The generals had been consistent—publicly—since at least the 2002 presidential election in their assertions that they would never allow power to go to anyone who did not soldier through the liberation war. However, as we have seen, some were negotiating otherwise.

Ask most soldiers now—remember, the 'soldiers' won the 2017 coup against the Mugabeite pen-pushers, pedants and bribe-taking police—and they will say 'Mugabe ordered it'. Many others will agree that he alone decided to strike cobra-like at the MDC and any ZANU (PF) traitors. Some will say that Mugabe never forgot Tsvangirai's 'betrayal' of the alleged 2002–3 moment of agreement. He was *still* furious about Tsvangirai rejecting the unity olive branch offered through his emissaries back then, resolving never to let the inconsistent Tsvangirai sit beside him. Alternatively and/or additionally, he was enraged at indications of American or British troops crawling around the borders of his Zimbabwe. Blair had been foolish enough in 2004 to ask Mbeki for assistance on an instructive little invasion.[55] There were enough signs of American forces around Africa to keep the Zimbabwean military wondering about Botswana, and there was lots of money and free advice–and advisers–going the opposition's way. He was furious, and wanted Tsvangirai and his whole party to disappear.

The more conventional–and Mugabe-aligned anti-soldier–view is that the dazed and defeated Mugabe was wandering around after a bruising defeat and near calamity. He was willing to call it a day. His partner Grace was worried about their children being teased at school. But he was shaken into alert wakefulness by the other members of the JOC (its weekly meetings would suggest in any case that all of these decisions were made together: a fly on the walls could remember accurately). Was he frog-marched to the barracks with a warning such as this: 'If you go, we go, and we don't want to travel to The Hague and lose our ill-gotten gains while you lose yours'? No one would have to tell him that.

The answer is somewhere between. Money links the gun and politics. It ties the party–state, civilian–military webs into a huge Gordian knot. Tom Burgis charts the ins and outs of Billy Rautenbach's complicatedly gained $100 million. Rautenbach contributed it to ZANU (PF)'s war chest and thus the execution, torture and uprooting of thousands to ensure Mugabe's victory. It is thus hard to find qualitative differences between the two ideas: there is no gap to mind; the resource curse is a killer.[56] Perhaps by 2008 Mugabe epitomised the fusion of soldier and politician. With his imagined Gumbo–Hamadziripi coup resolved in 1978, it had only taken him three decades to tie the knot fully. Quelling the 'people's army' in 1977 had started the process of creating his un-people's army, whilst chasing an illusory, legless, liberal ideology.

A chronological look at some perspectives on the movements before the run-off might shed some light on the options presented. Remember, the 'counting' of the March results took an unconscionable time–from the end of March to May's start—and there were many publicly released unofficial counts in the air.

On 3 April Stephen Chan raised the c-word yet again—quickly. The generals had pushed a tired and testy Mugabe to the wall. He had 'contemplated conceding defeat with a degree of grace' (pun intended or not, Grace's children were rumoured to be tired of school bullies). They discussed a coup, apparently, to ditch Mugabe or make his puppet strings public. Chan does indicate that there were 'two most extreme generals' who went for what would have been called a militarily assisted transition, but the idea was resisted by their comrades in the High Command. Who were they? Perhaps they are the current ruling duo. No matter, history was stopped for a moment when 'word came up, hard and clear from South Africa, that they were not to do that'. Chan asserted that diplomatic pressure from south of the Limpopo 'had a huge influence in turning back the course of what would have been a rigged election towards a murky compromise negotiated in back rooms'. Nevertheless, one might 'still see the retirement of Robert Mugabe ... slouch[ing] off into the ignominy of history'.[57] Chan notes that 'the rank and file of the security forces voted, it is said, 70 per cent against Mugabe'. I met one as the voting was under way in Mbare. He was proud to have voted once at his barracks and once using his home address, thus neutralising his input. However, as Michael Holman, an old hand at journalism on the continent, commented in *Prospect*'s online version of Chan's story, Chan's sources were unknown. Holman wondered if 'senior members of the opposition have encouraged the wishful thinking of Professor Chan and other analysts' with their 'stream of half-truths and calculated distortions'. Mugabe, the veteran of Ian Smith's vengeance back in the 1960s, was 'many things: a corrupt, vain, and brutal dictator', but to suggest he was a 'malleable coward undermines our understanding, both of the man and the Zimbabwe crisis'. Chan did have a memory of many other unification attempts, however. This one might have worked.

Would the man who made a point of surrounding himself with dullards yield to defeat so easily?[58] He would be back in form after a good dinner at the table with the vacant setting (a space reserved for Tongogara's ghost, they say),[59] a sound night's sleep, morning exercise, and downing his cocktails of Chinese and Western meds. That is (roughly) what happened in 2000 when he lost his referendum (he had yet to learn how to cook the ballot books). Mild acquiescence first, followed by fire and fisticuffs. He may have learned this in the 1970s too, dealing as he was with the Western imperialists' visits all the way to Quelimane and the 'ultra-leftists' threatening him from the camps he was about to claim.

What Chan does not tell us is that Mbeki's advisers themselves were not of one mind. Should they push forward the GNU idea—coup or not—to forestall the wider violence foretold? The other option was to stay out and follow the newly crafted Kariba constitution to the letter, chaotic consequences or not. That was the chosen path. It could have been, however, that Mugabe decided for that path for them.

Mugabe's fury about Mbeki's unity plans may have festering since the 2002–3 conversations (recall Moyo's note on the 'South Africa and Nigeria' effort). It is said that Mbeki's trip north in the near interregnum between the first election and the aftermath entailed waiting days at the Meikles Hotel. The South African president—still reeling from his non-violent, but hurting, unseating by his party at the end of 2007, finally jumped on a plane to confront Mugabe at the Bulawayo International Trade Fair, only to be brushed away.

In any case, the South Africans did not have to back up such a move with a degree of force. Allowing the constitution to rule postponed an intra-ZANU (PF) backlash. The carnage came. Mbeki's unity dream unfolded—but after the killing fields, not to fend them off. Never would Chan's concoction of 'very brave people ... consign Mugabe and his hardliners to history and, immunities scorned, to The Hague'. You'd have to believe in hell and hope for James Joyce's vision of eternity to think Mugabe would get his just deserts then and there.

By 19 June—just over a week before the run-off and three days before Tsvangirai and his party decided that more deaths could not justify him stepping into the starting blocks—Oxford political scientist Blessing-Miles Tendi saw at least some generals pressuring Mugabe to guarantee the run-off's legitimacy. This would lead to a GNU with 'sections of the opposition in order to garner the international community's approval'. Then they would consecrate a successor 'not too long into Mugabe's term'. The anointed one would be Mnangagwa.[60] Would that have been a coup? Would it have washed their—or Mugabe's—hands of the previous week's blood?

Tendi's retrospective five years later took a longer historical view. The plotting history was short but intense, starting with the second DRC war—when Mugabe supported Kabila against his erstwhile Rwandan allies. The UK concluded the military training programme that had bonded their relations since 1980. The IMF cut its dollars, perhaps due to their being too fungible. The 2002–3 case followed shortly. Ideas about unity, let alone decent elections, had fallen by the wayside. Thus, Tsvangirai and company interpreted the 2008 moment as a 'de facto *coup d'état*'—but incorrectly. 'A military junta' did *not* rule. How could a group with such 'unstable ideological commitment … to ZANU (PF)' do a coup?[61] Mugabe still called the shots, although it remained uncertain if he ordered their 2008 variety.

It might be wise to turn to 2007 for a bit more backdrop. That year witnessed the closest thing to a coup yet. The decree of death had just dismissed three of its highly ranked military suspects. Even though they were decorated posthumously with national hero status, it was unlikely their survivors would carry out another for at least a decade.

8

FROM CONSPIRACIES TO THE REAL COUP'S CUSP

2007–17

At the very, very least 170 MDC supporters, as well as those in ZANU (PF) who voted for their MP but not Robert Gabriel Mugabe for president, were killed in the most vicious of ways during Operation Makavhoterapapi. Billy Rautenbach paid for the Zimbabwe party–soldier–state's orgy of violence.[1] Besides those murdered, hundreds more were chased from their homes, raped, burned, beaten and battered. Last chapter's vignette on Saviour Kasukuwere's modus operandi serves only as a snippet of such. In 2018 Derek Matyszak, a most assiduous and accurate Zimbabwe watcher, and I had a long email discussion about their number.[2] We thought the Armed Conflict Location and Event Data Project would have the best numbers. It counted 170 fatalities and 794 violent 'events' in the Zimbabwe of 2008, constituting 18.8% of Africa's state-initiated violence that year.[3] Yet just over a year later a person much closer to the scene riposted 'hah'. 'Only 17 in every province? There would have been more than 170 in Kwekwe's killing fields alone.' Kwekwe is the notoriously violent home area for the man who runs the al-Shabaab gang there, ran Operation Makavhoterapapi, and would be president within a decade.[4]

Another 'inside' report on the pre-election intimidation accepted Morgan Tsvangirai's estimate of 386, and noted 'incidentally and

ironically' the highest level of violence in the three Mashonaland provinces, where ZANU (PF) did very well in the parliamentary division
of the 'harmonised' elections, combining municipal, parliamentary
and presidential contests. The report did not explain the losses in the
presidential count, the one really infuriating ZANU (PF)'s managers.
The Electoral Institute for Sustainable Democracy in Africa (EISA)
reported ZANU (PF) winning 72.73% of the parliamentary *seats* in
Mashonaland West. The Zimbabwe Election Support Network
(ZESN) report records only 52.8% there for Mugabe in the *presidential*
poll, against Tsvangirai's 42.1%.[5] Similar traits showed in the other
Mashonaland provinces: in Mashonaland Central Tsvangirai got
approximately two-thirds of the presidential ballots while Mugabe
gained less than a third. In Mashonaland East Mugabe's approximately
55% beat Tsvangirai's 41%. As ZESN opined, many voted ZANU
(PF) at the parliamentary level, then 'switched to the MDC or independent presidential candidate'.[6] That, with the election as a whole,
convinced Eldred Masunungure that Zimbabweans were partaking in
a 'silent revolution'.[7]

However, the *counter*-revolution was far from quiet. If God ordained
your rule, holy vengeance follows defeat.[8] As Masunungure summarised, the violence spread from

> Mashonaland ... to other provinces and from the rural areas ... to the
> urban centres. In a tragic sense, the whole country was unified, in
> violence, and its pattern was the same, indicating a central point of
> organisation and execution. The bloody crackdown was reportedly
> orchestrated and systematically executed by soldiers, police, state secu-
> rity agents, ZANU (PF) militia [the Taliban force] and veterans of the
> liberation war. The violence took the form of intimidation, kidnapping,
> torture, arson and murder of opposition or suspected opposition lead-
> ers, activists, and supporters.

As one 'participant observer' put it, 100% of the 'Green Bombers'
militia were called to arms–remember, 'Tyson' had just recruited
nearly 7,000 of them–and even more junior 'students' in the 'Border
to Border' Gezi National Service. The 'Taliban' cells would knock
door to door, forcing youth to join. Former Ethiopian dictator
Mengistu Haile Mariam was a key adviser–perhaps the operational
brain–behind the 2008 crackdown. Exiled to Zimbabwe with his loss

of regime in 1991, he has assisted the Zimbabwean security boffins since at least 2001, fearing that an MDC win would have him repatriated. He helped plan Operation Murambatsvina too.[9] Along with Jonathan Moyo—back in Mugabe's graces—he was said to be one of the select few who could call on Mugabe whenever they pleased. Apparently the campaign was ordered on high, but provincial commanders were given some leeway, as Danny Stannard said was the case in Gukurahundi too.[10] In some cases the commanders let the youth loose for a free for all, their actions ranging from rounding up their peers, to rampant gold panning and wanton killing of opposition supporters and those only vaguely suspected of allegiance to the 'puppets' camp'. Rape, houses burned—some belonging to 'any person the ZANU (PF) thugs hated'—even 'wars' between the 'MDC armies'[11] and the other side's militias (including night-time raids by the former). Some provincial commanders had to negotiate to dampen down both sides.

Thousands headed for the protection of Harvest House and even the South African embassy. Ambassador Makalima negotiated with some churches to host them. He also invited retired South African generals to see the results of the run-off for themselves.[12] When their president arrived to see the films taken on their visit, he did not bat an eye.

As discussed in the last chapter, there remain many arguments regarding who fired the starting pistol for Operation Makavhoterapapi. At least five different reasons emerge for Mugabe ordering his troops and militias to crack down, with little need for the generals' encouragement.

First: he was livid with reports of American and British troops massing in Botswana. Furious, he ordered the crackdown. As discussed, Tony Blair (for whom Mugabe invented the moniker 'Tony Bliar') had investigated a military intervention. He was stupid enough to consult South Africa's president about it.[13] Those who counter this say there were no more foreign soldiers in the region than usual.

Second: a story circulated about unprecedented degrees of British 'democracy support'. There was always plenty of that, but 'Zimbabwe Democracy Now' seemed beyond the pale. Real journalists were angry about its fake news. It was the project of a Mayfair consultancy called G-3, directed by a retired senior MI6 operative with years of Zimbabwean experience. Some of Mugabe's operatives fed it their own altered versions of reality. Mugabe would have been furious at that too, and would have seen the MDC–Labour Party alliance nosing in on 'his Zimbabwe'. The MDC would have taken the brunt of that anger. Such minor details did not bother military intelligence very much: the focus was on the spread of military bases across the continent, perhaps to Botswana.[14]

Third: the MDC elements armed and fighting, even foraying to rural ZANU (PF) redoubts, could have been perceived to be part of the first, larger military threat. In some cases, as noted above, there were negotiations to ratchet down the violence on both sides during Operation Makavhoterapapi itself. To be sure, some Democratic Resistance Committees were in operation, ostensibly to resist the harder repressive tactics of the party-state. Their training had been outside the country.

Fourth: the ZANU (PF) voters who had supported their MPs but not Mugabe as president would also have to learn a very political lesson. Mugabe remembered this well during his 2018 interview with the *Zimbabwe Independent*.[15] After denying that Tsvangirai had pulled out of the run-off due to the casualties caused by ZANU (PF)'s murder and mauling, saying, 'No, he knew we would be better,' he explained *bhora musango* (the tactic of voting ZANU (PF) for the MPs and for Tsvangirai as president):

> [It was] again, a disease amongst us. … The likes of (General) Mujuru were fed up with me, they said I was preventing them from benefitting from companies, so they said 'let's get rid of Mugabe'. Our supporters were told 'ah, you don't have to vote for the president.'

Mugabe claimed he had not considered retiring then, and thus the story that the military forced him to continue with the race could not have been true. ('Ah no. Ah no. Mutasa is lying. We all said there's got to be a repeat in accordance with the constitution.') This answer avoided the issue of who ordered Operation Makavhoterapapi. He denied the violence in any case. If he lied about that, why not about everything? He could pick from a wide array of alternative facts.

The fourth is unlikely to have triggered Mugabe's rage at the MDC, but may have raised his overall irascibility. This observer had the fortune to attend the twentieth anniversary of the Southern African Political Economy Series Trust, started in 1987 when ZANU (PF) appeared to some leftist political economists as the best bet for some form of socialism, or at least radicalised state capitalism. Ibbo Mandaza was and is the leading light there, indeed since arriving in Maputo in the late 1970s a key intellectual in ZANU (PF)–and learning quickly that Tongogara dealt with intellectuals summarily. In the late 1990s, after advising Morgan Tsvangirai he would be torn to shreds if he lit the smouldering oppositional torch, Mandaza worked on many fronts to ease a transition within the ruling party. This included trying to persuade the retired, very rich and still very influential head of the armed forces, Solomon Mujuru, to abandon Mugabe, who blamed Mujuru for *bhora musango*.

The December 2007 conference had invited Mugabe's one-time blue-eyed boy to speak and effectively launch the Mavambo Kusile Dawn Party. Mujuru did not want to be involved directly. However, the 'technocratic' economist Simba Makoni, who had left the ruling party while it lurched with the new millennium's start, waxed and waned. He hesitated to take that meeting's bait. He arrived at the last moment, with nervous organisers pacing madly, muttering that he was no Simba (lion), but Chicken Little. Makoni's speech was misty, mystical and mythically nostalgic about how Zimbabwe's political values had changed for the worse in the past decade and a half. After many meetings, the backroom reformists could only persuade Makoni to commit to the idea by planting their story in the *Financial Gazette* after the year's turn.[16] Some pundits thought the new party would ruin the MDC's chances (already lessened because its plans to recombine with a splinter group went awry over allocation of seats), so was thus a ZANU (PF) ruse. Others thought the idea would spur wavering ZANU (PF) voters to move away from paterfamilias to less-known families.[17] Makoni gathered around 8% of the 2008 vote: if in his absence half had gone with the MDC, victory would have been harder for the rulers to steal.

If the South Africans thought Makoni would win, some of his mathematically challenged gurus misled them. He did add a fly to the electoral ointment. One day during the campaign a couple of colleagues and I headed to the Headlands in search of Makoni on his farm. MDC activists and war vets at the nearby town were equally hospitable, albeit with different explanations for the tough times. One group blamed ZANU (PF) while the ZANU (PF) war vets blamed global warming. Neither were as interesting as the farmer walking up the road to a ZANU (PF) rally with a portrait of local candidate and elderly ruling party doyen Didymus Mutasa emblazoned on his new T-shirt.[18] The journalist urged us to stop. She asked where he was going. He answered, 'To the ZANU (PF) rally.' Why? 'Mutasa and Mugabe have been good to us, we have land.' Yes, the journalist remembered that in 1992 there was a lot of land reform in the area, much of it organised by the secretary to the then minister Eddison Zvobgo. 'What about Tsvangirai and the MDC?' she asked. 'Yes, he is good: he has helped the unions; he has been leading the opposition bravely and that is a good thing.' As for Makoni (who was running as an independent)? 'Yes, he is a very smart man, an intellectual who lives nearby and knows ZANU (PF) works and how Mugabe is, and how to fix it.' The next question: 'OK, you think all of these people are good but you are going to vote for Mugabe and Mutasa?' He laughed: 'What is on my T-shirt might not be in my heart.' We laughed together, but it was not a good enough story for the newspaper. There was surely more uncertainty about the result of this election than any since 2000. That was when the wave of 'change' looked almost unstoppable–until the ballots were 'counted', and later, invented.

Fifth: Mugabe was still seething at Tsvangirai for taking the white democrats' advice and abandoning the 2002 unity gamble. Some say he had sworn never to trust him again. (Tsvangirai's inability to make a decision until consulting the USA or minor liberal powers annoyed his South African interlocutors–and many of his colleagues too. They did not appreciate an agreement made and then cancelled after a phone call to one embassy or another, as one South African negotiator put it. One of his colleagues decided it would be a good idea to commit his first promises to paper.)

Sixth, and relatedly: there were public indications of efforts to forge a pre-electoral united front–some from within ZANU (PF). Indications that such moves started again emerged soon after the 11 March 2007 'Save the Nation' prayer meeting organised by the clergy Mugabe would later say were 'political entities ... no longer spiritual', thus on 'quite a dangerous path'.[19] That rally eventuated in one young MDC member dead–and his funeral banned[20]–and bludgeoned, blood-spattered opposition leaders with their images all over the world.[21] Nine days later Stephen Chan discounted effective opposition and surmised a 'palace coup' on the horizon. 'Key figures in Mugabe's own Zanu-PF party' would be willing to 'sacrifice the old man to keep in power themselves'. Sure, 'the strongest factions in the party are led by figures closely associated with the security forces'; thus they would be more likely to be successful than the party's civilian side. It would still be an 'authoritarian government', but it might be *sans* 'the old man's paranoia'. Regardless of how Mugabe would go, 'as the symbol is removed, no matter how, the world will take a deep breath and begin to help rebuild Zimbabwe'.[22] Chan was not speaking in 2017, but more than a decade before. In some political ventures, a day is a long time. Coups can take decades. Sometimes they can get a trial run in a year.

A few days later, after some neighbours visited Mugabe to express their 'embarrassment', he told the 'west' to 'go hang ... [because] here are persons who went out of their way to effect a campaign of violence and we hear no criticism at all of those actions of violence, none at all'.[23] SADC anointed South African president Thabo Mbeki to mediate his northern neighbour's political fray. He assured the *Financial Times* that Mugabe would step down in peace when the free and fair elections would happen: 'You see,' he lectured, 'President Mugabe and the leadership of (the ruling) ZANU-PF believe they are running a democratic country'.[24]

Just nine days later Professor Chan weighed in again, in South Africa's *Mail and Guardian*.[25] 'Frantic realignments' in ZANU (PF) were taking place, he wrote:

> Powerful actors on all sides in Zimbabwe are realising that the worst must not be allowed to happen. If their interests are to survive, the future has to be rescued from the hands of the current president. The last sacrifice in the struggle for national liberation will be Mugabe himself.

The first possibility he outlined would entail two factions with lots of soldiers in each (Mujuru versus Mnangagwa, but collaborating for some reason) entailing a desperate Mugabe enrolling the Green Bombers to his side but gaining only bloody defeat. Next: a posse of AU leaders riding to Harare, ultimatum and safe haven in hand. Ibbo Mandaza, closer to the scene, may have seen the same thing coming– which he did not. He announced to the South African Institute of

International Affairs in Johannesburg (around the same time as the ANC was holding its wintry pre-Polokwane conference, in June, where some of its Zimbabwe negotiators were shaking their heads in disbelief that a man like Mugabe could exist) that Mugabe would be gone by September.

Coincidentally or not, efforts to hasten that move were well under way—but not very carefully. That would be reason number seven. It would make sense if it was the *real* one. It would also make sense if Mugabe would never trust a soldier again.

Reason Seven: 'Operation 1940' angered Mugabe so much that he forced the soldiers to make amends. This failed coup is so underreported (except for a very comprehensive Wikipedia entry started, notably, in late 2017 and edited as late as 12 October 2020)[26] that some people who were probably in it deny it ever happened. If Mugabe was angry with the soldiers who tried and failed (vowing not to fail again better, as Samuel Beckett might have put it, but to succeed), they would have had to demonstrate zeal at his command. A failed coup is a misdemeanour more severe than *bhora musango*. However, as with most Zimbabwean mists of reality, the conceit of thinking one controls the concept of veracity rather than mere verisimilitude constructs much conjecture. Aside from the hints Ibbo Mandaza dropped at SAIIA, Stephen Chan's musings, and the later news about a general in a car meeting a train too coincidentally at a crossing near Marondera, there are a few newspaper reports and some personal advertisements. However, they do indicate serious shenanigans. As well, University of KwaZulu-Natal students from Zimbabwe reported an unusual number of soldiers' burials at provincial heroes' acres. This would not be coincidental.

Someone—perhaps a retired CIO agent or army officer—told somebody in the French intelligence offices of the plans for Operation 1940, scheduled for 15 June 2007 at 19.40 (that made sense because most soldiers would be at home with their pay, although another report said the coup was scheduled for 2 June).[27] Apparently two military planes stocked full of bombs were stopped in the process of fuelling at an airbase near Harare—the target for the bombs being Zimbabwe House and Mugabe's Borrowdale Brook Blue Roof.[28] The arrests—mostly fall guys probably because the guilty ones did the arresting—happened on 29 May.

Journalists reported that anywhere from 400 to 700 soldiers were on call for the show. The first page of a list of 481 'active 2007' I was given bears remarkable similarities to the first page of a supposed six pages (the last five did not appear: that first one only goes up to 47) that accompanied a 2011 story on their leaking to the opposition-friendly SW Radio Africa.[29] A data records transcriber at Charlie India Oscar gave that list to the station—aka 'an external radical group or external government led by Lance Guma'. Controversy about breaches of state security followed. SW Radio Africa head Gerry Jackson deflected them with the argument that the CIO was 'not used to protect national security and to safeguard Zimbabweans' but for 'Mugabe and ZANU (PF) to cling to power with force and intimidation', and given it is 'administered directly through the Office of the President' there was no legislative framework to cover it. She hoped that readers would contact the station if the list held mistakes; otherwise, CIO operatives deserved exposure. One commentator questioned the list's authenticity and purpose, noting that one case of mistaken identification had led to the desecration of that person's father's grave.[30] Perhaps one comment was right: was the 'whistle-blower's' file related to a specific case in the past? That would be the 2007 missed coup.

Simon Chisorochengwe, #69 on the list, interested me because he 'shot to prominence via his well-publicized attempts to destroy the Zimbabwe Liberators' Platform (ZLP); a rival war vets association which is independent of ZANU (PF) interference and manipulation'.[31] The ZLP was the post-2000 reincarnation of *vashandi*. While reading that news snippet I remembered the severed brake cable Wilf Mhanda, ZLP's director, showed me one day in 2005. I also recalled the tale Wilf told me about the odd-flavoured sip of a flat beer he had left on the bar while going to the loo. On return the beer tasted bad: a neighbouring drinker said he saw someone lingering near Wilf's glass. Ricin killed Wilf, I was told years later—but that takes a short time to do its job; Wilf left this beer undrunk many years before cancer took him in May 2014. Four years after that, a South African newspaper pictured Chisorochengwe, minister counsellor at the Zimbabwean embassy, helping his boss explain away 1 August 2018, when soldiers mowed down half a dozen post-election demonstrators and bystanders.[32]

Some people thought Emmerson Mnangagwa was behind the 2007 event, not only because he called it 'stupid' (as he also did about the Tsholotsho efforts) when asked about it and alleged connections with Professor Moyo's new political party.[33] Also, some of the names of people seemingly associated with it were also on the Mnangagwa and Chiwenga side of the 2017 coup. For example, Major General Engelbert Rugeje was charged as a leader of the 2007 attempt. His accusations of treason disappeared when his trial was cancelled. In 2017 he was appointed national political commissar (but by 2019 had lost that post, carrying some blame for poor election results in 2018).[34] Somewhere between coups he got a PhD from the same School of Ethics at the Pietermaritzburg campus of the University of KwaZulu-Natal as did his boss. Air Vice-Marshal Elson Moyo, too, was said to be a leader, had the same shift of fate, was a negotiator under the 'Blue Roof' as Mugabe was facing his political death, and by 2020 was a full marshal. They say Elson is either the cousin or full brother to the late Sibusiso, famous for announcing 2017's semi-coup on TV, and July Moyo, local government minister and apparently Mnangagwa's right-hand man. Colonel Ben Ncube, of the army public-relations directorate, is also on the public lists of failed putschists.

Extra guards attended to most of the attempt's big names for a while. Few suffered after that. Brigadier General Armstrong Gunda, head of One Brigade and before that of the Presidential Guard, was the most prominent and well publicised—post-mortem. He was found dead in his car on a railway track near Marondera on 21 June. Reports say that after he had been tortured and killed, whoever battered his car in the King George VI service bays—not very well, if it was meant to simulate a train crash—took it and the body to Marondera. The first rumours had Gunda leading the coup. Later they changed to attest to his fall-guy status: since Gunda did not frequent Marondera often, retired general Mujuru was said to be behind the plot and needed Gunda gone. Alternatively, Gunda's car and remains might have been taken to Marondera to cast some doubt on Mujuru.[35] However, 'senior army officials' interviewed by *The Zimbabwean* in August had Mujuru—or 'a coterie of people connected to him'—behind it. Gunda would be the 'natural leader of the operation', said one, because having once been head of the Presidential Guard he would have known Mugabe's every move.

Other stories have retired Major General Gideon (or Taurai) Lifa, one of Mugabe's former aides-de-camp and a Brigadier General Fakazi Mleya (or Muleya) killed by lethal injection. All three suspects were buried at the National Heroes Acre, later receiving posthumous Grand Officer of the Zimbabwe Order of Merit medals.

At the funerals of Gunda and Mleya Mugabe proffered perfidious Albion as guilty. He reminded mourners that his team employed rougher tactics than its opponents. He returned to his philosophical treatise on the gun–politics dialectic. His reminiscences about his boyhood dog dying whilst chasing a buck followed thereafter.[36] Without backup, neither the buck nor the dog experience much of the consent side of Gramsci's dialectic. Aside from Britain, Mugabe did not discuss bases of support for the chaser or chased.

At least six relatively small fish were apparently arrested in the failed coup's wake, many not knowing why. One was a 21-year-old student, Rangarirai Mazirofa, imprisoned and tortured because he was too close to an army base, and related to the newly suspected ringleader, Albert Matapo.[37] The retired captain spent seven years in Chikurubi, the foul maximum-security prison. Matapo claimed on his release in 2014 that he had nothing to do with the coup, nor was he working for Mnangagwa, in his opinion worse than Mugabe. However, he had been establishing the United Crusade for Achieving Democracy (UCAD)–'a genuine political party. …The existing opposition parties are proxies of ZANU (PF),' but was asked about a 'United Democratic Front'. Perhaps the CIO and their peers had mistaken this UDF/UCAD for Jonathan Moyo's United People's Movement, but it was probably moribund by then. According to his interview in *The Zimbabwean* at the end of May 2014, more than 40 plain-clothed CIO and army intelligence officers took Matapo and six others from their party offices. They took computers and office goods, then 'blind folded us, stripped us naked, handcuffed, leg-chained us and [we were] thrown into unmarked vehicles', driving to his house to ransack it and take 'valuables worth US$10,000, jewellery worth thousands of pounds, computers and a S320 Mercedes Benz'.[38] Matapo must still be in the revolutionary party business: in late 2020 his name was on a security watch document allegedly leaked from the JOC, replete with more widely known activists.[39] A convoluted January 2021 webzine story has him somewhere in Sweden

155

fomenting revolution to the author's great displeasure. She seemed to have no idea of his years in prison.[40]

An MDC organiser also claims to have been taken in. State operatives grabbed Gilbert Kagodora from a meeting with Matapo. Held from 29 May to 4 June, he was beaten and accused of plotting to topple Mugabe in favour of Mnangagwa. Kagodora recalled a basement where military intelligence officers tortured Matapo and him with electrical rods. They asked about 'MDC terror camps' in South Africa, the opposition party's 'Democratic Resistance Committees' and their petrol bombers, and who led and financed the failed coup. Matapo was not as lucky. Another MDC activist, George Kawuzani, was detained, tortured and slain during the same period.[41]

Gunda's widow, who took out newspaper adverts marking her late husband's mysterious death, probably brought the most attention to this coup. More recently, however, the state-managed *Bulawayo Chronicle* celebrated her as an example of widows who pull themselves up by the bootstraps and succeed in business.[42]

In 2015–just after Joice Mujuru's 2014 defenestration–Bulawayo24 News published what looked to be the definitive report.[43] (It is notable that 2014 saw many of the 2007 coup stories revisited.) It says an intelligence report confirms Solomon Mujuru was the *éminence grise* behind the 2007 move. The aim: to cast aspersions on Mnangagwa. That would have involved the CIO, explained the arrest and long imprisonment of many innocents, and might even have led to Solomon Mujuru's 2011 death just about a month after SW Radio Africa received the long list. The Bulawayo 24 News article[44] says that Mossad–whose retired officers helped out in the 2013 elections with their Nikuv Election Machine–'connected the dots' to the French assistance. One source–said to be a 'retired officer in South Africa'–claimed that intelligence reports exonerating Mnangagwa led to 'the downfall of Joice Mujuru' in 2014. That was 'rooted in Mugabe's fear of a coup, like the one which almost cost him his rule in 2007'.

The 2014 Joice Mujuru drama was seven years away from 2007 though: Mugabe, until then the master of skulduggery in the party and the country at large, would have been suspicious of all from every side. Mugabe may have been so angry at the 2007 effort that he lashed out right away in 2008, fearing a Tsvangirai in the wings waiting for an alliance with one of Mugabe's erstwhile acolytes. Alternatively, the generals may have thought they had better seal their fealty forthwith with bowls of blood, even though they had been plotting all along.

The red baths of 2008 have entered mythological realms in other spheres too. A well-trodden tale has co-leaders of today's Zimbabwe clasping hands after they had rid the nation of Mugabe's scourge. Next step: their too-old nemesis himself. That accomplished, Emmerson would be the ruler for the first term and pass the legacy torch to Constantine (to be Constantino in 2016). That the promise was broken at the end of 2018 simply means that Mugabeism lives, in stereo and digital relief.[45]

In any case, the March 2008 election—at nearly the height of hyper-inflation[46]—was lost. With the Kariba constitution signed and the ballots cast, coup and unity plans were sidelined. With the shady results and the run-off's killing fields, however, the GNU the oft-enervated Statesmen to the south always wanted was on its way. As if enlisted by Thabo Mbeki, a corps of South Africa's pan-Africanist 'thought-leaders' ('revolutionary intellectuals' in the day) wrote in Mugabe's favour. The Reverend and President's Office director-general Frank Chikane even banged leader writers' heads to support the Zimbabwean 'revolutionary party'. There was no crisis, they chorused, nearly replicating Mugabe's words: only puppets intent on creating an Iraq could say the March election results were unreal.[47] This might have been to garner Mugabe's support while the South African foreign policy makers argued the benefits of pushing for a transitional government immediately or to weather the probable storm to follow the constitution. Mbeki lost that battle, apparently to his adviser Mojanku Gumbi. The storms did come. The 'transitional inclusive government' arrived, with mixed results.[48] Its minister of finance? Tendai Biti. He turned into a magic realist around then.

9

THE COUP INCARNATE

14–21 NOVEMBER 2017

The Geneva conference did not create a new state. The big deal was that Mugabe showed the world—and the Zimbabwean nationalist factions—that the soldiers held his hand in deference. The organisers wondered what would happen if Ian Smith did not sign over his power. The representatives of a holy Anglo-American alliance discussed the nature of a coup.

> Kissinger: The only difference is the nuance of whether the agreement by which he is replaced is signed by him or by someone else. If it is someone else, it would look like a coup.
>
> Crosland: The appearance of a coup will have enormous advantages in Britain—and would change the political atmosphere.[1]

Two score and a year later, politicians, diplomats and—later—academics would be considering the nature of another coercion-laced change in the configuration of Zimbabwean power. Soldiers had done (most of) the work.

Smith signed over his measure of power three years after Geneva's conference. His army generals threatened coups within minutes. Other Rhodesian security servants, embedded with Britain, saved Mugabe from a few. Rhodesia's new names and governors changed few British citizens' political views. Their concern about Rhodesia or Zimbabwe probably peaked in the '1968' era that kept on hanging on. Perhaps passions–about human rights and democracy and/or 'kith and kin' losing land–rose again when 'fast-track land reform' made millennial news.[2]

If we take coup-discourse seriously (it is often too earnest), we need to know when and why Mugabe decided to sign his resignation when he did. He handed in his resignation letter barely two days after rejecting his party members' quickly garnered vote to retire him. If the quality of the force behind his decision to vacate the party and country's presidium was sufficient to count as determinant, one could say safely that a *coup* facilitated a transition of power holders, albeit in the same party and arguably the same 'system' as before. There was a change 'within' power, but not one 'in' or 'of' it. Power stayed in the ruling party; perhaps it changed a bit: ZANU (PF) might have taken further steps towards the fullness of Ibbo Mandaza's 'securocrat state',[3] but the scrambling of the cartel-based contests over new patrons would create more insecurity among them, to trickle all over.[4]

If there is a 'credible threat' of force, does the letter of the law have to be broken for a transitional process to be a coup? Does the number of deaths matter? Or is it only their proximity to power and its wielders that matters? What makes 'soft' become 'hard'? I lack the dexterity and knowledge to argue complex legal ways of explaining (away?) a political question, considered in its historical and sociological context– but remember that the law is power's artefact. Given this book's history of many coups and conspiracies thereof, the mere success of this one lends it that name. Its relatively peaceful nature simply signifies its achievement while hiding its true colours. Furthermore, there seems a 'common sense' in Zimbabwe: nearly everybody except its protagonists and their apologists agree its intent and nature, whether they like it or not. The 'coup that is not a coup' chorus signals its ambiguous discomfort. This is the nature of truths and false truths.

Given the preceding pages' discussions of various veracities and their virtues, perhaps the 'very Zimbabwean' nature of those November 2017 days buttresses the case even more. I think there are at least two scraps of evidence and argumentation supporting the case that when Emmerson Dambudzo Mnangagwa, aka Ngwenya (Crocodile), was inaugurated for the first time (after waiting four decades) as president, Zimbabwe had experienced a coup.

Two ideas lend credence to the fading belief that the events of 11/17 were a 'militarily assisted transition' (MAT) with just a few guns' nudges. They are aside from the AU and SADC's diplomatic sleight of hand and the legal technicalities quickly handled by the hand-picked courts and political leaders glad to see Mugabe go by any (decent) means possible. SADC, quick to avoid the coup-word, commended Zimbabweans 'for conducting themselves in a steady, mature and peaceful manner during this historic transition and transfer of power'.[5] The apparent legalities followed by the coup-makers were behind SADC's acquiescence, but if keeping clear of the bounds measuring a 'house arrest' honour the law, then one could consider the law asinine.[6] The reasons offered are interpretative and evidential. They relate to that long-lasting but unreal division of labour between ZANU (PF)'s (and many of its interpreters') notions of the clear binaries of violence and peace, or 'the gun and politics'.

Such surreal perceptions arise directly out of what Benedetto Fontana might have essayed as the 'chronic absence ... of a hegemonic relation between the [Zimbabwean] ruling elite and the general population ... the failure of the ruling elites to establish a durable and stable hegemony over [Zimbabwe's] subordinate groups'.[7]

Perhaps they relate to Ernst Fraenkel's ideas on the 'Dual State', as he strove to understand Weimar Germany. It is a 'regime whose defining attribute is to disguise its true nature'. Its 'normative' side is relatively lawful and legitimate while it furthers its 'prerogative' side, which 'violates the same laws' and in so doing steers further from legality and legitimacy.[8] As states of emergency eventuate to coups, and when the force behind them necessitates as much cover as possible, the nature of this duality changes. 'Events' metamorphose to new structures.[9]

At the immediate level, the argument about the coupishness of the 11/17 soft, constitutional, *soupçon* coup–or the Jesuitical 'unexpected but peaceful transition', even managing to avoid the word 'military'[10]–relates to the weighting of head (consent) and hindquarters (coercion) in Gramsci's political centaur. Two moments in the coup's relationship to both popular and parliamentary forms of democracy are important for this consideration. The first instance of debate concerns the meeting of the two elements of the party-state's apparatuses of force. The first physical battle was between the military and the police, as Constantino Chiwenga landed from China to manage the military moves. The police tried to arrest him. (Is there a warrant of arrest?) They were proxies for two factions—Generation 40 versus Lacoste—in ZANU (PF)'s fractious elite. Zero fatalities, goes the tale: just a quick move with aviation uniforms at the airport completed the soldiers' job. On completion (but perhaps with more force than acknowledged) the relation between the victors of Round 1 and the 'people', and the institution purportedly representing them best—in Rounds 2a and 2b— was up for grabs. As for the various cabinet ministers roughed up a wee bit and the collateral damage between those moments, no one liked 'criminals' anyway.

The following few paragraphs should dispose of the idea that Zimbabwe's coup was special enough to be unique.[11] One cannot doubt the coup-like nature of the way Mugabe and his allies lost their jobs. The current president, first vice-president, associated 'war veterans' and hundreds of soldiers in their offices, on the streets, at the airport, and against the police and CIO all over, forced Mugabe and his 'criminal' consort to leave his throne and forget their chances to create a future in their image. Perhaps my 'exceptionalist' interpretation in a quickly penned *Transformation* article 'overstate[d] the Zimbabwe 2017 coup's differences from coups in other African countries'.[12] Aside from implicit comparisons with Samuel Doe's demise and Idi Amin's rise, this might have derived from the use of a term perhaps too specific to South African history—oft seen as incomparable by those buried within it—for those outside the arcane leftist theories of South African political economy to discern. 'A very Zimbabwean coup' made too much of the South African Communist Party's worn theory of 'colonialism of a special type' (with a nearly unique acronym, CST).[13] It is part of the peculiarly preternatural and indeed parochial South African mode of thinking that the whole world acknowledges and even reveres its multi-coloured rainbow.[14] Furthermore, the title of the article reveals the general albeit concrete nature of coups by channelling Chris Mullin's fiction.[15]

Nevertheless, particularities in the Zimbabwean case warrant bearing in mind. One cannot riposte with the banality that all coups are different, so they are all the same. A bit of every devil should come out in the detail, and it should be worth the digging. An equally clichéd (empiricist) idea is that careful detail can constitute the entirety of a devil's evil: but (the third cliché), the theorists wonder when, or if, quantity turns to quality.

Zimbabwe's late 2017 manic military moments–minute compared to Gukurahundi, but similarly dissimulated–straddle its unique qualities with continental and global commonalities, as are Zimbabwe's larger socio-economic structures. Its white-settler-colony status is not as marked as South Africa but sets it off from the subcontinent aside from Kenya. Indeed, Ibbo Mandaza's schizophrenic (and securocratic) state theories could spar very well with the CST perspective.[16] Ditto with the land question: never pushed so far in Kenya or South Africa. Industrialisation? Once the second most so on the continent, now a 'hustling' political economy like most,[17] but with more than memories of a strong trade union culture and politics.[18]

Aside from this structural liminality, there are many 'special' aspects to this coup. First must be Mugabe's age. His frailty meant that he was not failing better any more:[19] not all coups challenge an 'old man Machiavelli'.[20] As Trevor Noah observed of the tactics involved for a coup on a 93-year-old: 'Shhh,' the conspirators would have to whisper, 'don't wake him up!'[21] Contingency plans had to be constructed: his death in office would have sparked a fuse smouldering for ages. The factional friction's long festering roots add more specificity to the case. Blessing-Miles Tendi's carefully constructed chronicles–ranging from the mid-1970s to the coup–certainly add scholarly weight to that historical arsenal.[22] So far, this book has indicated the intricate and intimate relationship among ZANU (PF)'s three Cs, so the events of 11/17 should not be that surprising. It just took the Baader-Meinhof syndrome for the chips to fall and the conceit to turn to deceit.[23]

Perhaps that the Zimbabwean coup-makers cared to keep their work close to constitutional correctness, and (planned) popular inclusiveness, made it a little special. As soon as Chiwenga decided to put the coup machine in motion, he was on the phone asking for advice. That counsel was to keep profiles low and as constitutionally clean as possible. Lectures down south to Mnangagwa and Chris Mutsvangwa would have been similar.[24] Depending on how wide and deep the plans had spread, with Mnangagwa out of the country Chiwenga and company could have dumped him to deal with the 'criminals' around Mugabe in their own way: but they needed a civilian on top. Thus the political package. The long months of planning for some sort of non-electoral transfer of power, including meetings with members of the opposition parties, possibly British representatives, and the 'war veterans' (openly anti-Mugabe at least since 2016) meeting across ZANU and ZAPU lines–not to mention the mythical 2008 handshake–would also have worked against precipitous shifts. The increasingly incendiary Grace factor added a unique aspect to the 11/17 events.[25] How many coup templates include fears that the woman who whipped her son's girlfriend with an electrical cord–in another country–could be the next president?[26]

More theoretically, the 'very Zimbabwean' nature of the coup might be the eternal expression of the imagined bifurcation between the 'gun and politics' bedevilling Zimbabwean political discourse ever since Mugabe met the mad Maoists in London in the foggy January of 1976. One would need a long, wide and deep historical plough to go through African and other coups to test the hypothesis that the Zimbabwean coup-masters tried the hardest to hide the centaur's coercive hindquarters and to discern Machiavelli's influence therein. However, the times alone, as liberal democracy's veneer was fading with coups still unfashionable, would suggest as much.[27]

It is no wonder that I stumbled more than usual when that interviewer asked me if the MAT was really a coup.[28] My prevarication was not because I suddenly realised that my lack of interest in reading conservative tracts on the primordial-like prebendal and neo-patrimonial coupishness of Africans was a handicap: revisiting those boring undergraduate texts never occurred to me. I remembered one as interesting: Ali Mazrui's article on the lumpen militariat, arguing that army rule would set back the dictatorship of the African educated class stuck with me.[29] I had no time to challenge Mazrui's thesis with the master coup-maker's desire for educational qualification, albeit, they say, met with ghost writers.[30] Would that divert the journalist? No, I could only repeat the obvious hesitatingly because the question's obviousness gobsmacked me. It was a coup (implying that a political leader or group was replaced rather quickly via a degree of force somewhere between elections and war) because guns and soldiers were involved, and people were killed. Easy. Chester Missing's ventriloquist did not dither at the comical side of the interchange: the journalist was the 'asker of obvious questions' just as the truths I told were so transparent they could speak for themselves. Philosophical, legal and empirical discussions be damned.

The first example of the conceit–deceit dialectic in the popular coup rests within the way the notion of 'popularity' was constructed. With so many guns around, that is a delicate process. The two dimensions to the conceits and deceits of the big parade on 18 November follow. First, it was a joint venture of veterans of both ZAPU and ZANU's sides of the war. Their motivations may have been closer to 'civil society' than the 'politicians and soldiers':[31] their perceptions of the 'legacy' the putschists pretended to restore veered to various degrees from their commanders. This could indicate a problem with the argument that a single idea of the 'legacy' ruled the coup's discourse. The *vashandi* graduates' views would not be the only ones to differ from the coup's protagonists. Thus it would be a mistake to say that:

> [The coup] succeeded because soldiers from Zimbabwe's 1970s independence war subscribed to the coup's stated ideal to restore liberation struggle principles in the ruling Zimbabwe African National Union Patriotic Front party. ... Liberation war veterans in the military could not brook politicians without ideational and active participant connections to the independence struggle securing control of the state, hence their support for the coup.[32]

Not *all* war veterans shared the coup's 'stated ideal', and even those in 'control' had different ideological and strategic views along the spectrum from materialism to *Weltanschauung*.[33] If not there to start, they would show up later. What was important by 18 November (only five days from the announcement about Mugabe and his criminals needing a tough lesson)—with more time such shaky ideological moorings would bear less—is that their role in the coup led most visibly to its association with popular will.

'Tens of thousands' of happy marchers cheered the likes of Constantino Chiwenga, the man who did the dirty work of getting Emmerson Mnangagwa into the driver's seat from which he had been so unceremoniously deflected in early November. The rural marchers were bused in to the Zimbabwe Grounds in Highfield. Businesspeople and bus-company owners contributed to the cause. The country folk marched into the city to join the self-transported participants, who were middling classed and often pale—'whiteness' very evident on images heading 'west'. Their signs were finely printed; the photographs of their latest heroes intertwined with globally recognised cultural icons and tropes. 'Goodbye Lady Gaga', 'Leadership is not sexually transmitted', 'Mugabe NOTE that: Zimbabwe can Never Never Never be your Colony', and 'I want my son to be born into a free Zimbabwe' (held by a pregnant white woman beside a black man). The rural folk seemed to have made their own placards, some reading 'I am a history maker' and '18 November New Independence Day'.[34]

The interviews illustrated the people's hope, finally expressed in their focus on one man—gone soon, they dreamed—but laced with wishes for better governance in the next round, too. The MDC was in full support of the march and its members joining—but they did not wear party insignia. The YouTube videos—a permanent reminder of that glorious day—had the demonstrators dancing and laughing with the young-looking soldiers, some of whom must have fought a bit for this glimpse of freedom from Mugabe. Car owners and taxi passengers alike would have thanked the soldiers profusely: their actions so far had stopped the universally hated police roadblocks, the revenue from which trickled straight up to police commissioner Augustine Chiruri and then to Grace Mugabe. There were not many police around, although a couple managed to beat someone up in a side street.

A couple of YouTubes from that day are not so cheery.[35] South Africa's News24 put on a clip of just over a minute, as soldiers redirected what looked like thousands of marchers off a main street to a smaller one. A quick jump after about 40 seconds has a front row sitting or squatting, with a screenful of standing folks behind. Three or four men—one or two perhaps marshals with Zimbabwe-coloured scarves or flags draped around their necks, arms outstretched—stand as in argument, a soldier aims his rifle to the heavens. The next cut shows a couple of soldiers pacing in front of a huge semicircle, waving their arms downward to get all the people to sit. There is no voiceover. Al Jazeera's Tendai Marima got closer to the real thing, after they sat in one place.[36] She filmed the standoff. Just outside the central police headquarters, the crowd is packed and pouring out of the street. The State House, only a few minutes north, is the crow's desired location. The war veterans shared that aim. The scores of soldiers inside and outside their two or three trucks were grimacing more than grinning. Major General Sibusiso Moyo—he who had announced the coup a few days earlier without naming it—was on the back of a pickup truck flanked by a dozen soldiers, Brigadier General Anselem Sanyatwe beside him, and a worried leather-jacket-clad man holding the bullhorn emitting 'SB' Moyo's message. We do not hear what he said, but Marima's text records it: 'Go home, don't proceed to State House', he said, 'because we will finish the job'. He proceeded to say, 'The operation we are doing together as a country is a journey,' and, in Shona, Marima writes, 'We cannot go around the mountain in one day, but through your support we have covered a great distance.' Then the flick flashes over to the dominant portrayal: happy marching in the streets.

There are many stories around that event. They illustrate some of the tensions—the ways out of the ultimate meeting of the 'guns and politics' that so vex Zimbabwean political discourse—around the police headquarters moment. Chris Mutsvangwa, the man in charge of the war-vet contingent, was in Johannesburg apparently chatting up white Zimbabweans and Tweeting all over the place. The demonstrations were under the charge of his second in command, a serious former ZIPRA commander wearing none of the slightly mad flamboyance of Mutsvangwa, who took the 'restore' agenda at the noble end of the scale. Some war vets will tell you that State House was the plan; others that the endpoint was spontaneous—but do thousands of people turn on a dime and head in that direction? Someone told me that the demonstrators were in no mood to leave until they had either met Mugabe or deposited a message with a reliable messenger. Indeed, word has it, they were openly contemplating marching to the Blue Roof, the Borrowdale Brook mansion where Mugabe and the team of negotiators (in constant contact with the military) were figuring out what to do to make a clean exit, none at all, or what to pay for it. SB Moyo warned the crowd not to go that far—but he did not say what would await them if they did. If they had ignored his message and managed to get out of the police headquarters neighbourhood, not just the Presidential Guard but the whole National Reaction Force would have stopped them.

Brigadier General Sanyatwe, then head of the Presidential Guard (later promoted to Major General after heading up the shooting spree quelling rough post-2018 election demonstrations, and finally shuffled off as a retired Lieutenant General to the ambassadorship in Tanzania under suspicion of involvement in anti-Mnangagwa plots) ensured the Blue Roof was under control. According to a *New York Review of Books* report a few months later, on the 14th Sanyatwe had 'secretly renounced his allegiance to Mugabe and replaced troops loyal to the president with handpicked substitutes'.[37] Sanyatwe is renowned as one of Chiwenga's loyal protégés so would have been on that side of the fence for a long time. The secret renunciation would not have taken a second longer than Chiwenga's decision.

Perhaps Moyo's good crowd-control technique earned him the ministry of foreign affairs. True or false, there are two morals to these tales. One is: there is no such thing as a truly popular demonstration accompanying a coup. That the demonstrators did not manage to get past the police headquarters and to State House—let alone the Blue Roof—illustrates the moment when 'popular power' hits the Leviathan. We would need to see the drone's (undoctored) videos to know for sure. The second illustrates the Kissinger and Crosland bantering: get the blooming thing signed. Without it, the lies will proliferate and/or a full-on coup will follow.

The next day, well after his party had dumped him at the world's fastest leadership congress, Mugabe said at the end of one of the most surreal press conferences ever, 'See you at the special congress'.

The Leviathan was on more than standby. Its guns were at the ready. They stopped the protests. They were backed by good talkers, who retained the state's legitimacy even when the luck of their political interlocutors had run its course. Maybe the soldiers, no longer a people's army, *stopped* the Zimbabwean version of a popular storming of the citadel. Perhaps, their leaders not visible and in any case powerless, the masses did not know where to go after they had trod the streets. That is what happens when you have what Knox Chiteyo told the *Irish Times* is a 'military-guided popular revolt',[38] especially when it was a faction fight that went viral. The 'popular revolt' lasted for about a weekend; a faction of Zimbabwe's political–military complex—indeed, a small element within that faction, with few or no guns—led it. The men on horseback will not let go of their status as 'the liberators of the country' even when they say they are restoring the legacy of those who fought for freedom. The first sheen of their new polish wears off soon. There was one more attempt at people's power, via the nascent intelligentsia. After Sunday's press conference when Mugabe foiled the soldier–party alliance at the hastily called ZANU (PF) conference to send him packing, and Mutsvangwa's immediately texted message to Reuters that another march would follow on Wednesday, the university students tried. Thousands on campus marched, demanding delayed examinations and that the university rescind Grace Mugabe's ghost-written PhD. Along with that: the vice-chancellor's arrest. The university conceded on the exam issue. The coup-masters responded quickly: go back to your studies, they ordered. 'REMEMBER THAT ONE DAY OF EDUCATION LOST IS DIFFICULT TO RECOVER', they wrote. By the way, they added, Operation Restore the Legacy is finished.[39] Mutsvangwa announced that the war vets would hold a sit-in until Mugabe saw the light–but time would tell that this would not be necessary.

The first scene in the first act of the *popular* coup finished with those whimpers. Yet Mnangagwa–with good historical memory or not– played that tune with a line in the popular repertoire going back to the seedbed of liberal imperialism in the fourteenth century. The fired and exiled ex-vice-president had written to Mugabe just two days after his escape and told the man with whom his 'relationship has over the years blossomed beyond that of master and servant but to father and son' that his time was up. 'You and your cohorts will instead leave Zanu-PF by the will of the people and this we will do in the coming few weeks'.[40] By the 21st, Mnangagwa's second very public letter bore out his prediction two weeks previously. After the demonstrations and the quickly arranged party conference, Mnangagwa could be secure in his summoning of the popular will. The 'people of Zimbabwe ha[d] clearly spoken on this matter'. He then expounded his political theory:

> To me the voice of the people is the voice of God and their lack of trust and confidence in the leadership of President Mugabe has been expressed. Several groups including students, general workers, opposition party members, vendors, religious organisations and ordinary citizens led by our war veterans, our party members in Zanu PF, civic

society, and all races of colour and creed in Zimbabwe clearly demonstrated without violence their insatiable desire to have the resignation
of His Excellency, Cde Robert Gabriel Mugabe.[41]

The *vox populi, vox dei* duo has always been a contradictory one,
veering between direct democracy and the sovereign's protection from
the 'riotous masses'.[42] Although Mnangagwa glorified the demonstrators' voices–who, as Mugabe opined later, were just a few thousand
'noises ... well-organised by the opposition'[43] and the war veteran
leaders–he would not hedge his bets with his mentor at the next round.
Mugabe had rejected his party's voice on Sunday, so Mnangagwa and
his comrades moved on with the third part of the people's component:
Round 2b. That was the impeachment plan, worked out–but never
signed–with the two chairs of the latest and most publicly discussed
iteration of the constitution, Douglas Mwonzora (MDC) and Paul
Mangwana of the crumbling revolutionary party.[44]

Parliament might be a good democratic example of the people's
voices once removed and thus reflective of God's considered and
devolved wisdom. Common and other sorts of wisdom has it that a
very few cabinet members attended Mugabe's pre-impeachment session because Mugabe–and his 'criminal cohorts'–had already lost the
game. Sibusiso Moyo's television announcement, the demonstrations,
the disappearance of many in the G-40, the beating up and turning of
the ZANU (PF) Youth League leader, and the clear presence of soldiers
instead of the police on the streets: all would have been enough to
persuade the vast majority of the cabinet ministers to vote by not moving their feet. That would have been the signal to Mugabe that he had
lost the battle for the guns and minds. His cabinet would have known
that, and he would have known that without that support he would not
have survived the impeachment process. As Naunihal Singh might have
put it, 'everyone recognised that [Mnangagwa and company] had
power' already, Mugabe and company had lost it, so it could be for-
malised quickly and easily.[45] Mugabe would have little choice but to
take Kissinger and Crosland's advice. Signing the paper would avoid
the coup going further.

Democracy in its parliamentary form would *really* amplify God's
call, as the divine mode of earthly revelation shifted from one interlocutor to another. It is more certain than a motley demonstration,

even if the margins within it can be small. Thus, Mnangagwa said that 'parliament is the ultimate expression of the will of the people outside an election',[46] closer to God than the unmediated voice of the people. Mugabe's last official letter read in part, as parliamentary clerk Jacob Mudenda recited it to the legislative body ready to start a lengthy impeachment procedure: 'My decision to resign is voluntary on my part and arises from my concern for the welfare of the people of Zimbabwe and my desire to ensure a smooth, peaceful and non-violent transfer of power that underpins national security, peace and stability.'[47]

What if, though, there was more force behind the cabinet ministers' decision than heretofore acknowledged? That there were guards at the houses of every cabinet minister is not an indication that cabinet ministers are incarcerated in their own (or the state's) homes: it is part of their everyday security. However, if the soldiers were not the same as those on previous shifts and the ministers had not been told why, that would be a clear indication that the ministers were not free to leave. This tactic served true when the war vets met Mugabe in 1997, winning their pensions and land.[48] Five people in various occupations and countries, but all who would know, confirm that this is the case. Is that enough evidence of force to demolish the non-coercive side of the case against the 'coup' label? This moment was not the 'catalyst' many scholars argue is the cornerstone of a coup, when the soldiers make the crucial decision to embark on the process.[49] If Tendi is correct, the catalyst was when Mugabe refused to discuss matters with the generals, on 13 November. Did they decide then to employ force beyond, or to supplement, other means? One would think this was always part of the plan, but did need a trigger. Confining Mugabe to the Blue Roof, chasing his 'young' cronies, killing some security guards, and roughing up an intelligence operative (or many more) would be part of that. So too would be the airport confrontation when Chiwenga arrived from China, about which the quotient of violence has not been resolved.

The changing of the cabinet guard might just have been the icing on the cake—the body of public representation so sacred to the apostles and disciples of representative democracy, even though marred by recipes demanding arbitrary measures of the ingredients. Perhaps too it signified the straw that broke the already limping camel's back. The 'prerogative state' outweighed its normative twin. This sealed the fate of the Holy Trinity: stalled already for decades (or just since 2000 and the MDC's challenge), the ever-waning progressive or Caesarist side of a stalemated process of primitive accumulation, nation-state formation and democratisation had lost the battle to a Bonaparte.

The rest of this chapter will follow the coup as it wound its way through what Douglas Rogers called the 'astonishing' two weeks in November 2017[50]–more to see if any of this book's preceding chapters are of any assistance in unravelling its threads than to measure levels of surprise. One thing can be said at this point: when a crocodile finally awakens, watch out.[51]

The coup: a narrative

Is Grace Mugabe the starting point of the coup?[52] If so, perhaps it began with her pre-prepared University of Zimbabwe Sociology PhD, thus negating Kissinger's dictum that academic battles are small. If a PhD can arrive on a silver platter with a few coins for the scribes, why not a country?[53] However, it would be ridiculous to assert that she was the causative factor, given previous chapters' investigations. Perhaps she was a slower burning 'catalyst' than a missed meeting.[54] The woman she elbowed out of the vice-presidency got a deserved doctorate, but that did not help Joice Mujuru step to the top. At the end of 2014, three years after her husband's fiery death, the Joice Mujuru threat was gone.[55] Grace Mugabe survived: Mujuru was no longer in line for the top job, so if Robert Mugabe died Grace would not be dragged Gaddafi-like 'in the streets, with people laughing while my flesh sticks on the tarmac', as she surmised in one of her 2014 speeches.[56]

Instead, she focused on the new vice-president, Emmerson Mnangagwa. His arrival meant dumping the 2004 gender norm, which had brought Mujuru in and kept Jonathan Moyo and Emmerson Mnangagwa out as the Tsholotsho saga wound down. If their parting of ways was softened somewhat during the Joice versus Grace battle, it hardened again very soon.[57] Moyo and his colleagues decided to join with Grace and convince her elderly husband to think young. They would find out soon that Mrs Mugabe became the fly in their ointment.[58]

In a couple of years the first lady took direct aim at the Crocodile, whose fluid faction was now called Lacoste–after the reptile adorning the French clothing brand—instead of 'weevil'.[59] The 'Generation 40' or G-40 faction was purportedly directed by cabinet ministers Jonathan Moyo, Saviour Kasukuwere, Ignatius Chombo and Patrick Zhuwao (Mugabe's nephew). Police commissioner General Augustine Chiruri was involved more loosely given his Gamatox origins, being in the Mujuru camp in 2014. The military wing of the 'securocrat state' was Lacoste's reservoir of force and intelligence, while the civilian side of that equation was purportedly closer to the G-40. However, the boundaries between them were permeable (indeed penetrated), given the nascent forms of the networks emerging with Zimbabwe's power structure and systems of accumulation.[60] Nor should either of these institutions—nor 'factions'—be seen as unified entities with singular interests and purpose. In the drawn-out emergencies constituted by the interregna between one Bonaparte and the next, focus can often rest upon one individual who condenses and exaggerates all the tensions—the morbid symptoms—thereof. Dr Amai (mother) Grace Mugabe personified these exceptionally well.

Grace Mugabe's whipping of the young South African model indicated that the pressure was intense.[61] Perhaps emboldened by her escape or worried about her husband's mortality, her political presence seemed to expand. She paced Youth Interface rallies and church gatherings suggesting that Mnangagwa's snake-like head be hit hard, then removed.[62] The 'youth' aspect of the rallies indicated the importance G-40 placed on generational issues. ZANU (PF) youth gangs would swoop into schools to abduct schoolchildren to attend the 'Interface' rallies. One school head apparently told the drunken youth that they could only take the children—and the bus—if they used the services of the school's usual driver, who was sober. The students may have been pleasantly surprised by the break, but shocked by the first lady's behaviour.

Also in August, the Crocodile flew from a ZANU (PF) rally to a South African hospital, very ill: he was probably poisoned and he certainly believes so.[63] Meanwhile, Jonathan Moyo showed the Politburo long videos about Mnangagwa's indiscretions, later distributed to independent media.[64] Mnangagwa could only respond with oft-repeated allegations that Moyo was a CIA agent.[65] On 10 October the cabinet and civilian intelligence services were turned into G-40 redoubts, with the CIO's director replacing Mnangagwa as justice minister. This may have confirmed the common consensus that Jonathan Moyo controlled the CIO as well as being minister for higher education. A few days later Robert Mugabe warned armed forces commander Chiwenga that he should desist from anti-Grace moves or he would be killed, but (after many warnings to Mugabe about Grace's problems) Chiwenga ignored his commander-in-chief.[66] When, on 4 November, Lacoste members of a Bulawayo crowd booed and heckled Grace Mugabe's rude behaviour, the nonagenarian president himself suggested Mnangagwa be fired, saying to the assembly:[67]

> We are denigrated and insulted in the name of Mnangagwa. Did I make a mistake in appointing him as my deputy? ... You know nothing. ... If I made a mistake by appointing Mnangagwa ... tell me. I will drop him as early as tomorrow. We are not afraid of anyone. We can decide even here. ... If it has come to this, it is time we make a final decision.

He did. Mugabe fired Mnangagwa on 6 November. It was the last straw for Mugabe, but perhaps not the straw he intended.[68] The Crocodile was president by the 24th.

How did the G-40 think they could get away with sending off a man so close to the military, who also had Gukurahundi, winter 2008, and much more under his belt? Their plans to sideline Grace, by putting Sydney Sekeramayi in the place she wanted at the upcoming extraordinary congress, were unfolding. The police forces were on G-40's side, but could hardly be a reliable partner in a contest with a very good military force. G-40 might have figured the army younger soldiers would go with them. Social media (probably false—but believed by at least some soldiers) pointed to a plan involving Israeli soldiers and $15 million.

Many Zimbabweans thought the volatile former secretary had gained too much influence over her doddering husband and he should not have taken the bait to fire Mnangagwa. Yet it seems G-40 had a relatively precise date in mind: things had to move quickly if ZANU (PF)'s extraordinary congress (a year earlier than usual: Mugabe was *very* old after all) was going to be theirs for the taking and their candidate would be poised for the mid-2018 elections. Perhaps, too, the G-40 thought Mnangagwa's long relationship with the UK would have tainted him, thinking Zimbabweans' anti-British sentiment went beyond the jilted president.[69]

G-40, they tell us retrospectively, had planned to create three vice-presidencies at the December meeting, pushing the bumbling Phelekezela Mphoko (formerly ZAPU, keeping in mind that that forced unity with ZAPU in 1987 gave it a second vice-presidency) to third place. Dr Grace would have been in the second spot. The then defence minister, the quiet doctor Sydney Sekeramayi, would be first in line and so next up for Zimbabwe's presidential palace.[70] One presumes the next stage of factional struggles would have followed: perhaps the men in G-40 planned to rid the country of the unpredictable Grace when her husband left the mortal coil.[71]

None of this was to come to pass.

On his sacking, Mnangagwa took a quick trip to South Africa via Mozambique, where he consulted with presidents past and present.[72] In the letter cited above he warned the 'minnows … who plunder public funds and are used by foreign countries to destabilise the Party' and are 'brazenly protected in public by the First Lady thereby making a mockery of our public institutions' that he would be back soon.[73] War vets leader Chris Mutsvangwa followed him—and apparently met with members of the exiled white 'Rhodesian' community, including MDC supporters who found themselves in an anti-Mugabe alliance with some disaffected CIO members.[74]

As well as preparing Bulawayo war veterans from ZIPRA, as early as March (this coup had been in the works for quite some time) Mutsvangwa courted former ZIPRA intelligence head and contemporary ZAPU leader Dumiso Dabengwa for a vice-president position. Dabengwa refused to agree to anything until he had met Mnangagwa and they had signed all the papers. At their last meeting, Mutsvangwa said Dabengwa's posting would have to wait for the second term, in 2023. That would have meant, if Mnangagwa and Chiwenga had kept their 2008 promise, that Dabengwa would have been in the presidium with someone he disliked more than the Crocodile. Dabengwa said he would have retired from politics by then (he died in May 2019).[75]

The eventual coup-master's presence in China prompted the British press to guess that China was helping plan the events,[76] in turn provoking suspicion that the British were creating a diversion.[77] As early as

175

16 November, Reuters, seemingly following British thinking assiduously while bragging about the 'several years of Zimbabwean intelligence documents' that it accessed, forecast a GNU with such noble personages as Morgan Tsvingirai, Tendai Biti, and even Dabengwa taking top spots.[78]

The Crocodile—from South Africa, either in a Michelangelo Hotel apartment suite in Sandton reserved for such visitors or with the Zimbabwean computer executive in Ray Ndlovu's book, but in any case deep in conversation with his hosts[79]—with Chiwenga in China and Lieutenant General Philip Sibanda in Zimbabwe, rallied the troops in a week's time. The police's efforts to arrest Chiwenga on his return from China on 12 November failed spectacularly. The military were not surprised: it had many 'agents' within its parallel body. Indeed, some 'police' rushing to the arrest were long-time military moles; more were dressed in civilian airport uniforms, as widely reported. They surrounded the aircraft and stopped the police in their tracks. One person who was on a plane arriving simultaneously recalled soldiers checking everyone's passports while still sitting, and again at the door. When this person arrived at a flat near the centre of the city, she noticed a rather marked increase in the number of drones flying around.

Tendi situates the 'catalyst' the next morning, not at the airport but with a meeting Mugabe rebuffed.[80] Chiwenga, furious at his attempted arrest (presumably no surprise to him), asked Mugabe to postpone his normal morning meeting so they could have a later one with the officers. Mugabe said no. Chiwenga was even more furious. Was that when all the officers agreed to use necessary force? Did they tell Mugabe? I prefer a processual approach: if on the next day Mugabe had not accused the officers of treason his house may not have been under siege that night.

The rest of the 13th was most interesting as far as 'legacy' goes. General Constantino Chiwenga, commander, Zimbabwe Defence Forces, read out Operation Restore Legacy's three pages to the press. The speech was later on YouTube, not the state-run ZBC-TV: in true coup fashion, that would be taken soon.[81]

The speech (edited, I was told, during a media engagement with one very animated Mnangagwa supporter from the Zimbabwean diaspora, by the late Major General Trust Mugoba)[82] did not lay out Mugabe's retirement ultimatum directly. It was barely implied. Whether the statement suggests a turning point direct to a coup *against a particular leader* is still open for question. The 'counter-revolutionaries' around Mugabe would have felt the heat through their laptops though. The events of the past few days were an intra-party affair, Chiwenga said to the many security forces leaders around him (excepting police commissioner Chiruri, whose forces had just been embarrassed) and the cyber-audience. However, given ZANU (PF)'s intimate ties with the state, this was a big deal. What happened in ZANU (PF) affected the whole country.

> It is with humility and a heavy heart that we come before you to pronounce the indisputable reality that there is instability in ZANU-PF and as a result anxiety in the country at large. ... It is pertinent to restate that the Zimbabwean defense forces remain the major stockholder [*sic*] in respect to the gains of the liberation struggle [and] ... it is common cause that any instability within the party naturally impacts on their [the people's] social, political and economic lives. ... We are obliged to take protective measures.

Are 'protective measures' tantamount to a coup? We know by now that when 'counter-revolutionaries' appear in Zimbabwe's history the axe falls. We also know who has wielded the weapon. They were always for maintaining order and hierarchical harmony; here too those traditions were to be maintained. The difference resides in the fact that the leader—or one captured by counter-revolutionaries but redeemable—is the one seen as disrupting a natural construction of power. What then is a counter-revolutionary in such a situation? A definition is brought to the fore three times.

First, the 'revolutionary party's ... gallant fighters' spirited hope of seeing a prosperous Zimbabwe', but also the hope of leaving behind 'inheritance and legacy [*sic*] for posterity' has been destroyed (mostly in the 'past five years'). All of this was 'a direct result of the machinations of counter revolutionaries who have infiltrated the Party and whose agenda is to destroy it from within'. Note: 'infiltration' means these forces are from outside originally. The second time the commanding officer introduces the notion is to invoke Mugabe's very own 'Zimbabwe will never be a colony again' discourse. The 'counter revolutionary infiltrators who are now effectively influencing the direction of the Party' are 'seriously challeng[ing]' this idea. Again, they are infiltrators–indeed, neo-colonisers. Our revolution is 'being hijacked by agents of our erstwhile enemies who are now at the brink of returning our country to foreign domination'. Finally, 'the known counter revolutionary elements who have fermented the current instability in the Party must be exposed and fished out'. The members of G-40 might as well have been under the spotlight. Their absence from history is evidenced by their ignorance of the crises in the party's history that the soldiers had resolved. And the list is only partial (and partially accurate):

> The formation of FROLIZI, the attempt to remove the late Cde Chitepo from his position of Chairman at the Mumbwa bogus Congress in 1973, the Nhari-Badza rebellion, Ndabaningi Sithole rebellion soon after the death of Cde Chitepo, the Vashandi 1 and 2 as well as the rebellion that led to the death of the late ZIPRA Commander, Cde Alfred Nikita Mangena, among others are cases in point.

The G-40 group was thus corralled with all the rebels of the past. 'We' however were the ones who *made* history (history, regardless of how accurate, is made by the victors): therefore the 'current shenanigans by people who do not share the same liberation history of Zanu-PF Party are not a surprise to us'. Furthermore–and importantly for coup-talk, 'all these rebellions were defused by the military, but at no point did the military usurp power'. The politics–gun dialectic was drawn out once again. It would be about to reach its snapping point.

The operation was not named 'legacy' at the time, but the statement did contain the word 'legacy' thrice, and proxies aplenty.[83] Its first mention in the statement notes the freedom fighters' historically imbued hopes to see a 'prosperous Zimbabwe' for their 'legacy for posterity'. Second, Chiwenga read out that ZANU (PF)'s recent 'gossiping, back-biting and public chastisement' was 'undoing its legacy built over the years'. This was a party matter but such 'manner of doing business' stretches across society (as any party–state complex would!). It has a 'direct impact on the lives of every citizen ... regardless of political affiliation'. Third, the statement fingers the 'known counter revolutionary elements' who will destroy the party's heritage. Those 'who have fermented the current instability in the Party ... must be exposed and fished out'. The armed forces will protect 'our legacy

... those bent on high-jacking [*sic*] the revolution will not be allowed to do so'.

Chiwenga made it clear—indeed 'restated'—that the forces under his command constituted the 'major stockholder' so they would have to protect the stocks. They had done this in the past when 'people who ... attempted to destroy the revolution from within' during the liberation war were stymied. These included some of the phenomena discussed in this book—especially the Mgagao Declaration and the 'two' *vashandis*—the second never having taken that name before. The operation that would restore the values of the past laid out the choices for the next few days and the historical template—in perfectly distorted hindsight—justifying them.

Emmerson Mnangagwa was not named. Even Mugabe himself was only mentioned twice, quoted on his anti-imperialist stance, and noticed by his status as *the only one* commander-in-chief. It was clear, however, that 'counter-revolutionary infiltrators' and purgeists surrounded him and had to be flushed out. 'When it comes to matters of protecting our revolution, the military will not hesitate to step in.' If the president and the party would not remove them, the soldiers would. They would try to keep the process running 'amicably and in the ruling Party's closet', as they had during the liberation war. The next few days would see few of these friendly and hidden aspirations.

Perhaps if Mugabe had agreed to have the purgers around him removed he might have remained president until death retired him. That chance came and passed. The next day ZANU (PF) spokesperson Simon Khaya Moyo told Chiwenga off. Mugabe, he said, had 'recently reminded the military of its "subordinate place"', but 'yesterday's ... reprehensible conduct' had demonstrated that such 'wise counsel not only went unheeded but was flagrantly flouted in deference to factional politics and personal ambitions'. The revolutionary party would '"never" succumb to any threats', 'least of all those deriving from conduct that is inconsistent with the tenets of democracy and constitutionalism'.[84] Chiwenga's unsigned letter did not represent all the armed forces, thus it was 'an outrageous initiation of professional soldiership'. It suggested 'treasonable conduct ... meant to incite insurrection and violent challenge to the constitutional order'. Khaya Moyo invoked the gun and politics trope: 'This', he sermonised, 'is what happens when the gun seeks to overreach by dictating to politics and norms of constitutionality.'[85]

This was either the last grass or the last gasp, depending on the exact timing of the military troops immobilising the police force's special support unit at Chikurubi, and confiscating weapons.[86] Arguments about killing take place here. Some say none–the brutal torturing or nearly killing of CIO and police officers being sufficient violence–while others speak of numbers in the mid-thirties and more still up to 63.[87] A few have suggested that after the police support unit was attacked and raided, the ammunition therein was taken by the soldiers, and remains on one of Chiwenga's farms. The soldiers knew they could persuade no longer; force would have to follow–a tactic many of them preferred anyway. Operation Restore Legacy (apparently named by General Sibanda) began in earnest after Khaya Moyo's challenge. Armed personnel carriers rolled onto the streets, the acting CIO direc-tor scooted to Mugabe's house but was stopped and beaten by army officers, and the royalist couple was 'arrested' under the palatial Blue Roof.[88] Soldiers rounded up various G-40 cabinet ministers–shooting at one or two Israeli security guards and finding $15 million at the finance minister's house (that some say was readied to pay Israeli mer-cenaries in Zambia, who quickly stilled), but failing to catch Jonathan Moyo and Saviour Kasukuwere, who escaped to Blue Roof.[89]

The armed forces announced their actions early the next morning via the recently overtaken state television broadcaster. Major General Sibusiso Moyo–veteran of many UN missions around the continent, said to have played a big role in ridding Angola of Jonas Savimbi and thus well respected within the African military and diplomatic com-munity, and soon to take over the foreign affairs portfolio–announced the shift in power dynamics and denied a coup. It was just a quick attempt to target 'criminals around [Mugabe] who are committing crimes that are causing social and economic suffering in the country in order to bring them to justice', and to keep Mugabe secure. 'To both our people and the world beyond our borders,' the youngish military officer announced, 'we wish to make it abundantly clear that this is not a military takeover of Government.' All the military forces are 'doing is to pacify a degenerating political, social and economic situation in our country which if not addressed may result in violent conflict'. As for the 'other Security Services' (that is, those in the police and civilian intelligence services), 'we urge you to cooperate for the good of our country. Let it be clear that we intend to address the human security threats in our country. Therefore any provocation will be met with an appropriate response.'[90]

Thus was settled the question of the gun and politics–and sleight of hand–as far as the armed forces and their exiled 'political' ally in South Africa were concerned. As discussed in the previous section, Mnangagwa and his speechwriters near and afar dressed it all up with the voices of the people and God, but Moyo's short speech was clearer. His colleagues would decide when 'we have accomplished our mission' and thus when everyone else can 'expect that the situation will return to normalcy'.

Many of Mugabe's colleagues and friends (not that he had many) visited the Blue Roof over next few days. They included long-time confidant Father Fidelis Mukonori, information secretary George Charamba (the recipient of Grace Mugabe's public barbs at a rally whilst her husband slept on the podium), Gideon Gono, former governor of the reserve bank, and Kenneth Kaunda, Zambia's guitar-playing past president who had left power without a fuss. They all tried to persuade Mugabe to give up the ghostly apparitions of power, but failed. Some say that when Mugabe was taken to a university graduation ceremony on the 17th a few senior CIO officers told him he had no more legs to stand on (and theirs were shaky too: in the next few months many had to disappear).

While the military and 'popular' demonstrations were unfolding, Mnangagwa's comrades were speedily turning the party's memberships around from their recent G-40 shuffling. By Sunday evening the party had voted Mugabe out. The press conference at which the watching world expected Mugabe to cave in to his once beloved party proved surprising. To the assembled military commanders' stoically hidden shock and horror, Mugabe refused to accept his party's verdict. Toward the end of his mumbled speech–live, after some argument over the generals' preference for a pre-recorded version[91]–he acknowledged that ZANU (PF)'s handling of its disunity left 'something to be desired':[92]

Open public spurts [*sic*] between high-ranking officials in party and government exacerbated by multiple conflicting messages from both the party and government made the criticisms [of lack of unity] levelled against us inescapable. ... The way forward cannot be based on swapping by cliques that ride roughshod over party rules and procedures.

Perhaps with his young spouse in mind, he continued with a plea for the party to come to terms with generational transitions:

[The party must] go back to the guiding principles ... of traditions ... served by successive generations who have shared ideals and values which must continue to reign supreme in our nation. ... [ZANU (PF) needed a] new ethos ... nourished by an abiding sense of camaraderie [to override the recent] era of victimisation and arbitrary decisions. Our inter-generation conflict must be resolved through a harmonised melding of old established players as they embrace and welcome new ones through a well-defined sense of hierarchy and succession.

Minutes later, after dropping some of the papers he or an assistant had prepared, he told viewers and soldiers that he would see them at the December conference and apologised for 'a very long speech'. This feint would prove to be Mugabe's last. (There are two different interpretations of this move, however. One is that the soldiers encouraged him to say 'no' in order to gainsay those who were accusing the soldiers of a coup: he could say goodbye without soldiers by his side. The other is that Chiwenga coached him to prevaricate because Chiwenga was dithering too, with second thoughts about the Crocodile already.)[93] In any case, the coup-makers had other plans up their sleeves. Their last gambit would prove the prominence of parliament.

While the generals were utilising their force of arms as quickly and quietly as possible and the war vets were moving the masses, the parliamentarians were planning Mugabe's impeachment. Douglas Mwonzora and Paul Mangwana worked out a pact, but it was never finalised. The MDC would co-operate if Mnangagwa signed an agreement that included guarantees of internationally observed free and fair elections in mid-2018, but Mangwana said that his principals would not agree to such an infringement of sovereignty. In any case, Mnangagwa himself—still south of the border—had not signed.[94]

Plans were in motion nonetheless. Independent MP Themba Mliswa—once in ZANU (PF), once expelled; but in a conversation admitting 'once in the party, always in the party'[95]—tabled the motion on Monday 20 November. If the impeachment process had gone on,

Mugabe could have taken many legal options to slow it down (some MDC MPs relished the thought of his total exposure).[96] Mnangagwa told the world that he would return to Zimbabwe when it was safe for him, but in the meantime invoked the divine nature of *vox populi*. *Vox concilii* would come later. Where did the soldiers go?

The impeachment process was set to go ahead anyway. Mugabe rolled over before it could start, for the reasons above: his cabinet meeting was too poorly attended. Mugabe resigned. He signed. The Crocodile swam home, praising his 'father' all the time–and parliament's ability to be God's ventriloquist did not have to be tested. Rory Stewart, then the British minister responsible for Africa, rushed to Zimbabwe excitedly to discuss 'the need for an all-inclusive political process and elections which meet Zimbabwean and International standards' in this once 'one of the wealthiest countries in Africa'. There 'could be an opportunity for progress' over the horizon, he added.[97] Morgan Tsvangirai said he wanted an all-inclusive process too, indeed using the same words,[98] after telling the *Financial Times*, 'This is not a job for Zanu-PF alone.' Tendai Biti agreed, speaking the language of the 2009–13 transitional inclusive government in which he had been finance minister. 'We need a road map that establishes this transitional authority to ensure that the next election is free, fair and credible, and accepted by all Zimbabweans,' he said.[99] However, ZANU (PF)'s internet security minister (previously finance, and justice) Patrick Chinamasa had already told the world that such ideas were non-starters: 'We were correcting our own mess, we have the majority in Parliament, we can expel the President alone and we are the ruling party, so where does a coalition come in? We don't need them.'[100] Indeed, he told the war vets much the same, personally removing the chairs set for them at the inauguration's stage.[101] The coup had eaten up the official opposition *and* the war veterans, chewed well, and spat them out. A good number of commissioned soldiers, too, thought the positive side of the recent events soured when 'the party' took over. The MDC realised this very quickly, giving up GNU aspirations the next day.[102]

On his neatly prepared inaugural on the 24th President Emmerson Dambudzo Mnangagwa promised to revive the economy in a Paul Kagame–Deng Xiaoping sort of way, if everyone would work hard. And he would pay back the white farmers ... open up for business ...

get all those corrupt cronies to repay the money … and so on. He might have been reading a World Bank script.

Actors ranging from the ZANU (PF)-approved chief justice to a SADC and AU only too happy to accept a soft coup if it rid them of the Mugabe thorn wiped their hands.[103] It would have been simply too inconvenient for SADC to admit this had been a coup: if labelled a coup, something would have had to be done. There was neither the stomach nor capacity for any of that. Besides, an intervention from inside the ZANU (PF) had accomplished something a semblance of electoral processes could not. And thanks to a couple of decades of social movement and MDC struggles for democracy–from the media to demonstrations to parliament–the coup-makers faced constraints that ended up acting in their favour–for a while.[104] Furthermore, the sheer frustration with Mugabe shared by the vast majority of Zimbabweans would have approved his removal by just about any means possible. The way was clear for a new cabinet packed with the sorts of people one would expect after a coup: soldiers–even before they were retired, although that little error was fixed a week or so later. Mnangagwa, one-time justice minister and lawyer, perhaps in a rush to pacify the already restive generals, had not read the constitution's clauses regarding non-parliamentarian appointments.[105] He had to assure Chiwenga that his vice-presidency did not mean loss of oversight over the armed forces: so, unconstitutionally but unchanged, Chiwenga was both a VP and minister of defence.[106] Intelligence and Politburo changes also altered the balance towards the military. Maybe, though, one cannot go further than activist, lawyer and aid worker Brian Kagoro's words: 'this was a coup over who runs petrol stations' … and, one might add, access to foreign exchange, mineral resources, taxi cabs … and farms?

By the end of 2017 and at 2018's start, Zimbabwe's soft coup left its people with as many questions about the future as the past. The elections of July the next year might have answered them positively, but the response of the soldiers to the protests of 1 August–at least six killed–put paid to that. So too would the welcoming of New Year 2019. The *really* morbid symptoms of Zimbabwe's extended 'emergency' would not take long to appear.

10

FROM COUP TO COVID

LUMPEN LEADERS AND REALLY MORBID SYMPTOMS

For the kleptocrat, ruling by licensing theft rather than seeking consent, money can achieve most of what needs to be done. For everything else there is violence.[1]

In their original sense, the moments between one ruler and another—the interregna—make up a short and precise gap. When the difference between one old king and a new queen amounted to much there may have been a sense that a qualitatively new order would appear when the interregnum ended. Given nearly a century of Gramsci—with translations to English at about the same time as Rhodesia's Pearce Commission—the interregnum has changed into something longer, wider and deeper. It is the way taken out of an organic crisis and into a new system of power and politics, perhaps even all the way to a new mode of production. As we experience the trials of living within one, it seems longer than ever imagined.[2] We might even be stuck in a permanent purgatory. Covid has made it worse: the symptoms are medically morbid indeed. The point turning out of it could be worse than imagined. Coups seldom—if ever—turn into new modalities of power and accumulation.

If the Zimbabwean case is an example, the turn deepened the tendencies leading to them. The words of the past linger, but also take on new meaning in a new era. New names mean new realities. If the new era does not arise, the words just blur with even more ambiguity–even duplicity–than before. The names go back to an unclear past. Maybe they were just *noms de guerre*.[3]

As Mugabe faced the certainty that his political end was near, he may have recalled some of his words from previous tight situations. While in the gilded prison under the Blue Roof, with drones circling overhead and his negotiators in direct contact with the military headquarters (they were more messengers than mediators), was he *compos mentis*? Would those words gain a new clarity with the passage of time and the inevitability of a near eternity turning back on itself? Percy Zvomuya wondered if his words at the Geneva conference in 1976 came back to haunt him.[4]

Zvomuya says Mugabe made a 'rousing speech', although he does not reference it.[5] It must have been to a large crowd–'rousing' needs big numbers–of international civil servants, journalists, sympathetic religious folk, and perhaps NGO workers. The location might have been in a church hall, a university lecture theatre, or in a Palais des Nations conference room. Mugabe explained–or did he expound? 'Any vote we shall have shall have been the product of the gun ... the gun which produces the vote should remain its security officer–its guarantor.' Sounded radical enough for the children of the 1960s and 1970s, not too ideological for the UN officers from relatively new 'non-aligned' states, and it fused Mugabe and the guerrilla soldiers. However, to the television interviewers from the 'West'–in a one-on-one mode but to thousands more in the false intimacy of the TV screen–he pushed another truth. 'We', he said–meaning the politicians of his liking, in ZANU–'are responsible for guiding the war ... we are the head of the army ... we derive our support from the masses of the people who support the armed struggle and are actually in agreement with the armed struggle.'[6] Consent and coercion wrapped up better than any Gramscian cultural theorist or post-Marxist articulator of contingency could do it. Had he read his Machiavelli yet?[7]

One presumes he read *The Prince* he borrowed–and kept–from the Zimbabwe Institute of Development Studies (note: there are few steps between stealing or burning books and faking PhDs, and larger ones to fraudulent elections and burning books; plagiarism sits in the middle).

He may have mused such matters during the few days in mid-November when history had not caught up to him yet. Had he uttered them few would have listened. His words as Sunday 19 November closed signified his last effort to beat history. He lost. It did not last. He no longer controlled the guns and was not about to trust the masses. The time had passed him for that. Nor did the soldiers, who only wanted the appearance of enthusiastic consent for a day or so: the time was either too soon or would never arrive.

Mugabe welcomed reporters a few months after his resignation. No longer of much consequence, his new masters allowed him to spout. After all, all the countries and institutions that mattered had accepted his downfall with unequalled glee albeit slippery qualifications, even after visits to the Blue Roof.[8] John Ray of ITV, for example, managed to get him at his 94-year-old best. Ray queried, 'Mnangagwa said you were a father to him ... what kind of a son has he been to you?' Mugabe laughed, 'Of course, sons will not always be obedient ones to the father ... he has got his own character ... and it's a character that I did not quite see. I did not know about him.' Was his route to power legal? Of course not, Mugabe replied. 'He was an imposition of the army. And we are saying let's get that position corrected.' Mugabe had only resigned to save the nation–not his family–from bloodshed:

> [Mnangagwa] wasn't elected. Let's get that corrected. In not wanting to be democratic he has betrayed the whole nation. We are topsy-turvy. We used to be the pride of SADC but we are not that anymore. We are a disgrace, not just to ourselves but to SADC, to the community. Why did we do this, just for the glory of an individual?[9]

Ray and his sometimes animated subject covered a lot of ground. Zimbabwe compared to the rest of Africa? 'We are not that bad ... our people don't starve, they have land, education ... we are the model.' But did you ruin the model? Ninety per cent of your people are unemployed. 'It's only now that it's doing that. ...' And later, when more problems are admitted: one person (he) could not have done all of this: 'Nooo. That is not one person. How can you say one person? One person was leading a party and the party had its own programme.'

Ray's penultimate line hit on the violence and politics question vexing Mugabe all his political life. Violations of human rights? 'We have been accused of that. Yes, on that side, some errors were done, they continue to be done, human rights, that's a very difficult area, I agree, we offended, ah oh, in regard to that. ...' Ray interrupted before Mugabe could go on, to quelling the remnants of *vashandi* perhaps, maybe to Gukurahundi, perchance Operations Murambatsvina and Makavhoterapapi. He might even have expounded on his favourite ballots and bullets analogies. Ray asked: 'Is that in terms of elections?' Mugabe, with the shoe beginning to go on a new foot, replied: 'In terms, no, I think it is not elections but it is terms of how we handled other people, the opposition etc. etc.' Ray wanted clarification: 'The violence?' Mugabe agreed: 'The violence yes...'

Ray's last question evoked the truth and false truths dialectic. Mnangagwa has declared free and fair elections, he said. Mugabe replied: 'Promises! A promise is not the reality, it's just a promise. If it's ... Fine! It's a good start and I'm prepared to join him in making the process, the promise, a reality. ...'

One imagines Mnangagwa was not keen to take up the offer. Mugabe may have been with a 'new' party at the time.[10] Later, on the eve of the July election, he announced to a large gathering of journalists and others over a tedious ninety minutes that he would likely vote for Nelson Chamisa of the MDC,[11] while rumours and blurry videos circulated attesting to his material support for that cause. All for the cause of democracy and freedom of speech.

What if John Ray had asked Mugabe, 'What kind of ruling class or mode of accumulation did you nurture?' Would Mugabe have remembered his 1977 advice to his newly concocted Central Committee? After he had dispelled the *vashandi* movement and burned the books of its marxisant college, he urged his comrades to

> read and understand what the fathers of [scientific socialist] theory actually say ... [and] examine the theory in the light of our history and the environment of our country. Only in this way can we evolve from the pure ideology of socialism a workable practical ideology for Zimbabwe.[12]

A couple of months before his March 2018 interviews to various media–including the *Zimbabwe Independent*[13]–the IMF produced a study of the world's 'shadow economies'.[14] If he or Ray had read it, they would have found that as of 2015 Zimbabwe had the world's third-largest 'shadow economy', at 60.6% of GDP, 'after Bolivia at 62.3% and Georgia at 64.9%.[15] They might have discussed whether the IMF

Working Paper's authors' decision not to include 'illegal' activity in their models would make a difference, and what the absence of the word 'class' meant in such a paper. They could have debated the notions of 'informal economy', the old Marxist idea of a 'reserve army of labour' or the more open one of 'hustling'.[16] If Mugabe had lived for a few more years, he might have read the stunning, deathly sober analysis of Brian Raftopoulos, Godfrey Kanyenze and Mabel Sithole, in which the IMF paper's shadow economy ranking is far from the only startling point.[17] It is required reading for anyone wanting to discern the long-term process of Zimbabwe's degeneration. But it too is slightly reticent to invoke the idea of class formation and primitive accumulation, be the latter delayed or stayed by the former, saying only that ZANU (PF) did not want to foster a 'business class' that would be 'independent of its patronage'.[18] For Zimbabwe, we need more analysis of how this 'patronage-dependent' formation works. How can one analyse this 'class' (to stretch the concept)? How does it relate to particular 'godfathers'–big men–during the Mugabe years and now in the realm of 'politics'? How, in the words of Zimbabwean activist Brian Kagoro as the events of 11/17 unfolded, could a coup be simply the result of a struggle to control a bunch of petrol stations? Perhaps there needs to be an 'African' method of class analysis.

During the days approaching this book's closure, Tom Burgis's *Kleptopia: How Dirty Money Is Conquering the World* made up my supplementary reading. As noted above, Burgis writes about Billy Rautenbach's munificence to the macabre military mode of Zimbabwe's 2008 elections. He and his Zimbabwean connections seem small players amidst the ones from Australia to New York and Hong Kong. Nor did Tony Blair help them out, as he did the president of Kazakhstan in soft-selling his massacre of protesting oil workers. Given his dismissal of the Zimbabweans' claims regarding land and his queries to Mbeki about launching a war against Mugabe from south of the Limpopo, it is hardly likely Blair could charge the Zimbabwean securocrats $13 million for his services, as Burgis claims he gained from Nursultan Nazarbayev.[19] Burgis does not discuss the late John Bredenkamp, a Zimbabwean resembling Rautenbach but in orders of magnitude. His relationships with British Aerospace Engineering, South African arms dealers, Emmerson Mnangagwa and the Democratic Republic of the

Congo raise a myriad of speculation that will most likely remain in the lands of mysteries.[20] It couldn't be that some Bredenkamp largesse made its way to the $90 million Burgis says Blair made in the first decade of his post-prime ministership, could it?[21] If so, it might explain why when, after an email exchange with Bredenkamp and me bearing uncanny similarity to one between him and Boris Johnson, he was in Zimbabwe when I called his UK office in mid-2008–during ZANU (PF)'s 'mini-Gukurahundi'.[22]

Rautenbach paid a few hundreds of millions of dollars to grease a few Zimbabwean coercive election wheels in return for mineral and agricultural rights–but he failed to manage Gécamines very well.[23] There are thousands around the world like him, from the friends of the Trumps and the Johnsons across to Central Asia and Brazil. Burgis calls them the Kleptocrats: it's not a new label but they do seem to have enjoyed their Utopia lately. Even those who do not break the law as blatantly as those in Burgis's book do little more than suck wealth out of the ground or buy into pre-existing technology. They do not add value to the process of production, as do 'real capitalists'. Chrystia Freeland extends the idea of 'rent-seeking' from its bureaucratic bias to the world of the post-Soviet-style oligarchs to define them. Some of her plutocrats actually innovate; she likes them more than she does those who plunder.[24] As Zimbabwe's post-coup years slide into the Covid era, one might revive examination of this class formation, and its relation to politicians and securocrats such as Mugabe and his successor.[25]

Well before 2021 rolled in, Zimbabwe demonstrated what was becoming a global truism: Covid exposed the weaknesses in countries' political and economic structures vividly.[26] Zimbabwe's first victim, at the end of March 2020, was the relatively wealthy son of a rich ZANU (PF) businessman, a ruling party-friendly broadcaster. Just in from New York, where he probably got the coronavirus, Zororo Makamba encountered an extremely ill-prepared medical system and died too soon. His brother was not shy about letting the media know: had their money and timing been right, an entrepreneurial medical supplier might have sold them a ventilator for $120,000.[27] A few months later, corruption implicating Mnangagwa's family and not a few health ministry officials was discovered in the procurement chain. The journalist who spread the news with his well-Tweeted social media presence began a long time in and out of jail.[28] The public-gathering proscriptions made good excuses for the state to clamp down on demonstrations: the 'July 31 Movement' thereby got off to an almost invisible start as the ruling party's acting information secretary conflated demonstrators with virus-carrying traitors and encouraged militia to defend their country.[29]

As the Mnangagwa moment stretched into the time of Covid, at the start of 2021 the pandemic soared to new heights. Up to the end of February 2021, Zimbabwe recorded 36,058 coronavirus cases, with 1,463 fatalities.[30] More than half occurred since the start of the year, when the recovery rate had already declined from 82% to 71%.[31] The tales circulating about Zimbabwe's ruling class and Covid are scarifying. By mid-January 2021 at least three of Zimbabwe's cabinet ministers had died of Covid. One was Sibusiso Moyo, the foreign affairs minister whose Chatham House session started me thinking about various versions of veracity.[32] Where, the social media rumour mongers asked, did these important politicians get the virus? The answer? At a grand party hosted by Kudakwashe Tagwirei. His involvement in many 'joint ventures' with the state, global capital, and local 'agricultural empowerment' schemes would score well on Burgis's long list of kleptocrats.[33] One of his more recent investments is a private hospital:[34] reports are that such institutions charge $3,000 for Covid treatment[35]– unless the rich too will get the free Chinese vaccines–indeed, forced to, like their poorer compatriots.[36]

During the panic accompanying the elite's succumbing, ZANU (PF) information secretary Nick Mangwana Tweeted an ambiguous message. Someone's message (since removed) claimed that some doctors kill 'political players'. Mangwana, a psychiatric nurse and until his move to Zimbabwe the head of ZANU (PF)'s UK branch, wrote that 'this is what's leading to the unfortunate conspiracy theory' that 'political activists hiding behind medical qualifications' are eliminating 'certain political players' in hospitals. He followed that with, 'in fact not just political players but medical assassins'. This message did not say he believes the conspiracy tales, but it attracted sufficient umbrage for him to apologise–a bit–and delete. If one of the state's main propagandists cannot craft a sensible Tweet, what does this say about its ability to sieve more sensitive information? Intentional or not, a ruling party's chief propagandist should not have typed it.[37] If it is true that while still in the UK he Tweeted that the images of soldiers killing demonstrators in the post-2018 election wake were fake news, he may be the perfect person for the job.[38]

Towards the end of February Tagwirei starred in a Burgis-like exposé of Zimbabwe's cartels and kleptocrats. With the uncertainty of the post-coup scramble, they were scrabbling too.[39] Yet Tagwirei might save one of the putschists' promises—compensating the long-suffering white farmers for the 'improvements' on their long-gone farms. Another of the companies in which he is involved is part of Kuvimba, a new state–private mining consortium hoping to raise at least $1 billion. That will go towards the $3.5 billion agreed to keep that constitutional promise. Presto, global capital will trust Zimbabwe's fealty to private property once again.[40]

Tales such as these bring to mind two African intellectuals and their immediate sociological responses to clear indications of Zimbabwe's crisis. I would label Thabo Mbeki and George Charamba as 'intellectuals' in the Gramscian sense. Such politicians and propagandists craft the political, ideological and policy-wonking ways to work through the combinations of coercion, corruption and consent by which the class of which they are a leading stratum tries to gain and maintain hegemony. They can even be soldiers when the consensual side of the classic dialectic wears thin. The immediacy of Mbeki and Charamba's invocation of Karl Marx's most viciously Victorian disapprobation of a social group could reveal the theoretical depths of their class analysis.

As noted previously, Mbeki's 2001 'advice' to Zimbabwe's 'party of revolution' was extremely critical. It boiled down to the fact that ZANU (PF)'s governance was so bad in the 1980s and 1990s that a ragged band of lumpenproletarians took control. The resultant 'land reform' exacerbated the devastating economic results of the 1990s structural adjustment policies, and this aggravated ZANU (PF)'s factional tendencies. How, Mbeki asked, did the war-vet section of this most disreputable of classes get to occupy the 'position ... as the "true" representative of the revolutionary project in Zimbabwe'? This sub-class had 'achieved a level of autonomy' so powerful that it weakened ZANU (PF)'s 'capacity ... to influence and lead the masses of the people'. Far from being 'bound by the practices normal to a party of revolution' they thus used 'force against the people, rather than the education and persuasion of these masses to support the revolutionary cause'.[41] To accuse a former teacher of neglecting his duties and allowing the untutored mass to take control must have been insult added to injury–if indeed Mugabe read the paper.

Mbeki did not deign to theorise the concept. Fortunately, some of his party's intellectuals did so nearly twenty years later when preparing its discussion documents for the 2020 National General Council meetings.[42] One of the papers in that collection spent considerable time on the 'lumpen' concept, expanding it far beyond its original base in the poorest of the poor. The discussion of this somewhat ideational stratum begins with a brief look at the expansion of the black South African middle class.[43] Between 2004 and 2013 it had 'more than doubled from 7% to 14% of the black population', and by then made up 'between 48% to 52% of the national total'.[44] Given that this class has had a lot of influence in 'social upheavals' in the history of world revolution, 'revolutionary vigilance requires that the ANC must always have keen interest' in its dynamics–'especial [sic] the black segment of this community'.[45] It is a heterogeneous class, but it seems to have one worrisome propensity: all of its layers ranging from the 'petty bourgeoisie' to the bureaucratic bourgeoisie, the political elites and the 'parasitic comprador bourgeoisie (many of whom rely on connections in state structures)' have been tempted by and tainted with 'a preponderance of greed, crass materialism and conspicuous consumption'.[46]

From there a jump occurs from the material–'objective', in the language of old Marxism–world to one more subjective. 'Significant swathes' of this 'middle strata' make up a 'veritable community of lumpen elements', in 'various spheres of human endeavour, including in the grey area between legality and illegality or in fully-fledged criminal networks'. Lumpens were part of the surplus, unemployed proletariat at capitalism's origins. They were doubly alienated from labour and productive activity in society: workers with work were alienated from the products of their labour, but the unemployed did not even have that–'unemployment was a curse' in their lives. Now, according to the discussion paper–and here it becomes normative rather than analytical–unemployment is 'a status issue [sic] a badge lumpens wear with honour'. Not working has been 'elevated to a virtue, a value they worship. Lumpens have a disdain for people who live their lives out of their honest labour.' Why? 'Because they (the lumpens) live better lives without working.' The ANC intellectual(s) here say(s) 'Marx castigated them as "parasitic criminals"', and it seems the 'valuable body of knowledge' on the lumpens 'concurs with the view of former president Thabo Mbeki'.[47] Someone has done Mbeki's work for him.

The lumpen elements thus defined inhabit various socio-economic groups: they are no longer determined by their long-term unemployment. Well entrenched in the parasitic bureaucratic bourgeoisie, they may be trying to capture state institutions so they can assist their own accumulation projects; similarly, so may those higher up in the state. Trade union leaders can swindle their members and their investment arms. Religious leaders might use their churches for 'spiritual deceit' with larcenous intent. Youth and student leaders can be as corrupt, so too can civil society groups demanding 'empowerment cuts'. Just ahead of the criminals on the list come the 'leaders of local protest movements who use distressed communities' grievances to worm their way into political, bureaucratic or procurement opportunities'. These lumpen cut across many classes—although very few are in the private sector. None, apparently, are leading the state. The worst among this gallimaufry are

> the more cunning … [who] profess a populist radicalism—often combined with narrow nationalism—that takes advantage of the slow progress in social transformation to legitimise their criminal enterprise … some of them position themselves publicly as sworn enemies of, and fighters against, the remnants of the colonial capitalist establishment. … this pseudo-revolutionary militancy is used to shield some of the worst cases of corruption.[48]

For the writer of this ANC document, the Economic Freedom Fighters epitomise this tendency. For Mbeki in 2001, for the 'party of revolution' to his north the only way to be saved from EFF-ism (not yet invented in South Africa) would be full engagement in the election process, swallowing the IMF medicine, and ignoring the racists as long as they could work with their capital and skills. ZANU (PF) did none of this. Mbeki forgot his prescriptions. He changed his mind on the land question once, but headed back when the idea hit South Africa too hard.[49] Since Mugabe did not follow Mbeki's advice, should we take it that the lumpen elements now pervade ZANU (PF)? When some of them rise to the top they might be called the lumpen-bourgeoisie.

It is not fair to compare George Charamba with Thabo Mbeki. Aside from the relative lack of power of a ZANU (PF) scribe beside the president of Africa's most pivotal of states, the latter has not had to face Grace Mugabe's public rage.[50] Mbeki did however face his own party dumping him. In contrast, the winners of the coup graced Charamba with more than a ringside seat in the process: he was one of the chosen to go to the Blue Roof to persuade Mugabe to accept his fate. He kept his job from the first republic to the second. For a while, his column marking the resurrection of his employer was penned under the moniker 'Bishop Lazarus', and he quoted the Bible as assiduously as only the recently converted can. Before becoming the president's spokesperson one of his information secretary jobs was to write the 'Manheru' column, therein having some time to wax theoretical in a milder version of the Mugabeist rhetorical style.[51] As I noted in this book's introduction, Charamba even utilised Gramsci to condemn the MDC for following unmoored Western ideologies instead of ZANU (PF)'s legacy. It was doomed, he wrote a few weeks after ZANU (PF)'s 2013 election 'victory',[52] to perpetual electoral ignominy due to an artificially imposed liberalism, hardly matching ZANU (PF)'s deeply rooted worldviews. The MDC could only create ephemeral movements, rhetoric and so on, which could only show the 'truth' because it was so wrong.[53] Of course, he failed to recall ZANU (PF)'s non-ideological means of ensuring victory, as if one of Habermas's ideal speech communities was the forum for it all. The commonality between Charamba and Mbeki is their penchant for calling out the lumpen. Before we see how Charamba employed Marx's insult, a couple of events that could be construed as coup-consolidations intervene. Indeed, if we see coups as a process—that is what turns events into structures—the killings of July 2018 and January the following year can be perceived as the doses of repression necessary to seal the conquest of November 2017. The concurrent confusion could be part of a process of hegemonic dissembling.

Five years after Charamba's Gramscian interlude, in mid-2018, much had been swept under the MAT (aka Militarily Assisted Transition). The coup: all but forgotten as a family spat. The mid-year election was about to conclude inconclusively. The two-thirds parliamentary majority to change the constitution was short by one seat with an uncertain count due to a data clerk's error; the presidential election was almost too close to count so finally a presidential victory at 0.7% past the run-off edge won the day ... sort of. However, it took so long to get to the tally that a raucous demonstration started as the count wavered. When it was over, the soldiers–not police; they gave up–killed at least six protesters and innocent bystanders. One observer recalled what she thought were ZANU (PF) youth handing out MDC T-shirts to vaga-bondish youth and prepping them up with booze and drugs; others saw the police dancing with oppositionists; someone told me there were 'professional demonstrators' (and dead) but did not know who paid them nor how much they got. Some MDC leaders had uttered pro-vocative encouragements for supporters to go street-side if they did not win: but when the shooting started MDC leader Nelson Chamisa was in the country saying prayers. The ZANU (PF) provincial head-quarters building seemed to be in danger. The police officer in charge was not able to handle things (by then quite a few of his number had skedaddled from their new masters, and others were still in the rural areas) so started the procedure to call in the soldiers, hardly trained in public-order mode. Either Chiwenga or Mnangagwa gave the requisite order for the soldiers to arrive: the commission of inquiry, headed by South Africa's most indecisive former president ever, could not muster the trail.[54] The most notable of viral videos and pictures was Zinyange Auntony's, of one seemingly masked soldier aiming straight off the screen, with his laughing or grimacing mate about to clap him on the shoulder.[55] At the time that photograph seemed as iconic as Eddie Adams' of Vietnamese Brigadier General Nguyễn Ngọc Loan shooting Nguyễn Văn Lém,[56] but there won't be any follow-up because the Zimbabwean soldier's face is covered, we don't see the victim, and this was not an American war. Mnangagwa ignored Motlanthe's milque-toast recommendations.[57]

What more could go wrong? The nicely packed courts let the MDC's challenge to the election count go–focusing on the count this time did not work, and the violence and intimidation (better hidden in this election than ever) before and during the election seems unquan-tifiable. Chamisa's refusal to recognise the election results was a thorn in ZANU (PF)'s side, so the work began on an age-old promise to get rid of it: factions were encouraged, fanned and split off; parliamentary funds were postponed; overactive members were rounded up and beaten. All that was political seemed on the way to wrap-up, folded into corruption, coercion and Christian escapes.

One problem for the 'second republic' remained, however: the economy. By the end of 2018 material life was worsening; 2019 promised more of the same. Efforts to re-dollarise were stop and go. The cabals would not disappear to favour the whiz-kid econometrician finance minister's calculator. Inflation at over 200% brought back memories of the hyper-2007–8 days. The unions (starting with nurses and doctors) were stepping up to the plate. The ZCTU called a stay-away (with what degree of consensus is uncertain). Two weeks into the new year, a few (dark) hours before flying off on a $74,000 per hour Boeing 787 Dreamliner plane ride to Russia and some of those post-Soviet enclaves where Tony Blair liked to offer his public relations services, followed by the ever-alluring Davos, Mnangagwa announced a 150% rise in the price of petrol.[58]

Did he foresee the chaos to ensue when the strikers struck and the soldiers shot? Likewise, would he be aware that leaving his vice-president, coup-master Dr Constantino Chiwenga,[59] to manage things meant that the confusion would channel to many deaths? At least seventeen, in fact, and as many rapes. The Human Rights Forum counted 1,803 violations, from the murders and rapes to beatings and police-dog bites. Dragnets arrested 654.[60] Twenty-six people and more were 'disappeared' from their township homes.[61] The well-known unionists, MDC members (5 MPs, 10 councillors and perhaps 200 ordinary members) and civil society leaders were put on trial for treason, subversion and inciting violence.[62] Indictments, trials and convictions persecuted en masse. This could be Zimbabwe's January *jambanja*, meaning 'violent argument' but later associated with the 2000+ land invasions and state-sanctioned violence.[63]

The confusion is the thing: police and soldiers may have been both encouraging and quelling the looting and rioting. Defence force chiefs say their uniforms had been stolen so the violence went even beyond 'rogue soldiers'.[64] Some were stoking the rebellion. Indeed, ZANU (PF) party chefs may have been handing out uniforms to youth. Who bought the approximately half-dozen new Nissan Hardbodies in which party youth drove up to the MDC headquarters to burn it up with petrol–and the twenty others? Why did 'real' soldiers rush to the townships to discipline fakes, who were marching in new uniforms with rifles pointed at each other's backs, rampaging houses and telling the occupants to get into the city? Unlike the whitewash commission after the post-election shootings just six months before, nothing has been called about the January *jambanja*. The most comprehensive report so far is clear on the regime's renewed authoritarianism, but with the added confusion of split security forces and inchoate opposition–and that in Bulawayo, the ethnic dimensions of the violence against shopkeepers was marked.[65]

The theoretical thing is this: what kind of ruling group presides over such devastating, nearly uncontrolled, coercion? As it was unfolding, Charamba was with his boss in a very cold Baku, Azerbaijan–no doubt tired, not at his loquacious best–and the state-run *Sunday Mail*'s journalist had to file a story from the president's spokesperson on the mess.[66] Charamba theorised thus: 'The progenitors and perpetrators of the violence are lumpen elements, not workers.' The stayaways turning into the 'orgy of violence' were planned by the MDC, which is thus a lumpen party (and which would be held responsible for the damage caused by the rioters). Workers' interests had nothing to do with the stayaway cum insurrection. As for the trade union congress once behind the MDC, Charamba opined that the 'member-less and moribund ZCTU cannot claim to have galvanised or mobilised workers'. Seemingly confused, though, he thought that the January *jambanja* reactivated the '1999 structures which unleashed violence on society, where MDC and ZCTU had that filial relationship', as if they had been sleeping for two decades. Charamba promised that the state's 'response to the violence thus far was a foretaste of things to come', including changes in 'certain constitutional provisions that were being abused by some political elements'. Was this a promise for a state of emergency? If this was the best theory the ruling party's head intellectual could come up with on the fly, it seems that lumpen thinking has informed it. Blame the opposition, controlled by lumpen elements. What do the psychologists call this? Projection?

The only thing he missed was the foreigners. For that, a 'brief' came out of the foreign ministry just as the ANC delegation came in to see what was up at the end of February.[67] Not just lumpen, these protests were 'an instrument of choice for subversive elements', they being 'particularly the MDC, rogue NGOs, hostile CSOs and Hostile Intelligence Services (HIS)'. The Centre for Applied Nonviolent Action and Strategies (CANVAS), set up by people who helped over-throw Slobodan Milošević twenty years ago, seemed to be of special concern.[68] They all are 'keen to effect regime change in Zimbabwe or force the consummation of a GNU or an NTA [National Transitional Authority]'. The brief notes the 'opposition's penchant for violence': they would raise the ante high enough to bring in the foreign troops under the R2P (Responsibility to Protect) Principle.

This was the document raised in my questions to foreign minister Sibusiso Moyo, at the Chatham House meeting in the middle of 2019. At the time, seven recruits of the foreign agents, up to no good in the Maldives for a CANVAS conference, had been arrested and charged with treason.[69] This was in advance of another demonstration planned by the opposition, called off just after it was banned. A few demonstra-tors who had arrived in the cities' centres before their arterial roads were blocked felt the heavy hand of the law, now a more certain entity for its guardians than six months before.[70] Moyo's answer regarding the omnipresence of truths and their murkier alternatives started this book's foray into lies and legacies.

The next time I encountered Charamba's words was when I was driving to a hermitage to write the penultimate draft of this book, in September 2020. Johannesburg's Radio 702 was hosting an interview with him, about his government's announcement that it would com-pensate the land-lost farmers of old, as discussed regarding Kudakwashe Tagwirei above. At that time it was unclear where the money would come from. Charamba said that if funds were short, the displaced farmers could take over new settlers' land not farmed productively. I suppose those unproductive peasants were not much better than lumpen. The interviewer asked if Charamba thought this would be enough to satisfy Western governments and investors, still concerned about Zimbabwe's human rights deficit. Charamba answered that 'the West' is never concerned with human rights when it came to money, and cited places like Saudi Arabia or China. Brian Kagoro, introduced above with the line about the string-pullers behind the coup's stage, was interviewed next. What did he think of this compensation programme? 'Black lives don't matter.' Perhaps Kuvimba will solve these problems.

What then do Mbeki's, Charamba's and the ANC's NGC thinkers' theoretical additions to the sociology of African politics and ideology perform for this study's interpretation of one once-powerful man and his country? For the lumpen (except for the luxuriating segments the ANC thinkers worry about), everything is an emergency. The *kukiya-kiya* social economy means always on the edge–in the alternative facts between law and hustling.[71] The most adroit hustlers rise to the top– but even for the fastest talkers and dealers that climb does not go far without some forceful assistance. In many ways this is the birthplace of some weapons of the weak.[72] If they are celebrated too much, Friedrich Hayek's camp is the next step–perhaps surrounded by the palisades of the mafioso-style oligarchs advised by Tony Blair. When the weak become strong in this way their politics is paranoia writ large–from the imperialists to their puppets all over they see threatening emergencies in every challenge. Sometimes the weak become too strong. James C. Scott's gently anarchist *Seeing Like a State* ended up with a salute to Hayek's 'voluntarism', without noticing that Hayek thought little of the subalterns' use of the state to create a social democracy with fuller freedoms.[73]

Did Mugabe then create a 'lumpen' party–state complex, or vice versa? Is there an answer beyond saying the only way out of the question is to research and think further? The conditions in the interregna as modes of production and power move are usually morbid. They may or may not move on to recognisable–and even 'progressive'–forms. What is the legacy of a man like Mugabe in this emergency interregnum? Was he ever a progressive Caesar or always a dictatorial Louis Napolean Bonaparte, albeit with a hustling lumpen rather than an 'absolutist' state? The copout answer: the process is dialectical–and so far in Zimbabwe no one has arisen who will bend the stick too far from the one planted fifty years ago. One answer will turn on the question: *après Mugabe quoi*? *Le déluge* or *la disette* and *la sécheresse*? Storms make greener pastures.

EPILOGUE

ON THE OCCASION OF A HARARE BOOK LAUNCH

As I was about to begin a long-delayed ultimate draft of this book I received an unexpected invitation to Harare. After a long absence, mostly due to Covid, the opportunity could not be missed. Besides the overdue visit, the offer to review Godfrey Kanyenze's *Leaving So Many Behind*[1]—live!—was impossible to refuse. All of 3 March 2022 was taken up in the sumptuous Meikles Hotel's conference room with well over 100 participants of many generations discussing the themes of Kanyenze's *tour de force*. Panels and Zoom presentations started with comprehensive analyses of Zimbabwe's many economic dead ends and their global context. They continued with focus on his passionate and determined arguments about the need for thorough and democratic dialogue concerning the political interventions that could create the conditions for productive and fairly distributed wealth. More about that later: for now, a short survey of what remains of Mugabe's legacy is in order. Just under four days of conversation and reading can unravel a lot of recent history, but transforming them to a concise compendium is suitable punishment for so much neglect.

A short walk around Harare's Unity Square the morning after the launch served notice of some of the changes to, and continuity with, the 'Second Republic's' inheritance from the leading light of Zimbabwe's first political iteration. Situated with the Meikles across Jason Moyo Avenue to the south and Zimbabwe's parliament buildings to the north, the park hosted its usual visitors, from the sleeping homeless to professionals striding toward the stock exchange and lawyers' offices to the east, and the flower stalls facing the hotel. But the twenty or so police officers, most wearing helmets, masks and bulky bullet-proof vests, some reposed together on the grass while others struck a more alert pose, seemed something menacingly different.[2]

So too were the many ZANU (PF) posters advertising the merits of municipal and parliamentary candidates for the by-elections to come in a few weeks. Elections are nothing new in Zimbabwe, but by-elections on such a scale are: give or take 130 seats up for grabs, depending on various legal disputes. They were a preview to the national round around the bend in 2023. That needs some explaining. So too does the 'new' party contesting the plebiscite. Thus the final 'political' portion of this book, to be followed by 'economics' including their agrarian dimension, and a review of the Holy Trinity excursions in the era of Putinism whilst discussing the book launch that occasioned my latest visit to the reincarnation of *Kleptopia* on the fringes of the world economy.[3]

The new party was the Citizens Coalition for Change (CCC). Emerging from the embers of the original MDC, it appeared on January 24 while the ostensibly Covid-delayed by-elections approached at the end of March, as if erstwhile MDC-A leader Nelson Chamisa had single-handedly conjured it. Twenty-eight seats would be contested by incumbent and aspirant parliamentarians.[4] VP Constantino Chiwenga, who promised to crush the CCC like lice 'on a flat stone and then flatten it to the extent that even flies will not make a meal out of it',[5] was a vicious critic. Slightly less visceral *Herald* opinion columnists challenged the MDC's constitutional and other malfeasance,[6] as did one-time MDC activists maintaining their antipathy to Chamisa and wishing for the old days to return, but writing for the same paper.[7] So too did leftists of various angles from the old and new party, bemoaning that the new generation bore no trace of their influences during the days of Munyaradzi Gwisai's International Socialist Mondays at the University of Zimbabwe, complementing the mobilised trade unions: they worried about what they saw as Chamisa's evangelically inspired and neoliberal authoritarian populism[8] and hoped there would be enough space for the likes of Tendai Biti to keep within the CCC ambit after its congress. Yet there was good reason for the party's new name, although it may have been formed with unseemly, unstructured, and again unconstitutional, haste.

The MDC-A had been betrayed by Thokozani Khupe and Douglas Mwonzora, breaking off from the Chamisa group almost certainly with ZANU (PF)'s help. They took the MDC-A label while the Morgan Richard Tsvangirai House was conveniently emptied by the ruling party-state's armed contingent, but within no time they split, suffixed to A and T. Given the ruling party's compliant judiciary and the former MDC-A's legal laxity, there was little choice but to form a new entity in order to meet ZANU (PF)'s reticence to call by-elections that would reconfigure the opposition seats Mwonzora had emptied.[9] Chamisa's MDC-A/CCC also lost access to parliamentary funding;[10] yet the invention of crowd-funding would at least enable both leaders and individual candidates to gain such resources. The latter had never been served well by the centre. Thus Chamisa's call 'to everyone who is progressive ... Zapu come ... It's not about positions, but the change we want for the people of Zimbabwe ... There is enough space for everyone ... [but] ... Once bitten twice shy. We are going to make sure that we don't allow ZANU (PF) to infiltrate us'.[11]

Falling prey to prediction is never good for an academic observer of politics, but at the time of writing it is hard to foresee much electoral or other of Fortuna's grace for the MDC renegades: being ZANU (PF) playthings cannot work for long. The only questions to ask are why the Chamisa contingent did not see the playground taking shape long ago, and how many infiltrators from the other side it still holds. As this book makes clear, Mugabe's legacy (and formation) included constant fissuring congruent to the divide and rule tactics of those in power. Such politics do not make lasting commitments and purpose.

It remains to be seen if the party wasting in Mugabe's wake will undertake another coup, or revert to its tried route of uniting while electoral threats loom. Along with restive junior officers, the G-40 leftovers may find the allies for whom they lurk.[12] If party spokesperson Christopher Mutsvangwa is emblematic (recall his feverish role in the coup), the paranoia inspired by such probability spreads far and wide: 'there is an unspoken alliance', he says, 'between CCC, some MDC elements and some people who may manifest themselves as ZANU (PF)'. Of course, it has manifested on social media.[13] All this may prove the old adage that coups follow coups, although not as clones. Another mode of duck walking may be invented. It is likely to entail much shedding of blood.

As for the economic dimensions of post-purgatorial invocations, changes in the bus, kombi and taxi industry since 2019 suffice. Belarus and China have sold 432 buses to the 'partially privatise[d]' Zupco since Emmerson Mnangagwa's visit to the remnants of Soviet empire during Zimbabwe's January 2019 *jambanja*.[14] As the president commissioned a new arrival of shiny coaches, he said that Zupco should 'operate at the highest level of efficiency in line with our vision of a modern, highly integrated multi-modal transport which can play a key role in the development of our economic and social sectors ... given that we have now transitioned from stabilisation to growth, the workforce should not spend valuable productive time waiting for transport'. The investors, 'including sons and daughters of our country', he said, will 'create jobs as well as lower the cost of bus procurement in foreign currency as many of the parts can be sourced locally'.[15] The latter part of this statement appeared unlikely in the immediate term, given the fully built appearance of the buses on show. Moreover, as a local logistics graduate put it, the sons and daughters are 'them' (i.e., the party-military securocrats), and they also own many of the kombis that returned to service after their mid-Covid banning. In mid-February 'they' raised the fare for buses from 50 to 80 Zimbabwean dollars (the low informal exchange rate being 200 to US$1; those with bigger connections getting 250), while for kombis the fare was 100.[16] Meanwhile, the small and often battered *mushikashika* (referring to their dodgy and dangerous characteristics) take a host of legal and other risks.[17] However, the laws are mostly honoured in the breach because the tiny taxis are owned by officers of the law and sovereign security. You don't have to follow the law if it is you. This may be an example of the particular blend of 'hustling' and the securocrats' economy that is shaping Africa's urban economy. Perhaps the world's, too, as 'gig economies' bring what is left of a working class to the crumbs of the plutocrats' well-polished tables.[18]

Considerations of the agrarian dimensions of Zimbabwe's political economy take us to Tendai Murisa's presentation at the sumptuous book launch presaging this postscript. The post–Fast Track Land

Reform Programme (FTLRP) era will last a long time, as any reader of Marx in the original would know: primitive accumulation does drag on. Murisa's words sounded nearly a praise-poem version of De Soto's peon to the (creative) destruction of dead capital,[19] but the paper on which his talk was based is more nuanced—a sad, almost tragic, recognition of the difficulties of moving from the form of capitalist agriculture often signalled as 'economic dualism'[20] and by others as a 'vernacular' form of tenure,[21] to something fairer in the mists. The slow pace of post-white-commercial farm reform is replete with various military-private attenuations to models of classical mode of primitive accumulation. The corruption-ridden and inefficient 'Command Agriculture' meant for the aspiring-plus yeomanry[22] to the more straightforward land grabs portrayed in Murisa's paper indicate the shades between black and white within such processes. No doubt a brief article in *The Herald*, blaming the banks for not regarding 99-year leases as credit-worthy, is but one example of ideological blame rather than uncertainty.[23] The ambiguity of Shonhe and Scoones' summary is clear enough: the new agricultural modalities are blends of 'populist rhetoric [and] ... liberalized, market-oriented policies ... also result[ing] in the return of state (and military)-led corporatist interventionism and authoritarianism': and it is all 'framed in terms of a commitment to a "developmental state"' in the Chinese mould. The process is 'contingent, politically mediated' and abounding in the many stripes of 'social differentiation'.[24]

The celebration of *Leaving So Many Behind* raised these issues and many more. Kanyenze adds much needed weight to discussions of Zimbabwe's recent economic history. His sweep *and* detail make some sense of the increasingly frenetic economic policies of Zimbabwe's ruling group as it waded through the travails inherent in the phases of Mugabe's cobbled model of factional accumulation. As *Leaving* took us to the policies following the FTLRP, Kanyenze could only comment that those behind them (probably Mugabe himself) must have thought they were alchemists.[25] Indeed, as Adebayo Olukoshi ended his keynote presentation on the global economic ideologies that structured at least the early phases of Zimbabwe's paths to its current netherworld (today's 'austerity for prosperity' worse by far than the devastating 1990s' structural adjustment, Kanyenze warns[26]) he ended on a plaintive note. Africa's ruling groups—the 'leadership core', he said—must develop policies that enable people's self-respect and dignity. It struck me that *this* book's pages resonate with that: the 'leadership' many of the launch's participants harked towards is actually not that different from Zimbabwe's, and much of its peers around the world. Many of Zimbabwe's progressive intelligentsia would agree with Takura Zhangazha's concerns about how a progressive core can emerge from a culture mandating leadership based on the materialism that extols wealth 'no matter how it was acquired' and gives those with it 'a mandate not only to lead but to be chosen to lead.' Worse, in many cases those with such resources 'choose those that would lead'.[27] Kanyenze, Olukoshi, Zhangazha, and many others are looking for a 'progressive' *class* on which to hinge their leaders.

This is what Gramsci meant by his 'organic intellectuals', but in Zimbabwe, and much of Africa, the class—be it an industrialising (or otherwise job-creating) bourgeoisie or a vibrant proletariat—in which they must be rooted and help lead is buried within the uncertainties of 'development's' long, unevenly articulated interregnum. What sort of hegemony and nation-state formation can be crafted on such slender bases? It is hard to find a deeply rooted ideology arising from the distortions of colonialism and its thereafter, which have stalled the process eventuating in a foundational class structure.

Moreover, the rise of finance capital and its contradictions, one of which is its articulation with the enclave warlords and oligarchs described in Burgis' *Kleptopia*[28]—which, remember, includes Billy Rautenbach and the tale of his support for Mugabe[29]—have led to the 'morbid symptom' of Putin's war against Ukraine. London financiers chose not to—or, blinded by the ideologies celebrating their pursuits, could not—see this coming. As this book shows, the Zimbabwean securocrats are much like their Belarusian peers. After (and excepting) Gukurahundi, the increasingly 'intra' ethnic dimension of 'Shona' ruling group politics has yet to reach the South African nadir of July 2021:[30] 'nation-state construction' is nearly as hard as progressive primary accumulation processes. And for the global paragons of liberal democracy? The last few decades have perverted the particularly American perception that its highest aspirations are cradled in the USA's arms into a paranoid fantasy.[31] Can more be expected for an

African leader's dreams? Zimbabwe and its global context remind us that change is the constant within development's Holy Trinity. It is very hard to ameliorate the violence aligned with it.

Perhaps one can expect more from Africa's dreams and the nightmares surrounding them. Fela Kuti's somewhat chastised and sanitised reincarnation could transform it.[32] We might not have to change species to work it out, but we will have to do more than envelop ourselves with new names.[33]

NOTES

PROLOGUE—INTERREGNA: BEYOND THE LIMINITY OF LEGACIES

1. ThoughtCo, 'Does the catholic church still believe in purgatory?' *Learn Religions*, 26 August 2020, available at: learnreligions.com/does-the-catholic-church-still-believe-in-purgatory-4096467. (I accessed all links December 2020 to February 2021.)
2. My efforts to move away from the authorial mode of evading 'I' are part of this book's transitional condition. I will embark on the first-person mode in due course–but switch back often. It is foreign to an academic from the old school of supposedly detached objectivity.
3. Zabala 2020; Stahl 2019.
4. Pollitt 2017.
5. Radar, 'Jonso can pee all he wants–from outside', *The Herald*, 2 December 2017, available at: https://www.herald.co.zw/jonso-can-pee-all-he-wants-from-outside/.
6. Moore 2016b.
7. Moore 2018b; cf. Tendi 2020.
8. Moore 2019; Adebajo 2021.
9. Mullin 1982.
10. James Hamill, 'Mnangagwa and the military may mean more bad news for Zimbabwe', The Conversation, 16 November 2017, available at: https://theconversation.com/mnangagwa-and-the-military-may-mean-more-bad-news-for-zimbabwe-87646; Melissa Mayntz, 'Duck species list', The Spruce, 17 September 2020, available at: https://www.thespruce.com/duck-species-list-385436.
11. Matyszak forthcoming; Charles Laiton, 'Army intervention constitutionally correct: High Court', *Newsday*, 25 November 2017, available at: https://www.newsday.co.zw/2017/11/army-intervention-constitutionally-correct-high-court/; Jason Brickhill, 'Coup and constitution in Zimbabwe part 1: the mili-

tary action is profoundly unconstitutional', Oxford Human Rights Hub, 18 November 2017, available at: https://ohrh.law.ox.ac.uk/coup-and-consti-tution-in-zimbabwe-part-1-the-military-action-is-profoundly-unconstitutional/ and 'Coup, constitution and the court: Zimbabwean constitutional court white-washes flawed rigged elections', Oxford Human Rights Hub, 24 August 2018, available at: http://ohrh.law.ox.ac.uk/coup-constitution-and-the-court-zim-babwean-constitutional-court-whitewashes-flawed-rigged-elections/.

12. 'Almost news with Chester Missing', eNCA, 17 February 2019, available at: https://www.youtube.com/watch?v=__NKeFDxTw4.

13. Moore 2017: 22–3; David Moore, 'Zimbabwe: a future finely balanced between democracy and militarisation', The Conversation, 28 August 2018, available at: https://theconversation.com/zimbabwe-a-future-finely-balanced-between-democracy-and-militarisation-102214.

14. Ibbo Mandaza, 'When cabinet has become redundant amid a growing securo-cratic culture', NewsHawks, 12 February 2021, available at: https://thenews-hawks.com/when-cabinet-has-become-redundant-amid-a-growing-securocra-tic-culture.

15. Julia Cassaniti, a colleague at Clare Hall, Cambridge, helped me recognise the Baader–Meinhof moment. Ann Pietrangelo, 'What the Baader-Meinhof phe-nomenon is and why you may see it again … and again', healthline, 17 December 2019, available at: https://www.healthline.com/health/baader-meinhof-phe-nomenon.

16. Moore 2013.

17. Mhanda 2011; Saul 1979, 1980, 2016; Moore 1995, 2014c, 2016a; Mazarire 2011; cf. Makanda 2014.

18. Lisa O'Kelly, 'Chris Mullin: "I dedicated the book to Jo Cox"', The Guardian, 30 March 2019, available at: https://www.theguardian.com/books/2019/mar/30/chris-mullin-friends-of-harry-perkins-political-thriller-interview.

19. 'Editorial: Here comes the Second Republic!' Bulawayo Chronicle, 25 August 2018, available at: https://www.chronicle.co.zw/editorial-comment-here-comes-the-second-republic/.

20. Zamchiya 2020; also David Moore, 'A false new dawn for Zimbabwe: what I got right, and wrong, about the mood', The Conversation, 2 August 2018, avail-able at: https://theconversation.com/a-false-new-dawn-for-zimbabwe-what-i-got-right-and-wrong-about-the-mood-100971 and 'Fantasy that Mnangagwa would fix Zimbabwe now fully exposed', The Conversation, 22 January 2019, available at: https://theconversation.com/fantasy-that-mnangagwa-would-fix-zimbabwe-now-fully-exposed-110197.

21. David Moore, 'Zimbabwe now: post-coup, mid-Covid; continuing crises, cor-ruption, and confusion', African Arguments: Debating Ideas, 24 November 2020, available at: https://africanarguments.org/-2020/11/24/zimbabwe-now-post-coup-mid-covid-continuing-crises-corruption-and-confusion/. Cf.

Ray Ndlovu, 'Covid-19 breaks Zimbabwe, health minister denies disaster', Biznews, 25 January 2021, available at: https://www.biznews.com/briefs/2021/01/25/covid-19-breaks-zimbabwe.

22. Although, as my good friend and colleague Joost Fontein (2018, 2022) might say, Mugabe's death could mean more than his life. See 'Burying Bob', The Thinker, 84, 2, 2020, 4-11, available at: https://journals.uj.ac.za/index.php/The_Thinker/article/view/210.

23. Matyszak 2016 is the ultimate and most detailed exposition of ZANU (PF)'s 2014 expulsion of its vice-president, Joice Mujuru. Tendi's 2020 pointillist technique is similar but with fuzzier depth of field on Mujuru's late husband, the kingmaker turned against the king who may thus have met a flame-engulfed death.

24. Southall 2013.

25. In mid-2008, Thabo Mbeki, the soon-to-be-ousted South African president, pushed his Zimbabwean counterpart into a 'government of national unity'. This was after ZANU (PF) killed around 170 MDC voters and even some who voted for ZANU (PF) MPs but not the president, in the June 'run-off' after a March election the opposition candidate had won, but not according to the rulers' count a majority. The GNU lasted from early 2009 to the mid-2013 election. Moore 2018b; Raftopoulos 2013; Abey 2015. More in Chapter 5.

26. Southall 2013: 349–50.

27. Tendai Biti, 'MDC: Collapse of education system an indictment of ZANU PF: MDC Press Statement', SW Radio Africa, 13 October 2008, available at: www.swradioafrica.com/pages/mdconeduc131008.htm.

28. Robert Gordon, 'Academic advocates', Southern African Review of Books, March–April 1995, 3–5.

1. INTRODUCING INTERPRETATIONS: 'MEN' BECOMING HISTORY; EVENTS BECOMING STRUCTURES

1. Zabala 2020: 156; Gramsci 1971: 276. Reproduced with the kind permission of McGill-Queen's University Press, Lawrence and Wishart, and International Publishers. Readers wishing to avoid 'interpretation' (or theory) may jump to 'facts' in the next chapters.

2. Robert Gordon, 'Academic advocates', op. cit.

3. Kirk Helliker, 'Grace Mugabe's thesis does not meet minimum academic requirements', Mail and Guardian, 30 January 2018, available at: https://mg.co.za/article/2018-01-30-grace-mugabes-thesis-does-not-meet-minimum-academic-requirements/; Lex Vambe, 'Chiwenga PhD raises a stink after SA professor is killed by hitman after uncovering academic fraud at KZN university', PaZimbabwe, 3 December 2018, available at: https://www.pazimbabwe.com/business-49496-chiwenga-phd-raises-a-stink-after-sa-professor-is-killed-by-hitman-after-uncovering-academic-fraud-at-kzn-university.html.

4. Compagnon 2011; Moore 2008b.
5. Southall 2013: 259.
6. Bratton 2014; Shumba 2017.
7. David Moore, 'Zimbabweans must draw on years of democratic struggle to stop a repeat of Mugabe's militarism', The Conversation, 22 November 2017, available at: https://theconversation.com/zimbabweans-must-draw-on-years-of-democratic-struggle-to-stop-a-repeat-of-mugabes-militarism-87961; David Moore, 'Thinking after Zimbabwe's con-coup: now, then, and then again', *Zimbabwe Briefing: A Crisis in Zimbabwe Coalition Report*, 13 July 2018 [December 2017], available at: https: //www.zimbabwebriefing.org/single-post/2018/07/13/Thinking-after-Zimbabwe%E2%80%99s-ConCoup-Now-Then-and-Then-Again. Derek Matyszak has also employed this metaphor. Surely many others have too. I did not see his until well after I had used it! 'Après moi le déluge: Succession and the ZANU PF party constitution', Harare: Research and Advocacy Unit, July 2012, available at: http://www.archive.kubatana.net/html/archive/demgg/120730rau.asp?sector=DEMGG&year=2012&range_start=631. Matyszak left the 'I am the state' idea to the side, presuming perhaps that his readers would make the connection. It is worth elaborating.
8. Rowen 1961; Herman 2005.
9. Moore 2018b: 6.
10. For those uninitiated to Zimbabwean politics, this phrase refers to Gukurahundi, Shona for the storms and chaff metaphor. It has come to mean the near genocide in the 1980s, committed by ZANU (PF) against thousands of people in the Matabeleland and Midlands provinces: Doran 2017; Cameron 2018. It has precedents: ZANU (PF) labelled 1979 the 'year of the people's storm'.
11. Kriger 2012.
12. Moore 2014a and 2014b.
13. Tendi 2020.
14. David Moore, 'Bill Freund 1944–2020: a professor who wore the weight of history lightly', The Conversation, 14 September 2020, available at: https://theconversation.com/bill-freund-1944-2020-a-professor-who-wore-the-weight-of-history-lightly-145652.
15. Saul 2020a and 2020b. Saul is a key driver of this particular intellectual project since its germination in his 1980 post-graduate seminar at York University, followed by his supervision of my doctoral dissertation. Saul's involvement with Frelimo and its support for the *vashandi* movement that Mugabe thought was a coup and is the essence of this book's third chapter led to our–continuing–interest: Moore 1990; Saul 1979, 2016.
16. Cf. Tomás 2021.
17. 'Mozambique sees militia violence dwindle as military gains steam', Africanews, 9 February 2021, available at: https://www.africanews.com/2021/02/09/mozambique-sees-militia-violence-dwindle-as-military-gains-steam//.

18. Geoffrey York, 'In South Africa, it's bullets over ballots as political attacks spread', *Globe and Mail*, 9 October 2017. The numbers? 'At least 40 in KwaZulu-Natal', according to York. During Zimbabwe's coup? In the mid-thirties, three good sources have advised me. Others say few were killed, but around twenty agents in the Central Intelligence Organisation (which along with the police forces, albeit heavily infiltrated by military intelligence, was with the losing side of the coup) were beaten to near death. The publicly announced number killed is two cabinet members' security guards.

19. Hali Healy, 'Xolobeni and Somkhele: More assassinations feared as state drags its feet', Daily Maverick, 29 November 2020, available at: https://www.dailymaverick.co.za/article/2020-11-29-xolobeni-and-somkhele-more-assassinations-feared-as-state-drags-its-feet/.

20. Zamchiya 2020; David Moore, 'Zimbabwe now: Post-coup, mid-Covid; continuing crises, corruption, and confusion', African Arguments: Debating Ideas, 24 November 2020, available at: https://africanarguments.org/2020/11/24/zimbabwe-now-post-coup-mid-covid-continuing-crises-corruption-and-confusion/.

21. White 2003.

22. Fontein 2018; Tendi 2020.

23. Grinin 2010: 95, 116–17, 122.

24. Marx 1963 [1852].

25. Antonini 2020.

26. Saul 2020a: 155.

27. Vladimir Lenin, 'Letters from afar: the first stage of the first revolution', 7 March 1917, available at: https://www.marxists.org/archive/lenin/works/1917/lfafar/first.htm.

28. Pula 2018: 25.

29. Ndlovu-Gatsheni 2015.

30. Chitando 2020: 7–9.

31. Kriger 2020: 1131.

32. Matyszak 2016: 6.

33. Leonard Cohen, 'Anthem', in *The Future* (New York: Columbia, 1992), available at: https://www.azlyrics.com/lyrics/leonardcohen/anthem.html.

34. Zabala 2020.

35. 'Almost news with Chester Missing', eNCA, 17 February 2019, available at: https://www.youtube.com/watch?v=__NKeFDxTw4.

36. Brenner 1977; Bernstein 2010 is as good as one can get on the 'agrarian question' at the root of capitalist transformations today.

37. Moore 2003a, 2004, 2014b.

38. Mann 1999, 2005.

39. Perelman 2000; Desai 2012; Barbalet 2019: 31; Roberts 2020.

40. Gellner 1997.

41. Wade, quoted in Moore 2017a: 267–315.
42. Ferguson 2015.
43. Desai and Heller 2020: 1261.
44. Ibid.: 1261–2.
45. Applebaum 2020; cf. Watkins 2020.
46. Webber 2008; Barbalet 2019.
47. Gavin Jacobson, 'An examination of hegemony and power in The H-Word', *New Statesman*, 17 June 2017, available at: https://www.newstatesman.com/culture/books/2017/06/examination-hegemony-and-power-h-word.
48. Arrighi 1983, 2007, 2010; Cox 1981, 1983, 1987; Frank 1998; Wallerstein 2003.
49. Graeber 2018; Nathan Heller, 'The bullshit-job boom', *New Yorker*, 7 June 2018.
50. Gramsci 1971: 238, 242–3.
51. Gramsci 1971: note, p. 97. Perhaps given that this book examines a particular country in the 'Third World' a typo in the 1999 e-version of *Prison Notebooks* is more than a coincidence. The phrase following the one quoted above goes like this: 'They correspond to the NGOs and junior officers in the army, and also partly to the higher officers who have risen from the ranks.' Besides the inadvertent prediction of global civil society and its missionaries, Gramsci also made us realise that the military needs hegemony too. On how the development industry is a microcosm of larger hegemonic battles, see Moore 2007.
52. Priestland 2012–equally so is the case if soldiers or merchants gain too much power, or a devilish duo arises.
53. Friedman 2015.
54. Gramsci 1971: 182.
55. Moore 2019: 86–7.
56. Gramsci 1971: 367.
57. Richard Bourke, 'Burke and India', *Open*, 9 September 2015, available at: https://openthemagazine.com/essays/open-essay/burke-and-india/; Bourke, 2017; cf. Marx 1853.
58. Eagleton 2018: 17.
59. Timothy Garton Ash, 'The future of liberalism', *Prospect*, 9 December 2020, available at: https://www.prospectmagazine.co.uk/magazine/the-future-of-liberalism-brexit-trump-philosophy.
60. Wolpe, 1972: 428, in Moore 2019: 85–emphasis in Wolpe's original.
61. Moore 2019: 101; 'Traditional authorities, and the new peasants in ZANU-PF's Zimbabwe', Custom Contested, available at: http://www.customcontested.co.za/ chiefs-and-zanu-pf/
62. British Embassy Harare, 'Five Fold Increase of Chevening Scholarship Awards to Zimbabwe', 28 August 2015, available at: https://www.gov.uk/government/news/five-fold-increase-of-chevening-scholarship-awards-to-zimbabwe-2.
63. Unless otherwise noted, the acronym MDC refers to the Movement for

Democratic Change more or less in its original form, minus splinters, led by either Morgan Tsvangirai or, after his February 2018 death, his successor, Nelson Chamisa.

64. Nathaniel Manheru, 'Zim: Keeping the eye on the ball', *The Herald*, 30 August 2013, available at: https://www.herald.co.zw/zim-keeping-the-eye-on-the-ball/. Thanks to Brian Raftopoulos for sending this to me on its publication. Moore 2014a: 102–3.

65. Matyszak 2017; Gramsci 1971: 248.

66. Gramsci 1971: 248.

67. Dubbeld 2019: 133.

68. Fontein 2009, 2010.

69. Rutherford 2017.

70. Anderson, P. 2017: 147.

71. Foster-Carter 1978: 74.

72. Moore 2003b.

73. Friedman 2015, chapter 4.

74. Mann 1999, 2005.

75. David Moore, 'So what's a post-coup pre-election like? Zimbabwe's democracy after Mugabe–Phase I', *Zimbabwe Briefing: A Crisis in Zimbabwe Coalition Report*, 27 July 2018, https://www.zimbabwebriefing.org/single-post/2018/07/27/So-what%E2%80%99s-a-post-coup-pre-election-like-Zimbabwe%E2%80%99s-Democracy-after-Mugabe-%E2%80%93-Phase-I.

76. Most of this paragraph is from Marx 1972 [1867].

77. Marx in Barbalet 2019: 31.

78. Mkandawire 2015, 2020; Pitcher et al. 2009.

79. Richard Joseph, 'Prebendalism and dysfunctionality in Nigeria', Africaplus, 26 July 2013, available at: https://africaplus.wordpress.com/2013/07/26/prebendalism-and-dysfunctionality-in-nigeria/.

80. Ekeh 1975, albeit even with over 1,600 citations ignored by most of the above, is a good antidote.

81. Leys 1994: 44–5.

82. Adebajo 2010.

83. Cramer 2006.

84. Jameson 1986: 311, 321.

85. Edgar Lawrence Doctorow, 'Four characters under two tyrannies', *New York Times Book Review*, 29 April 1984, available at: https://www.nytimes.com/1984/04/29/books/four-characters-under-two-tyrannies.html.

86. To borrow from the title of Moore 2015b. Munyikwa 2019, for Gramsci applied to post-1980 Zimbabwe.

87. Stahl 2019 appears to have inspired investigations of interregnums (*sic*).

88. Zabala 2020.

89. Ian Murray, 'Covid-19 underscores media's responsibilities when "the first casualty of war is truth"', Ethical Journalism Network, 8 April 2020, available at: https://ethicaljournalismnetwork.org/covid-19-underscores-medias-responsibilities-when-the-first-casualty-of-war-is-truth.

90. Chatham House, 'Zimbabwe's international engagement', 12 July 2019, available at: https://www.chathamhouse.org/events/all/members-event/zimbabwes-international-engagement.

91. 'Sibusiso Moyo: Zimbabwe foreign minister dies from Covid-19', BBC, 20 January 2021, available at: https://www.bbc.com/news/world-africa-55731440.

92. See page 166 for details of how S. B. Moyo averted a worrisome move within the 18 November 2017 marches favouring 'Operation Restore Legacy'.

93. Apparently Ambassador Melanie Robinson, a veteran of the development industry, was tutoring the nuances of World Bank-speak assiduously to Zimbabwe's new leaders. See 'How Britain's foreign aid bonanza has created a new Goliath, towering over the Foreign Office', Daily Telegraph, 25 May 2019. In 2020 these two wings of the UK state merged: which one won?

94. United Nations, 'Plundering of DR Congo natural resources: Final report of the Panel of Experts (S/2002/1146)–Burundi', 2002/1146, available at: https://reliefweb.int/report/burundi/plundering-dr-congo-natural-resources-final-report-panel-experts-s20021146.

95. This event will constitute part of Chapter 7. More detail is in Moore 2022.

96. Pindula, 'Nick Mangwana', 27 August 2020, available at: https://www.pindula.co.zw/Nick_Mangwana; New Zimbabwe, 'Moyo attack in London: it's the kind that forces the army out—gvt', 12 July 2019, available at: https://www.newzimbabwe.com/moyo-attack-in-london-its-the-kind-that-forces-the-army-out-gvt/.

97. John Banville, '"My ties to England have loosened": John le Carré on Britain, Boris, and Brexit', The Guardian, 13 October 2019. As if to prove the point, le Carré convinced his editor that he maintains a 'sort of faith in certain kinds of idealistic people'. His combination of this with clear recognition of 'human frailty' and an ability to 'see through people, not just in a political sense [but to] the nub' of their motivations suggests why he sold many tales. Alison Flood, 'John le Carré: new novel set amid "lunacy" of Brexit with UK run by "10th-raters"', Irish Times, 9 September 2019. Sisman 2015 is the biography.

98. Bauman 2012.

99. Theophanidis 2016–Agamben to Žižek; Gramscian efforts include Stahl 2019 and Worth 2019. Babic 2020 and Abrahamsen et al. 2020.

100. Femia 1981: 46–7.

101. The paper examined left-wing terrorism in the late 1960s and 1970s in Italy, West Germany and the USA. Supervisor Jorge Nef knew first hand of Chile's end of interregnum. Theophanidis 2016: 120 discusses the monsters: Žižek

probably *thought* Gramsci used it, thus it became part of the currency, e.g., Ken Davie, 'Now is the time of monsters', *Mail and Guardian*, 6 September 2019, available at: https://mg.co.za/article/2019-09-06-00-now-is-the-time-of-monsters/.

102. Gramsci 1971: 275–6.
103. As with Gilbert Achcar's excursion to Gramsci's coded version of immediate Italian politics: 'Morbid symptoms: what did Gramsci mean and how does it apply to our time?' *International Socialist Review*, 108, 2017, available at: https://isreview.org/issue/108/morbid-symptoms.
104. Mhanda 2011; Saul 1979, 1980, 2016; Moore 1995, 2014c, 2016a; Mazarire 2011; cf. Makanda 2014.
105. Jackson and Rosberg 1982.
106. Saul 1974.
107. Zabala 2020. A deserved nod to Molobye 2020, citing Zabala's 'The difference between right and left-wing populism', Al Jazeera, 17 January 2017, available at: https://www.aljazeera.com/opinions/2017/1/17/the-difference-between-right-and-left-wing-populism, which led to *Being at Large*.
108. Laclau 1997; Laclau and Mouffe 1985. Cf. Townshend 2004; Wenham, 2003.
109. Williams 2015; Alexander and Macgregor 2020.
110. Finlayson 2010; Primera 2018: 221.
111. Zabala 2020: 4.
112. In Jackson 2019: 49–50.
113. Primera 2018: 222.
114. Ndlovu 2020.
115. Agamben in Damai 2005: 258.
116. White 2015.
117. Brian Raftopoulos, 'Zimbabwe: deepening authoritarianism, dissipating alternatives', African Arguments: Debating Ideas, 1 December 2020, available at: https://africanarguments.org/2020/12/zimbabwe-deepening-authoritarianism-dissipating-alternatives/.
118. Agamben 2005: 1.
119. Ibid.: 15; Hett, 2018, for a careful study of fascism's rise in Germany.
120. Scarnecchia 2006.
121. In Zabala 2020: 119. The double quotes are Zabala's references to Benjamin.
122. Ndlovu-Gatsheni 2020.
123. Kitsepile Nyathi, 'Gruesome evidence jolts Zimbabwe to act on organised mining gangs', *The East African*, 15 December 2019, available at: https://www.theeastafrican.co.ke/tea/news/rest-of-africa/gruesome-evidence-jolts-zimbabwe-to-act-on-organised-mining-gangs-1432944; Moore and Mawowa 2010.
124. Burgis 2015 indicates that Zimbabwe shares this undefined mode of accumulation with many other African countries.

125. Terence Chitapi, 'Two decades of dithering: Where is Zimbabwe's agrarian bourgeoisie?', *African Arguments: Debating Ideas*, 15 December 2020, available at: https://africanarguments.org/2020/12/two-decades-of-dithering-where-is-zimbabwes-agrarian-bourgeoisie/.

126. Ranger 2004, 2013: 37ff.; Limb 2011; Moore 2015a: 317–19; Cobbing 1977; Phimister 2003, 2012; Beach 1984.

127. Doran 2017; Cameron 2018.

128. Sithole 1979.

129. Moore 2018a: 266.

130. Applebaum 2020: 50, after Ivan Krastev and Stephen Holmes, 'How liberalism became "the god that failed" in Eastern Europe', *The Guardian*, 24 October 2019.

131. Moore 2016b.

132. Compagnon 2011.

133. Stuart Doran, 'Why the international community turned a blind eye to the Gukurahundi', Centre for Innovation & Technology Lecture Series, available at: https://www.youtube.com/watch?v=dKlZ12WDfgACITE.

2. MUGABE'S ENDS

1. Ndlovu 2020: 284.

2. David Moore, 'When the state is the man and that man is Mugabe, a new era begins with his fall', The Conversation, 21 November 2017, available at: https://theconversation.com/when-the-state-is-the-man-and-that-man-is-mugabe-a-new-era-begins-with-his-fall-87868.

3. Chabal 2012. Cf. Hindess 2015.

4. 'Conceit', Merriam-Webster.com Dictionary, Merriam-Webster, 22 December 2020, available at: https://www.merriam-webster.com/dictionary/conceit.

5. 'Hands off Zimbabwe, Mugabe tells Blair', *The Guardian*, 2 September 2002, available at: https://www.theguardian.com/environment/2002/sep/02/greenpolitics.Zimbabwenews.

6. 'Mugabe twists knife into Mnangagwa', Bulawayo24, 25 February 2019, available at: https://bulawayo24/index-id-news-sc-national-byo-156949.html. The following lines rely on this source for detail.

7. Andrew Donaldson, 'Mugabe kids won't be washing their watches with Champagne anymore', Independent Online, 18 November 2017, available at: https://www.iol.co.za/news/opinion/mugabe-kids-wont-be-washing-their-watches-with-champagne-anymore-12063650.

8. See Chapter 7. Also Moore 2022.

9. See Chapter 3.

10. Daoud 2015: 31, 137, wherein Harun Uld el-Assas asks why death 'didn't make sense' for his ageing mother.

11. David Moore, 'When the state is the man and that man is Mugabe, a new era begins with his fall', The Conversation, 21 November 2017, available at: https://theconversation.com/when-the-state-is-the-man-and-that-man-is-mugabe-a-new-era-begins-with-his-fall-87868'.

12. Fontein 2010, 2018, 2022.

13. David Moore, 'Robert Gabriel Mugabe: a man whose list of failures is legion', The Conversation, 6 September 2019, available at: https://theconversation.com/robert-gabriel-mugabe-a-man-whose-list-of-failures-is-legion-121596. See also 'Gone but not forgotten: the consequences of forty years in power', Review of African Political Economy Blog, 22 October 2019, available at: http://roape.net/2019/10/22/gone-but-not-forgotten-the-consequences-of-forty-years-in-power/#_edn3.

14. Marquez 1981.

15. Ovenden 2020: 173–9; Anderson 2015. In 1977 a guerrilla leader, Teurayi Ropa, supervised the burning of all the books at the *vashandi*'s Wampoa College, established to challenge the 'old guard's' narrow nationalism. In 2004 Ropa, aka Joice Mujuru, became Zimbabwe's vice president. Mhanda 2011: 179.

16. Fontein 2022.

17. SAFM Sunrise, 6 September 2019, available at: http://www.safm.co.za/sabc/home/safm/schedule/details?id=302e24a1-1d1b-4330-9f4b-abeb161f4afa&title=SAfm-Sunrise.

18. Interview with Biti, Harare, August 2004; Tendi 2008: 387; Mhanda 2011; Saul 1979, 1980, 2016; Moore 1995, 2014c, 2016a.

19. Stephen Chan, 'Zimbabwe's tense countdown', New Statesman, 3 April 2008 and 'Exit Mugabe', Prospect Magazine, April 2008.

20. Kriger 2008a: 3; Moore 2018a: 266; Chris McGreal, 'Beaten for voting the wrong way: how Zanu-PF is taking revenge in rural areas', The Guardian, 16 April 2008, available at: https://www.theguardian.com/world/2008/apr/16/zimbabwe.

21. Burgis 2020: 49, 51, 73.

22. Kriger 2008a: 4.

23. Electoral Institute for Sustainable Democracy in Africa, 'African Democracy Encyclopaedia Project, Zimbabwe: 2008 presidential election results–second round', available at: https://www.eisa.org/wep/zim2008results6.htm.

24. Raftopoulos 2013.

25. Moore 2014a.

26. Tendai Biti, 'MDC: collapse of education system an indictment of ZANU PF: MDC press statement', SW Radio Africa, 13 October 2008, available at: www.swradioafrica.com/pages/mdconeduc131008.htm.

27. Eagleton 2018: 17; Moore 2012, 2019, 2020a.

28. Mills et al. 2019.

29. In 2007 Sisulu wrote an introduction for the publication of the 1999 Catholic

Commission for Justice and Peace and Legal Resources Centre's report on Gukurahundi. A good part of her contribution examined why so many Zimbabwean and global citizens knew little and did nothing about it. Cf. Doran 2017; Cameron 2018.

30. Tinashe Nyamunda, 'Speaking ill of the dead? The uncertain legacy of Robert Mugabe', In the Long Run, 18 September 2020, available at: http://www.inthe-longrun.org/articles/article/speaking-ill-of-the-dead-the-uncertain-legacy-of-robert-mugabe/.

31. Ruth Murambadoro, 'Mugabe and the tradition to not speak ill of the dead', Africa is a Country, 18 September 2019, available at: https://africasacountry.com/2019/09/do-not-speak-ill-of-the-dead 2019.

32. Solly Mapaila, 'Mugabe's legacy—"A few steps forward and many backward"', Umsebenzi Online, 26 September 2019, available at: https://www.sacp.org.za/content/mugabes-legacy-few-steps-forward-and-many-backward.

33. Prof. Everisto Benyera, 'Reflecting on Robert Mugabe's legacy', SABC News, 6 September 2019, available at: https://www.youtube.com/watch?v=j0IWNyofhJY.

34. Dande et al. 2020.

35. Zenzo Moyo, 'Robert Mugabe's tattered legacy: an educated man who refused to learn', City Press, 13 September 2019, available at: https://www.news24.com/citypress/voices/robert-mugabes-tattered-legacy-an-educated-man-who-refused-to-learn-20190913.

36. Percy Zvomuya, 'The accidental dictator: even Mugabe's mother said he shouldn't have been president', The Citizen, 9 September 2019, available at: https://citizen.co.za/news/south-africa/insight/2176711/the-accidental-dic-tator-even-mugabes-mother-said-he-shouldnt-have-been-president/.

37. Percy Zvomuya, 'What's left of Zimbabwe? Part III: too late for change', New Frame, 30 August 2018, available at: https://www.newframe.com/whats-left-zimbabwe-part-iii-too-late-change/.

38. Moore 2012; Mhanda 2016 [1978].

39. Percy Zvomuya, 'Unlearning the Zimbabwean lesson,' New Frame, 17 April 2020, available at: https://www.newframe.com/long-read-unlearning-the-zimbabwean-lesson/.

40. More details in Chapter 3.

41. Ellert and Anderson 2020: 327–56.

42. White 2011, 2015.

43. Interview with Edgar Tekere, Mutare, September 2004.

44. National Archives, UK. FCO 106/753, 'Bishop Muzorewa', 4 July, 25 November and 14 December 1981.

45. Percy Zvomuya, 'Part II: unlearning the Zimbabwean lesson', New Frame, 24 April 2020, available at: https://www.newframe.com/long-read-part-two-unlearning-the-zimbabwean-lesson/.

46. Austin 2020: 16.
47. Ibid.: 12–19.
48. Shamuyarira (1960); Moore 1990: 88–115.
49. Interviews with Joshua Nkomo, Harare and Bulawayo, April 1985, March 1986.
50. Bango and Tsvangirai 2011; Tendi, 2008, 2010; Moore 2010b.
51. Blessing-Miles Tendi, 'How intellectuals made history in Zimbabwe', *Counterpoints*, Africa Research Institute, 2010, available at: https://africaresearchinstitute.org/newsite/wp-content/uploads/2013/03/How-intellectuals-made-history-in-zimbabwe.pdf.
52. Priestland 2012.
53. Interviews with Dennis Grennan, Hexham, August 2007, September 2008. Moore 2014c: 307–10, 2015b: 35–40, 2016a: 173, 176. Thanks to Tony Humphries for information on the Africa Centre and Sally Mugabe's role there.
54. Interview with Richard Cashmore, Twickenham, January 1986.
55. Ranger 1980.
56. Moore 2015b: 40; interview with David Sanders, Cape Town, July 2014.
57. Phimister 1987.
58. David Coltart was a dedicated anti-Communist at the University of Cape Town. Delighted to learn at Phimister's history lectures that Mugabe was no Marxist, Coltart organised a public meeting for the Zimbabwean students' group and Mugabe. The South African regime did not approve. Coltart 2016.
59. Kriger 1988, 1992.
60. David Caute, 'The road to Independence', *London Review of Books*, 21 November 1985, available at: https://www.lrb.co.uk/the-paper/v07/n20/david-caute/the-road-to-independence.
61. Interviews with Terence Ranger, Manchester, November 1985, and David Caute, London, November 1985, August 2014. Email correspondence with David Caute, April 2017.
62. Sellström 2002: 204.
63. Per Wästberg, email, 2 January 2021.
64. According to Danny Stannard of Rhodesian intelligence, who knew Sithole–and Mugabe–well, the former ZANU leader was epileptic, not an alcoholic. Interview, Newmarket, September 2014.
65. Itai Dzamara, 'Veteran writer urges Mugabe to go', *The Standard*, 6 May 2005, available at: https://www.thestandard.co.zw/2005/05/06/veteran-writer-urges-mugabe-to-go/; Amnesty International, 'Whereabouts of Zimbabwean journalist remain a mystery five years later', 9 March 2020, available at: https://www.selmastories.se/artikel/per-wastberg-mugabe-firade-sin-seger-med-orden-de-som-lider-av-sitt-nederlag-kan-bega%cc%8a-sjalvmord-ifall-de-onskar/.
66. Johanna Stenius, 'Per Wästberg: "Mugabe celebrated his victory with the words: those who suffer from their defeat can commit suicide if they wish"', extract

from Wästberg's *Semaforen och lodlinan: en memoar (1995–2005)*, Selma Stories, 2017, available at: https://www.selmastories.se/artikel/per-wastberg-mugabe-firade-sin-seger-med-orden-de-som-lider-av-sitt-nederlag-kan-bega%cc%8a-sjalvmord-ifall-de-onskar/.

67. National Archives, UK. FCO 36/1785. Part B, 'Political parties in Rhodesia–ANC operations outside Rhodesia: Dick Cashmore to Mr Barlow, Rhodesia Department: Comments on the Price of Détente', 7 June 1976, in Moore 2016a: 175.

68. National Archives, UK. Letter from R. A. R. Barltrop to St. C. Duncan, Esq. Central African Office, Whitehall, DO 183 183 Fed. AD/20, 22 September [1962], as in Moore 2015b: 34.

69. Southern 2020: 7.

70. National Security Archives (1976), 'State Department, Text of Telegram 76Maputo000785 ADP 150 Confidential, CodeL Solarz: Meeting between Congressman Solarz and ZANU leader Edward [sic] Mugabe. NSC-06/020W, declassified 7/19.1990'. George Washington University, Washington, DC. In Moore 2014c: 310–11.

71. Trevor Grundy, 'Who put Mugabe into power?' PoliticsWeb, 15 September 2019, available at: https://www.politicsweb.co.za/opinion/who-put-mugabe-into-power.

3. KNOWING MUGABE

1. Saul 1979, 2016; Moore 1990, 1995, 2014c, 2016a.

2. Mhanda 2011: 81–92, 278–83.

3. Wheen 2009; Gopal 2019; Cf. Abrahamsen 2020.

4. Tor Sellström, 'Interview with Per Wästberg', Nordic Africa Institute Interviews, 28 February 1996, available at: https://nai.uu.se/library/resources/liberation-africa/interviews/per-wastberg.html.

5. National Archives, UK. 'H. W. Chitepo, First Southern African Barrister', DO 35/7726, CA 207/63/2, 1954. See Karekwaivanane 2017, on Zimbabwean lawyers and law.

6. National Archives, UK. 'H. W. Chitepo, First Southern African Barrister', DO 35/7726, 'Onward Telegram from Commonwealth Relations Office', 1 March 1960.

7. National Archives, UK. 'H. W. Chitepo, First Southern African Barrister', 24 August 1960.

8. National Archives, UK. FCO 36/14 'Confidential and Guard' (1030/11), British Embassy, Washington, DC, 29 March 1967.

9. Zambia Information Services, 'Dear Mr Vorster ... details of exchanges between President Kaunda of Zambia and Prime Minister Vorster of South Africa', Lusaka 1971.

10. Chung 2006: 132 puts the count at 70. The 60–250 spread is from Tendi 2017, 2020: 34–8, 42–52. Mhanda does not make an estimate: see 2011: 48–9.

11. White 2003.

12. Interview with Kenneth Kaunda, Durban, October 2005.

13. Zimbabwe Detainees Defence Committee, 1976, *The Price of Détente: Kaunda Prepares to Execute More ZANU Freedom Fighters for Smith*. In National Archives, UK. FCO 36/1785. Part B 1976, 'Political Parties in Rhodesia–ANC Operations outside Rhodesia', in Moore 2016a: 175.

14. National Archives, UK. 'FCO 36/1785. Part B 1976, Political Parties in Rhodesia–ANC Operations Outside Rhodesia, Dick Cashmore to Mr Barlow, Rhodesia Department: Comments on the Price of Détente,' 7 June 1976, in Moore 2016a: 175.

15. Per Wästberg, 'Var finns Robert Mugabe?' (Where is Robert Mugabe?), *Dagens Nyheter*, 1 June 1975, cited in Sellström 2002: 205.

16. Simpson et al. 1981: 75–7.

17. National Archives, UK. Cypher/Cat A: Immediate Commonwealth Office to Accra. Telno 1351. 9 November 1967 (IR 5/7/-), 'Confidential'. Moore 2005a: 158–9ff.

18. Dorril 2000: 475, 722.

19. Interview with Dennis Grennan, Hexham, August 2007; Moore 2014c: 307–10, 2015b: 35–40, 2016a: 173, 176.

20. 'Britain and Rhodesia: Route to Settlement', seminar, 5 June 2005, Institute of Contemporary British History, 2008, available at: http://www.kcl.ac.uk/innovation/groups/ich/witness/diplomatic/Rhodesia2.aspx/), 120–1.

21. Ibid., 121.

22. David Moore, 'Zimbabwe's struggles in Zambia: counter hegemonic discourses and their discontents', Conference on 'Zambia: Independence and After: Towards a Historiography', University of Zambia, Lusaka, 11–13 August 2005.

23. State Department telegram: 'Secret Lusaka 01612 2415187–August 24 1975,' National Security Archives, George Washington University, Washington, DC.

24. Zukas 2002.

25. Interview with Henry Hamadziripi, Harare, October 1984.

26. Artefacts, 'Lorenz, Erhard', n.d., available at: https://www.artefacts.co.za/main/Buildings/archframes.php?archid=2125.

27. Skype interview with Nigel Wakeham, July 2013. Nigel Wakeham, Consultant Architect, available at: https://www.consultant-architect.co.uk/profile.

28. John Matshikiza, 'With the lid off', *Mail and Guardian*, 14 April 2000, available at: https://mg.co.za/article/2000-04-14-white-veteran-of-a-black-war/.

29. Interview with Bente Lorenz, Lusaka, August 2005.

30. Interview with Mark Chona, Lusaka, August 2013.

31. Rachel Sylvester, 'A licence to kill? Oh heavens, no!' *Daily Telegraph*, 24 April

2003, available at: https://www.telegraph.co.uk/culture/3593236/A-licence-to-kill-Oh-heavens-no.html.

32. Trevor Grundy, 'The Men who Saved Zambia's Cash', Cold Type, June 2012, available at: http://www.coldtype.net/Assets.12/PDFs/0612.ColdType.pdf; Trevor Grundy, 'Professor Michael Faber: an obituary', Politics Web, 11 April 2015, available at: https://www.politicsweb.co.za/opinion/professor-michael-faber-an-obituary.

33. Colin Leys, 'Letters: the African university', *London Review of Books*, 2 August 2018; Mahmood Mamdani, 'The African university', *London Review of Books*, 19 July 2018. The Commonwealth Secretariat's oral history website states that Wicken was a 'British public servant' while Julius Nyerere's Personal Assistant 'from 1960 until the 1990s': chrismoffat, 'Joan Wicken', Commonwealth Oral Histories, 3 July 2015, available at: https://commonwealthoralhistories.org/explandict/joan-wicken/.

34. National Archives, University of Stirling, 'Archives and Special Collections: Peter Mackay', https://libguides.stir.ac.uk/archives/mackay.

35. Jennings 2002.

36. Lionel Cliffe, 'Joan Wicken: an unsung figure who worked alongside Julius Nyerere in the building of Tanzania', *The Guardian*, 21 December 2004.

37. National Archives, UK. 'Visit by Dennis Grennan, Private Secretary to President Kaunda, to UK', DO 209/125, 1966.

38. National Archives, UK. FCO 36/122, 'Rhodesia Political Affairs: Mr Dennis Grennan', 1967.

39. State Department telegram: 'Secret Lusaka 01612 2415187–August 24 1975,' National Security Archives, George Washington University, Washington, DC.

40. Meredith 2002: 35.

41. National Archives, UK. 'PREM 19/3592, Visit to London by President Mugabe', 28 September 1988.

42. London Metropolitan Archives, City of London, 'African Jubilee Year: Official Launch for Garvey Centenary Scope', LMA/4462/H/03/008, 1987; Mrs Sally Mugabe opens an art/craft exhibition at Africa Centre, GLC/DG/PRB/05/003, 1986; Unveiling of the Mandela bust on the South Bank; Boateng, Paul, GLC/DG/PRB/05/371, 1981–1985. Thanks to Tony Humphries for finding the depositary. He worked at the Africa Centre at the same time as Sarah Mugabe.

43. The archival material below is online. National Archives, UK. FCO 36/717, 'Registered file concerning application to reside and work in the United Kingdom: Mrs Sarah Francesca Mugabe, Ghanaian-born wife of Robert Mugabe (detained in Rhodesia), residing in London following completion of her studies', 1969 Jan 01–1970 Dec 31 Closed Until 2005', available at: http://discovery.nationalarchives.gov.uk/details/r/C10911219. I recount parts of this tale in 'Exposing Mugabe of the past', *Zimbabwe Independent*, 14 December 2007,

available at: https://www.theindependent.co.zw/2007/12/14/exposing-mugabe-of-the-past/.

44. This foreshadowed his advice to Tony Blair to keep his England so Mugabe could 'keep my Zimbabwe': 'Hands off Zimbabwe, Mugabe tells Blair', *The Guardian*, 2 September 2002, available at: https://www.theguardian.com/environment/2002/sep/02/greenpolitics.zimbabwenews.

45. 'Mugabe denounces Amnesty report on torture', Associated Press, 21 November 1985, available at: https://apnews.com/article/ed9dec7d6fec142be545522 070977285.

46. Per Wästberg, email, 2 January 2021.

47. Martin and Johnson 1981: 209.

48. Baumhögger et al. 1984, vol. II, doc. 35: 39.

49. Ibid., doc. 36: 39.

50. Martin and Johnson 1981: 209; Ranger 1980: 78–85; Simpson et al. 1981: 94–6.

51. Frankfurt 2017; Sarajlic 2019; Barber 2020; Zabala 2020.

52. Per Wästberg, email, 2 January 2021.

53. National Archives, UK. CP 020/2921, 'Record of Meeting Between the Secretary of State for Foreign and Commonwealth Affairs and Mr Mark Chona held at the FCO on Friday, 13 February at 1:30 P.M.', 24 February 1976.

4. *VASHANDI*: THE OUTSIDE VIEW

1. Crosland and Kissinger Letters, Crosland Papers. London School of Economics and Political Science Special Collections. CC HK>AC 21/10/76. Thanks to Sue Onslow for informing me of this, and the LSE library for permission.

2. Scarnecchia 2021 is the hallmark.

3. Sebenius et al. 2018.

4. Lionel Cliffe's writing on the 'generations' of the aspiring Zimbabwean rulers is foundational, as was his university teaching, and writing in general, in eastern and southern Africa: Moore 2016a.

5. Henry Kissinger, 'Letter to Anthony Crosland', Crosland Papers.

6. In Burton and Keefer 2011: 691.

7. 'Mugabe one-on-one interview', *Zimbabwe Independent*, 23 March 2018, available at: https://www.theindependent.co.zw/2018/03/23/mugabe-one-one-interview/.

8. In Burton and Keefer 2011: 723.

9. In Burton and Keefer 2011: 722.

10. In Burton and Keefer 2011: 693.

11. Interview with Dennis Grennan, Hexham, September 2007.

12. Julius Caesar, Sparknotes, available at: https://www.sparknotes.com/nofear/shakespeare/juliuscaesar/page_22/.

13. Interview with Mark Chona, Lusaka, August 2013.

14. In Burton and Keefer 2011: 625–6. Reinhardt was one of the first black American ambassadors. He became director of the US Information Agency in 1977, and was later a professor at the University of Vermont. https://en.wikipedia.org/wiki/John_Reinhardt.

15. In Burton and Keefer 2011: 621.

16. Interview with Frank Wisner, Washington, November 2013, in Moore 2016a: 182.

17. Wisner, 2013, in Moore 2014c: 315.

18. United States of America Department of State, 'State Message, from Amembassy Lusaka to Sec. State Washington, Geneva to Wisner, "Basis for African Unrealism in Geneva"', 25 October 1976, Freedom of Information Act.

19. National Archives, UK. FCO 36/1785, Part B 1976, 012/1 CP/ 011/2, 'Political Parties in Rhodesia–ANC Operations outside Rhodesia: Note from Jeremy Varcoe: Lusaka High Commission, 29 June'; partly in Moore 2016a: 176. One should note many observers' careless use of ethnic labels. That ZIPA and the imprisoned group that would later co-operate with Mugabe in ZIPA's elimination were often condensed into a 'Karanga–radical/terrorist' whole indicates the inadequacy of such analysis. Warner 1981:235 states unequivocally that 'the differences between the ZIPA Military Committee and ZANU's traditional leadership were ideological and political, not ethnic'. This MA thesis is a most astute analysis of the Zimbabwean liberation war, its main premise being the importance of ethnicity during the struggle. That a man destined to be the head of Australia's intelligence service could make such a judgement is a sorry reflection on the care of his British predecessors. Thanks to Norma Kriger for reminding me of this work.

20. 77 cadres of the African National Council (Zimbabwe) at Morogoro Camp, 'Memorandum to the OAU Liberation Committee (and the governments of the Frontline States)', 24 August 1976, p. 2. Courtesy of Enos Malandu, Harare, March 1986.

21. National Archives, UK. FCO 36/1785, Part B 1976, 'Jeremy Varcoe: Lusaka High Commission, to Barlow. 13 July'.

22. National Archives, UK. FCO 36/1786, Part C 1976, 'Political Parties in Rhodesia–ANC Operations outside Rhodesia: JC (Jeremy) Varcoe to JC Harrison Esq., Rhodesia Department. 29 September'; Moore 2016a: 178.

23. 'CTV News Archive: 1976 interview with Robert Mugabe', available at: https://www.youtube.com/watch?v=BSU--J9MMGs.

24. In Burton and Keefer 2011: 626–7.

25. National Archives, UK. CP/020/16, 'Rhodesia Conference. Info Immediate Lusaka, Maputo, Gaborone; Info Priority Pretoria, Washington, UKMIS New York, Yr Tel No 289:', 20 October 1976.

26. Interview with Hashim Mbita, Dar es Salaam, January 1997.

27. National Archives, UK. 'Mozambique: Internal Situation', CP 020/267/1, 11 October 1976.

28. Centre Party Memorandum, 'Action to Prevent and Economic and Political Collapse', BC 969 Mitchell Collection F 4.3 'Détente: Settlement and the Interim Government, 1975–1977'.
29. In Burton and Keefer 2011: 601.
30. Nyadzonya Raid, Pindula, available at: https://www.pindula.co.zw/Nyadzonya_ Raid, 9 August 2019.
31. National Archives, UK. 'Mozambique: Alleged Massacre of Rhodesian Refugees', CP/020/367/1, 23 August 1976; Dhada, 2020.
32. In Burton and Keefer 2011: 687.
33. Leo Zeilig, editor of Roape's blog, fronted my long obituary of Mugabe with a December 1976 photograph of Mugabe visiting Nicolae Ceauşescu. David Moore, 'Gone but not forgotten: the consequences of forty years in power', Review of African Political Economy Blog, 22 October 2019, available at: http://roape.net/2019/10/22/gone-but-not-forgotten-the-consequences-of-forty-years-in-power/#_edn3.
34. Deletant 2011.
35. Norman 2018: 113–14.
36. Interview with Iden Weatherall, Harare, September 2004.
37. United States of America Central Intelligence Agency, 'Special National Intelligence Estimate: Rhodesia, Looking Ahead', Secret, SNIE 72.1–1–77 (Freedom of Information Act). 29 January 1977, 8–15. Moore 2014c: 312.
38. Interview with Frank Wisner, November 2013, in Moore 2014c: 315.
39. Eric Rosenbach and Aki J. Peritz, 'Confrontation or collaboration? Congress and the intelligence community', Belfer Center, Harvard University, 2009, pp. 36–7, available at: https://www.belfercenter.org/sites/default/files/legacy/files/IC-book-finalasof12JUNE.pdf.
40. National Archives, UK. FCO 36/4208, 1979, 'K D Evetts, Esq', CP/011/1, 4 January.
41. National Archives, UK. FCO 36/4208, 1979, 'ZANU (MUGABE), 6 and 15 February.
42. National Archives, UK. FCO 36/4208, 1979, 'ZANU (MUGABE) Potboiler', CP/011/1, 1 March.
43. Shubin 2017: 228, 230–1 reports Nkomo going directly to Moscow for help after his failed talks with Smith in May 1976: he does not mention ZIPA, nor ZANU during the 'paper' Patriotic Front, but does note Nkomo's duplicity in his memoir.
44. Saul 2016.

5. INSIDE *VASHANDI*–THEN OUT

1. The next few pages derive from Moore 1990, 1995, 2012, 2014c, 2016a, 2020b, many conversations since 1984, and Mhanda 2011.

2. Mhanda 2011: 280.
3. 'Zimbabwe People's Army', interview with ZIPA Political Commissar Dzinashe Machingura by the Mozambique Information Agency, 22 September 1976.
4. Interviews with *vashandi* members, Harare and Bulawayo, November 1984, April 1985 and March 1986.
5. Chung 2006: 133, 151; Mhanda 2011: 195.
6. 'Comrade Mugabe lays the line at historic Chimoio central committee meeting', *Zimbabwe News*, 9, 5–6, July–December 1977, p. 13.
7. 'Zimbabwe African National Union Central Committee Report', *Zimbabwe News, sp. issue, ZANU (PF) Second Congress 8th–13th August*, 1984; cf. Mhanda 2011: 173.
8. Moore 1990: 126, 152–3.
9. Gumbo in 1979, in Mhanda 2011: 172–3.
10. Mhanda 2011: 193.
11. Given the experience in Zambia and *vashandi 1* it is hard to believe more executions would have taken place.
12. Moore 2014b.
13. Mazarire 2011: 572, 576–8; Tendi 2017, 2020: 34–8.
14. Mukonori 2017; Pollitt 2017.
15. Chung 2006: 161. Chung joined the camps after the Chitepo assassination, along with fellow University of Zambia lecturer Sam Geza. Zambian authorities jailed their comrade Lionel Cliffe for instigating student demonstrations against Zambia's foreign policy vis-à-vis Angola: he shared cells with some of Chitepo's alleged murderers (Moore 2016a: 172). Geza joined the *vashandi* group and lectured at Wampoa College. He was married to Mugabe's sister. She divorced him on his incarceration. Both Geza and Chung had high positions in the post-1980 government–Chung as education minister until structural adjustment hit hard; Geza in the land resettlement programme and transport, until similar ideological roadblocks hit those departments.
16. Ibid.: 161, 149.
17. Ibid.: 174.
18. 'BBC interview: Robert Mugabe before Geneva conference 1976: "We are dedicated to Socialism"', available at: https://www.youtube.com/watch?v=yfRyx RzOg7o, and in Simon Bright's documentary, *Robert Mugabe: What Happened?* Bristol and Cape Town: Zimmedia, 2012. The website I found while writing the first draft of this book had disappeared by the time the second draft was in progress. I do not recall the BBC entitling the YouTube with reference to Mugabe's alleged socialism, which, as a careful viewing would reveal, Mugabe considered about as seriously as the next question, about elections.
19. National Archives, UK. Prem 16/1092, 'Note for the Record'. London, 6 May 1976.
20. National Archives, UK. FCO 36/1854, 'FM Maputo to Routine FCO Tel No 121 of 9 June, Info Dar es Salaam Gaborone Lusaka Cape Town UKMIS New York; Dar es Salaam Tels Nos 197 and 198: Rhodesia', 15 June 1976.

21. Philip Warhurst Collection, Killie Campbell Archive, Durban. 'Highly Confidential: A Plan for Rhodesia', Centre Party, 24 June 1976.
22. National Archives. UK. Prem 16/1096, GR 175, Cypher/Cat A FM Maputo, 26 September 1976.
23. Johnnie Carson, email, 12 June 2019.
24. National Security Archives. 1976. 'State Department, Text of Telegram 76Maputo000785 ADP 150. Confidential, CodeL Solarz: Meeting between Congressman Solarz and ZANU leader Edward [sic] Mugabe', NSC-06/020W, declassified 7/19.1990. George Washington University, Washington, DC.
25. National Archives, UK. FCO 36/1853/1976, 'P M Laver Esq, Rhodesia Department, FCO, ROBERT MUGABE', 26 July.
26. National Archives, UK. FCO 36/1785. Part B 1976, 'Political Parties in Rhodesia–ANC Operations Outside Rhodesia'. P. J. Barlow in London to CRL Chassiron Esq., CP/011/02 97 29 July. Moore 2016a: 177.
27. Moore 2016a: 177; National Archives, UK. FCO 36/1785. Part B 1976, 'Political Parties in Rhodesia–ANC Operations outside Rhodesia'. Record of Meeting between Officials of Rhodesia Department and a Zimbabwean Delegation at the FCO on Friday 27 August. CP/011/02 108.
28. Moore 2016a: 177; National Archives, UK. FCO 36/1785. Part B 1976, 'Political Parties in Rhodesia', 'Letter from Mugabe, C.P. 279, Quelimane, Province de Zambesia, to C. R. L. de Chassiron, Second Secretary, British Embassy, MAPUTO. 24 August.
29. Moore 2016a: 177; National Archives, UK. FCO 36/1785. Part B 1976, 'Political Parties in Rhodesia', 'Jeremy Varcoe: Lusaka High Commission, to Barlow', 13 July.
30. National Archives, UK. FCO 36/1786. Part C 1976, 'Political Parties in Rhodesia–ANC Operations outside Rhodesia', JC (Jeremy) Varcoe to JC Harrison Esq., Rhodesia Department. 29 September.
31. Moore 2016a: 179; National Archives, UK. FCO 36/1786. Part C 1976, 'Political Parties in Rhodesia–ANC Operations outside Rhodesia', 'Mozambique Information Agency, Special Edition, September 22–People's War in Zimbabwe'.
32. Kriger 1985, 1988, 1992 portrays more complexity.
33. Mhanda 2011: 139–40.
34. Note the date of Ted Rowlands' 26 September 1976 report (endnote 22) about Joshua Nkomo's worries regarding who 'controlled' Mugabe.
35. Chung 2006: 137–9, 158.
36. Chung 2006: 153–70 for a first-hand account of the conference. Even Jane Fonda and Tom Hayden visited to show their support.
37. Mhanda 2011: 151–64.
38. 'ZIPA Denounces the Geneva Perfidy', Zimbabwe People's Army, 1976, Private Collection of Carol Thompson, cited in Moore 1990: 214; Warner 1981: 229.
39. Baumhögger et al. 1984, vol. II, doc. 206 (a): 222.

40. Ibid. 206 (b): 222.
41. Moore 2012.
42. Levi Mukarati, 'It wasn't all success at the front', *Sunday Mail*, 18 August 2019, available at: https://www.sundaymail.co.zw/it-wasnt-all-success-at-the-front.
43. Mhanda 2011: 159.
44. National Archives of Zimbabwe, *c*.1979. 'Chitepo College Curriculum: "Detente and United Front"', Zimbabwe African National Union. Thanks to Tim Scarnecchia for this.
45. Doran 2017: 644.
46. National Archives, UK. FCO 36/1871, 'Visits to Southern Africa by Ministers and Officials of the Foreign Office', 'Sir David Ennals: Maputo', 2–3 April 1976; 'Mozambique No. 3. CSQ 093/1(139) 1977'; FO 93/207/4–7, 1978–82.
47. Mhanda 2011: 175.
48. These documents (and Foot's reply to Minty) are in the Judith Hart papers at the People's Archive, Manchester. Chris Mullin, 'Private and Confidential: International Department. The Labour Party, ID/19756/76/163–Report from Rhodesia/Zimbabwe', June 1976. 'Abdul Minty: Revised Strategy for the Zimbabwean Liberation Struggle', 8 June 1976; 'Michael Foot: Strictly between Ourselves', 12 June 1976.
49. Wilfred Mhanda, aka Dzinashe 'Dzino' Machingura, 'A Treatise on Zimbabwe's Liberation Struggle: Some Theoretical Problems', ROAPE Blog, 29 March 2016, [Cabo Delgado: April–May 1978], available at: http://roape.net/2016/03/29/a-prison-notebook-mhandas-treatise-on-zimbabwes-liberation.
50. National Archives, UK. FCO 36/1750, 'Political Relations between Mozambique and Rhodesia', DR Upton Rhodesia Dept, CP 3/367/1, 20 October, 1975.
51. National Archives, UK. FCO 73/245 S/S, 'Records of Conversation 1977: Part 1. Mr. Crosland. 3 February 1977.
52. Sisman 2015: 137–45.
53. Interview with Stephen (Frank) Miles, Oxted, September 2004. Michael Smith, 'Stephen Miles: highly regarded diplomat who helped save Tanzania from a military coup', *The Independent*, 12 June 2013, available at: https://www.independent.co.uk/news/obituaries/stephen-miles-highly-regarded-diplomat-who-helped-save-tanzania-military-coup-8656189.html.
54. Henry Kissinger, 'Letter to Anthony Crosland.' Crosland Papers. London School of Economics and Political Science Special Collections. CC HK>AC 21/10/76.
55. Burton and Keefer 2011: 723.
56. Ellert and Anderson 2020: 143–5, having reproduced 'XYB 5254/1, XYO 2499/1, XYO 2500/1–ZIMBABWE PEOPLE'S ARMY (ZPA): HIGH COMMAND & CENTRAL COMMITTEE', Special Branch Headquarters, 'Special Branch Headquarters, SALISBURY, June 1976, most of which was gained from 'various sources including capture debriefing'.
57. Ellert and Anderson 2020: 146.

NOTES

58. National Archives, UK. FCO 36/1926, CP 011/1, 'Rhodesia: The Patriotic Front', 'Confidential Mr Mansfield', 8 February 1977.
59. National Archives, University of Stirling, 'Archives and Special Collections: Peter Mackay', available at: https://libguides.stir.ac.uk/archives/mackay.
60. Diana Mitchell and Robert Cary, 'Eshmael Ephial Mtshmalyeli Mlambo', *African Nationalist Leaders–Rhodesia to Zimbabwe*, 1977, available at: http://www.colonialrelic.com/biographies/eshmael-ephial-mtshmayeli-mlambo/.
61. Ranger 2004.
62. Makanda 2014: 78–9.
63. Ibid.: 84–5.
64. Ibid.: 83.
65. Moore 2015a. What are 'near-delusional bombings' and why was Masipula spelled correctly at times and as masiphula at another? How can one think that Chung (2006) and Mhanda differ on the *vashandi*'s leaders, and that they 'are of the same stable'? Is 'we agreed to their proposal and voluntarily abandoned our plans to go to England date and page references' in Mhanda's book? Makanda 2014: 83–4, 88.
66. Ranger 1980.
67. Mhanda, 'A Treatise on Zimbabwe's Liberation Struggle'.
68. Makanda 2014: 88.
69. Morris 2020.
70. Makanda 2014: 87.
71. One of the younger soldiers on *vashandi*'s fringes, in 1985 working in one of the state's media outlets, told me that Mhanda and his peers were too cautious. He thought Muammar Gaddafi would be a good ruler for Zimbabwe. He later confessed to his friends that the CIO employed him. Few are able to maintain the imperatives of *vashandi* for long.
72. Chung 2006: 141–3.
73. Makanda 2014: 85–7.
74. Moore 2009: 49. After William Kentridge's *I Am Not Me: the Horse is Not Mine*, which also concerns Stalin's show trials, portraying Bukharin's pathos graphically. Kentridge's work is, in his own words, a 'comedy of a world at odds with itself ... of inversion ... where logical argument is a sure sign of duplicity and lying is explained away as strategy.' Tate Gallery, 2008: available at: https://www.tate.org.uk/art/artworks/kentridge-i-am-not-me-the-horse-is-not-mine-t14213.
75. Trevor Grundy, 'Who put Mugabe into power?' PoliticsWeb, 15 September 2019, available at: https://www.politicsweb.co.za/opinion/who-put-mugabe-into-power.
76. National Archives, UK. FCO 36/260, 'The Patriotic Front (Zapu-Nkomo Factor)', 'Records of interviews with Joshua Nkomo in Salisbury with Joshua Nkomo and Robin Renwick', Telegrams 487, Item 60, and 823, Item 73, 4 and 26 February 1980; Moore 2014d: 61–3.

77. National Archives, UK. FCO 36/260, 'Henderson: FM Washington 212100Z Feb 80 to Immediate FCO–Rhodesia: Nkomo's Views', Telegram No. 787 of 21 February, Priority Salisbury', 21 February 1980.
78. Gary Thatcher, '"The Russians' greatest reverse in Africa in years'", *Christian Science Monitor*, 22 April 22 1980, available at: https://www.csmonitor.com/1980/0422/042232.html, in Moore 2014d: 63.
79. Ellert and Anderson 2020: 356.
80. Interview with Dennis Grennan, Hexham, September 2008.
81. Interview with Mark Chona, Lusaka, August 2013.
82. Interview with Edgar Tekere, Mutare, September 2004.

6. COCKROACHES, KIDS AND COUNTING DOWN: 1980–2000

1. Alois Mlambo and Brian Raftopoulos, 'Zimbabwe's multilayered crisis', Chr. Michelsen Institute Brief, 9 (3), 2010, available at: https://www.cmi.no/publications/file/3727-zimbabwes-multilayered-crisis.pdf.
2. Meredith 1979; Ellert and Anderson 2020: 328–33.
3. The data in these paragraphs derive from Moore 2005b: 130–2.
4. Chagonda 2011, 2012.
5. Cf. Kriger 2008b.
6. Thus the title for Moore 2005b.
7. Vambe 2008.
8. Interview, Gweru, August 2004; Chung 2006: 99, 110, 161.
9. 'Patrick Kombayi', Pindula, 17 July 2020, available at: https://www.pindula.co.zw/Patrick_Kombayi#cite_ref-GREAT_1–0.
10. Tendi 2020b. Cf. Kriger 2020; Moore 2020a.
11. Moore 2016b; Stahl 2019.
12. Ranger 1980.
13. Chris McGreal, 'Zimbabwe's voters told: choose Mugabe or you face a bullet', *The Guardian*, 18 June 2008, available at: https://www.theguardian.com/world/2008/jun/18/zimbabwe.
14. Hoffman 1984.
15. Fontein 2018; Tendi 2020b: 264–96.
16. Chung 2006: 169.
17. 'Mugabe one-on-one interview', *Zimbabwe Independent*, 23 March 2018, available at: https://www.theindependent.co.zw/2018/03/23/mugabe-one-one-interview/.
18. 'Mugabe twists knife into Mnangagwa', *Bulawayo 24*, 25 February 2019, available at: https://bulawayo24.com/index-id-news-sc-national-byo-156949.html.
19. Interviews, Harare and Bulawayo, February 1986; White 2022: 101–6.
20. Ellert and Anderson 2020: 325–6.
21. Scarnecchia 2008.
22. Interviews, David Hemson, Hackney, January 1986 and Johannesburg, October

2017; Marxist Workers Party, 'What is SALEP and what work has it done?' available at: http://marxistworkersparty.org.za/?page_id=2343.

23. Churchill Archives Centre. The Papers of Neil Kinnock, KNNK 10/1/25, May–20 July 1985.

24. Percy Zvomuya, 'What's left of Zimbabwe? Part I', New Frame, 15 August 2018, available at: https://www.newframe.com/whats-left-of-zimbabwe-part-i/. Gwisai 2009: for his later role (among scores) in a Zimbabwean agricultural labour dispute that illustrates the 'ground of politics' fully see Rutherford 2017.

25. Churchill Archives Centre. The Papers of Neil Kinnock, KNNK 10/1/40, Jul 1988–May 1991, 24 October 1989.

26. Moore 2008a.

27. Moore 2016b.

28. 'Tongogara and the System', Financial Mail, 29 October 1976. Thanks to Shirley de Villiers for sending this to me.

29. Gelfand 1978.

30. BBC, 'Woman's Hour—Zimbabwe: Judith Garfield Todd', 23 November 2007' available at: https://www.bbc.co.uk/radio4/womanshour/03/2007_47_fri.shtml; British Pathé, 'London: Miss Judy Todd among speakers at a rally calling for overthrow of illegal regime in Rhodesia', 27 June 1996, available at: https://www.britishpathe.com/video/VLVA2ZJSVSJU4YIAUB4YP50MKBOM9-LONDON-MISS-JUDY-TODD-AMONG-SPEAKERS-AT-A-RALLY-CALLING-FOR/query/Todd.

31. Pritchard 2018: 52; Wood 2012: 78.

32. Wood 2012: 124, 128.

33. 'Uproar at the university: students clash as African mob tries to stop ceremony', Sunday Mail, 17 July 1966, Warhurst Collection, Killie Campbell Archives, Durban. Interview, Gerald Caplan, Toronto, September 2004. Lord Malvern was Godfrey Huggins, Southern Rhodesia prime minister from 1933 to 1953, then three further federation years. He described Rhodesian politics as a 'partnership' between blacks and whites, i.e., of horse and rider.

34. Wood 2012: 127.

35. Patrick van Rensburg, 'Obituary–John Andrew Conradie: Liberation War Hero in Zimbabwe', SARE with EWP (3), August 1999, 85–6.

36. Ranger 2013; Moore 2015a: 320.

37. Hughes, 2003. Shamuyarira 1960.

38. Interviews, Peter Mackay, Marondera, August 2005; Dennis Grennan, Hexham, September 2008; Joshua Mpofu, Cape Town, January 2014. Mackay 2008; Wood 2012: 128; Turok, 2003: 185; Peter Mackay Archives, University of Stirling, available at: https//libguides.stir.ac.uk/archives/MackayArchive Project.

39. Ranger 2013: 165.

40. Arrighi and Saul 1973.
41. The Arrighi Center for Global Studies, Johns Hopkins University, 'Giovanni Arrighi (1937–2009)', available at: https://krieger.jhu.edu/arrighi/about/giovanni-arrighi-1937–2009/.
42. Arrighi 1966: 64–5.
43. Ranger 2013: 161, in Moore 2015a: 319.
44. Nursey-Bray 1967. Interviews with Michael Holman, London, July 2019, Bulawayo, July 2018, London, August 2014, London, October 2013. *Black and White*'s nine editions are available at JSTOR's 'Struggles' section of the ALUKA site: www.jstor.org/stable/10.2307/al.sff.document.zimrevp2b1002 through to 1010\.
45. Sue Onslow, 'Interview with Malcolm Rifkind', *Commonwealth Oral Histories*, 8 January 2013, available at: https://commonwealthoralhistories.org/2013/interview-with-sir-malcolm-rifkind/.
46. National Archives, UK. FCO 36/57, 'Rhodesia Political Affairs–Internal–M. Holman', 1968.
47. Found by Ian Phimister in the Zimbabwean National Archives, 'Z 535, SECRET', *c.* 1969 and sent to Michael Holman.
48. Holman 2020: 18, 254–74.
49. Ellert and Anderson 2020: 130.
50. Eddison Jonas Mudadirwa Zvobgo, 'SPECIAL FEATURE: the armed struggle ZILA in full bloom and in full swing', *Zimbabwe News*, 1, 1 (January/May 1976), San Francisco, pp. 28–30, in Moore 2005a: 159–60.
51. National Archives, UK. FCO 36/766, Files 26 and 28, 'Policy and Activities of Amnesty International in Relation to Rhodesia: demand for release of political pensions and detainees, 1968–1971', in Moore 2005a: 162.
52. Nathan Shamyuria [*sic*], 'Liberation movements in Southern Africa', Eighth Annual Hans Wolff Memorial Lecture, Indiana University, Bloomington, 14 April 1977: 27, 31, in Moore 1990: 228.
53. Washington's solidarity magazine *Southern Africa* published Saul's 'Transforming the struggle in Zimbabwe' (1979) in April 1977. Saul remembered that Frelimo 'instructed' him to write a supportive article 'directly into liberation-movement support circles'. Email to Moore, 16 December 2014, in Moore 2016a: 179.
54. Ellert and Anderson 2020: 357–60. Oddly, the two former security service officers say ZIPRA soldiers were already undergoing joint training exercises with their Rhodesian counterparts 'and their leaders had doubtless been given an idea of what the operation might entail'. If so, their plans to eliminate Dabengwa and Masuku were flexible, or they were not included in this particular definition of 'leaders'.
55. National Archives, UK. PREM 19/3592, 'Visits by Mr. Mugabe, Prime Minister of Zimbabwe, to the UK', 'Record of a Conversation between the Prime Minister and the Prime Minister of Zimbabwe, Mr. Robert Mugabe, at 10 Downing Street on Friday 9 May 1980 at 1140'.

56. Alexander 1998: 153–54, 175–6.

57. Ibid.: 153.

58. National Archives, UK. PREM 19/3592, 'Visits by Mr. Mugabe, Prime Minister of Zimbabwe, to the UK', 'Dear Michael,' FCO to 10 Downing Street, 13 March 1981.

59. Cameron 2018.

60. Gukurahundi was not my main concern at Kew Gardens, but I could not ignore the related files, nor stop wondering why so many are removed or redacted.

61. Moore 2018a: 265. National Archives, UK. PREM 19/1154, 'Ewans (High Commissioner), Telno 810, 26 September 1983'.

62. Moore 2018a: 265. National Archives, UK. PREM 19/1154, 'Zimbabwe: General Review of Relations', 9 December 1982'. The underlined words in this quotation are penned in the original.

63. Moore 2020b: 457; Centre for Innovation and Technology, 'Breakfast club: interview with Dumiso Dabengwa', available at: www.cite.org.zw/videos/interview-with-dumiso-dabengwa/.

64. Doran 2017: 644.

65. Raftopoulos and Mlambo 2009.

66. Simon Allison, 'Gukurahundi ghosts haunt Mnangagwa', Mail and Guardian, 24 November 2017, available at: https://mg.co.za/article/2017-11-24-00-gukurahundi-ghosts-haunt-mnangagwa.

67. CCJP/LRC 2007 [1997]. Elia Ntali, 'Gukurahundi: can the man accused of opening the wounds heal them?' African Arguments, 4 June 2019, available at: https://africanarguments.org/2019/06/gukurahundi-zimbabwe-mnangagwa/.

68. Nyashadzashe Ndoro, 'Mnangagwa threatens to arrest people with cockroaches in their homes', Nehanda Radio, 6 March 2020, available at: https://nehandaradio.com/2020/03/06/mnangagwa-threatens-to-arrest-people-with-cockroaches-in-their-homes/.

69. National Archives of Zimbabwe, c.1979. 'Chitepo College Curriculum: "Detente and United Front"', Zimbabwe African National Union.

70. Interview with Danny Stannard, Newmarket, Cambridgeshire, September 2014.

71. White 2007.

72. Moore 2003b, 2008b.

73. Donatus Bonde, 'Student politics: sense and nonsense', Moto, November/December 1991, 5–6.

74. Mapanzure 2020.

75. Netsai Mushonga, 'Don't use "culture" to oppress women', Zimbabwe Standard, 22 April 2006, available at: http://www.kubatana.net/html/archive/opin/060422nm.asp.

76. Hodgkinson 2018: 131.

77. Ibid.: 363; cf Hodgkinson 2021 for students going abroad.

78. Mutambara 2017: 26.

79. Brian Raftopoulos, email, 17 January 2020.
80. Richard Poplak, 'The ageless, never-ending government/corporate collusion porno', *Daily Maverick*, 26 July 2017.
81. Cheater 1991: 205.
82. Scarnecchia 2006: 234.
83. Tinashe Chimedza, email, 20 November 2019.
84. Human Rights Watch 2006. Mkwananzi later led the MDC-linked Tajamuka/ Sesijikile, a social media 'movement'. He was suspended for a year for misappropriating donor funds for his Subaru: 'Tajamuka suspends leader for fraud', Newsday, 5 December 2017, available at: https://www.newsday.co. zw/2017/12/tajamuka-suspends-leader-fraud/.
85. Bond and Saunders 2005; Hodgkinson 2018; McCandless 2011; Moore, 2008b; Moyo 2018; Ncube 2010; Raftopoulos 2006, 2018; Rich-Dorman 2016; Saunders 2000; Zeilig 2006, 2007.
86. Interview with Patrick Kombayi, Gweru, August 2004.
87. Kriger 2005: 14–20, on ZANU (PF)'s coercive response to the ZUM challenge.
88. Nyarota 2006; Tekere 2007.
89. Interview with Latief Parker, December 2007, Cape Town. Thanks to Paul Brickhill for the introduction. Paul once wondered in his 'by the way' mode if I had ever heard of Latief Parker, who in addition to engaging in fascinating conversations wrote a blank cheque on learning that Paul and the Grassroots Bookstore co-operative were having problems paying the rent.
90. Charehwachaguma Chirombowe, 'Only Hunzvi understood Bob's psyche', *The Standard*, 17 December 2004, available at: https://www.thestandard.co. zw/2004/12/17/only-hunzvi-understood-bobs-psyche/, in Moore 2008b: 28–30.
91. Interview, Crispin Matawire, Mazoe, February 2005. Matawire's war name was David Todlana, with 'JV' as a nickname given his association while with ZAPU with the USSR and his somewhat authoritarian qualities. He was a key player in the *vashandi* movement and Wampoa College, and a good friend of 'Dzino' Machingura until they disagreed regarding the land issue after 1997. In 2000 Matawire and 400 veterans from Harare led some farm invasions. He gained a farm. When I interviewed him he was still a hospital administrator, and his Chinese tractor was not working.
92. Moore 2010a, 2012, from Thabo Mbeki, 'How will Zimbabwe defeat its enemies? A discussion document', African National Congress mimeograph, 10 July 2001, reprinted with minor alterations as 'The Mbeki–Mugabe Papers: A Discussion Document', *New Agenda*, 2nd Quarter, 2008, 56–75.
93. Interview, Morgan Tsvangirai, Harare, September 2004. Tsvangirai said: 'We knew they would never honour that agreement.'
94. 'IRIN interview with land expert Sam Moyo', The New Humanitarian, 14 August 2001, available at: https://www.thenewhumanitarian.org/fr/node/193915.

95. Moore 2008b: 28–30, based on Harare interviews, July–September 2004. Kriger 2003.

96. Mark Lobel, 'Short denied responsibility to Zimbabwe', *The Guardian*, 11 August 2003, available at: https://www.theguardian.com/politics/2003/aug/11/freedomofinformation.zimbabwe; Charles Crawford, 'Dead aid in Zimbabwe: that Clare Short letter fisked', Charles Crawford: Negotiating-Mediating, 2 February 2009, available at: https://charlescrawford.biz/2009/02/28/art826/.

97. Raftopoulos 2018: 71.

98. Moore 2010a.

99. Boyer-Bowyer and Stoneman 2000.

100. Moyo 2000.

101. Nest 2001; 'Plundering of DR Congo natural resources: final report of the Panel of Experts (S/2002/1146)', United Nations, 2002, available at: https://reliefweb.int/report/burundi/plundering-dr-congo-natural-resources-final-report-panel-experts-s20021146.

102. Shola Adenekan, 'Mark Chavunduka', *The Guardian*, 3 December 2002, available at: https://www.theguardian.com/news/2002/dec/03/guardianobituaries.

103. Marx 1963 [1852]: 338.

104. African Democracy Encyclopaedia Project, 'Zimbabwe: 2000 constitutional referendum results', June 2007, available at: https://www.eisa.org/wep/zimresults2000r.htm.

7. RUMOURS OF COUPS: 2000–7

1. Alan Rusbridger, 'Hugo Young: 1938–2003–off the record', *The Guardian*, 15 November 2008, available at: https://www.theguardian.com/books/2008/nov/15/politics.

2. Mbeki 2008 [2001]. Stephen Gelb remarked that this treatise coincided with Mbeki's efforts to establish the New Partnership for Africa's Development, which needed $60 billion to start.

3. Hugo Young, 'Mugabe faces coup plot', *The Guardian*, 21 May 2001, available at: https://www.theguardian.com/world/2001/may/29/zimbabwe.hugoyoung.

4. Jimmy Jamieson, 'Peter Longworth CMG interviewed on 18 January 2006', British Diplomatic Oral History Programme, 2006, available at: https://www.chu.cam.ac.uk/media/uploads/files/Longworth.pdf.

5. Hugo Young, 'The people of Zimbabwe have put us all to shame', *The Guardian*, 12 March 2002, available at: https://www.theguardian.com/world/2002/mar/12/zimbabwe.foreignpolicy.

6. Simon Allison, 'Analysis: The Khampepe Report, a crushing blow to SA's diplomatic credibility', *Daily Maverick*, 17 November 2014, available at: https://www.

dailymaverick.co.za/article/2014-11-17-analysis-the-khampepe-report-a-crushing-blow-to-sas-diplomatic-credibility/.

7. Tendi 2013: 834–35.
8. United Nations 2002; Nest 2001.
9. Allister Sparks, 'Zimbabwe: plots abound as Zanu-PF leaders try to shed Mugabe, pacify MDC', All Africa, 11 February 2003, available at: https://allafrica.com/stories/200302180512.html; Richard Chidza, 'Mugabe offered to retire', Newsday, 25 March 2016, available at: https://www.newsday.co.zw/2016/03/mugabe-offered-retire/.
10. Coltart 2016; Rahul Nagvekar, 'Not Free, not fair, not credible: did Britain back a Zimbabwean autocrat's re-election?' The Politic, 27 March 2019, available at: https://thepolitic.org/not-free-not-fair-not-credible-did-britain-back-a-zimbabwean-autocrats-re-election/.
11. David Smith, 'WikiLeaks cables reveal secret plan to push Mugabe out in Zimbabwe', The Guardian, 9 December 2010, available at: https://www.theguardian.com/world/2010/dec/08/wikileaks-cables-mugabe-coup-zimbabwe.
12. Sparks, 'Zimbabwe: Plots abound'.
13. 'Zimbabwe opposition chief seeks U.S. envoy', Washington Times, 27 January 2003, available at: https://www.washingtontimes.com/news/2003/jan/27/20030127-084531-2896r/.
14. In Tendi 2013: 835.
15. Emphasis mine. Only Moyo raised the question of force. Voice of America, 'Zimbabwe info minister blasts Mugabe critics–2003–01–19', available at: https://www.voanews.com/archive/zimbabwe-info-minister-blasts-mugabe-critics-2003–01–19; Russell Thompson, 'Zimbabwe distances itself from Moyo's comments', Mail and Guardian, 20 January 2003.
16. Basildon Peta, '"Final push" to rid Zimbabwe of Mugabe', The Independent, 1 June 2003, available at: https://www.iol.co.za/news/africa/final-push-to-rid-zimbabwe-of-mugabe-107149.
17. 'Zimbabwe opposition chief'.
18. Interview with Walter Kansteiner, Washington, DC, September 2004.
19. Colin Powell, 'Freeing a nation from a tyrant's grip', New York Times, 24 June 2003, available at: https://www.nyfftimes.com/2003/06/24/opinion/freeing-a-nation-from-a-tyrant-s-grip.html.
20. Rory Carroll, 'Bush backs Mbeki on Zimbabwe', The Guardian, 10 July 2003, available at: https://www.theguardian.com/world/2003/jul/10/zimbabwe.rorycarroll.
21. Suzanne Goldenberg, 'Zimbabwe calls Powell "Uncle Tom"', The Guardian, 2 July 2003, available at: https://www.theguardian.com/world/2003/jul/02/zimbabwe.suzannegoldenberg.
22. R. W. Johnson, 'Mugabe's shadow falls on Bush safari', Sunday Times, 13 July 2003, available at: https://www.thetimes.co.uk/article/mugabes-shadow-falls-on-bush-safari-8clldltmgdl.

238

23. Matyszak 2017; Moore 2018a: 264, 267.

24. Lenin Ndebele and Njabulo Ncube, 'Robert Mugabe ally to run for president "due to popular demand"', *Sunday Times*, 1 December 2019, available at: https://www.timeslive.co.za/sunday-times/news/2019-12-01-robert-mugabe-ally-to-run-for-president-due-to-popular-demand/.

25. Lance Guma, 'Kasukuwere exposed as violent political gangster', SW Radio Africa, 5 January 2012, available at: https://www.zimbabwesituation.com/old/jan6_2012.html.

26. Jonathan Moyo, 'Tsholotsho saga: the untold story', *Zimbabwe Independent*, 17 December 2004, available at: https://www.thestandard.co.zw/2004/12/17/tsholotsho-saga-the-untold-story-3/.

27. Matyszak 2016: 166, applies this concept to Mugabe but may take too negative a view of a tendency with two poles; Chris Bourn, 'The psychology of referring to yourself in the third person: the surprisingly smart science of a very dumb-sounding habit', *Mel Beta Magazine*, 2018, available at: https://medium.com/mel-magazine/the-psychology-of-referring-to-yourself-in-the-third-person-f82c7755d3f8.

28. Jonathan Moyo, 'Tsholotsho saga: the untold story', 17 December 2004; Basildon Peta, 'Final push'.

29. David Coltart, 'How Solomon Mujuru scuppered the Tsholotsho Declaration masterplan', 25 February 2018, available at: https//www.thestandard.co.zw/2018/02/25/solomon-mujuru-scuppered-tsholotsho-declaration-master-plan/. Sparks, 'Zimbabwe: Plots abound'.

30. Matyszak 2016.

31. Moore and Mawowa 2010.

32. Mbeki 2008 [2001]; Moore 2010a, 2012.

33. 'Hands off Zimbabwe, Mugabe tells Blair', *The Guardian*, 2 September 2002, available at: https://www.theguardian.com/environment/2002/sep/02/greenpolitics.Zimbabwenews.

34. McEwan 2019: 21.

35. Moyo 1988: 10.

36. Ibid.: 11.

37. Ibid.: 15.

38. Jackson and Rosberg 1982.

39. Moyo 1988: 15.

40. Ibid.: 16.

41. Ibid.: 199.

42. Jonathan Moyo, 'Tsholotsho saga: the untold story', 17 December 2004.

43. Matyszak 2016: 39–40, 44.

44. Tendi 2020b; Kriger 2020; Moore 2020a.

45. Jonathan Moyo, 'Full text of Moyo's reply to dismissal from government', Independent Candidate for Tsholotsho Constituency, 19 February 2005, available at: http://jmoyo.50megs.com/response.html.

46. Owen Gagare, 'Zanu PF politburo video exposé', *Zimbabwe Independent*, 11 August 2017, available at: https://www.theindependent.co.zw/2017/08/11/zanu-pf-politburo-video-expose/.

47. Mhanda 2011: 25. 'Prof Moyo denies fleeing liberation struggle', The Zimbabwe News Live, 21 February 2015, available at: http://www.thezimbabwenewslive.com/i-didnt-flee-struggle-prof-moyo/.

48. Interview, Harare, June 2000.

49. Jonathan Moyo, 'Tsholotsho saga: the untold story', *Zimbabwe Independent*, 23 December 2004, available at: https://www.theindependent.co.zw/2004/12/23/tsholotsho-saga-the-untold-story-2/.

50. Jonathan Moyo 'Full text'.

51. Actualités, '"Third way" runs into criticism', New Humanitarian, 31 August 2005, available at: https://www.thenewhumanitarian.org/fr/node/223559.

52. Nyambi 2016.

53. Matyszak 2016.

54. Ibbo Mandaza, 'Back to the future for Zimbabwe: Mnangagwa's false start', Independent Online, 19 November 2018, available at: https://www.iol.co.za/news/opinion/back-to-the-future-for-zimbabwe-mnangagwas-false-start-18178222.

55. Tendi 2013; Chan 2012.

56. Burgis 2020: 48–57. His 2015 book is Africa resource curse centric. The focus is London City by 2020.

57. Stephen Chan, 'Zimbabwe's tense countdown', *New Statesman*, 3 April 2008, available at: https://www.newstatesman.com/world-affairs/2008/04/mugabe-election-zimbabwe; Stephen Chan, 'Exit Mugabe', *Prospect Magazine*, 2 April 2008, available at: http://www.archive.kubatana.net/html/archive/opin/080402sc.asp?sector=OPIN&year=2008&range_start=421.

58. David Moore, 'Fantasy that Mnangagwa would fix Zimbabwe now fully exposed', The Conversation, 22 January 2019, available at: https://theconversation.com/fantasy-that-mnangagwa-would-fix-zimbabwe-now-fully-exposed-110197.

59. Victoria Brittain, 'A tale of two breakfasts', *The Guardian*, 10 May 2006, available at: https://www.theguardian.com/commentisfree/2006/may/10/arts.theatre; Peter Fabricius, 'Ghost returns to haunt Mugabe', *Mercury*, 11 December 2009, available at: https://www.pressreader.com/south-africa/the-mercury-south-africa/20091211/282638913687345. Note the source in Fabricius's piece: apparently from Zimbabwe Democracy Now.

60. Blessing-Miles Tendi, 'After Mugabe, who?' *The Guardian*, 19 June 2008, available at: https://www.theguardian.com/commentisfree/2008/jun/19/zimbabwe. In Tendi 2013, he seems to take a different view.

61. Tendi 2013: 831, 841.

8. FROM CONSPIRACIES TO THE REAL COUP'S CUSP: 2007–17

1. Burgis 2020: 48–57, 73, 277–8, 306–7.
2. Moore 2018a: 267–71; Derek Matyszak, 'Southern Africa Report 12: back to the future: legitimising Zimbabwe's 2018 elections', Institute of Security Studies, 17 November 2017, available at: https://issafrica.org/research/southern-africa-report/back-to-the-future-legitimising-zimbabwes-2018-elections.
3. Armed Conflict Location and Event Data Project, 'Zimbabwe', available at: https://public.tableau.com/profile/acled6590#!/vizhome/Zimbabwe_1/ProportionZiminTotal.
4. Moore and Mawowa 2010.
5. African Democracy Encyclopaedia Project, 'Zimbabwe: 2008 House of Assembly election results by province', EISDA, April 2008, available at: https://www.eisa.org.za/wep/zim2008results2.htm.
6. 'Report on the Zimbabwe 29 March 2008 Harmonized Elections and 27 June Presidential Run-off', Zimbabwe Election Support Network, 2008, available at: http://localhost/oldzesn/publications/publication_275.pdf.
7. Masunungure 2009: 86; Sachikonye 2011: 49–61.
8. Masunungure 2009: 86.
9. 'Mengistu hatched and directed Operation *Murambatsvina*', Zim Online, 20 February 2006, available at: https://www.zimbabwesituation.com/old/feb20a_2006.html.
10. Interview with Danny Stannard, Cambridgeshire, September 2014.
11. Wilkins 2013.
12. Celia W. Dugger, 'New signs of Zimbabwe attacks as Mbeki arrives', *New York Times*, 10 May 2008, available at: https://www.nytimes.com/2008/05/10/world/africa/10zimbabwe.html.
13. Tendi 2016. Interviews, London, August 2014.
14. Interviews, Harare, April 2019; London, July 2019; Johannesburg, May 2020.
15. 'Mugabe one-on-one interview', *Zimbabwe Independent*, 23 March 2018, available at: https://www.theindependent.co.zw/2018/03/23/mugabe-one-one-interview/.
16. Rangarirai Mberi, 'Interview with Makoni', *Financial Gazette*, 14 February 2008, available at: http://archive.kubatana.net/html/archive/elec/080214fingaz.asp?sector=elec&year=2008&range_start=1201.
17. Interview with Wilfred Mhanda, who took up the Mavambo Kusile torch and ran in Mbare, Harare, March 2008.
18. The graduate of the Christian Socialist Cold Comfort Farm is infamous for saying during a famine, for which a party card could gain food aid, that 'we would be better off with only six million [ZANU (PF)] people'. Trevor Grundy, 'Whatever happened to Didymus Mutasa?' Institute for War and Peace Reporting, 4 October 2006, available at: https://iwpr.net/global-voices/what-

ever-happened-didymus-mutasa. Ironically, Mutasa was not above offing people in his party who challenged him at the 2004 primaries (Moore 2008a).

19. MacDonald Dzirutwe, 'Mugabe warns Catholic bishops over politics', Reuters, 4 May 2007, available at: https://www.reuters.com/article/uk-zimbabwe-mugabe-bishops/mugabe-warns-catholic-bishops-over-politics-id UKL0430109020070504.

20. Andrew Meldrum, '"Emergency law" on streets as Mugabe bids to cling on', *The Guardian*, 18 March 2007, available at: https://www.theguardian.com/world/2007/mar/18/zimbabwe.andrewmeldrum.

21. 'EU presidency, Ban Ki-moon condemn Zimbabwe treatment of opposition leaders', *International Herald Tribune*, 12 March 2007, available at: http://archive.kubatana.net/html/archive/demgg/070312iht.asp?sector=CACT&year=0&range_start=1.

22. Stephen Chan, 'Farewell, Robert Mugabe', Open Democracy, 20 March 2007, available at: www.opendemocracy.net/democracy-africa_democracy/chan_mugabe_4450.jsp.

23. Ros Taylor, 'Mugabe says "go hang"', *The Guardian*, 16 March 2007, available at: https://www.theguardian.com/news/2007/mar/16/wrap.rostaylor.

24. 'Editorial: Mbeki says election key to Zimbabwe crisis', Reuters, 3 April 2007, available at: https://uk.reuters.com/article/us-zimbabwe-opposition-mbeki/mbeki-says-election-key-to-zimbabwe-crisis-idUSL0265387220070403.

25. Stephen Chan, 'Back to the future', *Mail and Guardian*, 12 April 2007, available at: http://archive.kubatana.net/html/archive/opin/070412sc.asp?sector=Demgg&year=2007&range_start=1291.

26. Wikipedia, '2007 Zimbabwean alleged coup d'état attempt', available at: https://en.wikipedia.org/wiki/2007_Zimbabwean_alleged_coup_d%27%C3%A9tat_attempt.

27. Tom Head, 'What happened with the last coup attempt against Robert Mugabe?' *The South African*, 24 November 2017, available at: https://www.thesouthafrican.com/news/last-coup-against-Robert-Mugabe; 'Coup plot details revealed', *The Zimbabwean*, 16 July 2007.

28. Moses Moyo, 'Coup attempt nipped in bud', *First Post*, 8 June 2007, available at: http://www.ocnus.net/artman2/publish/Africa_8/Coup_Attempt_Nipped_in_Bud.shtml.

29. Never Kadungure, 'Zimbabwe spy agency thrown into turmoil', Nehanda Radio, 3 July 2011, available at: https://nehandaradio.com/2011/07/03/zimbabwe-spy-agency-thrown-into-turmoil/.

30. '(New Zimbabwe) Radio publishes names of "CIO agents"', Maravi Blogspot, 1 July 2011, available at: http://maravi.blogspot.com/2011/07/newzimbabwe-radio-publishes-names-of.html.

31. Never Kadungure, 'Zimbabwe spy agency thrown into turmoil'.

32. Jonisayi Maromo, 'Zim ambassador rubbishes opposition crackdown reports',

The Independent, 8 August 2018, available at: https://www.iol.co.za/news/africa/zim-ambassador-rubbishes-opposition-crackdown-reports-16465111.

33. 'Zim soldiers "plotted coup"', News24, 15 June 2007, available at: https://www.news24.com/Africa/Zimbabwe/Zim-soldiers-plotted-coup-20070615; Dumisani Muleya, 'Mnangagwa grilled over UPM links', *Zimbabwe Independent*, 19 October 2007, available at: https://www.theindependent.co.zw/2007/10/19/mnangagwa-grilled-over-upm-links/.

34. Blessed Mhlanga, 'ED elbows out Rugeje', *Newsday*, 11 June 2019, available at: https://www.newsday.co.zw/2019/06/ed-elbows-out-rugeje/.

35. Marondera seems to be the scene of many a battle among military leaders: a widespread tale of many years standing has Chiwenga and Mujuru fighting in Marondera's streets over one or the other's cuckolding.

36. Our correspondent, 'Coup plot details revealed', *The Zimbabwean*, 16 July 2007, available at: https://www.thezimbabwean.co/2007/08/coup-plot-details-revealed/.

37. Clemence Manyukwe, 'Zimbabwe: student faces death for alleged coup plot', *University News*, 20 July 2008, available at: https://www.universityworldnews.com/post.php?story=20080717165223414.

38. 'Former army officer breaks silence on coup accusations', *The Zimbabwean*, 3 September 2014, available at: http://www.thezimbabwean.co/2014/09/former-army-officer-breaks-silence/; 'Army captain on "live" charges of attempting to remove president for croc disowns Mnangagwa', Zim Eye, 8 December 2017, available at: https://www.zimeye.net/2017/12/08/army-captain-on-live-charges-of-attempting-to-remove-president-for-croc-disowns-mnangagwa-despite-longest-chikurubi-prison-stay-since-1980/.

39. Desmond Chingarande, 'Securocrats scale up surveillance', *Newsday*, 23 October 2020, available at: https://www.zimbabwesituation.com/news/securocrats-scale-up-surveillance/#more.

40. Nomazulu Thata, 'Where is comrade Albert Matapo?' Zim Eye, 30 January 2021, available at: https://www.zimeye.net/2021/01/30/where-is-comrade-albert-matapo/.

41. 'Coup "plotter" freed, says general killed', New Zimbabwe, 1 March 2014, available at: http://www.newzimbabwe.com/news-14645-Coup+plotter+freed,+says+General+killed/news.aspx.

42. Richard Muponde, 'Dr Gunda a widow who picked up the pieces and moved on', *Bulawayo Chronicle*, 2 June 2018, available at: https://www.pressreader.com/zimbabwe/chronicle-zimbabwe/20180602/281599536182814.

43. Itai Mushekwe, 'President Mugabe fall out with Mujuru due to coup d'état', Bulawayo24 News, 16 January 2015, available at: https://bulawayo24.com/index-id-News-sc-national-byo-60935-pg-2.html. Derek Matyszak (2014, 2016) tells that tale best, so replication will not happen here other than to wonder why the dynamic Moyo–Crocodile duo fell apart (again) after her forced departure. She started a new party with a few ZANU (PF) has-beens thereafter.

44. Itai Mushekwe, 'President Mugabe fall out with Mujuru due to coup d'état'.
45. Philemon Bulawayo, 'ZANU-PF approves Mnangagwa re-election bid in 2023', *The Independent*, 15 December 2018, available at: https://www.iol.co.za/news/africa/zanu-pf-approves-mnangagwa-re-election-bid-in-2023-18517753.
46. Chagonda 2012.
47. Moore 2010b: 67–8.
48. Raftopoulos 2013.

9. THE COUP INCARNATE: 14–21 NOVEMBER 2017

1. Kissinger 2011 [1976]: 507.
2. Scoones et al. 2010.
3. Ibbo Mandaza, 'The political economy of the state in Zimbabwe', 'Securocrat state and Zim in transition', 'The making of a securocrat state in Zim', *Zimbabwe Independent*, 1, 8, 15 April 2016, available at: https://www.theindependent.co.zw/2016/04/01/political-economy-state-zimbabwe/, https://www.theindependent.co.zw/2016/04/08/securocrat-state-zim-transition/, https://www.theindependent.co.zw/2016/04/15/making-securocrat-state-zim/.
4. Maverick Citizen, 'Report on cartel power dynamics in Zimbabwe', Daily Maverick, 9 February 2021, available at: https://www.dailymaverick.co.za/article/2021-02-09-zimbabwe-explosive-cartel-report-uncovers-the-anatomy-of-a-captured-state/.
5. 'Statement by the Executive Secretary of SADC Following the Resignation of President Robert Mugabe', 24 November 2017, available at: https://www.sadc.int/news-events/news/statement-executive-secretary-sadc-following-resignation-president-robert-mugabe/.
6. Matyszak forthcoming will prove more sophisticated. Jason Brickhill, 'Coup, constitution and the court: Zimbabwean constitutional court whitewashes flawed rigged elections', Oxford Human Rights Hub, 24 August 2018, available at: http://ohrh.law.ox.ac.uk/coup-constitution-and-the-court-zimbabwean-constitutional-court-whitewashes-flawed-rigged-elections/.
7. Fontana 2004: 177.
8. Burgis 2020: 36–8, on Fraenkel.
9. Thanks to Brendan De Paor-Moore for this idea.
10. Pollitt 2017.
11. Tendi 2020a: 42.
12. See Tendi 2020a: 40.
13. Moore 2019. Stellenbosch University's Centre for Complex Systems in Transition is another, with undoubtedly coincidental parallels.
14. The very cosmopolitan Joost Fontein may be the first to coin this description of South African exceptionalism.
15. Mullin 1982.

16. Mandaza 1986.
17. Thieme et al. 2021.
18. Sachikonye et al. 2018; Chagonda 2011, 2012.
19. Apologies to Samuel Beckett. Chris Power, 'Samuel Beckett, the maestro of failure', *The Guardian*, 7 July 2016, available at: https://www.theguardian.com/books/booksblog/2016/jul/07/samuel-beckett-the-maestro-of-failure.
20. Tendi 2020a: 51.
21. 'Trevor Noah jokes about Zimbabwe', eNCA, 17 November 2017, available at: https://www.enca.com/life/entertainment/watch-trevor-noah-jokes-on-zimbabwe-situation.
22. Tendi 2020a: 51–60, 2013, 2016, 2017, 2020.
23. Anina Rich and Sarah Maguire, 'What is the Baader-Meinhof phenomenon?' The Lighthouse, available at: https://lighthouse.mq.edu.au/article/july-2020/What-is-the-Baader-Meinhof-Phenomenon.
24. 'Douglas Rogers says Chris Mutsvangwa played key role in defacto military coup', Voice of America, 15 November 2019, available at: https://www.voazimbabwe.com/a/christopher-mutsvangwa-role-in-military-coup/5166379.html.
25. Rutherford 2019; Rudo Mudiwa, 'On Grace Mugabe: coups, phalluses, and what is being defended', Africa is a Country, 28 November 2017, available at: http://africasacountry.com/2017/11/on-grace-mugabe-coups-phalluses-and-what-is-beingdefended.
26. Jason Burke, 'Grace Mugabe says she acted in self-defence in hotel incident', *The Guardian*, 11 September 2017, available at: https://www.theguardian.com/world/2017/sep/11/grace-mugabe-self-defence-hotel-incident-gabriella-engels.
27. Moore 2016b.
28. 'Almost news with Chester Missing', eNCA, 17 February 2019, available at: https://www.youtube.com/watch?v=__NKeFDxTw4.
29. Mazrui 1973: 1.
30. Chiwenga 2015; 'Moyo fails to back Chiwenga thesis claims', *The Herald*, 12 July 2017, available at: https://www.herald.co.zw/moyo-fails-to-back-chiwenga-thesis-claims/.
31. McCandless 2011.
32. Tendi 2020a: 39, 67. The phrase 'as well as party members who had been sidelined' ends the first section of the quote but I am not sure what it means.
33. Tendi 2013: 841–3.
34. 'Top posters from Zimbabwe's historical protest', eNCA, 19 November 2017, available at: https://www.enca.com/africa/in-pictures-top-posters-from-zimbabwes-historical-protest.
35. 'WATCH: Tens of thousands stopped by soldiers on way to State House in Harare', News24, 18 November 2017, available at: https://www.youtube.com/watch?v=fgUuEU0vb8g.

245

36. Tendai Marima, 'Zimbabweans demand Mugabe's resignation at Harare rally', Al Jazeera, 19 November 2017, available at: https://www.aljazeera.com/news/2017/11/19/zimbabweans-demand-mugabes-resignation-at-harare-rally.

37. Joshua Hammer, 'Zimbabwe: enter the Crocodile', *New York Review of Books*, 22 March 2018, available at: https://pulitzercenter.org/reporting/zimbabwe-enter-crocodile.

38. Jason Burke and Emma Graham-Harrison, 'Zimbabwe in chaos as Mugabe fails to announce resignation', *Irish Times*, 19 November 2017, available at: https://www.irishtimes.com/news/world/africa/zimbabwe-in-chaos-as-mugabe-fails-to-announce-resignation-1.3297861.

39. Geoffrey York, 'Student protest crackdown shows Zimbabwe's military still firmly in charge', *Globe and Mail*, 23 November 2017, available at: https://www.theglobeandmail.com/news/world/zimbabwes-military-cracks-down-on-studentprotests/article37063823/.

40. 'Full statement: "I'm not going anywhere … Zanu-PF is not your personal property," Mnangagwa tells Mugabe', News24.com, 8 November 2017, available at: https://www.news24.com/news24/Africa/Zimbabwe/full-statement-im-not-going-anywhere-anywhere-zanu-pf-is-not-your-personal-property-mugabe-tells-mugabe-20171108.

41. 'Full statement: Emmerson Mnangagwa's plea for Mugabe to resign', TimesLive, 27 November 2017, available at: https://www.timeslive.co.za/politics/2017-11-21-in-fu/.

42. Hamburger 2008: 74; Ernest Aggrey, 'Is the voice of the people; the voice of God?', Modern Ghana, 22 February 2016, available at: https://www.modernghana.com/news/676340/is-the-voice-of-the-people-the-voice-of.html.

43. 'Robert Mugabe tells ITV News Zimbabwe "must undo disgrace" of "military takeover"', ITV News, 6 March 2018, available at: https://www.youtube.com/watch?v=yJG74nnDNAk.

44. Interviews with Douglas Mwonzora, Johannesburg, December 2017, Harare, January 2018; Nielsson 2014.

45. David Fickling, 'This was no coup. But it comes far too close: interview with Naunihal Singh', *Washington Post*, 8 January 2021, available at: https://www.washingtonpost.com/business/this-was-nocoup-but-it-comes-far-tooclose/2021/01/07/f4bb3ef2-50f4-11eb-a1f5-fdaf28cfca90_story.html.

46. Jan Bornman, 'Mnangagwa calls parliament the "ultimate expression" of Zimbabweans' will as Mugabe impeachment looms', News24, 21 November 2017, available at: https://www.news24.com/Africa/Zimbabwe/mnangagwa-calls-parliament-the-ultimate-expression-of-zimbabweans-will-as-mugabe-impeachment-looms-20171121.

47. 'Robert Mugabe's resignation letter in full', Al Jazeera, 21 November 2017, available at: https://www.aljazeera.com/news/2017/11/21/robert-mugabes-resignation-letter-in-full.

48. 'IRIN interview with land expert Sam Moyo', The New Humanitarian, 14 August 2001, available at: https://www.thenewhumanitarian.org/fr/node/193915.
49. Tendi 2020a: 39–45, 63, 67.
50. Rogers 2019.
51. Ndlovu 2018.
52. Rutherford 2019; Rudo Mudiwa, 'On Grace Mugabe: coups, phalluses, and what is being defended'. This section relies on an updated, altered version of Moore 2018b.
53. Desmond Chingarande, 'Revealed: how Grace got her "fake" PhD', The Standard, 18 February 2018, available at: https://www.zimbabwesituation.com/news/revealed-how-grace-got-her-fake-phd/; Kirk Helliker, 'Grace Mugabe's thesis does not meet minimum academic requirements', Mail and Guardian, 30 January 2018, available at: https://mg.co.za/article/2018-01-30-grace-mugabes-thesis-does-not-meet-minimum-academic-requirements/.
54. Tendi 2020a: 41, 44, 61.
55. Ibid.: 51, 57; Fontein 2018, 2022.
56. Peta Thornycroft, 'Grace Mugabe claims Joice Mujuru plans to kill her "Gaddafi-style"', Daily Telegraph, 14 November 2014, available at: https://www.telegraph.co.uk/news/worldnews/africaandindianocean/zimbabwe/11241242/Grace-Mugabe-claims-Joice-Mujuru-plans-to-kill-her-Gaddafi-style.html.
57. Tendi 2016.
58. Interview with Saviour Kasukuwere, Harare, December 2018.
59. Nyambi 2016. Elder nationalist Didymus Mutasa said he would use the pesticide Gamatox to eliminate the youthful 'weevils'—associated with Emmerson Mnangagwa—trying to take some of his farms, which in turn he had taken from white commercial farmers. These became the labels in the Joice Mujuru vs. Grace Mugabe factional battles. Matyszak 2016.
60. Kriger 2012.
61. Jason Burke, 'Grace Mugabe says she acted in self-defence in hotel incident'.
62. Gosebo Mathope, 'Watch: four times Grace Mugabe slammed Mnangagwa in scathing speeches', The Citizen, 11 November 2017, available at: https://citizen.co.za/news/news-africa/1728839/watch-six-times-mugabe-slammed-mnangagwa-in-scathing-speeches/.
63. Tendai Mugabe, 'Mnangagwa clarifies poisoning statement', The Herald, 6 October 2017, available at: https://www.herald.co.zw/mnangagwa-clarifies-poisoning-statement/.
64. 'VP Mnangagwa Politburo Presentation', YouTube, 11 August 2017, available at: https://www.youtube.com/watch?v=3ZXqwFvPLPQ.
65. 'VP Mnangagwa roasts Prof Moyo', Newsday, 13 October 2017, available at: https://www.newsday.co.zw/2017/10/vp-mnangagwa-roasts-prof-moyo/.
66. MacDonald Dzirutwe, Joe Brock and Ed Cropley, 'Special Report: "Treacherous shenanigans"—the inside story of Mugabe's downfall', Reuters, 26 November

2017, available at: https://www.reuters.com/article/us-zimbabwe-politics-mugabe-specialrepor/special-report-treacherous-shenanigans-the-inside-story-of-mugabes-downfall-idUSKBN1DQ0AG.

67. 'Mugabe threatens to sack VP as wife booed at rally', Agence France-Presse, 5 November 2017, available at: https://www.news24.com/news24/Africa/Zimbabwe/mugabe-threatens-to-sack-vp-as-wife-booed-at-rally-20171104; Moore 2018b: 10.

68. Bernard Mpofu and Elias Mambo, 'Mnangagwa's great escape: the details', *Zimbabwe Independent*, 10 November 2017, available at: https://www.theindependent.co.zw/2017/11/10/mnangagwas-great-escape-details/. Chiwenga had gone to China as planned ages before. Mugabe had hastened chief of staff Major General Trust Mugoba (in charge of military operations) to his acceptance of a long-delayed appointment as the head of the AU standby force: his delays were suspicious.

69. Blessing-Miles Tendi, 'Zimbabwe: the UK's misguided role in the rise and fall of Mnangagwa', African Arguments, 8 November 2017, available at: http://africanarguments.org/2017/11/08/zimbabwe-the-uks-misguided-role-in-the-rise-and-fall-of-mnangagwa/.

70. Elias Mambo, 'Mnangagwa faction faces decapitation', *Zimbabwe Independent*, 15 September 2017, available at: https://www.theindependent.co.zw/2017/09/15/mnangagwa-faction-faces-decapitation/.

71. Rudo Mudiwa, 'On Grace Mugabe: coups, phalluses, and what is being defended'.

72. Farai Mutsaka, 'Zimbabwe's Mnangagwa describes risky escape after firing', *The Independent*, 13 January 2018, available at: https://www.iol.co.za/news/africa/zimbabwes-mnangagwa-describes-risky-escape-after-firing-12713362.

73. 'Full statement: "I'm not going anywhere … Zanu-PF is not your personal property," Mnangagwa tells Mugabe'.

74. Rogers 2019. Interviews, Johannesburg, September 2019.

75. Moore 2020b, 2018b: 12. Interview with Dumiso Dabengwa, Bulawayo, January 2018. David Moore, 'A tribute to Zimbabwean liberation hero Dumiso Dabengwa', The Conversation, 30 May 2019, available at: https://theconversation.com/a-tribute-to-zimbabwean-liberation-hero-dumisodabengwa-117986.

76. Tom Phillips, 'Zimbabwe army chief's trip to China last week raises questions on coup', *The Guardian*, 16 November 2017, available at: https://www.theguardian.com/world/2017/nov/16/zimbabwe-army-chief-trip-china-last-week-questions-coup.

77. Moore 2018b: 12; Interviews, Bulawayo, January 2018.

78. 'Factbox: Morgan Tsvangirai (likely prime minister), likely players in potential post-coup Zimbabwe unity government', Reuters, 16 November 2017, available at: https://www.firstpost.com/world/factbox-likely-players-in-potential-post-coup-zimbabwe-unity-government-reuters-4213505.html.

79. Ndlovu 2018; interviews, Harare and Johannesburg, July 2018; Angelique Serrao, 'Online publications dig into Mnangagwa's connections to SA business-man', News24, 28 November 2017, available at: https://www.news24.com/news24/SouthAfrica/News/online-publications-dig-into-mnangagwas-connec-tions-to-sa-businessman-20171128.

80. Tendi 2020a: 39, 43–6, 61, 63.

81. 'General Chiwenga latest press conference 13 Nov 2017', YouTube, 13 November 2017, available at: https://www.youtube.com/watch?v=DnX ybgPIRqc.

82. Interviews, Johannesburg, November 2017.

83. Statement by General Constantino Chiwenga, Commander, Zimbabwe Defence Forces, Monday 13th November 2017, available at http://www.veritaszim.net/node/2256. His full name is Constantino Guvheya Dominic Nyikadzino Chiwenga. Up until 2016 he had been Constantine Chiwenga, but decided to accentuate his Italian tastes–it is said that his house is a direct copy of a Tuscan castle he visited in Italy–with the 'o'. He also added Nyikadzino, meaning he is destined to rule. Tendi 2020a: 61.

84. 'Zanu-PF warns army general,' TimesLive, 15 November 2017, available at: https://www.dispatchlive.co.za/news/2017-11-15-zanu-pf-warns-army-gen-eral/.

85. Mungwari 2018: 6; 'Zimbabwe: army chief accused of "treasonable conduct"', BBC, 14 November 2017, available at: http://www.bbc.com/news/world-africa-41991425.

86. Tendi 2020a: 48–9.

87. Ibid.: 49; interviews in Harare, Bulawayo and Johannesburg, July and October 2018, December 2020.

88. MacDonald Dzirutwe et al., 'Special Report: "Treacherous shenanigans"–the inside story of Mugabe's downfall'.

89. James Thompson, 'Hide and seek for Zanu-PF's G40 faction', TimesLive, 16 November 2017, available at: https://www.timeslive.co.za/news/south-africa/2017-11-16-hide-and-seek-for-zanu-pfs-g40-faction/.

90. 'Full statement from the Zimbabwe defence forces', Eyewitness News, 15 November 2017, available at: https://ewn.co.za/2017/11/15/official-state-ment-from-the-zimbabwe-defence-forces.

91. Moore 2018b: 14.

92. 'President Mugabe addresses Zimbabwe', YouTube, 19 November 2017, avail-able at: https://www.youtube.com/watch?v=yKTmqKswH-E.

93. Interviews, Harare, February 2019. Ibbo Mandaza, 'Back to the future for Zimbabwe: Mnangagwa's false start', Independent Online, 19 November 2018, available at: https://www.iol.co.za/news/opinion/back-to-the-future-for-zimbabwe-mnangagwas-false-start-18178222.

94. Interview with Douglas Mwonzora, Harare, January 2018.

95. Interview with Themba Mliswa, Johannesburg, August 2018.

96. Interview with Teresa Makone, Harare, January 2018.

97. 'Rory Stewart returns from Zimbabwe', United Kingdom (UK) Government, 28 November 2017, available at: https://www.gov.uk/government/news/rory-stewart-returns-from-zimbabwe.

98. MacDonald Dzirutwe, 'Zimbabwe opposition wants inclusive political process after military intervention', 20 November 2017, available at: https://www.reuters.com/article/us-zimbabwe-politics-opposition/zimbabwe-opposition-wants-inclusive-political-process-after-military-intervention-idUSKBN1DK16W?il=0.

99. David Pilling, 'Robert Mugabe's fall offers faint hope to Zimbabwe opposition', *Financial Times*, 22 November 2017, available at: https://www.ft.com/content/c547e042-cf12-11e7-b781-794ce08b24dc.

100. Bernice Maune and Thapelo Lekabe, 'Mugabe has resigned as parliament moved to impeach him', *The Citizen*, 21 November 2017, available at: https://citizen.co.za/news/news-africa/1734903/live-report-zim-military-commander-reveals-mnagagwa-expected-back-in-country/.

101. Interviews, Bulawayo and Harare, February 2019.

102. Stephen Jakes, 'Mnangagwa will not have a GNU with Tsvangirai–MDC official', Bulawayo24 News, 22 November 2017, available at: https://bulawayo24.com/index-id-news-sc-national-byo-122715.html.

103. Charles Laiton, 'Army intervention constitutionally correct: High Court', *Newsday*, 25 November 2017, available at: https://www.newsday.co.zw/2017/11/army-intervention-constitutionally-correct-high-court/; Solidarity Peace Trust, *Old Beginnings: The Political Context of Zimbabwe and a Report on Biometric Voter Registration (BVR): A National and Matabeleland Perspective*, February 2018, available at: http://solidaritypeacetrust.org/download/report-files/SPT-Old-Beginnings-February-2018-.pdf.

104. Moore 2017: 22–3.

105. 'Mnangagwa names new Zimbabwean cabinet', *The Citizen*, 1 December 2017, available at: https://citizen.co.za/news/news-africa/1746240/mnangagwa-names-new-zimbabwean-cabinet/; 'Zimbabwe: coup general appointed vice president', Deutsche Welle, 27 December 2017, available at: http://www.dw.com/en/zimbabwe-coup-general-appointed-vice-president/a-41918031.

106. David Coltart, 'Wither Zimbabwe?' *Financial Gazette*, 31 December 2017, available at: https://www.africanewshub.com/news/7895806-wither-zimbabwe.

10. FROM COUP TO COVID: LUMPEN LEADERS AND REALLY MORBID SYMPTOMS

1. Burgis 2020: 163. Reprinted by permission of HarperCollins Publishers Ltd © Burgis 2020.

2. Babic 2020; Stahl 2019.

3. Apologies to NoViolet Bulawayo: Bulawayo 2013; cf. Ngoshi 2016.

4. Percy Zvomuya, 'Have Mugabe's own words come back to haunt him?' Al Jazeera, 16 November 2017, available at: https://www.aljazeera.com/features/2017/11/16/have-mugabes-own-words-come-back-to-haunt-him.

5. It might have been Meredith 2007.

6. CTV News Archive, '1976 interview with Robert Mugabe', available at: https://www.youtube.com/watch?v=BSU--J9MMGs.

7. Hugo Tavera Villegas, 'Machiavelli and "political realism": Gramsci's interpretation of Machiavelli', unpublished paper, available at: https://www.academia.edu/26661127/Machiavelli_and_political_realism_Gramscis_interpretation_of_Machiavelli.

8. Anna K. Mwaba, 'When is a coup a coup?' Africa is a Country, 28 February 2018, available at: https://africasacountry.com/2018/02/when-is-a-coup-a-coup; 'Communiqué on the Visit of the Chairperson of the African Union Commission to Zimbabwe', African Union press release, 22 February 2018, available at: https://au.int/en/pressreleases/20180222/communiqu%C3%A9-visit-chairperson-african-union-commission-zimbabwe.

9. 'Robert Mugabe tells ITV News Zimbabwe "must undo disgrace" of "military takeover"', ITV News, 6 March 2018, available at: https://www.youtube.com/watch?v=yJG74nnDNAk.

10. Associated Press, 'New party forms in Zimbabwe with Mugabe's backing', News24, 5 March 2018, available at: https://www.news24.com/news24/africa/zimbabwe/new-party-forms-in-zimbabwe-with-mugabes-backing-20180305.

11. 'Former Zimbabwean Pres Robert Mugabe holds media briefing on the eve of July 30th polls', SABC News, available at: https://www.youtube.com/watch?v=cipP8WELnuE.

12. 'Comrade Mugabe lays the line at historic Chimoio central committee meeting', Zimbabwe News, 5–6, July–December 1977, p. 13, available at: http://www.aluka.org/action/showMetadata?doi=10.5555/AL.SFF.DOCUMENT.nuzn197707.

13. 'Mugabe one-on-one interview', Zimbabwe Independent, 23 March 2018, available at: https://www.theindependent.co.zw/2018/03/23/mugabe-one-one-interview/.

14. Leandro Medina and Friedrich Schneider, 'Shadow economies around the world: what did we learn over the last 20 years?' WP/18/17, International Monetary Fund, January 2018, available at: https://papers.ssrn.com/sol3/papers.cfm?abstract_id=3124402.

15. From Medina and Schneider, 'Shadow economies around the world: what did we learn over the last 20 years?', in Raftopoulos et al. 2021.

16. Thieme et al. 2021.

17. Raftopoulos et al. 2021.

18. For example, citing Mkandawire 2020.

19. Burgis 2020: 155, 161, 163, 165.

20. Netherlands Institute for Southern Africa and Pax Christi, 'John Arnold BREDENKAMP', 2004, available at: http://archive.niza.nl/docs/200503 291053497103.pdf; Christopher Thompson and Michael Peel, 'BAE linked to Zimbabwean arms dealer', *Financial Times*, 1 August 2008, available at: https://www.ft.com/content/c997119a-5f41–11dd-91c0–000077b07658;   Staff reporter, 'Smokes, sex and the arms deal', *Mail and Guardian*, 28 October 2008, available at: https://mg.co.za/article/2008-10-28-smokes-sex-and-the/; Open Secrets, 'Unaccountable: John Bredenkamp–agent of BAE systems', Daily Maverick, 18 June 2020, available at: https://www.dailymaverick.co.za/article/2020-06-18-john-bredenkamp-agent-of-bae-systems/.

21. Burgis 2020: 162–3; David Runciman, 'Deliverology', *London Review of Books*, 16 March 2016.

22. Bredenkamp replied to my work email on 'Make Mugabe an offer he can't refuse: the country's civil society groups need help from South Africa if civil war is to be averted', *Globe and Mail*, 9 April 2008. I surmised therein that he and Robert Mugabe might have shared a Christmas vacation in the West Indies, and that Mugabe should have been persuaded to stay. Many Zimbabweans to whom I spoke during the March 2008 election guessed much the same, although we did not debate the latter option. Bredenkamp's reply was similar to his riposte to Boris Johnson's, 'Cowardly whites who help Mugabe', *The Spectator*, 13 April 2002, available at: www.zimbabwesituation.com/apr12a_2002. html. Bredenkamp's is, 'I'm no Zanu-PF crony', 10 May 2002, available at: https://www.zimbabwesituation.com/old/may10_2002.html#link4. We agreed we could meet in England to discuss 'Zimbabwe's future, not its past'. When I called his office from the National Archives in Kew Gardens, as the MDC was debating the merits of pulling out of the run-off election or allowing more of its members to be killed, his secretary told me he was in Zimbabwe.

23. Burgis 2020: 56–7, 73, 276–8, 306–7, 336.

24. Freeland 2012.

25. Bratton 2014; Shumba 2017; Maverick Citizen, 'Report on cartel power dynamics in Zimbabwe'.

26. David Moore, 'Zimbabwe now: post-coup, mid-Covid; continuing crises, corruption, and confusion', African Arguments: Debating Ideas, 24 November 2020, available at: https://africanarguments.org/2020/11/24/zimbabwe-now-post-coup-mid-covid-continuing-crises-corruption-and-confusion/.

27. Staff writer, 'Makamba family fumes over Zororo's death', *Daily News*, 24 March 2020, available at: https://dailynews.co.zw/makamba-family-fumes-over-zororos-death/.

28. Edmund Kudzayi, 'Zimbabwe: Covid-19 drugs scandal lays bare the rot in the

system', *The Africa Report*, 23 June 2020, available at: https://www.theafricareport.com/30676/zimbabwe-covid-19-drugs-scandal-lays-bare-the-rot-in-the-system/; Frank Chikowore, 'Zimbabwean journalist Hopewell Chin'ono remanded in custody on fresh charges', Daily Maverick, 5 November 2020, available at: https://www.dailymaverick.co.za/article/2020-11-05-zimbabwean-journalist-hopewell-chinono-remanded-in-custody-on-fresh-charges/.

29. 'Chinamasa blasts the US ambassador during ZANU PF press conference', YouTube, 27 July 2020, available at: https://www.youtube.com/watch?v= HAopA2VMGHM.

30. Johns Hopkins University Coronavirus Resource Center, 'Zimbabwe overview', 28 February 2021, available at: https://coronavirus.jhu.edu/region/zimbabwe.

31. Reuters, 'Zimbabwe Covid-19 deaths pass 1,000 as infections surge', Sowetan Live, 25 January 2021, available at: https://www.sowetanlive.co.za/news/africa/2021-01-25-zimbabwe-covid-19-deaths-pass-1000-as-infections-surge/.

32. Farai Mutsaka, 'Fourth Zimbabwean cabinet member dies of COVID-19 in surge', *Washington Post*, 24 January 2021, available at: https://www.washingtonpost.com/world/africa/fourth-zimbabwean-cabinet-member-dies-of-covid-19-in-surge/2021/01/24/d6c51b52-5e4b-11eb-a177-7765f29a9524_story.html.

33. 'Kudakwashe Tagwirei', Pindula, 5 August 2020, available at: https://www.pindula.co.zw/Kudakwashe_Tagwirei; 'Trafigura to take 100% control of its Zimbabwe fuel import business', Reuters, 5 February 2020, available at: https://www.reuters.com/article/us-zimbabwe-trafig/trafigura-to-take-100-control-of-its-zimbabwe-fuel-import-business-idUSKBN1ZZ0QI.

34. Percy Zvomuya, 'Covid-19 shows what Zimbabwean nationalism means', New Frame, 31 March 2020, available at: https://www.newframe.com/covid-19-shows-what-zimbabwean-nationalism-means/.

35. 'Virus strikes Zimbabwe president Mnangagwa's inner circle', *Zimbabwe Mail*, 21 January 2021, available at: https://www.thezimbabwemail.com/main/virus-strikes-zimbabwe-president-mnangagwas-inner-circle/.

36. Jeffrey Moyo, 'No vaccination, no job: that's the warning from Zimbabwe's leader', *New York Times*, 26 February 2021, available at: https://www.nytimes.com/2021/02/26/world/no-vaccination-no-job-thats-the-warning-from-zimbabwes-leader.html.

37. Gibbs Dube, 'Zimbabweans attack govt. official for claiming that medical professionals are killing political players', VOA News, 15 January 2021, available at: https://www.voazimbabwe.com/a/medical-assassins-zimbabwe-nick-mangwana/5750378.html.

38. 'WARNING–DISTURBING PICTURES: UK Nurse (Nick) Ndabaningi Mangwana has watched as people were shot dead and called it fake news', Zim Eye, 7 August 2021, available at: https://www.zimeye.net/2018/08/07/uk-nurse-nick-ndabaningi-mangwana-has-watched-as-people-were-shot-dead-and-called-it-fake-news/.

39. Citizen Maverick 2021.
40. Godfrey Marawanyika, 'Zimbabwe to fund white farmers' compensation with mine revenue', Bloomberg, available at: https://www.bloomberg.com/news/articles/2021–01–07/zimbabwe-s-kuvimba-seeks-1-billion-for-2021-acquisitions-capex.
41. Moore 2010a, 2012, from Thabo Mbeki, 'How will Zimbabwe defeat its enemies? A discussion document', African National Congress mimeograph, 10 July 2001.
42. African National Congress (ANC) 2020.
43. See also Southall 2016.
44. ANC 2020: 4.
45. Ibid.
46. Ibid.
47. Ibid.: 5.
48. Ibid.: 6, 8.
49. Thabo Mbeki, 'What then about land expropriation without compensation? The national democratic revolution must resolve the intimately inter-connected land and national questions!' Thabo Mbeki Foundation, 25 September 2018, available at: https://www.dailymaverick.co.za/wp-content/uploads/TMF-NDR.pdf.
50. Blessed Mhlanga, 'Grace has captured Mugabe: war vets', Newsday, 31 July 2017, available at: https://www.newsday.co.zw/2017/07/grace-captured-mugabe-war-vets/?cn-reloaded=1.
51. Moore 2010b: 62–5.
52. Cf. Matyszak 2017.
53. Nathaniel Manheru (aka George Charamba), 'Zim: keeping the eye on the ball', The Herald, 30 August 2013, available at: https://www.herald.co.zw/zim-keeping-the-eye-on-the-ball/; Moore 2014a: 102–3.
54. Derek Matyszak, 'Emerson Mnangagwa exposed', ISS Today, 23 January, 2019, available at: https://issafrica.org/iss-today/emmerson-mnangagwa-exposed; Derek Matyszak, 'The Motlanthe Commission's anniversary of shame: the results of the inquiry into the 1 August 2018 shootings reveal Zimbabwe's lack of reform', Institute for Security Studies, 12 August 2019, available at: https://issafrica.org/iss-today/the-motlanthe-commissions-anniversary-of-shame.
55. Jason Burke, 'Zimbabwe election unrest turns deadly as army opens fire on protesters', The Guardian, 2 August 2018, available at: https://www.theguardian.com/world/2018/aug/01/zanu-pf-wins-majority-of-seats-in-zimbabwe-parliament-elections.
56. 'Eddie Adams' iconic Vietnam War photo: what happened next', BBC, 29 January 2018, available at: https://www.bbc.com/news/world-us-canada-42864421; David Simpson, 'Iwo Jima v. Abu Ghraib', London Review of Books,

November 2007, available at: https://www.lrb.co.uk/the-paper/v29/n23/david-simpson/iwo-jima-v.-abu-ghraib?

57. Derek Matyszak, 'Emerson Mnangagwa exposed' and 'The Motlanthe Commission's anniversary of shame'.

58. Erika Gibson, 'Zim president Mnangagwa's dream jet', *City Press*, 21 January 2019, available at: https://city-press.news24.com/News/zim-president-mnangagwas-dream-jet-20190121.

59. Now his dissertation is a book, entitled *Goose or Gander: The United Nations Security Council and the Ethic of Double Standards*, published by ZANU (PF)'s Herbert Chitepo School of Ideology.

60. 'On the Days of Darkness in Zimbabwe', Zimbabwe Human Rights NGO Forum, 6 February 2019, available at: http://www.hrforumzim.org/press-releases/daysofdarkness2/.

61. Jason Burke, 'Zimbabwe crackdown could last months, activists fear', *The Guardian*, 27 January 2019, available at: https://www.theguardian.com/world/2019/jan/27/zimbabwe-crackdown-will-continue-for-forseeable-future-activists-fear.

62. 'Zimbabwe police target trade union leaders in civil rights crackdown', International Trade Union Confederation, 23 January 2019, available at: https://www.ituc-csi.org/Trade-Unionists-Arrest-Civil-Right-Crackdown-Crisis-Zimbabwe.

63. Moore 2022, and 'Fantasy that Mnangagwa would fix Zimbabwe now fully exposed', The Conversation, 22 January 2019, available at: https://theconversation.com/fantasy-that-mnangagwa-would-fix-zimbabwe-now-fully-exposed-110197.

64. Columbus S. Mavhunga, Alaa Elassar and Dakin Andone, 'Zimbabwe accuses "rogue elements" of inciting violence against protesters', CNN, 19 January 2019, available at: https://edition.cnn.com/2019/01/19/africa/zimbabwe-violence-protesters/index.html; T. Kamhungira, 'ED goes after rogue soldiers and invites Chamisa, for talks', *Daily News*, 23 January 2019, available at: https://www.zimbabwesituation.com/news/ed-goes-after-rogue-soldiers-and-invites-chamisa-for-talks/.

65. 'Resurgent authoritarianism: the politics of the January 2019 violence in Zimbabwe', Solidarity Peace Trust, 20 February 2019, available at: http://solidaritypeacetrust.org/download/report-files/Resurgent-Authoritarianism-The-Politics-of-the-January-2019-Violence-in-Zimbabwe.pdf.

66. Mabasa Sasa, 'MDC and allies will be held accountable', *Sunday Mail*, 20 January 2019, available at: https://www.sundaymail.co.zw/mdc-and-allies-will-be-held-accountable.

67. The 'brief' made the Harare social media within hours, in advance of the ANC's visit to Harare to discuss the crackdown. ANA Reporter, 'Zanu-PF thanks ANC for demanding the removal of sanctions imposed on Zim', Independent Online, 31 January 2019, available at: https://www.iol.co.za/news/politics/zanu-pf-

thanks-anc-for-demanding-the-removal-of-sanctions-imposed-on-zim-19063265.

69. Carl Gibson and Steve Horn, 'Wikileaks docs expose famed Serbian activist's ties to "shadow CIA"', *In These Times*, 2 December 2013, available at: https://inthesetimes.com/article/wikileaks-docs-expose-famed-serbian-activists-ties-to-shadow-cia.

60. 'Zimbabwe: seven activists arrested, charged with treason,' Amnesty International, 31 May 2019, available at: https://www.amnesty.org/en/documents/afr46/0450/2019/en/.

70. 'Zimbabwe protests: opposition MDC backs down after police ban', BBC News, 16 August 2019, available at: https://www.bbc.com/news/world-africa-49366224.

71. Jones 2010.

72. Scott 1985.

73. Scott 1999. In a short correspondence with him after an Australian Hayekian and I debated his interpretation of East Asia, Hayek and Scott, Scott admitted he should have left Hayek out of his book. His postcard responses were charming.

EPILOGUE: ON THE OCCASION OF A HARARE BOOK LAUNCH

1. Kanyenze 2022.

2. I was later reminded that the gendarmerie had been there since the 'Occupy Unity Square' days ended with the March 2015 'disappearance' of its activist journalist leader, Itai Dzamara, which was never resolved. Kubatana, 'Zimbabwe: Statement marking six years since the disappearance of Itai Dzamara', 9 March 2021, available at: https://allafrica.com/stories/202103100621.html.

3. Burgis 2020.

4. Violet Gonda, 'Episode 2: Spotlight on Zimbabwean elections: New kid on the block or old actors in new costumes?', Hotseat, 7 March 2022, available at: https://youtu.be/KNSNiirwcJQ.

5. Sikhululekile Mashingaidze, 'A bloody road to Zimbabwe's 26 March by-elections', *Mail and Guardian*, 4 March 2022, available at: https://mg.co.za/africa/2022-03-04-a-bloody-road-to-zimbabwes-26-march-by-elections/.

6. Nobleman Runyanga, 'CCC: Old wine in old wineskins', *The Herald*, 16 February 2022, available at: https://www.herald.co.zw/ccc-old-wine-in-old-wineskins/.

7. Grace Kwinjeh, 'Zimbabwe: Chamisa lacks leadership qualities', *The Herald*, 10 March 2021, available at: https://allafrica.com/stories/202103100326.html.

8. Interviews with Moore, 3–5 March 2022; Colpani 2021, Gontijo 2021; Worth 2022.

9. Robert Tapfumaneyi, 'Zimbabwe: No-one can bar me from Harvest House—Chamisa', New Zimbabwe, 19 June 2020, available at: https://allafrica.com/stories/202006190272.html.

10. James Muonwa, 'Zimbabwe: Windfall as Zanu-PF, Mwonzora share $500m ahead of March by-elections', New Zimbabwe, 28 January 2022, available at: https://allafrica.com/stories/202201280256.html.

11. Lorraine Muromo, 'CCC links Chiwenga threats to violence outbreak', The Standard, 6 March 2022, available at: https://www.zimbabwesituation.com/news/ccc-links-chiwenga-threats-to-violence-outbreak/; SABC, 'Electioneering in Zimbabwe in full swing for by-elections', 6 March 2022, available at: https://www.youtube.com/watch?v=IZ7dnfJ2R6M.

12. ZimLive, 'Mnangagwa told to step down by military chiefs, claims Jonathan Moyo', Nehanda Radio, 27 February 2022, available at https://nehandaradio.com/2020/02/27/mnangagwa-told-to-step-down-by-military-chiefs-claims-jonathan-moyo/.

13. Miriam Mangwaya, 'CCC has infiltrated Zanu PF', NewsDay, 16 February 2022, available at: https://www.zimbabwesituation.com/news/ccc-has-infiltrated-zanu-pf/.

14. Moore 2022.

15. Zvamaida Murwira, '115 more Zupco buses commissioned', The Herald, 24 January 2022, available at: https://www.herald.co.zw/115-more-zupco-buses-commissioned/.

16. Herald Reporter, 'Zupco reviews fares', The Herald, 16 February 2022, available at: https://www.zimbabwesituation.com/news/zupco-reviews-fares/#more.

17. Garikai Dzoma, 'The $2000 mushikashika fine is cruel and heartless', TechZim, 3 September 2021, available at: https://www.techzim.co.zw/2021/09/the-2000-mushikashika-fine-is-cruel-and-heartless/.

18. Freeland 2012.

19. Chimhowu and Woodhouse 2006; De Soto 2000.

20. Ndlela 2019; Kanyenze 2022: 15–18, 108, 114, 124, 392, 407, 422.

21. Tendai Murisa, 'The past in the present: challenges of protecting customary tenure provisions—the Chilonga case', SIVI Institute, 13 February 2022, available at: https://www.sivioinstitute.org/.

22. Terence Chitapi, 'The state, new farmers and accumulation in Zimbabwe: the case of Command Agriculture in the Middle Sabi estate', 2021, MA Thesis, University of Johannesburg.

23. Raymond Madombwe, 'Zimbabwe: unlocking the value of 99-year leases', The Herald, 28 June 2021, available at: https://allafrica.com/stories/202106280300.html.

24. Shonhe and Scoones 2022.

25. Kanyenze 2022: 179.

26. Kanyenze 2022: 325–6.

27. Takura Zhangazha, 'On leadership in Zimbabwe: we cannot lead people backward', 19 February 2022, available at: takura-zhangazha.blogspot.com.

28. Burgis 2020.

29. Cf. Organised Crime and Corruption Reporting Project, 'Credit Suisse banked and financed Zimbabwean fraudster in deal that saved Mugabe', February 2022, available at: https://www.occrp.org/en/suisse-secrets/credit-suisse-banked-and-financed-zimbabwean-fraudster-in-deal-that-saved-mugabe.

30. Moore and Booysen 2022.

31. Anderson, K. 2017.

32. Neil Spencer, 'Fela Kuti remembered: "he was a tornado of a man, but he loved humanity"', *The Guardian*, 31 October 2010, available at: https://amp.theguardian.com/music/2010/oct/31/fela-kuti-musical-neil-spencer. Thanks to Emmanuel Sairosi for this reference.

33. Bulawayo 2013, 2022.

REFERENCES

Abrahamsen, Rita (2020), 'Internationalists, sovereigntists, nativists: contending visions of world order in pan-Africanism', *Review of International Studies*, 46 (1), 56–74.
————, et al. (2020) 'Confronting the international political sociology of the new right', *International Political Sociology*, 14 (1), 94–107.
Adebajo, Adekeye (2010), *The Curse of Berlin: Africa after the Cold War* (London: Hurst).
———— (2021), *The Trial of Cecil John Rhodes* (Johannesburg: Jacana).
Aeby, Michael (2015), 'Zimbabwe's gruelling transition: interim power-sharing and conflict management in Southern Africa' (doctoral thesis, University of Basel).
African National Congress (ANC) (2020), 'National General Council Special Edition: Let's Talk Politics—NGC2020 Discussion Documents', *Umrabulo* (November).
Agamben, Giorgio (2005), *State of Exception* (Chicago: University of Chicago Press).
Alexander, Jocelyn (1998), 'Dissident perspectives on Zimbabwe's post-independence war', *Africa* (68), 2, 151–82.
Alexander, Jocelyn and Joanne Macgregor (2020), '*Adelante!* Military imaginaries, the Cold War, and Southern Africa's liberation armies', *Comparative Studies in Society and History*, 20 (3), 619–50.
Anderson, David (2015), 'Guilty secrets: deceit, denial, and the discovery of Kenya's "migrated archive"', *History Workshop Journal*, 80, 1, 142–60.
Anderson, Kurt (2017), *Fantasyland: How America Went Haywire—A 500-Year History* (London: Ebury Press).
Anderson, Perry (2017), *The H-Word: The Peripeteia of Hegemony* (London: Verso).
Antonini, Francesca (2020), *Caesarism and Bonapartism in Gramsci: Hegemony and the Crisis of Modernity* (Leiden: Brill).

REFERENCES

Applebaum, Anne (2020), *Twilight of Democracy: The Failure of Politics and the Parting of Friends* (London: Allen Lane).

Arrighi, Giovanni (1966), 'The political economy of Rhodesia', *New Left Review*, 1 (39), 35–65.

———— (1983), *The Geometry of Imperialism: The Limits of Hobson's Paradigm* (London: Verso).

———— (2007), *Adam Smith in Beijing: Lineages of the Twenty-First Century* (London: Verso).

———— (2010), *The Long Twentieth Century: Money, Power, and the Origins of our Time* (London: Verso).

Arrighi, Giovanni, and John S. Saul (1973), *Essays on the Political Economy of Africa* (New York: Monthly Review Press).

Austin, Reg (2020), 'Zimbabwe: some reflections and hopes', *Indaba*, 108 (Vienna: Southern Africa Documentation and Cooperation Centre), 11–19.

Babic, Milan (2020), 'Let's talk about the interregnum: Gramsci and the crisis of the liberal world order', *International Affairs*, 96 (3), 767–86.

Bango, William and Morgan Tsvangirai (2011), *Morgan Tsvangirai: At the Deep End* (Johannesburg: Penguin).

Barbalet, Jack (2019), 'Primitive accumulation and Chinese mirrors', *Journal of Classical Sociology*, 19 (1), 27–42.

Barber, Alex (2020), 'Lying, misleading, and dishonesty', *Journal of Ethics*, 24, 141–64.

Bauman, Zygmunt (2012), 'Times of interregnum', *Ethics Global Politics*, 5 (1), 49–56.

Baumhögger, Goswin, Ulf Engel and Telse Diederichsen (1984), *The Struggle for Independence: Documents on the Recent Development of Zimbabwe (1975–1980)*, 7 vols. (Hamburg: Institute of African Studies, Africa Documentation Centre).

Beach, David (1984), *Zimbabwe before 1900* (Gweru: Mambo Press).

Bernstein, Henry (2010), *Class Dynamics of Agrarian Change* (Halifax: Fernwood Publishing).

Bond, Patrick, and Richard Saunders (2005), 'Labor, the state and the struggle for a democratic Zimbabwe', *Monthly Review*, 57 (7), 42–55.

Bowyer-Bower, Tanya and Colin Stoneman (eds.), (2000), *Land Reform in Zimbabwe: Constraints and Prospects* (Aldershot: Ashgate).

Bratton, Michael (2014), *Power Politics in Zimbabwe* (Boulder: Lynne Rienner).

Brenner, Robert (1977), 'The origins of capitalist development: a critique of neo-Smithian Marxism', *New Left Review*, 1 (104), 26–92.

Bulawayo, NoViolet (2013), *We Need New Names* (London: Chatto & Windus).

———— (2022), *Glory* (New York: Viking).

REFERENCES

Burgis, Tom (2015), *The Looting Machine: Warlords, Tycoons, Smugglers, and the Systematic Theft of Africa's Wealth* (London: William Collins).

———— (2020), *Kleptopia: How Dirty Money Is Conquering the World* (London: William Collins).

Burton, Myra, and Edward Keefer (eds.) (2011), *Foreign Relations of the United States 1969–1976, Volume XXVIII, Southern Africa* (Washington, DC: United States Government Printing Office).

Cameron, Hazel (2018), 'The Matabeleland massacres: Britain's wilful blindness', *International History Review*, 40 (1), 1–19.

CCJP/LRC (Catholic Commission for Justice and Peace and Legal Resources Centre) (2007 [1997]), *Gukurahundi in Zimbabwe: A Report on the Disturbances in Matabeleland and the Midlands, 1980–1988* (London: Hurst).

Chabal, Patrick (2012), *The End of Conceit: Western Rationality after Post-colonialism* (London: Zed Books).

Chagonda, Tapiwa (2011), 'The response of the working class in Harare, Zimbabwe to hyper-inflation and the political crisis, 1997–2008' (DPhil and Litt thesis, University of Johannesburg).

———— (2012), 'Teachers' and bank workers' responses to Zimbabwe's crisis: uneven effects, different strategies', *Journal of Contemporary African Studies*, 30 (1), 83–97.

Chan, Stephen (2012), *Southern Africa: Old Treacheries and New Deceits* (New Haven, CT: Yale University Press).

Cheater, Angela P. (1991), 'The University of Zimbabwe: university, national university, state university, or party university?' *African Affairs*, 90 (359), 189–205.

Chimhowu, Admos and Phil Woodhouse (2006), 'Customary vs private property rights? Dynamics and trajectories of vernacular land markets in sub-Saharan Africa', *Journal of Agrarian Change*, 6 (3), 346–71.

Chitando, Ezra (ed.) (2020), *Personality Cult and Politics in Mugabe's Zimbabwe* (London: Routledge).

Chiwenga, Constantine (2015), 'The predominance of an ethic of double standards in the United Nations Security Council Humanitarian Intervention Missions: a critical study based on the ethical concepts of mutual aid and equal recognition' (doctoral thesis, University of KwaZulu-Natal).

Chung, Fay (2006), *Re-Living the Second Chimurenga: Memories from the Liberation Struggle in Zimbabwe* (Uppsala and Harare: Nordic Africa Institute and Weaver Press).

Cobbing, Julian (1977), 'The absent priesthood: another look at the Rhodesian risings of 1896–1897', *Journal of African History*, 18 (1), 61–84.

REFERENCES

Colpani, Gianmaria (2022), 'Two theories of hegemony: Stuart Hall and Ernesto Laclau in conversation', *Political Theory*, 50 (2), 221–46.

Coltart, David (2016), *The Struggle Continues: 50 Years of Tyranny in Zimbabwe* (Johannesburg: Jacana).

Compagnon, Daniel (2011), *A Predictable Tragedy: Robert Mugabe and the Collapse of Zimbabwe* (Philadelphia: University of Pennsylvania Press).

Cox, Robert (1981), 'Social forces, states and world orders: beyond international relations theory', *Millennium*, 10 (2), 126–55.

———— (1983), 'Gramsci, hegemony, and international relations: an essay in method', *Millennium*, 12 (2), 162–75.

———— (1987), *Production, Power, and World Order: Social Forces in the Making of History* (New York: Columbia University Press).

Cramer, Christopher (2006), *Civil War is not a Stupid Thing: Accounting for Violence in Developing Countries* (London: Hurst).

Damai, Puspa (2005), 'Sovereignty, law, and play in Agamben's "State of Exception"', *CR: The New Centennial Review*, 5 (2), 255–76.

Dande, Innocent, Elijah Doro, Muchaparara Musemwa and Thembani Dube (2020), 'Remembering Mugabe', *South African Historical Journal*, 72 (2), 321–44.

Daoud, Kamel (2015), *The Meursault Investigation* (London: Oneworld).

Deletant, Dennis (2011), 'New evidence on Romania and the Warsaw Pact, 1955–1989', *Cold War International History Project e-Dossier No. 6* (Princeton: Woodrow Wilson School of Public and International Affairs, Princeton University).

De Soto, Hernando (2000), *The Mystery of Capital: Why Capitalism Triumphs in the West and Fails Everywhere Else* (New York: Basic Books).

Desai, Radhika (2012), 'Marx, List, and the materiality of nations', *Rethinking Marxism*, 24 (1), 47–66.

Desai, Radhika, and Henry Heller (2020), 'Revolutions: a twenty-first century perspective', *Third World Quarterly*, 41 (8), 1261–71.

Dhada, Mustafa (2020), *The Portuguese Massacre of Wiriyamu in Colonial Mozambique, 1964–2013* (London: Bloomsbury).

Doran, Stuart (2017), *Kingdom, Power, Glory: Mugabe, ZANU, and the Quest for Supremacy, 1960–1987* (Johannesburg: Sithatha Media).

Dorril, Stephen (2000), *MI6: Inside the Covert World of Her Majesty's Secret Intelligence Service* (New York: The Free Press).

Dubbeld, Bernard (2019), 'After revisionist Marxism: reanimating the critique of capitalism in South African studies', *Transformation* (100), 128–52.

Eagleton, Terry (2018), *Why Marx was Right* (New Haven, CT: Yale University Press).

Ekeh, Peter (1975), 'Colonialism and the two publics in Africa: a theoretical statement', *Comparative Studies in Society and History*, 17 (1), 91–112.

REFERENCES

Ellert, Henrik, and Dennis Anderson (2020), *A Brutal State of Affairs: The Rise and Fall of Rhodesia* (Harare: Weaver).

Femia, Joseph (1981), *Gramsci's Political Thought: Hegemony, Consciousness and the Revolutionary Process* (Oxford: Clarendon Press).

Ferguson, James (2015), *Give a Man a Fish: Reflections on the New Politics of Distribution* (Durham, NC: Duke University Press).

Finlayson, James Gordon (2010), '"Bare life" and politics in Agamben's reading of Aristotle', *The Review of Politics*, 72, 97–126.

Fontana, Benedetto (2004), 'The concept of Caesarism in Gramsci,' in Baehr, Peter and Melvin Richter (eds.), *Dictatorship in History and Theory: Bonapartism, Caesarism, and Totalitarianism* (Cambridge: Cambridge University Press), 175–96.

Fontein, Joost (2009), 'Anticipating the tsunami: rumours, planning, and the arbitrary state in Zimbabwe', *Africa*, 79 (3), 369–98.

———— (2010), 'Between tortured bodies and resurfacing bones: the politics of the dead in Zimbabwe', *Journal of Material Culture*, 15 (4), 423–48.

———— (2018), 'Political accidents in Zimbabwe', *Kronos*, 44, 33–58.

———— (2022), *The Politics of the Dead in Zimbabwe 2000–2015: Bones, Rumours and Spirits* (London: James Currey).

Foster-Carter, Aiden (1978), 'The modes of production controversy', *New Left Review*, 1 (107), 47–77.

Frank, Andre (1998), *ReORIENT: Global Economy in the Asian Age* (Berkeley: University of California Press).

Frankfurt, Harry (2017), *On Bullshit* (Princeton: Princeton University Press).

Freeland, Chrystia (2012), *The Plutocrats: The Rise of the New Global Super Rich and the Fall of Everyone Else* (London: Penguin).

Friedman, Steven (2015), *Race, Class and Power: Harold Wolpe and the Radical Critique of Apartheid* (Pietermaritzburg: University of KwaZulu-Natal Press).

Gelfand, Michael (1978), *A Non-Racial Island of Learning: A History of the University College of Rhodesia from its Inception to 1966* (Gwelo: Mambo Press).

Gellner, Ernest (1997), 'Reply to critics', *New Left Review*, 1 (221), 81–118.

Gontijo, Caio (2021), 'Bolsonaro: a ridiculous Caesar?', *Notebooks*, 1 (1), 142–57.

Gopal, Priyamvada (2019), *Insurgent Empire: Anticolonial Resistance and British Dissent* (London: Verso).

Graeber, David (2018), *Bullshit Jobs: A Theory* (New York: Simon & Schuster).

Gramsci, Antonio (1971), *Selections from the Prison Notebooks*, ed. and trans. Quintin Hoare and Geoffrey Nowell Smith (London: Lawrence & Wishart).

Grinin, Leonid (2010), 'The role of the individual in history: a reconsideration', *Social Evolution and History*, 9 (2), 95–136.

REFERENCES

Gwisai, Munyaradzi (2009), 'Revolutionaries, resistance, and crisis in Zimbabwe', in Zeilig, Leo (ed.), *Class Struggle and Resistance in Africa* (Chicago: Haymarket), 219–51.

Hamburger, Philip (2008), *Law and Judicial Duty* (Cambridge, MA: Harvard University Press).

Herman, Eleanor (2005), *Sex with Kings: 500 Years of Adultery, Power, Rivalry, and Revenge* (New York: HarperCollins).

Hett, Benjamin (2018), *The Death of Democracy: Hitler's Rise to Power* (London: Windmill).

Hindess, Barry (2015), 'Review of *The End of Conceit*', *European Review of International Studies*, 2 (3), 144–6.

Hodgkinson, Dan (2018), 'Marked out: an oral history of Zimbabwean student activism, 1954–2016' (doctoral thesis, Oxford University).

——— (2021), 'Politics on liberation's frontiers: student activist refugees, international solidarity, and the struggle for Zimbabwe', *Journal of African History*, 62 (1), 99–123.

Hoffman, John (1984), *The Gramscian Challenge, Coercion and Consent in Marxist Political Theory* (Oxford: Basil Blackwell).

Holman, Michael (2020), *Postmark Africa: Half a Century as a Foreign Correspondent* (London: EnvelopeBooks).

Hughes, Richard (2003), *Capricorn: David Stirling's African Campaign* (London: Radcliffe Press).

Human Rights Watch (2006), *Zimbabwe 'You Will Be Thoroughly Beaten': The Brutal Suppression of Dissent in Zimbabwe*, 18(10A) (New York: Human Rights Watch).

Jackson, Robert H., and Carl Rosberg (1982), *Personal Rule in Black Africa: Prince, Autocrat, Prophet, Tyrant* (Berkeley: University of California Press).

Jackson, Robert P. (2019), 'Violence and civilization: Gramsci, Machiavelli, and Sorel', in Rae, Gavin and Emma Ingala (eds.), *The Meanings of Violence: From Critical Theory to Biopolitics* (New York: Routledge), 48–64.

Jameson, Fredric (1986), 'On magic realism in film', *Critical Inquiry*, 12 (2), 301–25.

Jennings, Michael (2002), '"Almost an Oxfam in itself": Oxfam, ujamaa and development in Tanzania', *African Affairs*, 101 (405), 509–30.

Jones, Jeremy L. (2010), '"Nothing is straight in Zimbabwe": the rise of the *kukiya-kiya* economy 2000–2008', *Journal of Southern African Studies*, 36 (2), 285–99.

Kanyenze, Godfrey (2022), *Leaving So Many Behind: The Link Between Politics and the Economy in Zimbabwe* (Harare: Friedrich Ebert Stiftung and Weaver Press).

Karekwaivanane, George (2017), *The Struggle over State Power in Zimbabwe: Law and Politics since 1950* (Cambridge: Cambridge University Press).

REFERENCES

Kriger, Norma (1985), 'Struggles for independence: rural conflict in Zimbabwe's War of Independence' (doctoral thesis, Massachusetts Institute of Technology).

────── (1988), 'The Zimbabwean War of Liberation: struggles within the struggle', *Journal of Southern African Studies*, 14 (2), 304–22.

────── (1992), *Zimbabwe's Guerrilla War: Peasant Perspectives* (Cambridge: Cambridge University Press).

────── (2003), *Guerrilla Veterans in Post-war Zimbabwe Symbolic and Violent Politics, 1980–1987* (Cambridge: Cambridge University Press).

────── (2005), 'ZANU (PF) strategies in general elections, 1980–2000: discourse and coercion', *African Affairs*, 104 (414), 1–34.

────── (2006), 'From patriotic memories to "patriotic history" in Zimbabwe, 1990–2005', *Third World Quarterly*, 27 (6), 1151–69.

────── (2008a), 'Can elections end Mugabe's dictatorship?' *Association of Concerned Africa Scholars Bulletin*, 79, 2–6.

────── (2008b), 'Zimbabwe's parliamentary election of 2005: the myth of new electoral laws', *Journal of Southern African Studies*, 34 (2), 359–78.

────── (2012), 'ZANU (PF) politics under Zimbabwe's "power-sharing" government', *Journal of Contemporary African Studies*, 30 (1), 11–26.

────── (2020), 'Biographies of two "big men" in Zimbabwe: a review essay', *Small Wars and Insurgencies*, 31 (5), 1130–6.

Laclau, Ernesto (1977), *Politics and Ideology in Marxist Theory* (London: New Left Books).

Laclau, Ernesto, and Chantal Mouffe (1985), *Hegemony and Socialist Strategy: Towards a Radical Democratic Politics* (London: Verso).

Leys, Colin (1994), 'Confronting the African tragedy', *New Left Review*, 1 (204), 33–47.

Limb, Peter (2011), 'Terence Ranger, African studies and South African historiography', *Historia*, 56 (1), 1–25.

Mackay, Peter (2008), *We Have Tomorrow: Stirrings in Africa, 1959–1967* (Norwich: Michael Russell).

Makanda, Arthur P. T. (2014), 'Reading Dzino: memories of a freedom fighter', in Hove, Mediel and Kgomotso Masemola (eds.), *Strategies of Representation in Auto/biography: Reconstructing and Remembering* (New York: Palgrave Macmillan), 78–96.

Mandaza, Ibbo (ed.), (1986), *Zimbabwe: The Political Economy of Transition 1980–1986* (Dakar: CODESRIA, 1986).

Mann, Michael (1999), 'The dark side of democracy: the modern tradition of ethnic and political cleansing', *New Left Review*, 1 (235), 18–48.

────── (2005), *The Dark Side of Democracy: Explaining Ethnic Cleansing* (Cambridge: Cambridge University Press).

Mapanzure, Rangariayi (2020), 'Writing dictatorship, rewriting African writing: mythology, temporality and power' (doctoral thesis, University of the Witwatersrand).

Marquez, Gabriel Garcia (1981), *Chronicle of a Death Foretold*, trans. Gregory Rabassa (New York: Alfred A. Knopf).

Martin, David and Phyllis Johnson (1981), *The Struggle for Zimbabwe: The Chimurenga War* (London: Faber & Faber).

Marx, Karl (1963 [1852]), *The Eighteenth Brumaire of Louis Bonaparte* (New York: International Publishers).

———— (1972 [1867]), 'Part VIII: the so-called primitive accumulation— Capital Volume I', in Tucker, Robert (ed.), *The Marx–Engels Reader*, 2nd edition (New York: Norton), 431–38.

Masunungure, Eldred V. (2009), 'A militarised election: the 27 June presidential run-off', in Masunungure, Eldred V. (ed.), *Defying the Winds of Change* (Harare: Weaver Press), 79–97.

Matyszak, Derek (2016), *Succession and the ZANU (PF) Body Politic* (Harare: Southern African Political Economy Series).

———— (2017), 'Back to the future: legitimising Zimbabwe's 2018 elections', *Southern Africa Report 12* (Tshwane: Institute of Security Studies).

———— (forthcoming), 'Handling the crocodile', unpublished manuscript.

Mazarire, Gerald (2011), 'Discipline and punishment in ZANLA: 1964– 1979', *Journal of Southern African Studies*, 37 (3), 571–91.

Mazrui, Ali A. (1973), 'Lumpen proletariat and lumpen militariat', *Political Studies*, 21 (1), 1–12.

Mbeki, Thabo (2008 [2001]), 'The Mbeki–Mugabe papers: a discussion document,' *New Agenda*, 2nd Quarter, 56–75.

McCandless, Erin (2011), *Polarization and Transformation in Zimbabwe: Social Movements, Strategy Dilemmas and Change* (Lanham, MD: Lexington Books).

McEwan, Ian (2019), *The Cockroach* (London: Jonathan Cape).

Meredith, Martin (1979), *The Past is Another Country: Rhodesia 1890–1979* (London: Andre Deutsch).

———— (2002), *Robert Mugabe: Power, Plunder and the Struggle for Zimbabwe* (Johannesburg: Jonathan Ball).

Mhanda, Wilfred (2011), *Dzino: Memories of a Freedom Fighter* (Harare: Weaver Press).

Mills, Greg, Olusegun Obasanjo, Tendai Biti and Jeffrey Herbst (2019), *Democracy Works: Turning [or Re-Wiring] Politics to Africa's Advantage* (London: Hurst).

Mkandawire, Thandika (2015), 'Neopatrimonialism and the political economy of economic performance in Africa: critical reflections', *World Politics*, 67 (3), 563–612.

———— (2020), 'Zimbabwe's transition overload: an interpretation', *Journal of Contemporary African Studies*, 38 (1), 18–38.

REFERENCES

Mlambo, Alois (2014), *A History of Zimbabwe* (Cambridge: Cambridge University Press).

Molobye, Remofilwe (2020), 'Authoritarian populism and xenophobic violence in South Africa' (honours thesis, Anthropology and Development Studies, University of Johannesburg).

Moore, David (1990), 'The contradictory construction of hegemony in Zimbabwe: politics, ideology and class in the formation of a new African state' (PhD thesis, York University (Toronto)).

———— (1995), 'Democracy, violence and identity in the Zimbabwean War of National Liberation: reflections from the realms of dissent', *Canadian Journal of African Studies*, 29 (3), 375–402.

———— (2003a), 'Zimbabwe's triple crisis: primitive accumulation, nation-state formation, and democratisation in the age of neo-liberal globalisation', *African Studies Quarterly*, 7 (2–3), 35–47.

———— (2003b), 'Zimbabwe: twists on the tale of primitive accumulation', in Smith, Malinda S. (ed.), *Globalizing Africa* (Trenton, NJ: Africa World Press), 247–69.

———— (2005a), 'ZANU (PF) and the ghosts of foreign funding', *Review of African Political Economy*, 103 (32), 156–62.

———— (2005b), '"When I am a century old": why Robert Mugabe won't go', in Southall, Roger and Henning Melber (eds.), *Legacies of Power: Leadership Change and Former Presidents in Africa* (Cape Town and Uppsala: Human Sciences Research Council Press and Nordic Africa Institute), 120–50.

———— (ed.) (2007), *The World Bank: Development, Poverty, Hegemony* (Pietermaritzburg: University of KwaZulu-Natal Press).

———— (2008a), 'Coercion, consent, context: "Operation Murambatsvina" and ZANU (PF)'s illusory quest for hegemony', in Vambe, Maurice (ed.), *The Hidden Dimensions of Operation Murambatsvina in Zimbabwe* (Harare and Pretoria: Weaver Press and the African Institute of South Africa), 29–48.

———— (2008b), 'Contesting civil societies in Zimbabwe's interregna', Centre for Civil Society Working Paper, University of KwaZulu-Natal, available at: http://ccs.ukzn.ac.za/files/moore-zim100.pdf.

———— (2009), 'Mamdani's enthusiasms', *Concerned African Scholars Bulletin*, 82 (Summer), 49–53.

———— (2010a), 'A decade of disquieting diplomacy: South Africa, Zimbabwe, and the ideology of the National Democratic Revolution, 1999–2009', *History Compass*, 8 (8), 752–67.

———— (2010b), 'Zimbabwe's media: between party-state politics and press freedom under Mugabe's rule', in Besada, Hany (ed.), *Zimbabwe: Picking up the Pieces* (London: Palgrave Macmillan), 55–79.

———— (2012), 'Two perspectives on the National Democratic Revolution

REFERENCES

in Zimbabwe: Thabo Mbeki and Wilfred Mhanda', *Journal of Contemporary African Studies*, 30 (4), 119–38.

———— (2013), 'Generations, class formations and elections in Zimbabwe: methodological notes for analysing the historical construction of political power and resistance in a new African state', *Sephis*, 9 (4), 38–44.

———— (2014a), 'Death or dearth of democracy in Zimbabwe?' *Africa Spectrum*, 49 (1), 101–14.

———— (2014b), 'Coercion, consent, and the construction of capitalism in Africa: development studies, political economy, politics and the "dark continent"', *Transformation*, 84, 106–31.

———— (2014c), 'The Zimbabwean People's Army moment in Zimbabwean history, 1975–1977: Mugabe's rise and democracy's demise', *Journal of Contemporary African Studies*, 32 (3), 302–18.

———— (2014d), 'Zimbabwe's democracy in the wake of the 2013 election: contemporary and historical perspectives', *Strategic Review for Southern Africa*, 36 (1), 47–71.

———— (2015a), 'Five funerals, no weddings, a couple of birthdays: Terry Ranger, his contemporaries, and the end of Zimbabwean nationalism— October 24 2013–January 3 2015', *Review of African Political Economy*, 42 (144), 316–24.

———— (2015b), 'Robert Mugabe: an intellectual *manqué* and his moments of meaning', in Ndlovu-Gatsheni, Sabelo (ed.), *Mugabeism? History, Politics and Power in Africa* (London: Palgrave Macmillan), 29–44.

———— (2016a), 'Lionel Cliffe and the generation(s) of Zimbabwean politics', *Review of African Political Economy*, 43 (S1), 167–86.

———— (2016b), 'An arc of authoritarianism over Africa: toward the end of a liberal democratic dream?' *Socialist Register: The Politics of the Right*, 52 (2016), 193–212.

———— (2017), 'After the very Zimbabwean coup: another inch for democracy?' *Amandla*, 55/56 (December), 1–29.

———— (2018a), 'Reading Zimbabwe internationally: little errors, larger truths', *South African Journal of International Affairs*, 25 (2), 263–72.

———— (2018b), 'A very Zimbabwean coup: November 13–24, 2017— context, event, prospects', *Transformation*, 97, 1–29.

———— (2019), 'Review article: articulations, more articulations … and accumulation', *Transformation*, 99, 81–112.

———— (2020a), 'Book review: "The Army and Politics in Zimbabwe: Mujuru, the Liberation Fighter and Kingmaker"', *South African Journal of International Affairs*, 27 (4), 574–6.

———— (2020b), 'Toward non-hagiographical reflections on Zimbabwe's "heroes": Dumiso Dabengwa's history', *Review of African Political Economy*, 47 (165), 449–68.

REFERENCES

——— (2022), 'Unravelling Zimbabwe's January *jambanja*: truth, lies, rumours, and conspiracies', in Brown, Chris, David Moore and Blair Rutherford (eds.), *New Leaders, New Dawns? South Africa and Zimbabwe under Cyril Ramaphosa and Emmerson Mnangagwa* (Montreal and Kingston: McGill-Queen's University Press), 237–72.

——— and Susan Booysen (2022), 'Denouement—from grey dawns to the shadows at dusk', in Chris Brown, David Moore and Blair Rutherford (eds.), *New Leaders, New Dawns? South Africa and Zimbabwe under Cyril Ramaphosa and Emmerson Mnangagwa* (Montreal and Kingston: McGill-Queen's University Press), 352–60.

——— and Showers Mawowa (2010), '*Mbimbos, Zvipamuzis*, and primitive accumulation in Zimbabwe's violent mineral economy: crisis, chaos, and the state', in Padayachee, Vishnu (ed.), *The Political Economy of Africa* (London: Routledge), 317–38.

Morris, John (2020), *Culture and Propaganda in World War II: Music, Film and the Battle for National Identity* (London: Bloomsbury).

Moyo, Jonathan (1988), 'Preface to management: towards the development of craft-literacy and craft-competence in Africa' (doctoral thesis, University of Southern California).

Moyo, Sam (2000), 'The political economy of land acquisition and redistribution in Zimbabwe: 1990–1999', *Journal of Southern African Studies*, 26 (1), 5–28.

Moyo, Zenzo (2018), 'Civil society, the state and democracy in Zimbabwe, 1988–2014: hegemonies, polarities and fractures' (doctoral thesis, University of Johannesburg).

Mukonori, Fidelis (2017), *Man in the Middle: A Memoir* (Harare: The House of Books).

Mullin, Chris (1982), *A Very British Coup* (London: Serpent's Tail).

Mungwari, Teddy (2018), 'Media framing of Zanu PF internal succession struggles: Mnangagwa and the military factor', *Journal of Mass Communication and Journalism*, 8 (2), 1–11.

Munyikwa, Hamadziripi (2019), 'ZANU-PF's long reign: a Gramscian perspective on hegemony and historic blocs', (doctoral thesis, University of Limerick).

Mutambara, Arthur (2017), *In Search of the Elusive Zimbabwean Dream: An Autobiography of Thought Leadership, Vol. I* (Johannesburg: Jacana Media).

Ncube, Cornelias (2010), 'Contesting hegemony: civil society and the struggle for social change in Zimbabwe, 2000–2008' (doctoral thesis, University of Birmingham).

Ndlela, Daniel B. (2019), *Economic Dualism in Zimbabwe: From Colonial Rhodesia to Post-Independence* (London: Routledge).

REFERENCES

Ndlovu, Ray (2018), *In the Jaws of the Crocodile: Emmerson Mnangagwa's Rise to Power in Zimbabwe* (Cape Town: Penguin).

Ndlovu, Siphiwe (2020), *The History of Man* (Cape Town: Penguin).

Ndlovu-Gatsheni, Sabelo (ed.) (2015), *Mugabeism? History, Politics, and Power in Africa* (London: Palgrave Macmillan).

———— (2020), 'The cognitive empire, politics of knowledge and African intellectual productions: reflections on struggles for epistemic freedom and resurgence of decolonisation in the twenty-first century', *Third World Quarterly*, DOI: 10.1080/01436597.2020.1775487.

Nest, Michael (2001), 'Ambitions, profits, and loss: Zimbabwean economic involvement in the Democratic Republic of the Congo', *African Affairs*, 100 (400), 469–90.

Ngoshi, Hazel Tafadzwa (2016), 'Carnivalising postcolonial Zimbabwe: the vulgar and grotesque logic of postcolonial protest in NoViolet Bulawayo's *We Need New Names* (2013)', *Journal of Literary Studies*, 32 (1), 53–69.

Nielsson, Camilla (2014), *Democrats* (Copenhagen: Upfront Films).

Norman, Denis (2018), *The Odd Man In: Mugabe's White-Hand Man* (Harare: Weaver Press).

Nursey-Bray, Paul (1967), 'Rhodesia: a university in crisis', *Mawazo*, 1 (2), 39–46.

Nyambi, Oliver (2016), 'Of weevils and Gamatox: titles, names, and nicknames in ZANU (PF) succession politics', *African Identities*, 14 (1), 59–73.

Nyarota, Geoffrey (2006), *Against the Grain: Memoirs of a Zimbabwean Newsman* (Cape Town: Zebra).

Ovenden, Richard (2020), *Burning the Books: A History of Knowledge under Attack* (London: John Murray).

Perelman, Michael (2000), *Classical Political Economy and the Secret History of Primitive Accumulation* (Durham, NC: Duke University Press).

Phimister, Ian (1987), 'Zimbabwe: the combined and contradictory inheritance of the struggle against colonialism', *Transformation*, 5, 51–9.

———— (2003), 'Doing violence to the past: Zimbabwe's new old history', *Kronos*, 29, 210–15.

———— (2012), 'Narratives of progress: Zimbabwean historiography and the end of history', *Journal of Contemporary African Studies*, 30 (1), 27–34.

Pitcher, Anne, Mary Moran and Michael Johnston (2009), 'Rethinking patrimonialism in Africa', *African Studies Review*, 52 (1), 125–56.

Pollitt, Russell (2017), 'An interview with the Zimbabwean Jesuit who mediated Mugabe's fall from power', *America: The Jesuit Review*, 14 December, available at: https://www.americamagazine.org/politics-society/2017/12/14/interview-zimbabwean-jesuit-who-mediated-mugabes-fall-power.

REFERENCES

Priestland, David (2012), *Merchant, Soldier, Sage: A New History of Power* (London: Allen Lane).

Primera, German (2018), 'Biopolitics and resistance: the meaning of violence in the work of Giorgio Agamben', in Rae, Gavin and Emma Ingala (eds.), *The Meanings of Violence: From Critical Theory to Biopolitics* (New York: Routledge), 209–28.

Pritchard, Joshua (2018) 'Race, identity, and belonging in early Zimbabwean nationalism(s), 1957–1965', (doctoral thesis, University of Cambridge).

Pula, Besnik (2018), *Globalization under and after Socialism: The Evolution of Transnational Capital in Central and Eastern Europe* (Palo Alto: Stanford University Press).

Raftopoulos, Brian (2006), 'The Zimbabwean crisis and the challenges for the left', *Journal of Southern African Studies*, 32 (2), 203–19.

———— (ed.) (2013), *The Hard Road to Reform: The Politics of Zimbabwe's Global Political Agreement* (Harare: Weaver Press).

———— (2018), 'State politics, constructions of labour, and labour struggles: 1980–2000', in Sachikonye, Lloyd, Brian Raftopoulos and Godfrey Kanyenze (eds.), *Building from the Rubble: The Labour Movement in Zimbabwe since 2000* (Harare: Weaver Press), 46–74.

Raftopoulos, Brian and Alois Mlambo (eds.) (2009), *Becoming Zimbabwe: A History from the Pre-Colonial Period to 2008* (Harare and Johannesburg: Weaver Press and Jacana Media).

Raftopoulos, Brian, Kanyenze, Godfrey and Mabel Sithole (2021) *Navigating Turbulence in Southern Africa: The Case of Zimbabwe*, Case Study, Cape Town: Nelson Mandela School of Governance, University of Cape Town.

Ranger, Terence (2004), 'Nationalist historiography, patriotic history and the history of the nation: the struggle over the past in Zimbabwe', *Journal of Southern African Studies*, 30 (2), 215–34.

———— (2013), *Writing Revolt: An Engagement with African Nationalism, 1957–67* (Woodbridge: James Currey).

Ranger, Terry (1980), 'The changing of the old guard: Robert Mugabe and the revival of ZANU', *Journal of Southern African Studies*, 7 (1), 71–90.

Rich-Dorman, Sara (2016), *Understanding Zimbabwe: From Liberation to Authoritarianism* (London: Hurst).

Roberts, William (2020), 'What was primitive accumulation? Reconstructing the origin of a critical concept', *European Journal of Political Theory*, 19 (4), 532–52.

Rogers, Douglas (2019), *Two Weeks in November: The Astonishing Untold Story of the Operation that Toppled Mugabe* (Johannesburg: Jonathan Ball).

Rowen, Herbert (1961), '"L'état c'est a moi": Louis XIV and the state', *French Historical Studies*, 2 (1), 83–98.

REFERENCES

Rutherford, Blair (2017), *Farm Labour Struggles in Zimbabwe: The Ground of Politics* (Bloomington: Indiana University Press).

———— (2019), '(Dis-)graceful leadership: on familial logics and politics in Zimbabwe', *Cahiers d'Études Africaines*, 49 (2), 625–54.

Sachikonye, Lloyd (2011), *When a State Turns on its Citizens: 60 Years of Institutionalised Violence in Zimbabwe* (Harare: Weaver Press).

Sachikonye, Lloyd, Brian Raftopoulos and Godfrey Kanyenze (eds.), (2018), *Building from the Rubble: The Labour Movement in Zimbabwe since 2000* (Harare: Weaver Press).

Sarajlic, Eldar (2019) 'Bullshit, truth, and reason', *Philosophia*, 47 (3), 865–79.

Saul, John S. (1974), 'The state in post-colonial societies: Tanzania', *Socialist Register 1974*, 11, 349–72.

———— (1979) [1977], 'Transforming the struggle in Zimbabwe', in Saul, John S. (ed.), *State and Revolution in Eastern Africa* (New York: Monthly Review Press), 107–21.

———— (1980), 'Zimbabwe: the next round,' *Monthly Review*, 32 (4), 1–43.

———— (2016), 'The ZIPA moment: Dzino, Mugabe, and Samora Machel', *Review of African Political Economy*, 43 (1), 145–66.

———— (2020a), 'The African hero in Mozambican history: on assassinations and executions—Part I', *Review of African Political Economy*, 47 (163), 153–65.

———— (2020b), 'The African hero in Mozambican history: on assassinations and executions—Part II', *Review of African Political Economy*, 47 (164), 335–45.

Saunders, Richard (2000), *Never the Same Again: Zimbabwe's Growth towards Democracy, 1980–2000* (Harare: Edwina Spicer Publishers).

Scarnecchia, Timothy (2006), 'The "fascist cycle" in Zimbabwe, 2000–2005', *Journal of Southern African Studies*, 32 (2), 221–37.

———— (2008), *The Urban Roots of Democracy and Political Violence in Zimbabwe: Harare and Highfield, 1940–1964* (Rochester, NY: University of Rochester Press).

———— (2021), *Race and Diplomacy in Zimbabwe: The Cold War and Decolonization, 1960–1984* (Cambridge: Cambridge University Press).

Scoones, Ian, Nelson Marongwe, Blasio Z. Mavedzenge, Jacob Mahenehene, Felix Murimbarimba and Chrispen Sukume (2010), *Zimbabwe's Land Reform: Myths and Realities* (Woodbridge: James Currey).

Scott, James C. (1985), *Weapons of the Weak: Everyday Forms of Peasant Resistance* (New Haven, CT: Yale University Press).

———— (1999), *Seeing Like a State: How Certain Schemes to Improve the Human Condition Have Failed* (New Haven, CT: Yale University Press).

Sebenius, James, Nicholas Burns and Robert H. Mnookin (2018), *Kissinger*

REFERENCES

the Negotiator: Lessons from Dealmaking at the Highest Level (New York: HarperCollins).

Sellström, Tor (2002), *Sweden and National Liberation in Southern Africa Vol II: Solidarity and Assistance 1970–1994* (Uppsala: Nordic Africa Institute).

Shamuyarira, Nathan (1960), 'Revolt of the intellectuals: eggheads join the NDP', *Central African Examiner*, 4 (2), 10–11.

Shonhe, Toendepi and Ian Scoones (2022), 'Private and state-led contract farming in Zimbabwe: accumulation, social differentiation and rural politics', *Journal of Agrarian Change*, 22 (1), 118–38.

Shubin, Vladimir (2017), 'Moscow and Zimbabwe's liberation', *Journal of Southern African Studies*, 43 (1), 225–33.

Shumba, Jabusile (2017), *Zimbabwe's Predatory State: Party, Military, and Business* (Pietermaritzburg: University of KwaZulu-Natal Press).

Simpson, Colin, David J. Smith with Ian Davies (1981), *Mugabe* (Salisbury: Pioneer Head).

Sisman, Adam (2015), *John le Carré: The Biography* (London: Bloomsbury).

Sithole, Masipula (1979), *Zimbabwe: Struggles within the Struggle (1957–1980)* (Salisbury: Rujeko Publishers).

Southall, Roger (2013), *Liberation Movements in Power: Party and State in Southern Africa* (Pietermaritzburg: University of KwaZulu-Natal Press).

——— (2016), *The New Black Middle Class in South Africa* (Johannesburg: Jacana).

Southern, John (2020), *A Class of its Own? Social Class and the Foreign Office, 1782–2020*, FCO Historians Occasional Paper No. 18 (London: Foreign and Commonwealth Office).

Stahl, Rune Møller (2019), 'Politics and ideology in nonhegemonic times', *Politics and Society*, 47 (3), 333–60.

Tekere, Edgar (2007), *A Lifetime of Struggle* (Harare: Southern African Political Economy Series).

Tendi, Blessing-Miles (2008), 'Patriotic history and public intellectuals critical of power', *Journal of Southern African Studies*, 34 (2), 379–96.

——— (2010), *Making History in Mugabe's Zimbabwe: Politics, Intellectuals, and the Media* (New York: Peter Lang).

——— (2013), 'Ideology, civilian authority, and the Zimbabwean military', *Journal of Southern African Studies*, 39 (4), 829–43.

——— (2016), 'State intelligence and the politics of Zimbabwe's presidential succession', *African Affairs*, 115 (459), 203–24.

——— (2017), 'Transnationalism, contingency, and loyalty in African liberation armies: the case of ZANU's 1974–1975 Nhari mutiny', *Journal of Southern African Studies*, 43 (1), 143–59.

——— (2020a), 'The motivations and dynamics of Zimbabwe's 2017 military coup', *African Affairs*, 119 (474), 39–67.

REFERENCES

——— (2020b), *The Army and Politics in Zimbabwe: Mujuru, the Liberation Fighter and Kingmaker* (Cambridge: Cambridge University Press).

Theophanidis, Philippe (2016), 'Interregnum as a legal and political concept', *Synthesis: An Anglophone Journal of Comparative Literary Studies*, 9, 109–24.

Thieme, Tatiana, Meghan E. Ference and Naomi van Stapele (2021), 'Harnessing the "hustle": struggle, solidarities and narratives of work in Nairobi and beyond: Introduction', *Africa*, 91 (1), 1–15.

Tomás, António (2021), *Amílcar Cabral: The Life of a Reluctant Nationalist* (London: Hurst).

Townshend, Jules (2004), 'Laclau and Mouffe's hegemonic project: the story so far', *Political Studies*, 52 (2), 269–88.

Turok, Ben (2003), *Nothing but the Truth: Behind the ANC's Struggle Politics* (Johannesburg: Jonathan Ball).

United Nations (2002), *Plundering of the Democratic Republic of Congo's Natural Resources: Final Report of the Panel of Experts (S/2002/1146)* (New York: United Nations).

Vambe, Maurice (2008), *The Hidden Dimensions of Operation Murambatsvina* (Harare: Weaver Press).

Wallerstein, Immanuel (2003), *Decline of American Power: The U.S. in a Chaotic World* (New York: Free Press).

Warner, Nick (1981), 'Times of darkness: ethnicity and the causes of division within the Rhodesian guerrilla groups' (MA thesis, Australian National University).

Watkins, Susan (2020), 'The fractured right', *New Left Review*, 2 (126), 119–25.

Webber, Michael (2008), 'Primitive accumulation in modern China', *Dialectical Anthropology*, 32, 299–329.

Wenham, Mark (2003), 'Laclau or Mouffe? Splitting the difference', *Philosophy and Social Criticism*, 29 (5), 581–606.

Wheen, Francis (2009), *Strange Days Indeed: The Golden Age of Paranoia* (London: Fourth Estate).

White, Luise (2003), *The Assassination of Herbert Chitepo: Texts and Politics in Zimbabwe* (Bloomington: Indiana University Press).

——— (2007), '"Whoever saw a country with four armies?": the battle of Bulawayo revisited', *Journal of Southern African Studies*, 33 (3), 619–31.

——— (2011), '"Normal political activities": Rhodesia, the Pearce Commission, and the African National Council', *Journal of African History*, 52 (3), 321–40.

——— (2015), *Unpopular Sovereignty: Rhodesian Independence and African Decolonization* (Chicago: University of Chicago Press).

——— (2021), *Fighting and Writing: The Rhodesian Army at War and Postwar* (Durham, NC: Duke University Press; Johannesburg: Jacana).

REFERENCES

Wilkins, Sam (2013), 'Ndira's wake: politics, memory, and mobility among the youth of Mabvuku-Tafara, Harare', *Journal of Southern African Studies*, 39 (4), 885–901.

Williams, Christian (2015), *National Liberation in Postcolonial Southern Africa: A Historical Ethnography of SWAPO's Exile Camps* (New York: Cambridge University Press).

Wolpe, Harold (1972), 'Capitalism and cheap labour power: from segregation to apartheid', *Economy and Society*, 1 (4), 425–56.

Wood, J. R. T. (2012), *A Matter of Weeks Rather than Months: The Impasse between Harold Wilson and Ian Smith—Sanctions, Aborted Settlements, and War (1965–1969)* (Bloomington: Trafford).

Worth, Owen (2019), *Morbid Symptoms: The Global Rise of the Far-Right* (London: Zed Books).

———— (2022), 'The great moving Boris show: Brexit and the mainstreaming of the far right in Britain', *Globalizations*, DOI: 10.1080/147477 31.2021.2025291.

Zabala, Santiago (2020), *Being at Large: Freedom in the Age of Alternative Facts* (Montreal and Kingston: McGill-Queen's University Press).

Zamchiya, Phillan (2020), 'Inside competitive electoral authoritarianism in Zimbabwe, 2008–2018', in Tendi, Blessing-Miles, JoAnn McGregor and Jocelyn Alexander (eds.), *The Oxford Handbook of Zimbabwean Politics* (Oxford: Oxford University Press).

Zeilig, Leo (2006), '"Increasing my value proposition to the struggle": Arthur Mutambara and student politics in Zimbabwe', *African Sociological Review*, 10 (2), 94–115.

———— (2007), *Revolt and Protest: Student Politics and Activism in Sub-Saharan Africa* (London: Bloomsbury).

Zukas, Simon (2002), *Into Exile and Back* (Lusaka: Bookworld Publishers).

INDEX

Note: Page numbers followed by '*n*' refer to notes

277

INDEX

Robert Gabriel Mugabe), 44,
52–3
Chikweche, Enoch (Munyaradzi
Gwisai), 107
Chimedza, Tinashe, 119
China, 8, 175–6
Chinamasa, Patrick, 129, 183
Chipoera, Parker, 75
Chirombowe, Charehwachaguma,
122
Chiruri, Augustine, 166, 173
Chisorochengwe, Simon, 153
Chissano, Joaquim, 82
Chitapi, Terence, 24
Chitepo, Herbert, 3, 46–8, 78
assassination of, 37, 48, 75, 89,
103
Lorenz (Bente) and, 52
Chitepo College, 90, 116, 117
Chiteyo, Knox, 168
Chiwenga, Constantino, 78, 131,
154, 163, 165, 171, 178–9,
180, 182, 184, 197, 235n35
arrest of, 162, 176
'doctoral degree', 203n3 203,
247n59
Mugabe on, 174, 176
Chombo, Ignatius, 173
Chona, Mark, 51, 52, 58–9, 64,
70, 99
Christie, Iain, 88
Chung, Fay, 77, 89, 104, 220n15
on Chitepo assassination, 103
on Mhanda, 80–1
CIA (Central Intelligence Agency),
49, 54, 137
National Intelligence Estimate
(NIE), 70, 71
CIO (Central Intelligence
Organisation), 103, 106, 116,
121, 131, 132, 152, 153, 155,
156, 174, 180

civil society, 32, 117, 119, 120,
140, 194, 197
and state relationship, 8–9
class analysis, 192–4
Clausewitz, Carl von, 15
Cliffe, Lionel, 220n15
coercion, 12, 24, 80, 186, 192,
198
Cohen, Leonard, 6
Cold Comfort Farm, 233–4n18
Cold War, 8, 24–5, 39, 44, 47,
50, 71, 73, 93, 115, 117
'colonialism of a special type'
(CST), 162, 163
Coltart, David, 129–30, 133, 134,
136, 137, 213n58
'Committee of Six', 108, 111
Commonwealth, 42, 83, 89, 128
conceit, 6, 11–12, 16, 21, 25,
101, 104, 105, 117, 165
birth of, 27–8
conceptual structure, 1–25
'great men' theories, 3, 4
historical narratives, 3–5
'Holy Trinity' theory, 6–7, 23
interregna, 15, 19–21
'modes of belonging', 12–14,
24
modes of production, 10,
12–13, 19, 25
'shadow economy', 188–9
state and civil society relationship, 8–10
theory of lying, 15–19
See also capitalism, ideology, and
intellectuals
'conjuncture', 4–5, 25, 59, 93,
117
Conservatives, 54
constitutional referendum, 101,
125, 132
Conversation, The (website), 35

INDEX

INDEX

INDEX

national identity, 134
National Intelligence Estimate
(NIE), 70, 71
National Reaction Force, 167
National Security Archives (George
Washington University), 51
National Union of Students, 49
nationalism, 34, 45
Nazarbayev, Nursultan, 189
Ncube, Ben, 154
Ndebele (ethnic group), 37, 107,
115, 138
Ndlovu, Ray, 176
Ndlovu, Siphiwe Gloria, 27
Ndlovu-Gatsheni, Sabelo, 36–7,
38, 75
neo-patrimonialism, 34
New York Review of Books, 168
New York Times, 130
News24 (South Africa), 166
NGO (Non-Governmental
Organization), 7, 32
Ngũgĩ wa Thiong'o, 33
Ngwenya (Crocodile). *See*
Mnangagwa, Emmerson
Dambudzo 'Ngwenya
(Crocodile)'
Nhamodzenyika (son of Robert
Gabriel Mugabe), 55
Nhari–Badza rebellion, 48, 77, 80
Nhongo, Rex. *See* Mujuru,
Solomon (Nhongo, Rex)
'Nick' Mangwana, Ndabaningi, 17,
18
Nigeria, 134, 136
Nkomo, Joshua, 34, 40, 42, 63,
70, 73
Mlambo on, 95
Young Turks, fear on, 82–3
on ZANU (PF) violence, 98–9
Noah, Trevor, 163
Nursey-Bray, Paul, 111

Nyadzonia/Nhazónia raid (9 Aug
1976), 69
Nyagumbo, Maurice, 42
Nyakadzinashe, James, 75
Nyamunda, Tinashe, 35
Nyarota, Geoffrey, 121
Nyerere, Julius, 48–9, 53, 75, 76,
82, 89, 93
on Mugabe's ZIPA leadership
status, 67–8

OAU. *See* Organisation of African
Unity (OAU)
Obasanjo, Olusegun, 34
Observer, The (newspaper), 56
Onslow, Sue, 50
'Operation 1940', 152–3
Operation Makavhoterapapi, 32,
145–7, 188
reason for, 147–52
Operation Murambatsvina ('Clear
out the trash'), 34, 102–3, 147,
188
Operation Quartz, 113
'Operation Restore Legacy', 16,
169, 176–80
'organic crises', 19–21
Organisation of African Unity
(OAU), 109
conference (July 1985), 106
Liberation Committee, 66, 76

Parade (magazine), 138
Park, Daphne, 52, 54, 121
parliament, 170–1
parliamentary election (2000), 132
'patriotic history', 24
Pearce Commission, 37, 112, 185
Pearce, Mick, 52
Peasant Consciousness (Ranger), 42
pensions, 122, 124, 171
Perelman, Michael, 7

289

INDEX

'Wars of manoeuvre', 9
Washington, 34, 49, 70, 129, 130
Washington Times, 129
Wästberg, Per, 42–3, 46, 57, 83
    Chitepo, views on, 48–9
    Maputo visit, 58
    Mugabe and, 42–3
    Swedish branch of Amnesty
        International (AI), 57
Weimar Germany, 161
Weltanschauung, 165
wheat production, fall of, 102
white farmers, 102, 107
White, Robin, 57
Whitehall, 43, 49, 53, 54, 55, 86, 87
Wicken, Joan, 53–4, 82, 110, 216n33
Willowgate scandals (1989), 121
Wilson, Harold, 54, 56
Wisner, Frank, II, 64–5, 66, 71
Wolpe, Harold, 10, 11
    'articulation of modes of
        production', 10, 12
Women of Zimbabwe (WOZA), 120
Women's League, 139
Workers Convention (Feb 1999), 124
World Bank Development
    Reports, 7
World Bank, 7, 102, 124, 184
World Economic Forum, 17
World War II, 53

Young Turks, 62, 80, 82–3
Young, Hugo, 127, 128
YouTube, 166

Zabala, Santiago, 21, 22
Zambia, 51, 58, 65, 75, 80, 84
ZANLA. *See* Zimbabwe African
National Liberation Army
    (ZANLA)
ZANU (PF). *See* Zimbabwe African
    National Union–Patriotic Front
    [ZANU (PF)]
ZANU. *See* Zimbabwe African
    National Union (ZANU)
ZAPU. *See* Zimbabwe African
    People's Union (ZAPU)
ZBC-TV, 176
ZCTU ('Zimbabwe Congress of
    Trade Unions'), 106, 107, 122,
    197, 198
ZESN (Zimbabwe Election Support
    Network), 32, 146
Zezuru (ethnic group), 93, 135,
    138, 139
Zhuwao, Patrick, 173
Zimbabwe
    American forces in, 141
    Americans embassy launch, 99
    economy, 102–3, 197
    election manifesto (2018), 13
    election team, 128
    farmworkers' strikes, 12
    fascism, 119
    January *jambanja*, 197–9
    liberation struggle, 45
    politicides, 3–4, 48
    post-coup years, 190–3
    'Second Republic', 2, 13, 197
    and Soviet Union, 115
    and United Kingdom (UK), 115
    See also conceptual structure;
        11/17 coup
Zimbabwe African National
    Liberation Army (ZANLA), 62,
    75, 77, 90, 113
    and ZIPRA unity, 76
Zimbabwe African National Union
    (ZANU), 71, 78, 165
    bi-annual meeting (1971), 48

293

INDEX